The National Interest on INTERNATIONAL LAW & ORDER

The National Interest on INTERNATIONAL LAW & ORDER

R. James Woolsey
editor

Transaction Publishers
New Brunswick (U.S.A.) and London (U.K.)

Originally published in *The National Interest.*

This book is printed on acid-free paper that meets the American National Standard for Permanence of Paper for Printed Library Materials.

Library of Congress Catalog Number: 2003042684
ISBN: 0-7658-0187-6 (cloth); 0-7658-0565-0 (paper)
Printed in Canada

Library of Congress Cataloging-in-Publication Data

The national interest on international law and order / R. James Woosley, editor.
p. cm.
Includes bibliographical references.
ISBN 0-7658-0187-6 (alk. paper) ; ISBN 0-7658-0565-0 (paper: alk. paper)
1. International law. 2. International relations. 3. Law enforcement. 4. Human rights. 5. United States—Foreign relations. I. Woosley, R. James, 1941- II. National interest.

KZ3410.N37 2003
341—dc21

2003042684

Contents

Introduction

My first day in an international law class some years ago, Yale Professor Leon Lipson opened with the following line: "This is the only class you'll take in law school in which there is a reasonable argument that the subject does not exist. The reason is that there's no sheriff."

Lipson's cautionary note is worth keeping in mind as one assesses the state of international law today, its role in preserving global order, and its relationship to our own national interest—not to speak of whether it is a positive or negative factor in advancing the prospects for the people of the world to secure the right to life, liberty, and the pursuit of happiness. (More below on the latter point—much confusion has resulted from attempts over the last two and a quarter centuries to improve on Jefferson's formulation.)

Sheriffs presuppose sovereignty. If you don't pay a legal debt that you owe me or if you burglarize my home, I have some reason to expect that the sheriff will enforce the law in such a way as to protect me—serve you with process or arrest you. I forgo coming after you with the family shotgun because you and I live as part of a polity, and that polity's government passes laws and exercises sovereignty within its borders in such a way as to enforce them, protecting my rights and yours.

Further, in this country, I agree to let the sheriff do his job and the courts to decide the matter because I have confidence that the laws dealing with debt obligations or burglary have been passed by my elected representatives and will be fairly enforced. Two and a quarter centuries ago, Americans did not have such confidence, rebelled, and founded a system of government that proceeded from the recognition that they had "inalienable rights" of which they had been "endowed by their Creator." They then set up a government "to secure these rights", and were confident that it would then "assume among the powers of the earth [a] separate but equal station…."

Until relatively recently most of us who thought about international law at all saw it anchored in these two principles: sovereignty and legitimacy. We were prepared to observe agreements we had made and also, with some caveats, to treat all nations according to customary principles of international law. We cast a somewhat jaundiced eye at dictatorships and autocracies. Since their power was not "derived from the consent of the governed", all were, in a sense, illegitimate in our eyes. It was often not prudent to make an issue of it, usually because some were of assistance against greater threats (e.g., the Soviet Union when it was our ally against Nazi Germany during World War II). Sometimes we needed to act in order to keep dictatorships or autocracies from taking advantage of their sovereignty to our detriment or that of others. In these latter cases, due to their illegitimacy in our eyes, we didn't see that international law particularly got in our way—whether the evildoers were Barbary pirates attacking shipping or Serbs killing Bosnian Muslims.

Most of us would have further felt that, in view of this history and the principles it bequeathed us, certain issues about international law were relatively clear, the first being that the primary actors on the international scene are nation–states. Our own state has participated in alliances to maintain collective security and to deter attack, but that was a practical and pragmatic multilateralism. The United Nations, on the other hand, was largely a place to talk.

Second, if we were at war and signed a temporary cease-fire, and the other party clearly violated it, we would not agonize over our right to renew hostilities.

Third, if anyone had speculated about what would happen if some American troops fighting in the Gulf in 1991 were accused of violating the laws of war—a Middle Eastern My Lai, so to speak—we would have assumed that they would have faced a court-martial by their commander.

Fourth, we expect to be subject to, say, French justice if we drove too fast on French roads, but not for our official actions as employees of the U.S. government.

Fifth, we would have regarded murderous foreign terrorists who had demonstrably tried to kill us as national enemies analogous to pirates or saboteurs, not as possessors of substantial procedural rights such as those held by prisoners of war or criminal suspects entitled to full due process. Human rights discussions would have been thought to deal with matters quite basic—along the line of Jefferson's life, liberty, and the pursuit of happiness.

But those who write, speak and cogitate about international law are infinitely creative, and in the last fifteen years or so, as evidenced by this collection, every one of these common-sense notions about international law has been seriously called into question. Much of this challenge has been in the context of other countries' attempting to constrain the United States—sometimes on the part of our allies, more frequently authoritarian or totalitarian adversaries. Some efforts have been blatant, others veiled. Some have sought to subject American citizens—including the Supreme Allied Commander of NATO and former Secretary of State Henry Kissinger—to judicial investigation by an international tribunal or to a foreign state's judicial process for decisions made in the course of their U.S. government service. Other states have been most persistent in trying to use arguments about international law to, *inter alia*, protect their oil companies' interests and constrain us from renewing hostilities against Ba'athi Iraq—even after it blatantly violated a 1991 cease-fire agreement.

Those who have written for *The National Interest* on these subjects have, on almost all points, defended common sense against these creative efforts to bring international and foreign law to bear on Americans in non-traditional ways and to restrict the ability of the United States to use force to protect itself and its allies. But the assault is relentless and there is a certain Horatio-at-the-bridge character to the defense chronicled here. Happily the editors have recruited a number of able Horatios over the years, and the battle goes on.

One of the most important assaults on common sense and accepted past principles of international law is the new International Criminal Court (ICC), the subject of much commentary in the pages that follow. The ICC reflects a unique relationship between law and reality. There are several ways that states and individuals have chosen to deal with the sheriff's absence and the fact that rogue states and terrorists are today largely the source of international conflict—i.e., that because of them we still live, internationally, in a decidedly Hobbesian world. One approach is to recognize that fact and facilitate the use of force when necessary against rogues, terrorists and the like. The reasoning of the proponents of the ICC appears to be different; since they wish the world as a whole were Lockean and not Hobbesian, their solution is to let their wish become the father of their worldview—in other words to pretend that we are all part of a collegial social contract and are citizens of an inchoate international entity.

The Court's supporters elide the fact that its writ does not effectively run to dealing with the leaders of rogue states—and take the position that its decisions should be enforced nonetheless against everyone else. This includes even citizens of sovereign states that have not agreed to be subject to the Court's jurisdiction. In a precursor of what they seek to bring about on a permanent basis, the wishful Lockeans noted that, in the course of the United States halting the ethnic cleansing of Kosovo by the Serbs, U.S. aircraft may have inadvertently bombed some civilian targets. Very well, their thinking ran, let's use an existing international tribunal to investigate the American NATO commander and decide whether to prosecute him. You say the United States hasn't agreed to that? Of what relevance is that?

Many Europeans, who are themselves in the process of surrendering some aspects of their nations' sovereignty to the European Union, are enthusiastic about the prospect of surrendering sovereignty to the Court or other international entities. Most of the European nations in the bloody 20th century, with Britain the noble exception, contributed in one way or another to making the tragedies of that century worse, either as predators, bystanders or ineffectively-resisting victims. After seeing many millions killed in the two world wars and many more enslaved during the Cold War, it is easy to understand why many

Europeans in the decades after World War II have come to the view that such surrenders of national sovereignty may be reasonable steps toward peace and security.

The ongoing process of forging a continent's nation-states into what may someday be a new country—Europe—has left many Europeans with a sense of pride at what they see as their progress (although this view is far from universal on the continent). They are welcome to their pride, but from the American perspective there are two rather aggravating aspects to all this.

First of all, it would be nice if our European friends would occasionally remember that we were of some assistance in seeing to it that they now have an opportunity to develop a United States of Europe that is united under terms other than those of fascist or communist fiats. Furthermore, the legal side of our assistance, such as the Nuremberg Trials, was not the starting point. Conducting the trials was relatively easy compared with, say, taking Omaha Beach—and the latter was the precondition for the former.

Second, we apparently need to remind them that we dealt with this issue in our own way between 1861 and 1865, when we resolved on the battlefield that we would have a continent-wide nation and that Federal sovereignty trumped state sovereignty. (Robert E. Lee, who had serious problems with the institution of slavery, nonetheless turned down the offered command of the Union Army in 1861 because he felt he owed primary allegiance to what he regarded as his sovereign homeland—the Commonwealth of Virginia.) If we should do any further sovereignty submerging—of the United States into some new entity—most Americans, if they think about it at all, would expect that it would be done only if we consent to it. A number of Europeans seem to believe that they are free to sweep us into the process even if we do not wish to be so swept. They have also forgotten, or do not care, that independence from the arrogance of European assertions of sovereignty over us is at the heart of our revolution and our polity's existence. In the pages that follow, noting Jeremy Rabkin's observation that the EU, not being quite a state, favors a world in which states are no longer central, Lee Casey and David Rivkin wryly observe that "Europe, however, is not the world."

There is a another, very fundamental, reason why on this side of the Atlantic most would balk at surrendering American citizens to the ICC's jurisdiction. The Court is just, in Alan Keyes' phrase, "out there" – a combination of prosecutor and judge unchecked and, in effect, unsupervised by elected officials, by the UN Security Council, or indeed by anyone at all. The American perspective on law is the polar opposite of this: we start with individuals' rights (endowed "by their Creator"), then to proceed to these individuals giving their consent to establish governments "to secure these rights." In constructing a government, as Michael Novak has put it (quoted herein by John Bolton) we operate according to the principle: "In God we trust—for everyone else, checks and balances." Madison's formulation in the *Federalist* (no. 51) is classic: "The great difficulty lies in this: you must first enable the government to control the governed; and in the next place oblige it to control itself." The ICC is squarely at odds with this entire way of thinking.

The ICC is addressed in a number of the essays below, and it lurks as the major contemporary challenge to our concept that one proceeds from pre-existing individual rights to the legitimacy of government, and that government must be constructed to make it supremely difficult to trample these rights. Other challenges come from the tendency of prosecutor-judges in several European countries to invoke "universal jurisdiction" in their own courts. This latter may enable individual magistrates not only to target those who have committed real crimes, such as General Augusto Pinochet (crimes, however, that their own now-democratic countries have chosen to deal with in their own sovereign ways), but also to harass former public officials from democratic nations—Henry Kissinger, for example. In any case, the sovereignty of nation-states to deal with their own citizens, other than under certain specific agreed exceptions, is under substantial siege. In this regard, however, sovereignty is ably defended by the contributors herein.

A second major assault on sovereignty is manifest in actions by the International Court of Justice (ICJ) in the Hague and the UN General Assembly that are at odds with the rights of democratic states to deter aggression and undertake effective steps in support of collective security. To this must be added, in the latter part of 2002 and early 2003, the efforts of some members, including permanent members, of the Security Council to thwart the effective enforcement of Security Council resolutions requiring Iraq's disarmament.

This is the same spirit that reigned in 1983, when a larger share of the UN General Assembly voted to condemn the United States for its overthrow of the Marxist government in Grenada than had voted to condemn the Soviet invasion of Afghanistan. The United States had acted in support of Barbados, Jamaica, and the Organization of Eastern Caribbean States (OECS) and to rescue American hostages held by the regime, but this seemed to count for little in the General Assembly. Then in 1986 the ICJ held that the United States was at fault for assisting El Salvador in taking action against Nicaragua in response to Sandinista support of rebels in El Salvador—this at the latter's request. The Court ruled, essentially, that steps taken by the United States in support of collective security pursuant to Article 51 of the UN Charter, after Nicaragua assisted in attacks on El Salvador, violated customary international law because only El Salvador had the right to respond and then only with "proportionate countermeasures."

These sorties by international institutions against the right of states to undertake effective steps in pursuit of collective security—moreover steps by democratic states in response to attacks by dictatorial ones—were harbingers of what has come about with regard to Iraq. A major question facing the community of nations in early 2003 is whether Iraq will be required to abide by its

1991 cease-fire commitment (reiterated in countless Security Council resolutions) to destroy its weapons of mass destruction and long-range missile programs, or whether the Security Council will limit the ability of the United States and its allies to bring this about so as to give Iraq the same type of pass given to Marxist Grenada and Sandinista Nicaragua.

Some long-sanctioned practices in dealing with certain classes of prisoners in the war against terrorism have also come under fire from those who maintain they are supporting the rule of international law. The Geneva Conventions (rooted in this regard in the Hague Convention of 1899) clearly set out the requirements for combatants to be treated as prisoners of war: responsible commanders, arms carried openly, insignia or uniform "recognizable at a distance", and operations conducted "in accordance with the laws and customs of war." As Jeremy Rabkin points out, efforts by NGOs and others to have all prisoners in the war against terrorism treated as POWs—even those who do not come within a country mile of these criteria—can, if successful, severely cripple our ability to defend ourselves against terror.

There is a consistent theme here: many who speak for the new approach to international law seem bound and determined to ignore the requirements of fighting successfully against the unconventional threats of our current era—rogue states' acquiring weapons of mass destruction, sponsoring covert attacks on others and cooperating with terrorist groups. In the absence of traditional armies crossing borders with flags flying, it is clear that democracies, as they seek to protect themselves, will face confused but determined opposition from many institutions that claim to be operating in the name of international law.

American law enforcement, as it came to be organized and administered before September 11, 2001, does not fare well in these pages. It is dealt several body blows in the volume's section on "Law Enforcement and Foreign Policy" with respect to its ability to protect us from the new range of threats we face.

William Wechsler characterizes Federal law enforcement "a dysfunctional mess," a view he also attributes to each group of experts that has examined it every few years. Wechsler's bill of particulars charges that law enforcement officials have too frequently refused to see themselves as part of the effort to preserve national security, have stayed aloof from enforcement of sanctions and covert action abroad even when their help could have been important, have elevated their individual cases above the need to cooperate on crucial matters with foreign governments, have jumped to make claims of interference at the drop of a hat, have resisted vital steps toward consolidation, and have made leaking to the press and the pursuit of public credit an art form.

Then, after that mild introduction, Ruth Wedgwood takes off the gloves. In a blunt and devastating critique she takes on the Clinton Administration, the FBI, and the approach of "treating terrorism as if it were simply another form of crime"—i.e., proceeding against terrorists chiefly by Federal prosecution under traditional standards and principles. She zeroes in on the Clinton Administration's decision in the spring of 1996 not to take advantage of information volunteered by the government of Sudan and neither to press the Saudis hard to jail Osama bin Laden when he left Khartoum in May, nor to intercept or divert his plane. She calls FBI Director Louis Freeh's advice on this matter "a fatal misjudgment", to which the White House deferred, causing the law to be read "in a narrow and needlessly self-constraining fashion." "Osama bin Laden," she points out, "enjoys no right to be a para-American." Wedgwood states that both the law of war's doctrine of anticipatory defense and the domestic law of conspiracy could have sanctioned action and that "[i]n March 1996, bin Laden clearly fulfilled these [conspiracy law] requirements." She adds that "[s]econdhand reports suggest that former President Clinton is now aware of this error, and considers it perhaps the worst mistake of his presidency."

The volume closes with seven essays on the debate over human rights. Readers will be drawn back, *inter alia*, to Hume, Kant, and the nature and purpose of government itself—subjects most of us last touched upon as undergraduates. But the editors have made the substance understandable and relevant by framing disputes among brilliant authors with graceful prose styles, different philosophical perspectives, and different views on concrete contemporary questions.

There is no way to do justice in summary to Francis Fukuyama's persuasive presentation of how the right interpretation of Hume, by Alasdair MacIntyre (my favorite modern philosopher from graduate study years ago), helps us understand that we cannot avoid judgment and striking balances in developing a defensible definition of human rights from natural rights. That balancing, in Fukuyama's hands, produces an outcome very much along Jefferson's life-liberty-pursuit-of-happiness lines.

For those who would rely solely on any single and undiluted basis for the concept of human rights the pitfalls become rather obvious. If we are to rely on religion the question arises, whose religion? Bin Laden has told us that, essentially, people have a right to one election once and that after that God (or rather bin Laden's interpretation of Him) will define their rights. The basic characteristics of human nature are relevant, but without balancing, if these are pushed too hard as the normative basis of rights, one ends up including nepotism and other natural human propensities that clearly do not deserve such status. The same may be said for the majoritarian view that whatever the nations of the world have put in treaties, especially those widely accepted, must govern. If similarly pushed to the extreme, this latter approach would include paid vacations as a "human right" (called for in Article 24 of the UN's Universal Declaration of Human Rights).

Owen Harries, Julian Pilon, and Irving Kristol close the volume with three remarkable pieces from the late 1980s. Although slightly dated now, they collectively make two key points. Harries tells the story of how much of the world's media ganged up against Singapore in the mid-80's on some human rights issues of less than Gulag-like dimensions, illustrating that what Tom Korologos once said of Congress can sometimes be said of the press as well: "They only do two things really well—nothing, and over-react." Pilon builds the case for liberty as a basic human right and wryly tweaks the Carter Administration for having evidenced on occasion that they did not regard the difference between free nations and dictatorships as having anything to do with the notion of human rights.

Kristol closes by melding both the theme of the overriding distinction between free (if flawed) governments and dictatorships with a case for not assuming that undiluted support for human rights is universally the proper approach. But if our tactics have meant that we have sometimes had to tack with wind changes, or even put into port for a time, our strategy has been clear. As Kristol puts it, "we do aim to 'make the world safe for democracy'—eventually. . . ."

Although some of our tactics and decisions can be faulted, it is worth noting that the United States has had a major hand in moving the world in the 86 years since it entered World War I, from one containing at most a dozen democracies (and at that point largely democracies for males only) to, today, one containing 121—over 60 per cent of the world's governments. Freedom House calculates that 89 of these are "free" and the other 32 only "partly free"—that is to say, they still have some deficits in, chiefly, guarantees of human rights. Along the way we have made our compromises, getting along with (in some cases even allying with) Chiang Kai-shek, various South Korean dictators, Franco, Salazar, Pinochet, and so on. But today Taiwan, South Korea, Spain, Portugal, Chile and many other once-dictatorial nations are democracies that either protect human rights well or are headed in that direction. Moreover our adversaries in the First and Second World Wars and the Cold War have largely joined the democracy/human rights movement, many "free", some "partly free": Germany, Austria, Hungary, Turkey, Italy, Japan, and, most recently, Russia.

We have, of course, not done this alone—Britain has been our key and indispensable ally throughout, as have been Canada, Australia, France and others. But it has been crucial that in all three world wars of the 20th century—two hot, one cold—we have made it clear that we were not fighting on behalf of our civilization against others or even our state against other states, but rather on behalf of freedom and against tyranny. Our support for human rights was our banner throughout. We fought World War I for Wilson's Fourteen Points, World War II for Roosevelt's and Churchill's Atlantic Charter, and the Cold War for the ideas expressed best by Truman, Kennedy, and Reagan (and in the Helsinki Final Act). Fighting under this banner had an important practical effect: it steered us away from reparations and vengeance and toward building democracy after World War II, and in the Cold War it helped us acquire some vital allies—Vaclav Havel, Lech Walesa, Andrei Sakharov, the Solidarity union—that were instrumental in making it possible for us to win without direct military conflict with the Soviet Union.

Within 86 years—a single lifetime—we have had a major hand in advancing the numbers of democratic governments by a literal order of magnitude. But there are 192 countries in the world, and in approximately a third of them there are still brave journalists being tortured, women being brutally suppressed and even mutilated, students demonstrating for freedom and being beaten by government thugs. The spirit that emanates from these pages would say: "Nearly two-thirds done, about a third to go." We may need on occasion to build slowly; but we build to last.

R. James Woolsey

Part 1

International Law

1

The Rocky Shoals of International Law

*Lee A. Casey and David B. Rivkin, Jr.**

Although international law has always been a consideration for American foreign policymakers, it has rarely commanded the focus of their attentions. Under the next president, this will have to change. Since the Cold War's end, a number of international organizations, human rights activists and states have worked to transform the traditional law of nations governing the relationship between states into something akin to an international regulatory code. This "new" international law purports to govern the relationship of citizens to their governments, affecting such domestic issues as environmental protection and the rights of children. Among other things, it would: nearly eliminate the unilateral use of military force; create the unattainable requirement of avoiding all civilian casualties in combat; promote the criminal prosecution of individual state officials by the courts of other states and international tribunals; and permit—or even require—international "humanitarian" intervention in a state's internal affairs. Recast as such, international law constitutes a real and immediate threat to U.S. national interests.

The impetus for extending the reach of international law stems from both our allies and our adversaries, who have chosen to use it as a means to check, or at least harness, American power. While each group has different strategic goals, from the perspective of both, the great "problem" of international affairs in the post-Cold War world is the unchallenged military, diplomatic, economic and even cultural predominance of the United States.[1] Our global antagonists, particularly China, would like to see the United States disengage from world affairs. For our allies, who continue to depend far too much on U.S.

---

*Lee A. Casey and David B. Rivkin, Jr. are partners in the law firm of Baker & Hostetler llp. Both have practiced before the International Court of Justice and the International Criminal Tribunal for the Former Yugoslavia.

This essay originally appeared in *The National Interest*, no. 62 (Winter 2000/01).

military might to wish for a new American isolationism, the great danger has become American "unilateralism"—an all-purpose term for U.S. action not sanctioned by the "international community." They do not want to prevent U.S. global engagement; they want to influence and control it.

Both our allies and our adversaries understand the value of international law in achieving their ends. Law and its rhetoric have always played a far more important role in the United States than in almost any other country. We are a nation bound together not by ties of blood or religion, but by paper and ink. The Declaration of Independence itself was, at its heart, an appeal to law—the laws of nature and of nature's God—to justify an act of rebellion against the British Crown. As Alexis de Tocqueville wrote in the early days of the American republic:

> [t]he influence of legal habits [in the United States] extends beyond the precise limits I have pointed out. Scarcely any political question arises in the United States that is not resolved, sooner or later, into a judicial question. Hence all parties are obliged to borrow, in their daily controversies, the ideas, and even the language, peculiar to judicial proceedings.[2]

Tocqueville was clearly prescient. Today almost every key policy issue in the United States is framed as a legal question. Law is our genius and our Achilles' Heel. If the trends of international law in the 1990s are allowed to mature into binding rules, international law may prove to be one of the most potent weapons ever deployed against the United States.

The good news is that international law, properly configured, should not be viewed as a burden for our foreign policy. Rather, it can function as a positive force, capable of promoting a more stable international environment and advancing our national interest. As the world's pre-eminent power, we have both the greatest opportunity and the most pressing need to shape international law. To do so successfully in the years ahead, though, will require a keen appreciation of how international law evolved over time and of what specific legal problems have confronted American foreign and defense policy over the last decade. Moreover, international law imperatives will have to be integrated into American statecraft. For just as war is too important to be left to the generals, international law cannot be left solely to the lawyers.

The Assault on the Westphalian Order

The current international order, in which the most important actor is the independent nation-state, dates from the 1648 Peace of Westphalia, which ended Europe's religious wars. Traditional international law, better described as the "law of nations," was built around this system. It was defined in 1758 by one of its early scholars, Emerich de Vattel, as "the science of the law subsisting between nations or states, and of the obligations that flow from it."

This law developed over time, primarily by the actual practice of states interacting with one another, and had little, if anything, to do with the relationship between citizens and their own governments. For this reason, the law of nations accommodated widely divergent domestic political systems, ranging from absolute monarchies to authoritarian and totalitarian regimes to democracies. It was not, moreover, enforceable through any regular legal or judicial process, but only by political means—up to and including war. In this manner, international law, which lacked the legitimacy enjoyed by law made by an elected and accountable legislative body, was fully compatible with the principles of self-government upon which the American republic was founded. Indeed, the Constitution itself recognizes the existence of the law of nations, and specifically gives Congress the authority to define offenses against that law.

In the aftermath of World War II, however, attempts to impose limitations on states through international legal strictures gained a new currency. The murderous policies of Nazi Germany and Imperial Japan prompted renewed international efforts to leash the dogs of war and, even more broadly, to impose a range of duties and obligations on sovereign governments. These endeavors involved not only limiting—through the UN Charter—the right of states to use force against other states, but also sought both to regulate the relationships between national governments and their citizens and to create tangible enforcement mechanisms, other than the use of raw political or military force. Thus, the conceptual foundation for the new international law was in place by the late 1940s. Because of Cold War imperatives, however, these efforts produced little effect in the way states actually behaved.

With the end of the Cold War things have changed. Activists, scholars, international institutions like the United Nations, and even a number of governments (including, episodically at least, the Clinton administration) have redoubled their efforts, championing a new international legal order by which states are subject to the will of the elusive "international community" at large. Non-governmental organizations (NGOs) have been the leading force in this process. They have been particularly active in promoting the adoption of international treaties and conventions, including the Rome treaty (which established the new permanent International Criminal Court, or ICC), the Land Mines Convention, the Chemical Weapons Convention and the Kyoto Protocol.

NGOs have also worked to steer and hasten the evolution of customary international law, an area where traditionally only state practice gave rise, at a rather glacial pace, to the emergence of legal norms. Now customs seem to be spawned overnight, through nothing more tangible than the convening of scholarly conferences or the publication of papers. Significantly, it is now alleged that states do not have any choice in deciding whether to comply with these newly minted international law norms. The NGOs have been arguing that they are able to represent public aspirations at both the national and global levels—that is, to speak for the (nonexistent) "global civil society"—better than any government. While these claims are quite obviously false—NGOs are not elected, not accountable to any body politic, and are not inherently better or worse than other special interests—such groups have had considerable success in shaping the new international law. These groups were omnipresent during the 1998 Rome Conference, which adopted the ICC treaty, and actually achieved mention as vessels of the "public conscience" in the Land Mines Convention.

The substantive body of the new international law that these groups have sponsored has a number of specific manifestations, not all of them entirely consistent with each other. These include claims that heretofore purely domestic public policy issues—such as the death penalty, abortion, gay rights, environmental protection, and the relationship between parents and children—must be resolved in accordance with "prevailing" international standards; that, with the possible exception of repelling armed attack, only the United Nations Security Council can authorize the use of military force; that the "international community" is entitled to intervene under a variety of circumstances in the internal affairs of states; and that the actions of individual civilian and military officials of states fall under the purview of international criminal jurisdiction.

At the core of these efforts is a frontal assault on sovereignty as the organizing principle of the international system. Proponents of the new order are not shy about saying so. Among the new international law's strongest supporters is Secretary of State Madeleine Albright, who has plainly stated,

> Great nations who understand the importance of sovereignty at various times cede various portions of it in order to achieve some better good for their country. We are looking at how the nation-state functions in a totally different way than people did at the beginning of this century.[3]

The Threat to the United States

Although the Clinton Administration has been generally supportive of the new international law, its key tenets create problems of the highest order for the United States. First, as a philosophical matter, any attack upon the principle of sovereignty threatens the very foundation of American democracy. Sovereignty is the necessary predicate of self-government. As Vattel wrote, a "sovereign State" is one that "governs itself, under what form so ever." Any limitation on sovereignty as an organizing principle, any "cession," to paraphrase Secretary Albright, is an abdication of the right of the citizens of the United States to be governed solely in accordance with their Constitution, and by individuals whom they have elected and who are ultimately accountable to them. To the extent that international law allows supranational, or extra-national, institutions to determine whether the actions of the United States are lawful, ultimate authority will no longer be vested in the American people, but in these institutions.

Thus, for all of its humanitarian and democracy-building rhetoric, the new international law is profoundly undemocratic at its core. Indeed, with its lack of accountability and disdain for democratic practice (as opposed to rhetoric), it arguably poses the greatest challenge to Francis Fukuyama's anticipated global triumph of liberal democracy. If the aspirations of today's international law proponents were ever to prevail, the resulting international system would not remotely resemble a community of democratic nations.

Second, as a practical matter, the new international law has the potential to undermine American leadership in the post-Cold War global system. Even more fundamentally, international law may well make the world safe for aggression, by imposing undue constraints on those countries that are willing to use force to deter and punish it. Although, as noted above, the new international law has a number of manifestations, those elements dealing with the use of military force, and the potential consequences for individual American officials who order or implement its use, are the most advanced and pernicious. As the world's pre-eminent military power, with global interests and responsibilities, the United States should be very concerned about any effort to create international judicial institutions capable of prosecuting individual soldiers, officers and elected officials in the chain of command.

The international criminal "norms" applied in these courts, both in the ad hoc criminal courts for the former Yugoslavia and Rwanda and in the International Criminal Court, are ambiguous in their meaning and remarkably fluid in their application. For example, one of the "war crimes" prosecutable in the ICC is defined as

> [i]ntentionally launching an attack in the knowledge that such attack will cause incidental loss of life or injury to civilians or damage to civilian objects or widespread, long-term and severe damage to the natural environment which would be clearly excessive in relation to the concrete and direct overall military advantage anticipated.

Whether any particular attack causes "excessive" civilian injuries or environmental damage is very much a matter of opinion.

This is, in fact, a crime that can be tailored to fit almost any circumstances, as was all but openly acknowledged by the prosecutor's office of the Yugoslav tribunal during its investigation of alleged NATO war crimes. This investigation was undertaken after a number of NGOs complained that NATO's 1999 air campaign against Serbia resulted in too many civilian deaths. As candidly noted in the report to the prosecutor,

> [t]he answers to these questions [regarding allegedly excessive civilian casualties] are not simple. It may be necessary to resolve them on a case by case basis, and the

> answers may differ depending on the background and values of the decision-maker. It is unlikely that a human rights lawyer and an experienced combat commander would assign the same relative values to military advantage and to injury to noncombatants. Further, it is unlikely that military commanders with different doctrinal backgrounds and differing degrees of combat experience or national military histories would always agree in close cases.[4]

The key underlying problem here is that injuries to noncombatants and their property—so-called "collateral damage"—are an endemic consequence of combat. As a result, the traditional law of war, *jus in bello*, although proscribing certain hostile actions toward civilians, eschewed overly rigid rules on collateral damage. Unfortunately, instead of continuing to rely on the broad, traditional *jus in bello* principles of proportionality and discrimination, the new norms have come to resemble American domestic regulatory law. These rules are overly prescriptive and proscriptive, to such an extent that ensuring full compliance has become almost impossible. This is particularly the case because the new international law seems to suggest that zero civilian casualties and no collateral damage are not only attainable outcomes in modern combat, but that these should be the norm. The combination of the unrealistic norms and unaccountable judicial bodies that would apply them is particularly problematic.

The American military is particularly vulnerable here. This is because U.S. military doctrine has always been attrition-oriented, emphasizing the intensive application of firepower and the use of "decisive force." It is inevitable that damage to civilian sites, and civilian casualties, will result. This is all the more likely given the growing American aversion to combat casualties, which forces our military commanders to rely more and more on air strikes and missile attacks. This raises the real possibility that American soldiers and officials will be considered subject to prosecution, even in situations where the intervention has been "humanitarian" in character, as with the air campaign against Serbia.

Significantly, while no prosecutions against NATO officials are currently planned, even the relatively tame Yugoslav tribunal did not give the alliance a clean bill of health. Indeed, the prosecutor's office declined to bring indictments, not because it concluded that no crimes were committed by NATO, but because "[i]n all cases, either the law is not sufficiently clear or investigations are unlikely to result in the acquisition of sufficient evidence to substantiate charges against high level accused or against lower accused for particularly heinous offenses." Future outcomes in the permanent ICC, a court that will be less dependent upon U.S. and NATO largesse than is the Yugoslav tribunal, may be very different. And the fact that the United States has not signed, and would not ratify, the ICC treaty will not prevent the ICC from pursuing Americans. The court claims to exercise a form of "universal jurisdiction" that will allow it to prosecute American citizens when their actions, or the effects of their actions, take place on the territory of a state that has signed the ICC treaty.

Moreover, the danger here is not limited to the potential actions of the ICC. Based on the "universal jurisdiction" theory—which suggests that any state can prosecute international humanitarian violations wherever they occur, whether or not that state's own citizens are involved—any state, or even a low-level foreign magistrate, can begin a prosecution against American military or civilian officials. This was, of course, the case with the former Chilean dictator, Augusto Pinochet, who traveled to England for medical treatment in 1998, and was very nearly extradited to Spain to stand trial for his actions during his rule in Chile.

Overall, there is no doubt that, insofar as they can successfully claim the right to prosecute military and civilian leaders for violations of the laws of war and international humanitarian norms, international judicial bodies and interested states will be able effectively to shape American policy. An American president would be far less likely to use force if there were a genuine possibility that U.S. soldiers or officials, including himself, would face future prosecution in a foreign court. Both our allies and our adversaries fully understand the importance of molding the new international law to fit their needs, and its power as an effective weapon against the United States.

Examples of this phenomenon are not difficult to find. Human rights activists, of course, have frequently made exaggerated claims that pre-existing international humanitarian norms require fundamental changes in U.S. foreign and domestic policy. States are also increasingly using the language of law as a means of shaping U.S. policy. In one of the most boldly cynical examples of this phenomenon, the People's Republic of China—desperate to prevent American deployment of even a limited anti-ballistic missile defense—has asserted that the 1972 Anti-Ballistic Missile Treaty between the United States and the Soviet Union remains in force (even though the Soviet Union disappeared a decade ago), and that it cannot be terminated by the United States because that treaty has assumed the status of "customary" international law.

Opportunities for the United States

All of these problems have led many conservatives, always skeptical of international law because of its ambiguous and supranational character, to reject it as law at all. Most notably, the dean of conservative constitutional lawyers, Robert Bork, has forcefully argued in these pages that even traditional international law is simply too indeterminate in its application and too subject to "non-legal"—i.e., political and diplomatic—criteria to be considered law. He also has attacked international law at a much more fundamental level, noting that the lack of any elected and accountable international law-making body deprives international law of the legitimacy inherently possessed by domestic law. As Judge Bork pointed out ten years ago, "There can be no authentic rule of law among nations until nations have a common political morality or are under a common sovereignty."[5]

On the facts, the conservative critics of international law are mostly right. Even traditional international law was not made by an elected, accountable legislature; was often ambiguous to the point of being unknowable; was not enforceable by regular judicial processes; and accorded totalitarian dictatorships the same legal status as democratic republics. But an unfair, unbalanced or nakedly political application of the law does not necessarily undermine its force and effect as law. Domestic examples of these faults are plentiful. Moreover, to the extent that international law, to be considered legitimate and effective, is expected to meet the standards that must be met by domestic law, it will necessarily fail.

It does not follow, however, that international law does not exist, or that the "rule of law" among nations is impossible, short of global governance. In fact, it is only when international law is expected to serve as the equivalent of domestic law, but on a global basis, that it appears ambiguous, ineffectual and illegitimate. And it is only comparatively recently that it has been expected to meet those standards—a task for which it is, and always has been, singularly ill-equipped. Nevertheless, international law does exist, and the United States, like other sovereigns, is bound by it. This much was fully recognized and accepted by the Founders of our Republic and the framers of the Constitution.

However, the United States is not required to accept the new international law, and would be foolish to do so. Rather, we should actively work to shape international law in ways that both support our national interests and that are consistent with our philosophical foundations. In this, we would simply be following the examples of other great powers, past and present, which have understood the importance and value of a favorable international legal system. An excellent example of such behavior is provided by the efforts of the great seventeenth and eighteenth-century maritime powers, Britain and the Dutch Republic, to mold the principle of "freedom of the seas" to their commercial and naval needs. As its dependence on maritime trade increased, the Dutch Republic argued for the broadest principle of free navigation—especially after its naval supremacy gave way to that of Britain. On the other hand, Britain's support for this international norm ebbed and flowed with its need to impose successful naval blockades on Continental aggressors, specifically, France and Germany.

The Restoration of International Law

To implement this active and national interest-driven approach to the development of international law would mean a significant change in the way American foreign policy is made. Restoring the "law of nations" must be one of the next president's most important priorities. To achieve this end, the new administration must consciously coordinate foreign policy and international law imperatives. The rules of international law are significantly affected by state practice. A state that consistently takes a particular position on the content or meaning of international law, and that acts commensurate with that position, can have a very important impact on the law's development. We need, in short, to approach the current problems posed by international law holistically, rather than one issue at a time.

To begin with, an adroit American public diplomacy is very important. We need to articulate clearly and consistently why we embrace particular international legal stances. While the United States should not shy away from invoking its national interests as a motivating force for its actions, whenever possible it should articulate a broader set of compelling normative principles. In particular, the United States should strongly espouse national sovereignty, the bedrock upon which democracy and self-government are built, as the fundamental organizing principle of the international system. In that regard, we should make clear to our European allies that our understanding of national sovereignty and independence is simply different than their own.

Throughout its history, the United States has taken a strong view of its rights as an independent sovereign; such a view is essential to our constitutional form of government. By contrast, over the past fifty years, the European states have come to accept increasing limitations on their sovereign rights, to the point of permitting significant elements of their foreign and domestic policies to be formulated by the European Union's bureaucracy in Brussels, rather than by their own elected national legislatures. It may well be accurate to say that, at least in Europe, a new form of sovereignty has developed—although these developments have not been without significant opposition. As Jeremy Rabkin has aptly noted, "as the EU is not quite a State, it favors a world in which states are much less central to international society than they used to be."[6] Europe, however, is not the world.

In this regard, it is essential to explain the role of American exceptionalism and the heroic component in our national civic culture. Our European allies may well be able to accommodate their national aspirations within the context of the European Union, looking back to the universalism of the Middle Ages; but the United States cannot. It was not a part of Charlemagne's empire or of medieval Christendom. An American president can motivate the American people to undertake a global leadership role—a role that continues to be critical to Europe's security—only by invoking patriotism, idealism and the national interest.

This is particularly true when the use of American military force may be involved. Our allies should understand that doctrines denigrating patriotism and national sovereignty inherently promote American isolationism. It is simply impossible to engage the U.S. military on the basis of the imperatives of multilateral institutions alone.

On a more practical level, senior U.S. foreign policymakers need to anticipate and take account of the international law implications of each and every foreign policy decision. Although clear statements by U.S. officials rejecting the worst excesses of new trends in international law will be important, this will not be enough to protect U.S. interests. The United States should avoid any action, however meritorious it may appear at the time, that would undermine traditional international law principles. On those occasions when the national interest or basic morality requires a violation of these principles, we should justify this by reference to a greater good—not by embracing the insupportable "new" international law.

This is especially true with respect to the "right of humanitarian intervention." The Clinton administration adopted this "right" as a pretext to justify NATO's air war against Serbia, and the new administration may well be tempted to invoke it again to justify further U.S. intervention in Yugoslavia, Iraq or elsewhere. This temptation must be resisted. The "right of humanitarian intervention" has no basis in the traditional law of nations. It violates the United Nations Charter, which prohibits interference in the internal affairs of member states. It is, in fact, nothing more than nineteenth-century colonialism—this time dressed in the language of law rather than of "progress" or the "white man's burden."

If the "right of humanitarian intervention" were established as a norm of international law, there would be neither limits to it nor means to support its neutral application. This fact surely has not been lost on weaker states that do not meet Western standards of democracy. Ultimately, the "right of humanitarian intervention" is not likely to produce a more just and safe world, but to impel vulnerable states to obtain weapons of mass destruction as a means of preventing Western intervention in their internal affairs. It is, of course, true that any sort of intervention by the United States and its allies fuels this particular fire. However, championing a new international law norm that permits, or even requires, humanitarian intervention suggests a much more immediate threat to these regimes. It implies that such intervention will be the rule rather than the exception. In a world where the designs for nuclear weaponry can be obtained on the Internet, this is not wise statecraft.

A better approach to dealing with "rogue" regimes would be to follow the traditional rules of international law. These permit self-defense, that is, action by a state against another that is threatening its national interests—a right that was fully incorporated into the United Nations Charter. The traditional rules give rogue regimes less reason to develop weapons of mass destruction. At the same time, they still permit significant scope for U.S. action. For example, if the next administration were to conclude that Saddam Hussein must finally be removed from power, it could avoid basing its action on a "right of humanitarian intervention" by recognizing an alternative Iraqi government and providing assistance in removing the dictator. A similar approach could have been employed against Milosevic.

In any case, when addressing international law issues, the United States should be consistent. It should only promote international law norms that it is prepared to obey. The Clinton administration's attempt to establish a "new" form of sovereignty, along with a "right of humanitarian intervention" and "international courts" to prosecute war crimes, arguably serves to some extent its foreign policy imperatives. However, these rules clearly would not be acceptable to the United States if they were applied to its own nationals or policies. Indeed, this was already clear when the Clinton administration found itself complaining bitterly about the inquiries of the International Criminal Tribunal for the Former Yugoslavia into NATO's Serbia campaign. That being the case, the United States should not have supported the creation of the Yugoslav tribunal in the first place.

Similarly, the United States was an early supporter of the permanent ICC. The Clinton administration's open enthusiasm for the project evidently led our negotiating partners to believe that the United States would ultimately sign the Rome treaty, even if all U.S. objectives were not achieved—in particular, guarantees that U.S. soldiers and officials could not be prosecuted without prior U.S. approval. In the end, when these guarantees could not be obtained, the American delegation (properly) refused to sign the Rome treaty and was left isolated from its allies.

This is an excellent example of how not to conduct U.S. foreign policy. An early and honest statement, for example, that the uniqueness of the U.S. Constitution and the long American tradition of independence precluded the subjection of American nationals to the ICC's authority would have better served the national interest and our international reputation. Moreover, a frank acknowledgment of this fact might well have undermined the ICC project in its early stages, avoiding the creation of a court that will automatically claim jurisdiction over American nationals. The only option now, of course, is to oppose vigorously the court's actual operations.

The United States must also oppose the increasingly exaggerated claims made in the name of the principle of "universal jurisdiction." Indeed, this new element of international law, which was invoked in an effort to extradite Augusto Pinochet to Spain, may be the most pernicious. The universal jurisdiction principle often is mistakenly traced to the Nuremberg trials. In fact, the International Military Tribunal at Nuremberg did not claim to exercise "universal jurisdiction" over the Nazi leadership. It instead justified its authority on the sovereign power of the conquered German state: namely, "the exercise of the sovereign legislative power [of Germany] by the countries to which the German Reich unconditionally surrendered; and the undoubted right of these countries to legislate for the occupied territories."[7] Under the traditional law of nations, universal jurisdiction is a narrow proposition, permitting all states to criminalize actions—like piracy—injurious to all and occurring outside the territory of any one state.

As expounded today, however, universal jurisdiction would permit the courts of any state to prosecute and punish the leadership of any other state for violations of international humanitarian norms. In this regard, the rule's proponents should keep in mind that any independent state, not just "right thinking" Western ones, would be entitled to prosecute such "violations" on a universal jurisdiction approach. Most recently, the courts of Yugoslavia tried (*in absentia*) and convicted the NATO leaders responsible for the spring 1999 air campaign against Serbia for crimes against humanity. (President Clinton was sentenced to twenty years' imprisonment.) This proceeding was obviously absurd. Yet, legally, it was just as "legitimate" as Spain's attempt to prosecute Pinochet.

As an alternative to expansive universal jurisdiction and the ICC, the United States should promote a renewed commitment to the prosecution of "international" crimes in national judicial systems. Under the traditional rules of international law, some national court system almost always has jurisdiction, either on the basis of territoriality (the country where the crime took place) or nationality (the citizenship of the accused), over crimes against the law of nations. For crimes committed beyond the borders of any state, the traditional universal jurisdiction principle would be available.

This solution, often derided by international humanitarian activists who are impatient with the whole notion of national sovereignty, shows real promise. Although states are often reluctant to prosecute their own nationals, concerted international pressure has produced results. For example, the Cambodian government is moving, albeit slowly, toward establishing a domestic tribunal to investigate and prosecute the crimes of the Khmer Rouge, and Libya was ultimately forced to surrender the individuals responsible for the terrorist attack on Pan Am Flight 103 over Lockerbie, Scotland. The Lockerbie case also demonstrates the potential flexibility of the "national" solution: the court that is trying the Lockerbie defendants has been convened in the Netherlands, but will apply the law of Scotland—the territory where the crime took place. Finally, in cases where the territory upon which the criminal acts took place has been militarily occupied (as in Kosovo), the Nuremberg model (courts established by the occupying or administering power) may be used.

At the same time, to make U.S. opposition to the ICC and to the expansion of universal jurisdiction more credible, the next president should seriously reconsider several attempts to subject foreign nationals to U.S. law. The enforcement of U.S. antitrust laws against foreign corporations is deeply resented in Europe and elsewhere. In addition, over the past decade the federal courts have increasingly entertained lawsuits, brought by U.S. citizens and foreign nations, arising out of acts taken in foreign countries by government officials and private citizens. These suits, brought under the 1789 Alien Tort Claims Act (which was originally passed to enable Americans to seek redress for piracy), have become vehicles for judicial examination of the internal policies of foreign states. Even the *Washington Post* argued, in an August 12 editorial, that this

> carries real dangers. The court system is designed to resolve disputes between people over whom the courts are actually capable of exercising authority. Here they are being used instead to convey moral messages and purvey essentially advisory opinions on questions of international human rights and foreign relations—not the courts' traditional province.

Along these same lines, Congress should temper its exuberance in allowing U.S. courts to consider claims brought by American nationals regarding terrorist acts overseas. Over the last few years, Congress has overturned the traditional principles of sovereign immunity, amending the Foreign Sovereign Immunities Act to permit civil suits against certain foreign countries (Iran, Syria, Libya, Iraq, North Korea, Sudan and Cuba) designated by the State Department as sponsors of terrorism against U.S. citizens. Under traditional legal principles, such foreign countries may be considered to have committed an act of war against the United States, entitling us to strike back at them or to bring a lawsuit at the International Court of Justice. It is not at all clear that converting an act of war into a subject for a civil suit, which can be brought by private litigants, is either good law or good foreign policy. A U.S. strategy of prompt reprisals against countries sponsoring terrorism—fully permissible under the traditional law of nations—should offer much more effective means of both deterring and punishing terrorism.

The restoration of the law of nations to its rightful place is an essential task for the next president. Accomplishing this goal will require a clear vision, sound public diplomacy, and a serious commitment to the rule of law in our international practices. Its realization would bolster American statecraft, enhance our global leadership position, and create a secure and prosperous international environment for the United States in the twenty-first century.

Notes

1. The State Department's Office of Media Reaction publishes analyses of foreign elite opinions that reveal a widespread preoccupation with alleged American "hegemony."
2. Tocqueville, *Democracy in America* (New York: Knopf, 1951), vol. 1, p. 280.
3. Quoted in Charles Trueheart, *Washington Post*, February 23, 1999.
4. Final Report to the Prosecutor by the Committee Established to Review NATO Bombing Campaign Against the Federal Republic of Yugoslavia, para. 50 (released June 13, 2000).
5. Bork, "The Limits of 'International Law'," *The National Interest* (Winter 1989/90), p. 10.
6. Rabkin, "Is EU Policy Eroding the Sovereignty of Non-Member States?," paper presented to the American Enterprise Institute, April 4-5, 2000, p. 3.
7. The Nuremberg Trial, *Federal Rules Decisions* (1946), vol. 6, p. 107.

2

International Law versus the American Constitution

*Jeremy Rabkin**

When major programs of President Roosevelt's New Deal were blocked by the Supreme Court during the 1930s, Roosevelt insisted that the Court must learn to apply a more "modern" view of the Constitution. Soon enough, a reshaped Court did adopt a much more permissive approach and scholars who liked the result spoke of a "living Constitution." We heard more about "evolving standards" and a "living Constitution" from defenders of judicial activism in the 1960s and 1970s. It seemed to offer the prestige of a higher law without the inconvenience of a fixed law. But sometimes we really want a constitution to have fixed and reliable limits. So, for example, many of those who once praised the "living Constitution" have, in recent months, invoked with great solemnity the "law" of impeachment, which, they say, was "fixed" by the Framers of the Constitution in the eighteenth century.

If nothing else, America's months of debate about impeachment remind us that many Americans care deeply about "the rule of law"—and disagree among themselves on what it means. Even those most devoted to defending President Clinton have appealed to arcane legal arguments about the proper application of the Constitution's provisions on impeachment.

But our own law may not be the only law that determines what happens in this country. At the very moment when Americans were so preoccupied with debates about the meaning of perjury or the requirements for impeachment, a series of events around the world offered a foretaste of what may become the next subject of heated legal debate for the United States: the proper reach of international law.

---

*Jeremy Rabkin teaches international law and American constitutional history in the Department of Government at Cornell University.

This essay first appeared in *The National Interest*, no. 55 (Spring 1999).

In Britain, the House of Lords decided last December that Augusto Pinochet could be held for extradition to Spain, where a magistrate sought to try the former Chilean dictator for tortures and murders committed by the Chilean government during Pinochet's period as chief of state. Meanwhile, halfway around the world, the government of Australia struggled to defend itself before a UN authority, which condemned the Australian government for allowing a uranium mine to be developed in the vicinity of an Australian national park. And here in the United States, the U.S. Supreme Court, after repeated displays of its own impatience with judicial second-guessing of capital sentences, suddenly ordered a halt to an execution in Texas and agreed to hear an appeal claiming that capital punishment in this case would violate international standards.

All these cases reflect the deepening insinuation of international law into the internal affairs of sovereign states. More than that, they raise sharp questions about the status of this emerging body of law. No one of these episodes marks a historic turning point in itself, but they are all straws in the wind. Lots of things are now rustling in that wind and it is gaining in force. We used to think that the Constitution would serve as a windbreak, but that is no longer so clear. To gauge the extent of the challenge it is necessary to look briefly first at the theoretical assumptions on which our Constitution was grounded, and in light of which it used to be interpreted on matters of international law.

The Traditional American View and Its Modern Rival

Resistance to international impositions has a long history in American political and constitutional thinking. Indeed, the United States was founded on a particular understanding of the limited authority of an external law applied to American society. For the American Revolution was a rebellion against the imposition of transnational law, the precise issue being whether the British Parliament possessed the rightful authority to make laws for the internal affairs of the colonies. The colonists insisted that, as they had never been represented in the British Parliament, they could not accept such authority. The British disagreed, and so brought on a revolutionary conflict.

Thus, when the Declaration of Independence asserts the "self-evident" truth that all men are "endowed by their Creator with certain unalienable rights," it proceeds almost at once to the conclusion that governments "derive their just powers from the consent of the governed." The specific grievances against British rule, enumerated in the body of the Declaration, make it plain that "just *powers*" are those constrained by law, and law derives from the enactments of elected legislatures. In short, no legislature, no real law.

The argument of the American Founders was not a sentimental plea for "participation." The Declaration speaks of consent to the "just powers" of government, not to its every particular action. The point of emphasizing constraints of law and legislative consent is that government remains, at some level, unavoidably about coercion: one submits to lawful government in the understanding that everyone else will be bound by the same law.

Americans were ready to recognize that law requires force to make it effective. Only five years after the end of the Revolutionary War, they adopted a new Constitution precisely to assure more reliable force to American government. The argument for the new Constitution as opposed to the Articles of Confederation was that reliable common policies required a common government, with its own army, its own sources of revenue and its own powers to make and enforce laws. But the underlying point was the same as in the Revolution: such powers are acceptable only if placed under the ultimate control of a common legislature.

Since the world as a whole has no legislature, this view might seem to leave no place for any sort of international law. But that was not quite the view of the Founders. The Constitution provided that treaties adopted by the United States (along with federal statutes) would be "the supreme law of the land." But it also stipulated that Congress should have the power to "define and punish offences against the law of nations"; and James Madison, often called the "father of the Constitution," thought it worthwhile to publish a lengthy and quite scholarly disquisition on the "law of nations" when he served as secretary of state under President Jefferson.

The founding generation and its successors did not see this as a threat to government by consent. On the contrary, some sort of international understanding is actually required by the doctrine of government by consent, since such government can only be effective if outside powers refrain from interfering in it. The Declaration of Independence itself appeals to such common understandings when it asserts the right of American states, "as free and independent states . . . to levy war, conclude peace, contract Alliances, establish Commerce and *to do all other Acts and Things which Independent States may of right do*" [emphasis added].

The "law of nations," as expounded in the leading European texts of that era, was focused on the relations of sovereign states, precisely with an eye to avoiding unnecessary affronts. It was concerned with such matters as security guarantees for diplomats and for nEUtral ships on the high seas. It was precisely to emphasize this focus of the "law of nations"—a law defining the way states deal with each other, and *not* how they govern at home—that Jeremy Bentham coined the term "inter-national law," just two years after the Framers convened in Philadelphia.

What made it seem plausible to speak of "international law" at the time of the American founding, and throughout the nineteenth century, was not only that this law was relatively undemanding, but that it was associated with a body of long-standing custom in inter-state dealings such that conformity with it could actually be expected of other states—or, if necessary, demanded.

In the background to expectations of conformity was the assumption that the violation of clear rules was an invitation to retaliation, perhaps even by force—so that the law was not, after all, entirely removed from force. International law was seen as the law that sovereign states were willing to accept *and also to insist upon*. Whether or not it was really or fully "law," it rarely entered into national courts, because (apart from disputes about private property seized in naval conflicts on the high seas) it rarely concerned the rights of individuals.

In this area, as elsewhere, America's founding doctrines seem to have exerted a lasting impression on subsequent American policy. The United States has generally held back from grand international schemes that might result in the imposition of international standards onto American domestic affairs. Most notably, the United States long refused to ratify international human rights conventions (along with labor standards proposed by the International Labor Organization). The Senate ratified a few human rights conventions in the past decade, but then only with severely limiting reservations, denying them any direct effect in domestic law. Critics have always complained that fuller participation would bind the United States to standards to which others would only pay lip service. In other words, for the critics these were not bona fide treaties at all but simply devices to shift fundamentally internal matters—how the American government deals with its own citizens—to international forums not directly accountable to the American people.

By now, this stance may seem less an expression of fundamental liberal principles than of particular American crochets, anachronistic survivals of eighteenth-century dogmas that make little sense even to other Western democracies. Certainly, the evolution of Europe's Common Market into the current European Union is a powerful challenge to the assumptions of the American Founders. The EU has an extremely ambitious regulatory agenda, reaching deeply into the internal policies of the member states. Yet it has no common army—and could not have, since some member states are committed to the NATO alliance and others are pledged to neutrality. The EU does not even have its own self-sustaining executive or law enforcement machinery, relying instead on the governmental machinery of the member states for ground-level enforcement and implementation of EU policies. And while it lacks the conventional elements of power or force, the EU also lacks a true legislature. There is a popularly elected assembly, called the European Parliament, but it is essentially an advisory body, with neither the power to tax nor the power to legislate.

What the European Union has, instead, is a central bureaucracy in Brussels (the European Commission) that elaborates new regulations. And it has a central court in Luxembourg (the European Court of Justice) that directs courts in the member states on the application of EU law. With the ready cooperation of national courts, this European Court has assumed the authority to hold even the acts of national parliaments invalid when they conflict (in the ECJ's view) with regulations of the Brussels bureaucrats or other requirements of EU treaty law. So half a continent is now governed by a curious collaboration of bureaucrats and judges, loyally supported by specialized interest groups that lobby the bureaucrats for favorable policies and then litigate before the judges to ensure their implementation by national governments.

It may be too soon to concede the success of this remarkable form of government, however—if indeed it can be considered a government. Even today, after decades of integrationist effort, European "law" does not mean the same thing in Greece or Italy as it does in Britain. While specialized interests lobby for specialized policy measures in Brussels, popular political protests still center on the elected governments of the member states. And European authorities, lacking the confidence of a direct electoral mandate, are wary of leaning too heavily on recalcitrant member states.

For the United States, at any rate, the problems of the EU are, for the moment, other peoples' problems. Indeed, by the classical principles of international law, the United States would have no clear right to object to how European states decide to share out their governing powers with neighboring states. The European Union, however, is only the most extreme instance of a larger trend that now does threaten to engulf the United States.

Pinochet's Revenge?

Former Chilean President Augusto Pinochet was sought by a Spanish magistrate wishing to try him for human rights abuses committed by the Chilean government while Pinochet was head of state. In September, with no prior warning, he was seized by British police, weeks after he had entered Britain—on a diplomatic passport for an arms-buying mission for the Chilean government. No one disputes that the military coup that brought Pinochet to power in 1973 was followed by nearly three thousand deaths or disappearances, the work of government security forces acting outside the restraints of due process. But it is also true that Chile has had a freely elected democracy since 1990 and that successive elected governments there have declined to challenge the amnesty law that protected Pinochet from domestic prosecution. Indeed, Chile's democratic government has declined even to challenge the constitutional scheme that made Pinochet commander-in-chief of the armed forces until 1997 and senator for life thereafter. So when British police arrested Pinochet, the Chilean government launched sharp and persistent protests and tried to assist Pinochet in his legal battle in the British courts.

The case for Pinochet's release turned on what had seemed a firm point of law. There has long been a customary rule of international law that courts of one country will not sit in judgment on the sovereign acts of, or the officials exercising sovereign power in, another country. As a matter of principle, to let courts in one country put the government of another on trial would be tantamount to an assertion by the first country that the second was actually subject to its authority and hence no longer fully sovereign: it would be, in effect, an attempt at conquest by courts. As a more practical matter, putting the government of another country on trial was assumed to be such a belligerent act as to be virtually an invitation to war. Thus the only exceptions to this rule until now have been cases where the home country of the defendant did not object—as in the Nuremberg trials (where the occupying Allied powers, which organized the trials, claimed to be the lawful government of Germany at the time), or in the more recent U.S. trial of deposed Panamanian dictator Manuel Noriega (whose successors were delighted to have him taken into U.S. custody and removed from their midst).

Now, of course, the world at large has no legislature to establish a new rule of international law, supervening the customary rules about sovereign immunity. Supporters of the Pinochet prosecution claimed that the rules had been changed by a succession of human rights conventions, by which governments around the world have promised to suppress and punish genocide, torture and other human rights abuses. But none of these treaties gives clear indication that it is supposed to supersede the customary rules of sovereign immunity, and certainly none gives explicit authority for third-party states to try government officials from other countries.

So in October Britain's High Court of Justice ruled unanimously that Pinochet should be released. On appeal in the House of Lords, a five-man panel split 3-2 the other way in early December. But in a subsequent appeal, Britain's Lord Chancellor directed that a new panel should be convened to reconsider this ruling. One of the three Law Lords making up the majority turned out to have been closely associated with fund-raising efforts for Amnesty International, a human rights advocacy group that had strongly advocated Pinochet's extradition and prosecution. The Lord Chancellor held that this made the ruling of the original panel look improper and Pinochet should therefore be accorded a new appeal before a new panel of Law Lords.

But it is hard to say why Amnesty International had any less right to participate in the judgment of Pinochet—for misdeeds committed in Chile, against Chileans—than the governments of Britain or Spain. In fact, both the British prime minister and his Spanish counterpart insisted that their governments were leaving the matter to the courts and taking no policy stand on the issues. Both declined to exercise the statutory powers that political ministers in either country could have invoked to stop the extradition process. So the whole momentous prosecution was supposed to be proceeding on the say-so of career prosecutors—that is, essentially, bureaucrats—in each country.

While the British courts were deliberating, the European Parliament sought to ensure that the prosecution would go forward. It adopted a resolution urging Britain to extradite, and other governments to take up the prosecution, if Spain finally declined to do so itself. This intervention of the European Parliament had its own ironic logic: a parliament that is not a real legislature demanded enforcement of a new international doctrine that is not a real law.

And clearly, it cannot be a real law. Weak and distant Chile will not go to war with Britain or Spain or the EU. But the notion that "international law" will now hold evil-doers of all lands to account is absurd. If "international law" requires the trial of Pinochet in an outside country, then it must require similar trials to hold accountable far worse butchers from many other places. Nothing in international law, however, says that only former dictators from small countries can be held to account in this way. There is no distinction in the relevant human rights treaties between dictators and democratic officials, between top officials of small countries and top officials of powerful countries, or even between former officials and currently serving ones. But no one expects EU countries to hold a top Chinese leader to account for massacres in Tibet, or to hold former Russian officials for extradition to Latvia—or American officials for extradition to Sudan, which has been threatening to charge them with war crimes for the bombing of an undefended aspirin factory last August. The European Parliament seems to have in mind a "law" that applies only to Pinochet.

Human rights advocates insist that the whole problem could be equitably handled if there were an international criminal court. And a UN conference did indeed come out with a treaty proposal to establish such a court in the summer of 1998. Its provisions were so vague and all-encompassing, however, that even the Clinton administration felt compelled to refuse its assent and the United States has since been lobbying other countries not to ratify the International Criminal Court (ICC) Statute. In effect, Spain's prosecution of Pinochet was a forcing of the issue by asserting the right of national courts to proceed in the name of the international community without waiting for the explicit agreement of other countries. It thus presents reluctant nations with the choice of submitting to the ICC (which does have a number of explicit procedural safeguards not recognized here by Spanish courts) or trusting to the vagaries of legal reasonings in the national courts of dozens of separate countries.

But even the ICC bids to force its jurisdiction on unwilling participants. The new court will be empowered to assert jurisdiction over war crimes and extreme abuses, not only when committed by nationals of signatory states, but also when committed against *victims* who are nationals of a signatory state. In theory, then, the ICC could be turned against the United States at the behest of Sudan, even if the United States does not itself ratify the treaty establishing the ICC. So we are back to the same basic problem. Either the ICC does not act, because its independent prosecutors have the bureaucratic nimbleness to avoid confrontation with a great power, or we have in store for us some troubling confrontations down the road.

Or would the United States finally agree to cooperate if its own citizens were called to account? Human rights advocates insist that the United States has nothing to fear because the ICC Statute acknowledges the right of home countries to conduct their own trials. But it also provides that if the trial result is judged to be inadequate or unsatisfactory, then the international prosecutor retains the authority to demand a new trial before the ICC. Then the United States would have to decide whether it would or would not go along if one of its own citizens were sought for a trial by the ICC.

Could the United States hand over an American citizen to an international tribunal, even for trial on the basis of acts committed while in the service of the U.S. government and even within the boundaries of the United States? A host of legal authorities have insisted that there is no constitutional objection to the U.S. government doing so. No one disputes that international tribunals violate guarantees in the U.S. Bill of Rights—such as the guarantee of trial by jury, which follows an English common law tradition that means nothing to international authorities. The argument is simply that if the United States can extradite its citizens to other countries for crimes committed in those countries, it can also extradite to international authorities for international crimes. But if it could do so for "war crimes," why not for other crimes? In that case, why not hand over drug dealers to an international drug court?—another venture that has received serious discussion. But then what do the guarantees in the Bill of Rights mean if they can be side-stepped any time our government finds it more convenient to have Americans tried by foreign authorities? We would then have a Constitution that can be amended without the bother of persuading three-quarters of the states to adopt a formal amendment.

Perhaps it will not come to that. But it is remarkable that we no longer feel the need for a constitutional boundary. Do we rely on public sentiment to stiffen the resolve of our government? If so, we may be misguided, for the new trend in international affairs is for transnational coalitions of advocacy groups to play on public sentiment in order to bolster the authority of international institutions.

Global Civil Society vs. Australia

That is just what happened in Australia at the same time the Pinochet case was proceeding through the British courts.

On November 30, 1998 the World Heritage Committee of Unesco voted to condemn the government of Australia for allowing a uranium mine to operate in close proximity to an Australian national park that had been designated as a World Heritage site. The committee agreed that the government of Australia should be given six months to defend the mine against findings of an international inspection team that the mine would endanger the scenic values of the Kakadu Park and its cultural significance for aboriginal people nearby. If Australia could not by then satisfy the committee, the park would be placed on the list of sites "in danger."

What made this episode remarkable was, in the first place, the willingness of this UN forum to enter into a confrontational dispute with a participating government. The World Heritage Convention essentially establishes a registry of sites in participating countries that are judged to be of special significance for the whole world. Essentially, it is the UN equivalent of a landmark registry, which has come to include such sites as India's Taj Mahal, America's Yellowstone National Park and France's Louvre Museum. A committee of representatives from twenty-one states, elected from all the states party to the convention, oversees the list. The committee not only decides which sites may qualify but purports to monitor their continuing safekeeping. Its only sanction for such purposes is to list a deteriorating site on a separate list of sites "in danger" and ultimately, if the dangers are not addressed, to de-list the site. No site has ever been de-listed.

Indeed, no site has ever been put on the "in danger" list except at the request of the home state. Some states have requested such listing as a way of dramatizing problems and seeking international financial assistance for corrective actions. But states that fear embarrassment have often resisted listing on the "in danger" list. Ecuador, for example, asked the World Heritage Committee to organize international assistance for what it admitted were serious problems in its management of its World Heritage site in the Galapagos Islands. But it specifically requested that the site not be listed as "in danger"—and it was not. The obvious reason to avoid such listing is that the whole scheme—such as it is—depends on the cooperation of the affected governments; a government that does not want to cooperate can simply walk away.

But the committee in this case took a very hard line because of another difference: within Australia itself, political opponents of the current conservative government were prepared to support—indeed, even invite—international intervention. The environmental spokesman for the opposition Labor Party actually wrote to the World Heritage Committee to urge it to take a tough stand. The networking skills of domestic opponents were altogether remarkable. Environmentalists, who seem to have opposed the mine in large part due to general opposition to nuclear power, managed to draw attention to the handful of aboriginal people who did oppose the mine, obscuring the majority view of local aborigines who stood to gain substantial payments from the mining company. Australian environmentalists have organized a separate Green Party, but with only two seats in the Australian parliament it is in itself a negligible threat to the government. But an Australian Green leader managed to make his case to important Green ministers in the governments of Western Europe and, in this way, secured a vote of the *European* Parliament urging Australia to shut down the mine. The same sort of back-channel mobilization has been credited with persuading the French government to take a tough stand against the mine through the French representative on the current World Heritage Committee.

The ultimate result is still uncertain but the pattern is clear. An international institution with no real authority has gained special leverage by acting as a bridge between opposition factions in one country and allies in other countries—over a matter that has no real connection to those other countries.

And this is not an isolated case. In its 1995 report, the UN Commission on Global Governance hailed the emergence of what it called "global civil society," which it saw as "best expressed in the global non-governmental movement." It did not mean business firms, churches or sports clubs—all of which are also "non-governmental." It meant advocacy groups. It noted that NGOs have proliferated at a remarkable rate over the past decade and praised their "vital assistance to the UN in the conduct of its work." Such organizations

> often provide independent monitoring, early-warning and information gathering services that can be especially useful in preventive diplomacy. They can serve as unofficial or alternative channels of communication and can help establish relationships that create the trust necessary to bridge political gaps.

Also, though the report does not quite note the fact, NGOs never have to face voters or bear any sort of accountability. It is not clear, in any case, who would be entitled to demand accountability from them, since they so often claim to speak for "humanity" or "the earth," constituencies that are not well equipped to demand any sort of direct accounting.

"Global civil society" is, in the older understanding, virtually an oxymoron. What makes a society "civil," in the classical liberal view, is a common government, able to enact and enforce common rules. The United Nations is not a government. What UN agencies seek is an authority that is somehow above government, without the accountability that actual governments have toward particular electorates or defined citizen bodies. Actual governments can be awkward for UN agencies. It is usually much easier to deal with constituencies that do not themselves have to pay UN bills or submit to UN directives. NGOs—a sort of phantom citizenry—are the perfect partners for the phantom authority exercised by UN agencies. So the UN and other international institutions have become great sponsors of NGOs, which figure prominently at UN conferences on global concerns. The World Bank, eager to deflect NGO criticism, has actually poured over a third of a billion dollars into NGO coffers in recent years. (And, not coincidentally, the European Commission in Brussels funds European NGOs on an even more lavish scale.)

Past Australian governments have cheerfully cooperated with NGOs working through international forums on other issues. Now the current government is finding it hard to ignore the World Heritage Committee, as local advocates demand adherence to the Committee's direction in the name of "international law."

Thinking Globally, Acting Locally

On December 12, 1998 the U.S. Supreme Court issued a stay of execution for Joseph Stanley Faulder less than thirty minutes before he was scheduled to die by lethal injection in Texas. The state of Texas was hardly acting with undue haste: Faulder had been on death row for twenty-one years. It was, in other words, the classic sort of death penalty appeal in America's endless litigation over capital punishment.

Faulder had been convicted for the brutal killing of a seventy-five year-old woman, leaving her to be found by her relatives "bludgeoned, bound with tape and Christmas wrapping paper, a knife protruding from her chest." Faulder never denied the charges. But years after his conviction he remembered that he was a Canadian citizen, something he had not mentioned to Texas officials at the time of his arrest, when he was found with a Colorado driver's license. So after many other failed appeals on other grounds, Faulder's lawyers launched the argument that his conviction violated the Vienna Convention on Consular Relations, which obligates signatory states, when they arrest a foreign citizen for a serious crime, to notify the nearest consulate of the defendant's home country. Texas officials, not knowing of Faulder's Canadian citizenship, did not notify Canadian officials until 1991—when he was deep into his various procedural appeals on other grounds.

What made the Supreme Court's intervention so notable was that a very similar case had been presented earlier in the same year. In that case, lawyers for a Paraguayan national, Angel Breard, who were appealing his death sentence in Virginia, persuaded the government of Paraguay to file claims before the International Court of Justice in The Hague, based on Virginia's failure to notify Paraguayan officials at the time of the trial. The ICJ asked Virginia to postpone the execution while the matter was considered by international authorities, and Secretary of State Madeleine Albright pleaded for Virginia to do so out of respect for international law. But Virginia refused and a last-minute attempt to appeal to the U.S. Supreme Court was denied by the justices.

The Faulder case followed the same script—earnest diplomatic entreaties from the Canadian foreign minister, followed by earnest entreaties from Albright, followed by the rejection of these entreaties by state officials in Texas. Only this time, the U.S. Supreme Court ordered the execution postponed to give itself time to consider the issues.

The Court may yet decide that the execution can go forward. The preamble to the relevant Vienna Convention stipulates that its purpose is to clarify "consular relations privileges and immunities" and "is not to benefit individuals but to ensure the efficient performance of functions by consular posts." In a survey conducted through U.S. embassies around the world, the State Department was unable to find a single case in which another country had overturned a criminal conviction in its own courts solely because a foreign defendant had not been advised of his rights to consult consular officials from his own country. And there seems to be no reason at all to believe that Faulder's trial would have turned out any differently if he had sought and received the opportunity to consult with a Canadian consulate before his trial commenced.

But none of that may matter. The United States remains one of the few countries in the Western world that still maintain capital punishment. And by no coincidence the state with the largest number of capital sentences is Texas, followed in second place by Virginia. And once again the specific case turns out to be the flashpoint of a larger international campaign. At the beginning of 1998, a UN special reporter issued a report condemning the United States for racist and abusive applications of the death penalty—ignoring the repeated judgments of U.S. courts, up to and including the U.S. Supreme Court, to the contrary. The European Parliament was—for once—not dragged into this dispute. But Amnesty International, taking time out from its advocacy for the prosecution of Pinochet in Europe, took notice.

An Amnesty report on human rights abuses in the United States, issued in 1998, devotes an entire chapter to abuses of the death penalty, which it asserts to be contrary to international law. Yes, it acknowledges, the U.S. Senate specifically inserted a reservation into its ratification of the Covenant on Civil and Political Rights, stipulating that the Covenant's death penalty restrictions were not accepted by the United States. But this reservation, according to Amnesty, conflicts with a subsequent ruling of the UN's Human Rights Committee about evolving standards of customary international law that must now make the U.S. reservation on this point unlawful. And, of course, Amnesty lawyers in Canada helped to organize the Faulder appeal, as other human rights groups had mobilized to resist the earlier execution of Angel Breard.

What Next?

So we have free-floating, evolving standards of "law" defined by international bureaucrats. We have organized advocacy groups in transnational coalitions. And we may soon have U.S. courts applying this law at the behest of these groups. In other words, all the elements of EU-style governance are already in place. Is this kind of government really consistent with the U.S. Constitution?

In at least three ways, the most prominent commentators have already promulgated legal theories that prepare the way. First, the latest *Restatement of Foreign Relations Law* (1987), a privately sponsored treatise that holds special prestige in an area of law with very little case law, asserts that there is now a federal common law of foreign relations, by which federal courts are empowered to impose their rulings on states and localities, even where there is no direct treaty or statute on which to rely but simply a federal court's notion of evolving international law. In domestic law, the notion of a free-floating judge-made common law of this kind was firmly repudiated by the Supreme Court in the 1930s. The *Restatement* argues, however, that international obligations of the federal government require a different approach for cases with an international dimension. Thus it has an entire chapter on "customary international law of human rights," which is supposed to be drawn from the spirit of existing treaties but applicable to the United States even where the Senate has not ratified the relevant treaty or has attached particular exceptions by reservation. Already a number of lower federal courts have relied on this "law" to allow suits against U.S. corporations (pursued in U.S. courts by U.S.-based advocacy groups) for supposed human rights or environmental depredations by their corporate subsidiaries in Asia and South America.

Second, the historic constitutional doctrine was that even formal treaties—let alone customary law, adopted without treaties—could not reach entirely domestic affairs. The treaty power and other foreign affairs powers of the federal government could only reach genuinely inter-national matters. The latest Restatement insists that such restrictions can no longer be maintained. And understandably so. If human rights conventions and the World Heritage Convention are bona fide treaties, then it is reasonable to say that what the U.S. Park Service does in Yellowstone National Park and what Philadelphia police do to Americans in Philadelphia are properly subject to international inspection—as indeed they have been over the past decade, though the binding effect of international interventions in these cases is much in dispute.

Finally, it was once clear doctrine that the treaty power could not be delegated to foreign bodies—that Senate ratification could bind the United States to the terms of an agreement, but not to subsequent extensions or extrapolations of the agreement by an international authority. While the *Restatement* skirts the issue, Professor Louis Henkin, who was the chief reporter for the *Restatement*, published in 1996 a new edition of his own treatise, *Foreign Affairs and the Constitution* (Oxford University Press), which explicitly repudiates such a non-delegation doctrine. Thus what the UN Human Rights Committee or the World Heritage Committee of UNESCO pronounces to be the law may well be taken as binding law for the United States (which is the case even though the United States is no longer a member of UNESCO). At least in Henkin's view, the Constitution does not forbid the United States from submitting to an arrangement in which this would be so.

World Order in a Post-Liberal World

Does any of this really matter? Before dismissing the significance of recent episodes, one ought to step back and look at the larger picture. Along with human rights treaties, we have begun to spin out a network of far-reaching new environmental treaties, culminating in the stupefyingly ambitious project of the Kyoto Protocol, which envisions international authorities empowered to enforce dramatic reductions in energy use among the world's major economies. The U.S. Senate has balked at ratifying this treaty, but its champions—in the Clinton administration and in a host of environmental advocacy groups—insist that it is necessary to avert global warming. The necessity is disputed by many respectable scientists and policy analysts. But surely this undertaking is at least as "necessary" as international supervision of parks policy in Australia or criminal justice in Texas. The ideology of global governance already has considerable momentum.

Meanwhile, there is continuing pressure to extend the terms of international trade agreements, which up until now have largely focused on reciprocal lowering of barriers to imports, while scrupulously refraining from imposing any standards for how goods entering into international trade are actually produced in their home countries. But President Clinton has repeatedly urged that the World Trade Organization must begin to develop standards that would prevent countries with unfair labor practices or unacceptably lax environmental controls from unfairly flooding the markets of countries whose own producers must observe higher standards.

At Kyoto, it was decided that if poor countries are not now willing to participate in energy reduction schemes, then a select group of richer nations should set them an example by taking one-sided commitments on themselves. We might see the European Union seek to negotiate such an approach to labor and environmental standards, which would apply to the United States and other affluent countries, even if rejected by China and India. And it is not altogether inconceivable that the United States would participate in such a venture, since it has already made limited—but precedent setting—commitments about internal labor and environmental standards in the NAFTA accords with Canada and Mexico. Clinton himself limned the vision in his latest State of the Union address: we must strive to give international trade "a human face," as earlier in this century we supplied a "human face" to interstate commerce at home. In plainer language, the New Deal for the U.S. economy must now be followed up with a New Deal for the world economy, with the United States itself fully accepting the new international controls this will require.

If the Constitution sets no barrier to such projects, then we may see the United States drawn deeper into a style of governance that looks very much like what the EU countries are now experiencing. True, it would not necessarily involve such a systematic program of integration or such powerful central institutions. But we could, like the Europeans, start by forswearing any notion of a super-legislature and end up with more and more governance by courts and bureaucrats, answering only to advocacy groups that are themselves unaccountable.

On the other hand, it may turn out that the American political system will summon a deep resistance to any such serious foreign intrusions. The United States has been a hold-out against many sorts of grand international ventures in this century—from the League of Nations to the Law of the Sea Treaty, from the Children's Rights Convention to the International Criminal Court. Perhaps the first time an international commitment imposes real cost or hardship in domestic affairs, without any direct U.S. legislative endorsement, Congress will rise up and sweep away all the grand visions of the law professors and the advocacy groups. In its domestic applications, international law may turn out to be the equivalent of those codes of proper political campaign tactics or proper journalistic practice, which are sponsored by well-meaning foundations, adumbrated by idealistic academics, endorsed by high-minded editorialists—and ignored by all real-world practitioners.

But the most likely development may not follow either of these alternatives. Lacking an international legislature or an international executive, champions of international law have maintained their credibility by learning to pick their spots—ducking out of sight when legal claims are strongly resisted, re-emerging in those settings where issue networks have prepared the way for success. It will, in other words, be a selective, inconsistent, bureaucratic sort of law, which has a lot of "give" along with its occasional "bite."

That is, after all, what should be expected from the demise of our founding constitutional traditions—a reversion to a pre-liberal world. Sovereignty was itself a concept of the Enlightenment and a part of the liberal vision of law and politics. There was certainly law of a kind in medieval Europe. As Enlightenment thinkers saw it in retrospect, the problem in the medieval world was not too little law but too much. There was the legal edict of the medieval emperors, battling with the opposing constitutional claims of the medieval church, and both in constant tension with a network of feudal relations with their own legal claims. It was also a world without distinct peoples—in the constitutional sense—and without legislatures, in the modern sense of lawmaking bodies. Above all the conflicting, often highly parochial legalistic claims, medieval Europe had a set of visionaries who conversed across borders in a common language unknown to ordinary people—Latin. And its most devoted visionaries talked endlessly about the unity of Christendom, a vision they sustained for centuries in the face of all evidence to the contrary.

This is not a world that any of the American Founders looked back on with nostalgia. But it seems to appeal very much to the champions of global civil society. It remains unclear whether the Constitution can still keep the United States from joining it.

3

International Crime and Punishment

*Alfred P. Rubin**

The idea of an international criminal court is supported by many people and now has moved from the lobbying of lawyers and moralists to an area of practical action. At the close of the Gulf War, the United States sent a team to investigate Iraqi atrocities with an eye to bringing those who committed them before an international tribunal authorized to apply international law to the acts of individuals. A recent Resolution of the United Nations Security Council calls for an investigation of at least equally repulsive atrocities reportedly committed in former Yugoslavia. Former United States Secretary of State Eagleberger even named a half dozen leaders of former Yugoslavia as fit defendants.

It can be argued that the failure to set up such a tribunal after the Gulf War was a failure merely of political will. But it can also be argued that the failure came about as a result of serious consideration, and that the inhibitions in setting up such a tribunal are inherent in the international legal order. If that is so, then there is no failure of will, but only a realization by those focusing on practicalities that the sort of tribunal envisaged by enthusiasts for international law could not achieve the goals its proponents have in mind. Before too much time of able people is consumed by the effort to establish an international criminal court, it might be well to examine the real obstacles to achieving their civilizing goal by this means in the current international legal order.

It is easy to define acts that are crimes under what is conceived to be international criminal law. National war crimes tribunals, military commissions, and courts martial have often enough tried and even executed persons for violating the "laws and customs of war" established in international practice.

---

*Alfred P. Rubin is distinguished professor of international law at the Fletcher School of Law and Diplomacy at Tufts University.

This essay originally appeared in *The National Interest*, no. 33 (Fall 1993).

"Common law" crimes can be created (or found inherent in the system) by tribunals authorized to do that, and prohibitions on retroactive "legislation" can be ignored or reasoned away, as was done by the victor's tribunals at Nuremberg and Tokyo with regard to the "crime" of planning and waging "aggressive war" and "crimes against humanity." Some other acts, like participation in the international drug trade, can be made "international crimes" by treaty or by consistent state practice accepted as law by the international community.

But the new crimes created for Nuremberg were defined by the victorious allies only in the context of Nazi and Imperial Japanese activities and were not applied to the Soviets, who also invaded Poland and the Baltic States by what were evidently pre-arranged "acts of aggression," and whose treatment of some national minorities might have been considered within any definition of "crimes against humanity" that had not been drafted to apply only to the defeated enemies. The treaties relating to drug trafficking reflect similar sensitivities. They do not provide "universal" jurisdiction, they oblige the treaty parties to exercise only their established jurisdiction against persons within that jurisdiction whose acts fit the treaty categories.

Those arguing for the establishment of an international tribunal frequently claim that crimes against humanity as defined for Nuremberg can now be defined without the restrictive language that made those proceedings seem hypocritical. That is so. But unless the law can be seen to apply to Israel's leaders as well as to leaders of various Arab factions, to George Bush (who ordered the invasion of Panama) as well as Saddam Hussein (who ordered the invasion of Kuwait), it will seem hypocritical again. This is not to say that Israeli and American leaders cannot defend their actions, but so can Arab leaders. Should any of them be obliged to?

This raises an even deeper problem. Who decides who are to be the prosecuting authorities, investigators, and judges, and who is to erect and supervise the facilities for punishment? Would the great powers trust the UN General Assembly's discretion in that selection? If so, presumably Israel's leaders and possibly our own would be the first indicted. Would the General Assembly majority be satisfied with the objectivity of the Security Council and its Great Power vetoes? Would the United States, which refused to appear before the International Court in the Hague to respond to Nicaragua's successful complaint, accept the judges of the International Court as impartial either as judges or as a body to select judges and prosecutors?

To solve these questions, advocates for such a tribunal frequently analogize their notion of international crimes to the international legal order's treatment of those who participate in the slave trade, "piracy" or "genocide." The analogy is misplaced. Despite the vigorous rhetoric, there has never been a coherent practice by states or other bodies to enforce the rules relating to the international slave trade, piracy and genocide as if they were part of some universal criminal law. National laws against what national legislators have called "piracy" or "slave trading" have been applied against persons within the traditional reach of national legislation, but the few attempts to apply such laws to the acts of foreigners that did not impact on the prescribing state have normally failed.

The reasons for this failure have to do with the structure of the state system on which the current legal order rests. For example, the Genocide Convention, which defines the crime and obliges states to punish it, limits the jurisdiction to the state in whose territory it happened (which never punishes the acts of its own officials) or an international tribunal which has not yet been established. That is as far as the states framing the Convention were willing to go. Thus, there have never been any trials for "genocide." There is no reason to expect states to agree to any greater transfer to international civil servants or others, of the authority to cite political leaders as "criminals" to be hauled before strangers and tried. Even "terrorists" regard themselves as "freedom fighters" or an "army of God" and deny to those outside their own movement the moral or legal authority to apply to their actions a purported "universal law" which they reject or whose application to their particular circumstances they refuse to acknowledge. In these circumstances, applying to them our version of what the criminal law should be is likely to create even deeper resentments and more violence.

Nonetheless, on 25 May (1993) the Security Council adopted a proposal to establish an International Criminal Court. It relies for enforcement on the provision of the United Nations charter requiring members of the UN to carry out some Security Council "decisions." But Bosnian Serbs are not represented in the UN except by Bosnians, against whom they are fighting. If the Serbs will not, and the Bosnians cannot, arrest the accused war criminals, who is bound to enforce the "decision"? What happens if they don't? And the tribunal's jurisdiction is to be restricted to events in the former Yugoslavia. Since the current international legal order rests on a notion of "sovereign equality" of states under the law, and the states that set it up are unwilling to submit themselves to its authority, the arrangement is inherently hypocritical; another "victor's tribunal" being set up belatedly by the winners of the Second World War.

There are many other practical and legal problems, some of which can be overcome; most of which cannot. Like the Kellogg-Briand Pact of 1928 legally renouncing recourse to war: it seems the product of enthusiasts, at best useful in providing a public relations rationale for hanging a few temporarily helpless villains, on deeper analysis, an embarrassment.

There are several other ameliorating actions that could be explored, none in the "criminal law" mode. International law is not a criminal law system; it is more akin to constitutional law, where enforcement rests on political counterpressures and foreseeable middle- and long-term reactions. A militarily organized movement that commits atrocities is likely to lose allies, unify its enemies, waste its energy in daring strikes of dubious military or political value, and ultimately turn on itself. The United States applied the laws of war in its own civil war 130 years ago not because "the law" compelled that application, but because it was in the interest of the United States to apply that law even if the overall framework of the international legal order did not require it. So held the United States Supreme Court in 1878.

From this point of view, Saddam Hussein has established a reputation as a person whose committed word is worthless and whose ability to lead by moral example and persuasion must be small. And those who believe that an ethnically "pure" Serbia or "Serbo-Bosnia" will be able to resume a level of economic activity that rests on contracts, property rights, mutual respect and the other things that make economic development possible and life bearable, are certain to be disappointed; as disappointed as the radical right in South Africa that thought that South Africa's international investors would not notice that apartheid was politically and economically destabilizing and its proponents not attractive associates even for hard-headed business-people.

In sum, the world would do better grappling with the tragedies of former Yugoslavia and the Middle East, acknowledging that violations of international morality and rules of law are not analogous to violations of national criminal law, but that no law requires anybody to do business with people whose behavior they regard as despicable, or to accept, in lieu of cash, the word of proven liars.

4

The Limits of "International Law"

*Robert H. Bork**

On October 25, 1983, armed forces of the United States invaded Grenada. President Reagan at once stated that our purpose was not only to protect Americans there but to "help in the restoration of democratic institutions" in a country where "a brutal group of leftist thugs violently seized power." Both the President and Secretary of State George P. Shultz said the operation was fully consistent with international law. Senator Daniel Patrick Moynihan disagreed: "I don't know that you restore democracy at the point of a bayonet." He said we had clearly violated international law. (Moynihan is the public official who most persistently invokes this law and his views deserve attention.) Soon, Harvard law professor Abram Chayes, who had served as legal adviser to the State Department in the Kennedy administration, wrote in the *New York Times* that among international law experts there existed "remarkably broad agreement that the United States' invasion was a flagrant violation of international law." On the same page, Eugene V. Rostow, a professor and former dean of the Yale Law School, wrote that "the American and allied campaign in Grenada is legitimized by classic precedents in international law, notably the Cuban missile crisis of 1962."

The American public, to the degree that it paid any attention, must have been quite mystified. High public officials and an undefined group of "experts in international law" were bitterly divided over the legality of what the United States had done. The pattern is familiar. Whenever an American President uses or subsidizes force against another country, the halls of Congress resound and the pages of newspapers sizzle with pronouncements by his political opponents (and his allies) that he is (and is not) a lawbreaker. Some months later, articles arguing both sides appear in scholarly journals. Since the public is

*Robert H. Bork is a senior fellow at the American Enterprise Institute.

This essay was originally published in *The National Interest*, no. 18 (Winter 1989/90).

assured that there is a law of nations but have no idea what it is, they are almost certain to come away with the impression that, according to a substantial segment of informed opinion, the United States is a habitual lawbreaker. Indeed, the U.S. appears to be a recidivist. That is no small matter.

People who deliberately break known laws are immoral. So it must be with nations. Or must it? The word "law" is a capacious one and before we accept a sense of guilt it would be well to inquire further. What, exactly, is international law? Is it law, at all? What purposes does it serve? In some of its branches, it is law in a conventional sense. If two nations dispute fishing rights in the sea under a treaty, they may submit the matter to an international tribunal and agree to abide by the decision. In addition, there are international conventions, some of long standing, that govern the treatment of prisoners of war, of diplomats, of the rights of neutrals, etc. But that is not the kind of international law about which politicians and scholars grow passionate.

In its grandest (or most grandiose) form, international law is about the use or support of armed force against another nation. Concerning that subject, there are a great many statements of principle that purport to be law. They may be found, for example, in the Charter of the United Nations, in the Charter of the Organization of American States, in any number of bilateral and multilateral treaties, and in custom. The rules of customary law, indeed, supposedly derived from the actual practices of nations, are said to be just as binding as any charter.

Most people find this rather perplexing. Nations regularly act in ways that, we are assured by politicians and scholars, constitute clear violations of international law ... and nothing happens. No police force goes into action, no grand jury indicts, no petit jury sits, no verdict is announced by a court or, if one is, the convicted party ignores it. Articles and books gradually appear contending vociferously, and sometimes learnedly, that there was, or that there was not, a law violation. What can it mean to say that rules like that are in some sense, in any sense, "law"?

Senator Moynihan has no doubts on that subject: "International law exists. It is not an option. It is a fact." Others are less sure; and it is not merely laymen who feel unease. Treatises on international law commonly open by addressing the question whether the subject contains much that can properly be called "law." Most writers seem a touch defensive, but they assure the reader that there is "law" there. Yet the explanations themselves tend to be more than a trifle elusive and often romantic. A very prominent international lawyer, Philip Jessup, once offered an argument better than most:

> The layman and the common lawyer who find it difficult to fit international law into their concept of "law" . . . usually are alike in asserting that there isn't any international law. They forget that law has many meanings. There is the law of gravity, the Sherman Anti-Trust law, the law of supply and demand, international law.

The passage confuses rather than clarifies. The law of gravity describes a force in the natural universe. The law of supply and demand is an observation about human behavior in markets. One who attempts levitation or tries to purchase more than anyone is willing to sell at a particular price would not be called a law violator. The Sherman Act is a rule made by a legislature with conceded political authority and is enforced by courts through damages, fines, and even imprisonment. The fact that all of these things are called "laws" demonstrates only that the word has been applied to things that have little or nothing in common.

Professor Michael Reisman of Yale notes that "Law is perforce a system of authorized coercion, and it can neither be conceived of nor operate without a supportive political system or power process. In the absence of a centralization of authoritative force and an effective monopoly over who can use it to maintain community order and values, individual actors must look to their own resources." Jessup recognized this problem but tried nonetheless to edge international law closer to the Sherman Act:

> In most cases the layman is impressed by the reality of breaches of international law and is not sufficiently aware of the reality of reliance upon it. He does not pause to wonder why foreign offices bother to maintain legal staffs, which are an expense and sometimes a hindrance to the execution of policy.

But the existence of legal staffs poring over issues of international law proves little about a law relating to international violence. Thousands of mundane commercial and political matters arise in international settings, where the meaning of "international law" is itself not a focus of controversy. But so long as there purports to be international law about the use of force, the most cynical and predatory government will employ a legal staff to engage in international "shystering" as the need arises. Jessup finally resorted to the argument that, since people called international lawyers are doing something, what they are doing must be international law:

> Impotent to restrain a great nation which has no decent respect for the opinion of mankind, failing in its severest test of serving as a substitute for war, international law plods on its way, followed automatically in routine affairs, invoked, flouted, codified, flouted again but yet again invoked. The Legal Adviser of the United States Department of State still sits at his desk ... in Washington and his counterparts sit at Downing Street, the Quai d'Orsay and the Wilhelmstrasse. It is not their task to frame policies. But can one say that the international law with which they deal has no reality?

In January of 1940, when Jessup's article appeared, one might have been inclined to say precisely that. One might have said it scores or hundreds of times since. The Soviets used force to crush movements toward freedom in Hungary, Czechoslovakia, and East Germany, and to seize Afghanistan. But it is not just a great power such as the Soviet Union that is immune to the blandishments of international law. Cuba and Nicaragua have armed and supported insurgency movements attempting to destroy democratic governments in Central America. China overran Tibet, India seized the Portuguese colony of Goa. The least one can say is that, in such cases, whatever reality this wraith called international law possesses is not visible to the non-expert.

This is not to deny that the *idea* of international law has real-world effects. It does. To see what those effects are, it is helpful to examine a pair of recent instances in which actions of the United States raised issues of international law. Two of the most spectacular such examples were the invasion of Grenada and our support of contra forces fighting the Sandinista regime in Nicaragua. The relevant facts cannot reasonably be disputed in either case.

The Nicaraguan revolution that deposed the dictator Anastasio Somoza in 1979 was made by a broad coalition, including the church, organized labor, professional and business groups, and peasants. Cuba, however, armed and advised the Marxist-Leninist Sandinistas who gradually removed democrats from positions of power, suppressed civil, political, and religious rights, and built a powerful army with arms and assistance from the Soviets and their allies. Nicaragua itself began supporting armed insurgencies designed to overthrow other democratic regimes. El Salvador was a particular target.

Alarmed, the United States began to support the Nicaraguan insurgency of the contras and to take other actions, such as the mining of harbors. Nicaragua struck back, using, among other tactics, international law. When the U. S. learned in the spring of 1984 that Nicaragua would file a claim in the International Court of justice (or World Court), a body established by the Charter of the United Nations as the UN's 44 principal judicial organ" and composed of judges from various nations, our government suspended its acceptance of the ICJ's jurisdiction as to disputes with any Central American state. The Court nevertheless decided that it retained jurisdiction and the United States then announced that it would not participate further because the dispute involved "an inherently political problem that is not appropriate for judicial resolution." The U.S. then terminated its qualified 1946 acceptance of the Court's compulsory jurisdiction.

This was hardly novel. At the time, only 47 of the 162 nations entitled to accept that compulsory jurisdiction did so-and nine of the fifteen judges on the ICJ came from nations that did not! The Court proceeded to hear only Nicaragua because the U.S. was absent and El Salvador's petition to intervene had been denied-although the ICJ's own statute gave El Salvador that right. At that point, it should have been obvious to anyone what the outcome of the case would be.

In the event, the fears of the United States were realized. The case proceeded in an odd way. Assuming that it had any jurisdiction to begin with, the ICJ clearly had none under the treaties invoked by Nicaragua—the Charters of the United Nations and the Organization of the American States—because the

U.S. had long before excepted issues arising under multilateral treaties unless all signatories were present. The Court claimed, nonetheless, that it could apply customary international law to the dispute. It found these principles binding despite their incorporation in provisions of the treaties that could not be applied. Customary international law is supposed to reflect the actual practices of nations, but the principles the Court applied were distinguished more for their continual violation by nations than for being followed. They were, moreover, principles hotly disputed among the scholars of international law. Despite these difficulties which, perhaps separately but certainly in combination, would seem to be insuperable, the Court went forward, making law as it went.

The ultimate difficulty with the ICJ's performance, however, was that the principles it fashioned turned out to be one-sided, wooden, and wholly unsuited to the realities of international conflict. The Court decided that merely arming rebels, even in combination with providing military advice and sanctuary for rebel leaders, does not constitute an "armed attack" and that only such an attack brings the issue of individual or collective self-defense into play.

Having found that Nicaragua had not engaged in an armed attack against El Salvador, according to the ICJ's definition, there was no reason whatever for the Court to go on to address the United States' claim that it was exercising the well-established right of collective self-defense. But the Court chose to do so and found this defense legally insufficient for a very odd reason:

> [It] is the State which is the victim of an armed attack which must form and declare the view that it has been so attacked. There is no rule in customary international law permitting another State to exercise the right of collective self-defence on the basis of its own assessment of the situation.

This was an entirely new procedural requirement, and it means that, even if El Salvador was under attack by Nicaragua and the entire world knew it, if El Salvador, for understandable reasons of prudence, did not wish to make a formal declaration of that fact, the United States could not respond by doing to Nicaragua what that country was doing to El Salvador. The ruling was triply odd since El Salvador had asked the U.S. to assist in its defense, President Duarte had repeatedly mentioned the Nicaraguan attack in press conferences, and El Salvador's rejected petition to intervene in the Court's proceedings had declared the existence of an attack.

It is customary for even those scholars who have pointed out the manifold deficiencies of the ICJ's performance—in its assumption of jurisdiction, its fact-finding, and its legal argument-to deny that they see bias or incompetence. But one must wonder whether an international tribunal can ever be entirely free of the foreign policy interests of the nations whose jurists sit on the tribunal. The ICJ judges, moreover, are elected by the UN's General Assembly and Security Council, often after a highly political process. In explaining the U. S. decision to terminate our acceptance of the Court's jurisdiction, Abraham D. Sofaer,* the legal adviser to the State Department, said: "One reasonably may expect at least some judges to be sensitive to the impact of their decisions on their standing with the UN majority." He continued, in rampant understatement, that the UN "majority often opposes the United States on important international questions." It did so on the question of our conduct with respect to Nicaragua.

Every lawyer with a national practice knows that if his corporate client is sued by a local plaintiff in certain state courts, the client is likely to have to eat what the bar calls "home cookin'." The lawyers for the commissioner of baseball were recently reminded of that. So, it would appear, was the United States in the International Court of Justice. But there appears to have been more to the matter than a politically inspired but perhaps aberrational decision. As Professor Reisman points out,

> the international law-making process has itself undergone change and has subtly, but steadily, sought to change international law with regard to certain unilateral uses of force. While it has not totally succeeded, it has accomplished enough to have made expectations of who and how the law is made and what the law is less certain than in the past.

This has much to do with the change in the nature of the UN General Assembly as many new nations were admitted. The Assembly began to operate on the assumption that what was said there was international law or evidence of it. These were largely have-not nations and they want an international law that implements their desires. The result, as Reisman says, is the inversion of many established rules about the use of force. The decision in *Nicaragua v. United States* is a case in point.

In any event, the entire episode of *Nicaragua v. United States* has a distinctly odd feel for those who fall into the category of what Jessup called the "common lawyer." No court of the United States would entertain a suit challenging the legality of our actions with respect to Nicaragua. Various radical groups tried to litigate our involvement there and elsewhere in Central America, but were not successful. Our courts, under one legal rubric or another, essentially agreed that this was an inherently political dispute, not fit for judicial resolution.

As much as could be said for all disputes about the use of force by one nation against another—but that is exactly my point about international law. We have not entrusted matters so gravely affecting our national interests, security, and foreign policy to American judges. Yet many argue we should entrust such matters to a Court sitting on another continent, made up predomi-

*Sofaer's own commentary on the ICJ decision is found as chapter 5 in this collected volume.

nantly of jurists from foreign nations, and elected by an international body dominated on such issues by Communist bloc and Third World nations. Perhaps the administration's objection to the proceedings should have been couched differently: "This is an inherently political problem which we are unwilling to submit to political judgment outside the American political process."

The U. S., of course, refused to honor the judgment of the ICJ by paying damages to Nicaragua. But that does not mean that no harm was done. Even before the Court's decision, Carlos Arguello, Nicaragua's ambassador to the Netherlands who filed the case in the ICJ, announced that a decision against the United States would "be a serious political and moral blow to them." And so it proved. That was true in the U.S. as well as abroad. International law scholarship, along with the rest of the American academic community, was partially politicized and for every professor who criticized the Court's opinion, another castigated the United States.

Thus, Herbert W. Briggs, an emeritus professor at Cornell, wrote in the *American Journal of International Law* that "An administration in Washington that takes satisfaction in invading Grenada, hijacking foreign planes in the Mediterranean, bombing people in Libya and attempting to overthrow foreign governments is unlikely to regard making the United States of America a fugitive from justice, dodging a Court decision, as a serious matter. In each case, the end is supposed to justify the means." The fact that the Mediterranean hijacking brought to justice in Italy PLO terrorists who had themselves hijacked the cruise ship *Achille Lauro* and murdered an American, or that the bombing of Libya was designed to (and did) deter Qaddafi's support of international terrorism—all this was deemed irrelevant. To which one can only reply that if the U.S. is a fugitive from justice for rejecting the jurisdiction of a biased court over matters vital to its security, then a large majority of the world's nations are in flight.

Except that there was no judgment by the World Court, much the same situation arose when the United States invaded Grenada. Grenada, a recently independent small island nation, had its government overthrown in a coup by Maurice Bishop and his revolutionary party in 1979. Developments followed much the same pattern seen earlier in Cuba and later in Nicaragua: the end to elections, freedom of the press, other political freedoms, and *habeas corpus*. A large number of political prisoners were held and the new regime engaged in rapid and heavy militarization with the assistance of arms and advisers from the Soviet Union, Cuba, and other nations of the Communist bloc. Grenada's neighbors, the other six island nations of the Organization of Eastern Caribbean States (OECS), were alarmed, since Grenada's military forces exceeded all of theirs combined and seemed to have no possible purpose other than to support subversion in order to overthrow their democratic governments. Factions existed within the Grenadan ruling party, however, and on October 13,

1983, Bishop was arrested and subsequently murdered, along with three of his cabinet and certain union leaders. It is thought that this coup may have been the work of even more hard-line Marxist-Leninists, but, in any case, chaos followed as no group seemed in control. Rioting, looting, demonstrations, shootings, and a round-the-clock curfew on the civilian population, enforced by threats to shoot on sight, left the island without a real government. The other nations of the OECS expressed serious concern, and the United States was concerned as well, for there were about one thousand Americans on the island, many of them medical students. As Richard Cheney, then a member of the congressional mission that later investigated, wrote:

> Cut off from the outside world, dependent on the People's Revolutionary Army for food and water, and confined to their quarters on pain of death, they were, the State Department employee [who had been trying without success to arrange their evacuation] believed, already hostages.

The OECS member nations, along with Barbados and Jamaica, met and decided to take military action, provided the United States would assist the effort, since their own military forces were meager. The U.S. agreed, and on October 25 the OECS mission, supported by Barbados and Jamaica, but consisting almost entirely of U.S. forces, invaded. When the fighting was over, a CBS News poll found that 91 percent of Grenadans were glad the U.S. troops had come. By December 15, U.S. armed forces had left the island, order had been restored, American and Grenadan lives very probably saved, and plans were underway for free elections so that the people of Grenada could choose their own government. One would have thought that outside the Communist bloc the American action would have been joyfully received.

One would have been quite wrong. Already, early in November, the UN General Assembly voted to condemn the action as a violation of international law. The majority was larger than that which had condemned the Soviet invasion of Afghanistan! The vote had been taken, moreover, without even allowing the nations of the OECS and the United States to present their case. Yet once more many of the U.S. international law academics responded in their own political fashion. No less than nine professors of international law, including Professor Chayes, signed a short article finding the U.S. "in egregious violation of international law" and stating that the lack of the "imprimatur" of the Organization of the American States would "raise serious doubts concerning the international legitimacy of any successor government." That the government ousted was a Communist dictatorship and that its successor would be freely chosen by the Grenadan people apparently raised no question in the professors' minds about the legitimacy of the former or the asserted doubtful legitimacy of the latter. The professors were not alone, of course. A number of politicians, along with Senator Moynihan, announced a U.S. violation of international law.

What are we to think about these pronouncements? Did the U.S. violate international law so that we are right to condemn the Reagan administration's international lawlessness? Are there known rules that lead reasonable people to firm conclusions about our actions in Nicaragua and Grenada? Or about Soviet and other nations' behavior around the world? If there are such rules that lead to firm conclusions, this fact is well hidden. The *American Journal of International Law* ran separate symposia on the Grenada invasion and our support of the Nicaraguan contras. The various experts took almost every position imaginable, from the assertion that the United States is a dangerous international outlaw to the contention that everything done exemplified our devotion to the rule of law. Some arguments, such as those by Professor John Norton Moore of the University of Virginia Law School, in defense of our action, seemed to me far more persuasive than others, but I quickly realized that I was judging not on grounds that might be called "legal" but rather on political and moral considerations. The "law" itself seemed infinitely flexible and indeterminate. This is due to a contradiction at the heart of the subject. Moynihan states the contradiction without seeming to realize that it is fatal to his idea that there is a solid body of law to which the United States must adhere:

> Manifestly, we cannot hold the rest of the world to a good many of the propositions relating to their internal conduct that we wrote into covenants and charters and declarations with such earnestness in the first half of this century. An ancient doctrine (going back at least to Grotius) is *rebus sic stantibus*, which denotes "a tacit condition, said to attach to all treaties, that they shall cease to be obligatory as soon as the state of facts and conditions upon which they were founded has substantially changed" (*Black's Law Dictionary*). For all that Chapter II of the charter of the Organization of the American States requires of members "the effective exercises of representative democracy," this is not going to be the political norm of this hemisphere or this world during the foreseeable future. It had once looked that way; it no longer does. Circumstances have changed. What has not changed—what the United States must strive to make clear has not changed—is the first rule of international law: *Pacta sunt servanda*, agreements must be kept.

But if the condition upon which the United States agreed to the OAS Charter—that the members would be democracies—has changed, why does not *rebus sic stantibus* relieve us of the obligation to keep the rest of the agreement? Moynihan's argument lacks all coherence.

The major difficulty with international law is that it converts what are essentially problems of international morality, as defined by a particular political community, into arguments about law that are largely drained of morality. I once listened to a professor of international law defend the United States' actions in Grenada. The argument seemed tortured and artificial, the most important considerations omitted. When he had done, I asked whether three factors that most Americans deemed relevant counted in international law. (1)

The Grenadan government consisted of a minority that seized control by violence and maintained it by terror. (2) It was a Marxist- Leninist regime and represented a further advance in this hemisphere of a power that threatens freedom and democracy throughout the world. (3) Finally, the people of Grenada were ecstatic at being relieved of tyranny and the ever-present threat of violence. The expert replied, somewhat sadly, that these considerations had no weight in international law.

A moment's reflection makes it clear that, in the real world, they could not. In order to be international, rules about the use of force between nations must be acceptable to regimes that operate on different—often contradictory—moral premises. The rules themselves must not express a preference for freedom over tyranny or for elections over domestic violence as the means of coming to power. This moral equivalence is embodied in international charters. The charters must be neutral and the easiest neutral principle is: No force. The fact that the principle will not be observed by those who simply see international law as another foreign policy instrument does not affect the matter.

But even the principle of neutrality is now being altered to the disadvantage of the United States and other democracies. The UN General Assembly, as Reisman notes, has begun to redefine the unlawful use of force so that those whom the General Assembly chooses to regard as struggling for "freedom and independence" may legally attack their own government, another nation may legally provide bases from which the attacks are launched—but the targeted state behaves illegally if it then attacks those bases! This reverses the older rule to the benefit, primarily, of Communist insurgencies supported by nations in the Communist bloc and to the detriment of the United States when it aids the nation under attack.

It might be said that we must I accept moral equivalence in international law in order to have rules that are acceptable to, and therefore may deter, Communist bloc nations and others from the use of armed force. The notion that it is worth keeping alive this idea of law in the power relations of nations because eventually that idea may tame the drives of aggressors is a bit like preaching the ideal of the rule of law to the Medellin cartel in the hope that one day the drug lords will be worn down by the rhetoric of idealism and submit to the law of Colombia. Even if one might hope that the aspiration of international law might one day lessen the amount of aggression in the world, there is the present reality that it does not, and that it imposes costs disproportionately on liberal, democratic nations.

The major cost is that, by eliminating morality from its calculus, international law actually makes moral action appear immoral. It can hardly be doubted that, in the American view, it would be a moral act to help a people overthrow a dictatorship that had replaced a democratic government by force, and to restore democracy and freedom to such people. Yet when our leaders act for such moral reasons, they are forced into contrived explanations. The implausibility of such explanations then reverses the moral stance of the parties.

International law thus serves, both internationally and domestically, as a basis for a rhetoric of recrimination directed at the United States. Those who disapprove of a President's actions on the merits, but who fear they may prove popular, can transform the dispute from one about substance to one about legality. The President can be painted as a lawbreaker and perhaps drawn into a legalistic defense of his actions. The effect is to raise doubts and lower American morale. The Soviets and other nations have no such problem.

As currently defined, then, international law about the use of force is not even a piety; it is a net loss for Western democracies. Senator Moynihan, speaking of international relations in Woodrow Wilson's time, said, approvingly, that "the idea of law persisted, even when it did not prevail." That is precisely the problem. Since it does not prevail, the persistence of the idea that it exists can be pernicious. There can be no authentic rule of law among nations until nations have a common political morality or are under a common sovereignty. A glance at the real world suggests we have a while to wait.

5

International Law and the Use of Force

*Abraham D. Sofaer**

Few legal issues are of greater significance to the interests of the United States, and of people everywhere, than the rules and the practices of nations concerning the use of force. The United States is committed to the principle that its conduct in international affairs—including the use of force-must be subject to law. The rule of law requires individual nations to subordinate their perceived needs to accepted standards of conduct based on the practice of nations. Lawyers play many important roles in connection with determining when and under what conditions nations may lawfully resort to the use of force. Among the most important of these roles is the function of advising government leaders—often themselves lawyers—on the legal principles applicable to proposed uses of force. To be effective in this role, lawyers must provide credible and practical guidance, based on the actual practice of nations, and consistent with legitimate political interests. Legal advisers in the United States have, since the adoption of the UN Charter, in general provided such advice, taking a "common- law" lawyer's approach that rests on a case-by-case application of widely accepted principles of international law to the particular facts of each situation. This approach has worked well to the extent lawyers have in fact been consulted for their advice.

The decision of the International Court of Justice (ICJ) in *Nicaragua v. United States* casts considerable doubt on this approach to the law relating to the use of force, particularly with regard to the right of collective self-defense. The ICJ has formulated and applied impractical and counterproductive rules, which have little or no basis in accepted international practices. These rules

*Abraham D. Sofaer is the George P. Shultz Distinguished Scholar and Senior Fellow at the Hoover Institution and was legal advisor at the Department of State from 1985 until 1990.

This article first appeared in *The National Interest*, no. 13 (Fall 1988).

may be in- tended to reduce the worldwide use of force, but in fact they reduce only the right to defend—collectively and effectively—against uses of force short of conventional warfare, which are in fact the most pernicious and widespread forms of aggression in the world today. Furthermore, the rules created by the ICJ for this purpose are so artificial, impractical, and counterintuitive that they threaten accepted principles of international law, as well as the stature of the ICJ itself.

The Lawyer's Role in Use of Force Decisions

Lawyers play important roles in the development and application of the law relating to the use of force. In addition to the judges and advocates that handle specific cases, scholars and the bar take a deep interest in this subject. We write, lecture, and lobby to advance our points of view. Legislators, many of whom are also attorneys, express their views through laws, resolutions, in hearings, or as influential individuals. Government lawyers have special responsibilities. We are sworn to uphold the law, and that includes international law, which is the law of the land. We have the duty to alert our leaders to applicable international rules of conduct, and to argue that the proper rules be respected. In doing so, however, we must rely on our ability to convince our clients to consult us, and to accept our advice. We can issue no writs; we can only seek to persuade. Political leaders are not always eager to talk to lawyers—even their own lawyers—about planned uses of force, and legal advisers through the years have occasionally been bypassed, or consulted inadequately, in such situations. Even when we are fully involved in the decision-making process, our advice is sometimes rejected in whole or in part.

To have any hope of influencing the political and military leadership, the lawyers in a government—any government—must have both a coherent and a convincing message. We must be able to explain why nations are bound by certain rules, and to demonstrate that the rules we propose as authoritative are reasonable, commonly accepted, consistent with prior practice, and fair in terms of the strategic challenges our leaders face. As Lawrence Hargrove recently put it, the "primary rules (governing the use of force], in order to work, must therefore be readily perceivable, by people bearing the actual responsibilities of government, to reflect the practical requirements of the world in which states must survive and conduct their affairs." The rules we advance as authoritative will fail to convince if they offend "the rough intuitions of responsible politicians" concerned with the safety of their citizens.[1]

The principles that the United States believes govern the use of force are in fact straightforward, sensible, and enlightened. The UN Charter contemplates an end to the threat or use of force by states against the territorial integrity or political independence of other states, unless the Security Council has authorized such action.[2] This represents a bold step toward peaceful relations among states by bringing, as Louis Henkin put it, "within the realm of law those ultimate political tensions and interests that had long been deemed beyond the control of law."[3]

The United States Position

The Charter expressly reserves in Article 51, however, the "inherent right of individual or collective self-defense." That provision is written in terms of defense against "armed attack" but the right of self-defense is termed "inherent," thus conveying the sense that it includes the right to defend those fundamental interests customarily protected. The United States has tried repeatedly to gain approval for collective UN action in using force, but that option became unavailable as a practical matter after the Korean War. Nevertheless, the United States has always assumed that Charter principles provide a workable set of rules to deal with the array of needs that potentially require the use of force, including such threats as state-supported terrorism and insurgencies, even if they are deemed not to amount to an "armed attack." General Assembly interpretive declarations make clear that "force" means physical violence, not other forms of coercion. But they also indicate that aggression includes both direct and indirect complicity in all forms of violence, not just conventional hostilities.[4] Our position has been that the inherent right of self-defense potentially applies against any illegal use of force, and to the extent the term "armed attack" is relevant in use-of-force issues that it should be defined to include forms of aggression historically regarded as justifying resort to defensive measures. Furthermore, the U.S. has assumed that it may lawfully engage in collective self-defense in any situation in which the nation assisted is entitled to act, and to the same extent. On the other hand, we recognize that force may be used only to deter or prevent aggression and only to the extent it is necessary and proportionate.

From Truman to Carter

The actions of presidents of the United States, and the positions taken by their lawyers, have consistently demonstrated this principled but practical approach to use-of-force rules. In his message to Congress requesting aid for Greece, President Truman announced the Truman Doctrine, which recognized the importance of the peaceful development of nations under the UN system, but called for the protection of free nations from "aggressive movements" seeking to impose totalitarian regimes. "This is no more than a frank recognition," he said, "that totalitarian regimes imposed upon free peoples, by direct or indirect aggression, undermine the foundations of international peace and hence the security of the United States."

When President Eisenhower sent U.S. forces into Lebanon in 1958 at President Chamoun's request, both the United States and Lebanon asserted a realistic definition of "armed attack." Secretary of State Dulles said: "[W]e do not think that the words 'armed attack' preclude treating as such an armed revolution which is fomented from abroad, aided and assisted from abroad."

In the wake of the Bay of Pigs debacle, which apparently went forward without legal screening of any kind, President Kennedy was careful to consult government lawyers during the Cuban Missile crisis. Then Legal Adviser Abram Chayes argued successfully for an approach that treated the matter as a threat warranting a quarantine, but not amounting to an armed attack. Professors Wright and Henkin criticized Chayes for his reliance on the Rio Treaty, but Chayes's response reflected an approach to use-of-force decisions that aptly describes what U.S. practice has been, when the lawyers have been consulted.[5] Chayes rejected the notion that law relating to the use of force was "a set of fixed, self-defining categories of permissible and prohibited conduct." He proposed instead what he called a "common-lawyer" approach in which international law is left open to a broad range of interpretation and emphasis, with terms that do not dictate conduct so much as orient deliberation, order priorities, and guide with- in broad limits. Using this practical and flexible common-law approach, Chayes argued the quarantine was a justified response.

This flexible but principled approach to the use of force had strong support among leading scholars of the day. Professor Julius Stone had criticized efforts to determine a "mechanical test of aggression, insulated from the merits of the situation in which States act ... , [a] juristic push-button device."[6] McDougal and Feliciano in fact explained the issue in terms strikingly similar to those used by Chayes:

> It is no more desirable to attempt to define aggression "once and for all" than it is so to define any other legal term or concept of inter national or municipal law. For observers with full awareness of the factors realistically affecting decision, the task of "defining aggression" is not appropriately conceived as one of searching for a precise, certain, and final verbal formula that would abolish the discretion of decision-makers and dictate specific decisions. It is rather, in broad outline, that of presenting to the focus of attention of the various officials who must reach a decision about the lawfulness or unlawfulness of coercion, the different variable factors and policies that, in differing contexts and under community perspectives, rationally bear upon their decisions; of indicating the interrelations of these factors and policies in context; and, perhaps, of making some lower-order generalizations about the relative weighting of pertinent factors and policies in different contexts. The task, again, is not so much to abolish, with quasi-magical arrangements of words, conflicts of national interests (more or less myopically perceived) as it is to clarify common, long-term interests in the maintenance of minimum public order.[7]

When President Johnson intervened in the Dominican Republic, no attack of any kind had occurred on the U.S. or its citizens. The danger to Americans there was serious, however, and a communist takeover was seen as a real possibility. Legal Adviser Leonard Meeker defended the intervention as justified to protect Americans "in imminent danger of life and limb from rioting mobs," and he argued that a continued U.S. presence was necessary to prevent anarchy. He rejected criticisms based on what he called "fundamentalist views about the nature of international law," as such views were "not very useful as a means to achieving practical and just solutions of difficult political, economic, and social problems." He called for a "practical idealism," in which international law could be read as consistent with efforts to prevent bloodshed and communist takeovers. He said that "an international law which cannot deal with facts such as these, and in a way that has some hope of setting a troubled nation on the path of peace and reconstruction, is not the kind of law I believe in." President Johnson added explicitly the justification of intervening to prevent revolutions by "evil persons who had been trained in overthrowing governments and establishing communist control."

The Vietnam conflict generated a great deal of legal debate about the use of force, and the legal adviser's office found the U.S. intervention to assist South Vietnam legally justified under the doctrine of collective self-defense. Further debate was prompted by the U.S. incursion into Cambodia. By this time, Chayes had changed his point of view. While purporting still to believe that "absolute" judgments about "legality" should be avoided in international law, his analysis became highly technical and much less oriented to the specific facts. He properly criticized the government for failing to consider the incursion's legality prior to its implementation. But his judgment on legality was controlled by what had become in his view "the essential guiding principle of world law and world order: to confine within the narrowest limits the situations in which we are prepared to condone or legitimate unilateral decisions to resort to force."[8] This guiding principle radically altered the practical approach and deliberative process Chayes considered proper as legal adviser, and which served the nation and world order so well at that critical time.

President Ford relied on Article 51 in ordering U.S. forces to attack Cambodian naval assets to secure release of the vessel *Mayaguez* and its crew. The seizure of a U.S. merchant vessel was deemed "a clear-cut illegal use of force" which UN Ambassador Scali asserted justified appropriate measures in self-defense. Similarly, President Carter used force in an attempt to rescue American hostages in Iran, arguing that the United States is entitled to seek to protect its citizens abroad "where the government of the territory in which they are located is unable or unwilling to protect them." Carter received the support of Professor Reisman,[9] and the limited use of force to rescue citizens has strong support in customary practice and scholarship.[10] Nonetheless, the President was condemned by some international law experts, who argued that by no stretch of the imagination was the seizure of Americans as hostages an armed attack, and therefore that the U.S. was precluded from using force to secure their release.[11]

The Reagan Years

The Reagan administration has continued to adhere to the practical but principled approach to use-of-force rules that has in general characterized United States policy since the UN Charter's adoption. The President has repeatedly made clear, moreover, that he will continue the policy of assisting nations in preventing non-democratic takeovers conducted by outside forces (as in Afghanistan) or fomented and aided by them.[12] The Grenada operation involved no armed attack on the U.S. but was justified as necessary to protect U.S. lives and to respond to invitations of the governor general and of members of the Organization of the Eastern Caribbean States. Chayes suggested that this action could not be distinguished from the Soviet invasion of Afghanistan,[13] and others also criticized it, including the American Bar Association Section on International Law. Legal Adviser Davis Robinson's defense, resting on the combined effect of all the unique circumstances supporting intervention, is an exemplary illustration of the U.S. common-law tradition.[14] As Edwin Yoder commented at the time:

> All the Grenadian operation has in common with recent Soviet enforcements of the Brezhnev doctrine, so-called, is the unpleasant use of military force. If force per se is to be condemned, if the legitimacy of its use under international law has nothing to do with intent or result, then it is anarchy merely disguised as law.[15]

We relied on the same approach in exercising our rights of self-defense by attacking facilities in Libya used to support terrorists. Before December 1985, we had exhausted virtually every measure short of force to convince Libya to stop supporting terrorists in attacks on Americans. Then came the mindlessly cruel attacks at the Rome and Vienna airports in which seven Americans were killed, including 11-year old Natasha Simp- son. Tunisian passports were found on the killers that were traced to Libyan officials, and Qadhafi praised the terrorists as heroes. Nevertheless, the President decided not to use force at that point, but instead to exhaust all remaining economic sanctions and to warn Libya one more time, explicitly invoking our view of the governing law. He said:

> By providing material support to terrorist groups which attack U.S. citizens, Libya has engaged in armed aggression against the United States under established principles of international law, just as if it had used its own armed forces.

Secretary Shultz explained our position in greater detail in January 1986, at the National Defense University:

> A nation attacked by terrorists is permitted to use force to prevent or preempt future attacks, to seize terrorists, or to rescue its citizens when means is available. The law requires that such actions be necessary and proportionate. But this nation has consis-

> tently affirmed the right of states to use force in exercise of their right of individual or collective self-defense. The UN Charter is not a suicide pact.

Despite these warnings, Libya organized and supported additional attacks, including the bombing of a Berlin disco in which two Americans were killed and over 100 people injured. We reliably knew that Libya was planning several more attacks. The purpose of the limited air strike was to convince Libya to halt this support for terrorist operations.

Most recently, we have used force in defensive actions in the Persian Gulf. Iran repeatedly engaged in placing mines in sea lanes with the attention of attacking U.S. public and flag vessels. We warned Iran that we regarded such mining as an armed attack that justified the necessary and proportionate use of force in self-defense. They persisted, openly asserting that they would make us suffer. For what? For exercising our right to navigate in international waters. We caught Iran laying mines and sank the vessel involved. Again Iran acted, this time firing a missile at a U.S. vessel. We destroyed a platform used for these military operations. Iran persisted in laying new mines, and one seriously damaged a Navy frigate, the *U.S.S. Roberts*, injuring ten crewmen. We destroyed two platforms, and then responded to Iranian attacks by sinking vessels of Iran's navy. If we deferred to such threats, we would have no end of Khomeinis and Qadhafis ordering us to give up exercising our rights. President Carter adopted the principle that we would exercise and defend our rights in international waters, including the Persian Gulf. President Reagan is determined to uphold that bipartisan policy. The limited scope of our actions, at each point, was wholly consistent with the legal advice the President received.

Nicaragua v. United States

The rules and expectations on which the United States has consistently relied in rnaking use-of-force decisions have been cast into grave doubt by the International Court of Justice in *Nicaragua v. United States*.[16] The background of this case is well known. El Salvador, unable to defend itself effectively against Nicaraguan-support- ed guerrillas, asked the U.S. to help in its defense. We assumed that Nicaragua's support of guerrillas for the purpose of destroying the government of El Salvador was a form of aggression against El Salvador, and that necessary and proportional responses, including force, could be taken collectively against such actions. This was precisely the position taken by Secretary of State Dean Rusk, in defending the legality of our actions against North Vietnam before the American Society of International Law in 1965. He said:

> In resisting the aggression against it, the Republic of Vietnam is exercising its right of self- defense. It called upon us and other states for assistance. And in the exercise of

> the right of collective self-defense under the United Nations Charter, we and other nations are providing such assistance.
>
> The American policy of assisting South Vietnam to maintain its freedom was inaugurated under President Eisenhower and continued under Presidents Kennedy and Johnson. Our assistance has been increased because the aggression from the North has been augmented. Our assistance now encompasses the bombing of North Vietnam. The bombing is designed to interdict, as far as possible, and to inhibit, as far as may be necessary, continued aggression against the Republic of Vietnam.

Significantly, Nicaragua did not disagree with us in these legal assumptions. Rather, it claimed it was innocent of having aided the insurgents in El Salvador, and therefore that our actions in aiding the contras had no justification.

The ICJ's opinion articulated a significantly different view of international law. While refusing unequivocally to determine that Nicaragua's conduct amounted to aggression, the court nonetheless found or assumed that Nicaragua had indeed supplied arms to communist rebels in El Salvador at least through early 1981. President Singh was willing to assume that Nicaragua's flow of arms to the rebels in El Salvador had "been both regular and substantial, as well as spread over a number of years and thus amounting to intervention." The court concluded, however, that a limited intervention cannot justify resort to self-defense. According to the court, customary law only allows the use of force in self-defense against an "armed attack," and an armed attack does not include "assistance to rebels in the form of the provision of weapons or logistical or other support." This ruling was without support in customary international law, or the practice of nations, which could not rationally be read to deprive a state of the right to defend itself against so serious a form of aggression. Recognizing this, the ICJ came up with the following solution: A state is not permitted to resort to "self-defense" against aggression short of armed attack,[17] but it may be able to take what the court called proportionate countermeasures."

This ruling arguably should not alone cause great concern. So long as a nation's inherent right to protect itself is recognized, whether one calls the actions "self-defense" or "countermeasures" need make no real difference. But the verbal play in which the court engaged had a purpose, egregiously transparent. Had the court called the defensive actions it allowed "self-defense," then Article 51 would explicitly have allowed such actions to be taken collectively as well as individually.[18] But by characterizing permissible defensive actions as "countermeasures," the court created a tautological rationale that enabled it to deny the right of joint action. "Countermeasures," the court found, can only be undertaken by the victim state, not by any other state, because such measures do not constitute self-defense.

The court went further in narrowing the right to collective self-defense. To be entitled to exercise collective self-defense, the court suggested, the victim must openly declare that it is under armed attack at the time of the attack, and must formally request assistance from the state seeking to justify its actions. The facts showed that the government of El Salvador had repeatedly and openly complained of Nicaragua's support for the rebels in that country. Furthermore, the uncontroverted Declaration of Intervention of El Salvador, filed with the court, confirmed that its president had asked the United States to come to his country's defense. But the court nonetheless ruled that El Salvador had failed to meet these new procedural requirements, and that this failure deprived U.S. actions of their potential justification as defensive measures.

Whether actions of the United States were necessary and proportional was treated by the court in a single paragraph. American actions were pronounced unnecessary because they were undertaken "several months after the major offensive of the armed opposition against the Government of El Salvador had been completely repulsed (January 1981), and the actions of the opposition considerably reduced in consequence." Thus, the court said, "it was possible to eliminate the main danger of the Salvadoran Government without the United States embarking on activities in and against Nicaragua."

The court's treatment of proportionality was similarly curt. Interestingly, the court made no finding that aid to the contras failed this test; in fact, United States aid to the contras was the same sort of aid the evidence demonstrated was extended by Nicaragua to the rebels in El Salvador. Rather, the court said it could not regard the actions relating to the mining of Nicaraguan ports, and attacks on port and oil installations, as satisfying proportionality, and that United States help to the contras continued long after any aggression by Nicaragua could reasonably have been presumed to have continued. Judge Schwebel detailed in his opinion, however, the similar measures of depredation engaged in by the insurgents in El Salvador, and he explained that an action is proportional when it is needed to halt and repulse an attack, not just when it corresponds exactly to the acts sought to be defended against. The mining of harbors could be expected to restrict the flow of arms from Nicaragua's suppliers, which were being passed on to the rebels in El Salvador, and the attacks on oil installations could similarly be expected to diminish Nicaragua's capacity to continue its aggression.

The decision, in short, ignored actual custom and practice, and relied on rules that were seemingly derived for the purpose of depriving the United States and El Salvador of inherent rights. Aggression, though undeniably present, was deemed irrelevant because it did not amount to an "armed attack." Defensive measures, though undeniably justified, were deemed "countermeasures" so they would not be jointly exercisable. Collective self-defense, though undeniably intended, was found imperfect for lack of unprecedented procedural requirements. Necessity and proportionality, though demonstrated by the desperate situation in which El Salvador found itself, were found lacking for reasons that might have reflected nothing more than the success of El

Salvador and the United States at preventing, through the acts condemned, further and more serious aggression.

Effects of the ICJ's Decision

Many international law academics and practitioners strongly believe that lethal support of the contras by the United States was inconsistent with our international obligations. Even those who take such a view, however, should consider whether the ICJ's conclusions are properly based, or seem likely to be effective in reducing resort to force in the world. In my view, the ICJ's rulings concerning the use of force create artificial distinctions and mechanical rules that are fundamentally inconsistent with the principled but flexible approach followed by the United States since the Charter's adoption.

The court's restrictive approach in defining "armed attack" could deprive states of the right of self-defense against the most common and dangerous forms of aggression in the world today. Our political leaders and military strategists cannot reasonably be expected to and will not accept the notion that self-defense applies only to armed attacks across borders in the formal sense, when the principal vehicles for competition against the democratic West through violence are state-supported terrorism and insurgencies. That the court might allow "countermeasures" even where self-defense is inapplicable may well demonstrate that the ICJ has not completely lost its grip on reality. But the distinction is artificial and creates undesirable uncertainty in an area of grave importance. Lawyers are unlikely to impress their political and military clients by assuring them that, although they may not be able to regard essential national security activities as "self-defense," they may nonetheless be allowed to engage in such activities as "necessary countermeasures."

The puzzlement that such an assurance is likely to cause will turn to disbelief as these clients learn the new rules of collective self-defense. While an ally may assist the victim state within the victim's territory, we lawyers must now explain, the ally may not act according to the ICJ against the aggressor state in the latter's territory. Furthermore, before acting to assist an ally in collective self-defense the ICJ would have the lawyer insist that his clients obtain from the victim state a public declaration that it is under attack, and a public invitation for the ally's assistance. At this point the client's eyes would assume that glazed expression associated with polite disregard.

But the lawyer would have even more to say. The court also expressed artificial and unrealistic standards in applying the accepted principles of necessity and proportionality. Rather than asking what in fact appears militarily necessary to deter the illegal conduct involved, the ally is supposed to do only that which seems sufficient to make it possible to preserve the victim state's independence. Furthermore, acts which are not strictly similar to those of the aggressor state will run a high risk of being condemned as disproportionate, even though they might be reasonably related to the threat involved. These are not the sorts of standards that are likely to convince, and at this point the lawyer is likely to have lost his case, or even worse to have lost his influence. Government lawyers do not get : for failing to convince. But they get ignored, thereby losing their capacity to help en that traditional and accepted use-of-force standards are maintained.

The court's proposed rules therefore, though undoubtedly well motivated, could reinforce the effectiveness of traditional and accepted standards of law. This is not because political leaders are slow witted, or averse to technical analysis, but rather because they would see through the court's rules as efforts to change the law rather than as guidance on the application of accepted rules of conduct.

Once the issue becomes the desirability of one set of rules over another, rather than their legitimacy, political leaders will feel free to challenge the court's premise that intervention and force would be minimized by its approach. They could reasonably conclude, in fact, that the court's rules are more likely to encourage conflict, intervention, and the unlawful use of force than are the rules and practices that reflect accepted norms of conduct. To construe restrictively the meaning of "armed attack," for example, would do wonders for the world if as a result unconventional forms of aggression became less frequent or more benign in their consequences. The court's ruling could have no such effect; rather, it can only limit—and is designed to limit—the use of force in responding to such forms of aggression. To the extent it succeeds in this objective, states which now sponsor terrorism and insurgencies will feel less pressure to stop.

The court's limits on collective self-defense are likely to have the same adverse effects. Refusing to allow an ally to join in "countermeasures" in the territory of an aggressor would not reduce the tendency of aggressors to sponsor internal subversion; rather such a rule would only diminish the capacity of relatively weak states to defend against aggression by relatively strong states. Where the victim state is not strong enough to use "proportional countermeasures" against the aggressor on the latter's territory, conflict would be limited to the territory of the victim state. If anything, the interests of peace would seem most clearly served by rules having a measured, deterrent effect on such aggression. Similarly, one is at a loss to understand what interest is served by the formalistic requirements that a state declare it is under attack and openly invite assistance from its ally. Apparently the court seeks to promote the goal of limiting the number of actors in a conflict. Once a state is forced to declare itself as under armed attack, however, and openly to invite an ally's assistance, the chances for diplomatic resolution may be reduced.

The problem of controlling conflict in this contentious world is not so easily dealt with as the court, and some international lawyers, assume. Political and military strategists intensely dispute which sets of rules and norms of conduct are most likely to preserve peace. The use of force is a central element in these calculations, and respected thinkers have cautioned against a world in which force can only be used in conventional war. Henry Kissinger has suggested, for example, that "in the missile age, the side which can add another increment of power without resorting to all-out war—or which can threaten to do so—will gain a perhaps decisive advantage over an opponent who does not have this ability." Ronald Reagan and George Shultz have made a similar point: "Diplomacy not backed by strength is ineffectual." We must adapt power to political circumstances to compete effectively with opponents who treat force as a continuation of politics by other means. Once it is established that state-sponsored terrorism and insurgencies can achieve their political objectives, their practitioners will get bolder, and the threat to our interests greater. The court's severe and artificial limitations on the right of self-defense would serve to encourage aggression by diminishing the capacity lawfully to deter.

The concepts of "armed attack" and "self-defense" are limitations which world leaders have accepted, and they provide a sufficient basis if reasonably construed to satisfy legitimate national security planning. But the right to self-defense is too fundamental for leaders to allow it to be subordinated to any scheme of world order based on theory and wishful thinking, however enlightened. Self-defense is not a production of lawyers to be modified as we please, but a concept lawyers have used to describe the situations and manner in which civilized nations have traditionally used force. It is a reflection of the fact that, despite the UN Charter, we still live in a world in which states are controlled by leaders who claim to get their marching orders directly from God; whose tolerance for pointless destruction is so monumental it can be explained only in pathological terms; or who are outright criminals—murderers, drug dealers, thieves. In dealing with the actions of such states, our leaders will continue to insist upon use-of-force rules that offer them, in clear and comprehensible terms, a sufficient degree of latitude to plan and act effectively to deter aggressors who would physically harm Americans or America's allies.

The most predictable result of the decision in *Nicaragua v. United States* will be a diminution in respect for the ICJ's pronouncements, and in its future potential as an instrument of reason in the cause of peace. At one point in his opinion, President Singh explained that the court could not allow itself "to miss a major opportunity to state the law so as to serve the best interests of the community." Yet, the ICJ's place in history will depend not upon its seizing opportunities to issue rulings attempting to narrow the inherent right of self-defense, but rather upon its development of a jurisprudence that retains the flexibility of the Charter's design, and leaves to statesmen the task of achieving the Charter's goals within the bounds of principles based on the actual practice of nations. The case against the ICJ's involvement in *Nicaragua v. United States* was cogently expressed by Chayes in his earlier days. He wrote:

> I suggest that most great disputes between states, even when they involve important legal elements, are not justiciable—and for much the same reason that most disputes between organs of our government not involving invasions of private rights are not justiciable. Courts do not exist to answer legal questions just for the sake of having an answer. They are specialized institutions. Acceptance of their judgments depends on a subtle complex of factors. Institutional characteristics limit the range in which they can effectively exercise authority. If judges go beyond those limits, the result is likely to be not vindication of the law, but erosion of judicial authority.[19]

Chayes likes to say that he has "already made a meal of those words in the Hague," where as counsel for Nicaragua he successfully persuaded the ICJ to risk the erosion of judicial authority he had predicted. Presumably, Chayes at some point also decided to eat his words about the common lawyer approach to use-of-force decisions. But the reasons he gave for the ICJ to decline jurisdiction remain valid. They go beyond separation of powers objections, and in the final analysis relate to the kind of international law the ICJ seems inclined to produce when it becomes involved in such issues, a law that this nation's leaders—of both parties and in both branches—will refuse to accept as the final word on protecting essential national security interests.

Perhaps the most dramatic evidence of this point was Congress' action after the court had issued its judgment on the merits. While some legislators criticized the U.S. on the basis of the ICJ's ruling, Congress provided $75 million in lethal aid for the contras. The reaction of the international bar—consisting on the whole of lawyers devoted to the rule of law—is also instructive. It has produced a range of commentary that is as divergent as it is impassioned. The decision has been hailed as "a positive model of judicial style," whose "quality of legal reasoning is admirable"; and it has been denounced as "a tragedy for world order." The judgment has been said both to misunderstand, and to uphold, international law. It has been characterized as "authoritative," "extremely persuasive," and "a misfortune of some magnitude" in its impact on the vitality of the law of the UN Charter governing force and self-defense."[20] Policy makers are particularly unlikely to defer to rules that are not only inconsistent with prior behavior, but also evoke such intense differences among persons expert in the field.

Continuity in American Policy

The United States properly refused to participate in the merits stage of the *Nicaragua* case, because the President had decided this nation could not allow its right to exercise self-defense to be regulated by the ICJ without its consent. This nation remains committed to the rule of law, however, and to the appropriate use of the ICJ. Our continuing support for the court is demonstrated by our willingness to take to chambers within it a maritime boundary dispute with Canada. We also continue to have over sixty treaties vesting the court with jurisdiction over disputes; and we are presently before a chamber of the court in a commercial dispute with Italy arising under one such treaty. We welcome the idea, moreover, of attempting to work out agreed areas of jurisdiction for the court, to which all permanent members of the Security Council would adhere. We are, in short, despite our rejection of the court's jurisdiction in the *Nicaragua* case, determined to work to preserve the court's role in the areas we believe it functions with authority and effectiveness.

Meanwhile, with respect to the use of force, the United States will continue to follow a principled but flexible approach: one that requires policymakers to grapple with and he guided by the traditional limitations on the use of force, while recognizing the legitimacy of protecting, effectively, not only American territory, but American citizens, interests, and allies. Lawyers must play an active role in the decision-making process, not by attempting to force policy to particular results through the assertion of artificial rules, but by insisting on the thorough evaluation of and respect for limitations based on accepted community practice.

Notes

1. John Lawrence Hargrove, "The *Nicaragua* Judgment and the Future of the Law of Force and Self-Defense," *The American Journal of International Law*, vol. 81 (1987), p. 137.
2. Article 2(4) of the Charter obligates all members "to refrain from their international relations from the threat or use of force against the territorial integrity or political independence of any state." Articles 39, 41, and 42 provide for collective action under Security Council auspices in response to unlawful uses of force.
3. Louis Henkin, *How Nations Behave: Law and Foreign Policy* (New York: Columbia University Press, 1979), p. 131.
4. See, e. g., *Declaration of Principles of International Law Concerning Friendly Relations and Cooperation Among States In Accordance with the Charter of the United Nations*, United Nations General Assembly Res. 2625 (1970).
5. Quincy Wright, "The Cuban Quarantine," *The American Journal of International Law*, vol. 57 (1963), p. 546; Louis Henkin, "Comment," in Chayes, *The Cuban Missile Crisis*, pp. 149-54.
6. Julius Stone, *Aggression and World Order: A Critique of United Nations Theories of Aggression* (Los Angeles: University of California Press, 1958), pp. 10-11.
7. Myres S. McDougal and Florentino P. Feliciano, *Law and Minimum World Public Order* (New Haven: Yale University Press, 1961), pp. 151-153.
8. Hammarskjold Forum, "Expansion of the Viet Nam War into Cambodia—The Legal Issues," *New York University Law Review*, vol. 45 (1970), p. 664 (comments of A. Chayes).
9. Michael Reisman, "Humanitarian Intervention," *The Nation*, May 24, 1980, p. 612.
10. The use of force for rescue, and perhaps for other purposes is widely approved. "It is increasingly accepted that a state may take steps to rescue victims or potential

victims in an action strictly limited to that purpose and not likely to involve disproportional destruction of life or property in the state where that rescue takes place." American Law Institute, *Restatement of the Law: The Foreign Relations Law of the United States*, vol. 2 (Minneapolis: ALI Publishers, 1987), p. 177. The U.S. and others strongly defended Israel's use of force in rescuing its citizens at Entebbe in 1976.

11. See Joseph H. Crown and John H. E. Fried, "A Legal Disaster," *The Nation*, May 24, 1980, p. 613; Benjamin B. Ferencz, "Rescue Mission Violated the U. N. Charter," *New York Times*, May 5, 1980 (letter to the editor).
12. W. Michael Reisman, "Old Wine in New Bottles: The Reagan and Brezhnev Doctrines in Contemporary International Law and Practice," *Yale Journal of International Law*, vol. 13 (1988), p. 180.
13. Abram Chayes, "Grenada Was Illegally Invaded," *New York Times*, November 15, 1983.
14. The letter from Robinson to Professor Edward Gordon was reprinted in "Contemporary Practice of the United States," *The American Journal of International Law*, vol. 78 (1984), p. 661.
15. Edwin M. Yoder, Jr., "The Legality of It All," *Washington Post*, October 28, 1983.
16. Military and Paramilitary Activities in and Against Nicaragua, 1986 ICJ Reports, p. 14 (Judgment on the Merits of June 27) (hereinafter, *Nicaragua v. U.S.*).
17. *Nicaragua v. U.S.*, pp. 93-94, 100-101. In these few sentences, the court resolved a forty-year debate about the meaning of Article 51 with absolutely no analysis. The majority view, backed by such scholars as Myres McDougal, Philip Jessup, Julius Stone, and others, concluded that Article 51 was inserted to ensure that regional self-defense organizations would not be paralyzed by a requirement that all collective responses to force be taken by the Security Council. The Article was meant to reaffirm, not constrain, the right of individual and collective self-defense under customary international law. The minority school, led by Professor Ian Brownlie, insists that Article 51 was inserted in order to create only the smallest exception to the ban on the use of force in Article 2, paragraph 4. The court adopts the minority view.
18. State practice and publicists support the view that a victim state's allies may assert the right of self-defense in those circumstances in which the victim state asserts it, presuming the consent of the victim state. Mutual defense agreements enshrining this principle include among others the Rio and Washington (North Atlantic) treaties.
19. Abram Chayes, "A Common Lawyer Looks at International Law," *Harvard Law Review*, vol. 78 (1965), p. 1409.
20. The international legal community is indebted to *The American Journal of International Law* for soliciting and publishing the views of 16 leading international law scholars of the ICJ's decision, edited by Harold G. Maier, in vol. 81 (1987)—including the comments of Richard Falk, John Norton Moore, Herbert W. Briggs, Tom J. Farer, John Lawrence Hargrove, and Francis A. Boyle.

Part 2

International Institutions and Global Order

6

After Guantanamo: The War Over the Geneva Convention

*Jeremy Rabkin**

British tabloids blasted the story around the world: The Americans had removed Al-Qaeda and Taliban prisoners to a secret torture camp in Cuba! Photographs showed prisoners gagged and shackled, and crammed into cells exposed to the elements. Amnesty International demanded immediate access to the scene of these abuses. Mary Robinson, the UN Commissioner for Human Rights, chimed in, along with other prominent human rights advocates and a supporting chorus of left-wing politicians in Europe. Unwilling to be left behind, the International Committee of the Red Cross (ICRC), self-declared "guardian" of the Geneva Convention on the treatment of war prisoners, weighed in with its own expressions of alarm and outrage.

The furor died down in less than a week as the actual facts became known. The prisoners, some of whom had been involved in a violent prison revolt in Afghanistan, had been restrained in transit but not within their prison cells in Guantanamo. Officials from the ICRC who visited the site soon confirmed that prisoners received adequate food and medical attention, and that their makeshift prison offered no less protection from the elements than the hastily constructed facilities set up for their American guards.

It was left only to wrangle about legal details. The ICRC, along with Amnesty International and Human Rights Watch, insisted that the prisoners deserved the full protections accorded prisoners of war under the Geneva Conventions. After some initial verbal clutter, the Bush Administration maintained that terrorists were not technically prisoners of war, but that they would

---

*Jeremy Rabkin teaches international law and American constitutional history in the Department of Government at Cornell University.

This essay first appeared in *The National Interest*, no. 68 (Summer 2002).

nevertheless be treated by the standards set down in the Geneva Conventions whenever possible. This did not satisfy the ICRC. "There are divergent views between the United States and the ICRC," officials in Geneva reported. They vowed to "pursue dialogue" on the legal issues even as they acknowledged that there was no humanitarian crisis at Guantanamo.

The whole episode could be chalked up to a characteristic expression of European carping at American "unilateralism," enabled, if not created, by irresponsible slash-and-burn journalism. But the fracas says something important about the changing character of international law. This episode should serve as a warning to the wise that the new version of international law advocated by those who have arrived after their long march through the institutions is likely to become a continuing source of mischief to the world, and much trouble to the United States.

Who Enacted the Laws of War?

The immediate source of law in the Guantanamo dispute is the third Geneva Convention of 1949, which concerns the treatment of war prisoners. Three other conventions were launched at the same time (on the treatment of wounded and sick combatants in the field; on the treatment of wounded, sick and shipwrecked combatants captured in naval war; and on the protection of civilians in occupied territory). The provisions in these four treaties were for the most part clarifications and elaborations of the Geneva Conventions of 1929, which in turn sought to elaborate and clarify standards agreed at The Hague Peace Conferences of 1906 and 1899. The underlying impulse for all of this is usually traced to the Geneva Convention of 1864, the first treaty to recognize a specially protected role for Red Cross medical services in wartime. (The International Red Cross had been established in Geneva only shortly beforehand and was instrumental in convening the 1864 conference.)

The dispute over the Guantanamo prisoners, then, is a dispute about treaty law—but treaty law with a history. It is worth our while to briefly review that history, for only in its light can we see how inventive the ICRC's current interpretation of the law really is.

That history can be traced much further back than the 19th-century conferences that gave formal recognition to restraints in the conduct of war. Clearly, restraint had not always been "accepted practice." In medieval Europe, the sacking of towns and fortresses was regarded as a necessary reward for soldiers after the rigors of a siege, and a useful warning to the next target to surrender short of a siege. As late as the 16th century, Spanish theologians claimed to be applying the principles of St. Thomas Aquinas in justifying massacre and rape as an acceptable form of punishment for those who took the wrong side in a just war. But unrestrained war of this kind seemed safely in the past by the mid-19th century. Wars had come to be the undertakings of professional armies, funded and directed by well-organized states that were generally eager to minimize injury to private property and ongoing commerce. It was already widely accepted, then, that states should respect certain limits and proprieties in war, especially in their treatment of enemy soldiers and civilians, even before the early treaty conferences in Geneva and at The Hague.

Geneva and The Hague were thought to be especially appropriate sites for conferences on the laws of war precisely because Switzerland and Holland were neutral states. By the 19th century, neutrality had achieved a considerable degree of moral prestige, as neutral powers were conceived by most European statesmen and jurists as standing aloof from the political intrigues and calculations of petty marginal advantage in the foreign ministries of warring states. The neutral power could thus be identified with the higher claims of humanity at large. The prevailing conception of war was so gentlemanly that both Hague Conventions contained provisions for releasing enemy officers on "parole"—that is, their word as gentleman not to escape or return to fighting, but be neutralized by their capture.

The same conferences that polished up humanitarian standards for captives also sought to lay down broader limitations on the conduct of war—for example, against the use of submarines to sink merchant ships even of the enemy power. Restrictions were also negotiated on the size of artillery shells and the types of rifle bullets that could be used in war.[1] Admiral Alfred Thayer Mahan, one of the American delegates to the 1899 Hague conference, cautioned (regarding a ban on dropping bombs from aerial balloons) that improved weapons, by "localizing at important points the destruction of life" might well "diminish the [overall] evils of war and [so] support the humanitarian considerations we have in view." But he was ignored by Europeans eager to experiment with what we would now call arms control.

Most of these experiments in mutual restraint were promptly abandoned amid the pressures of the First World War. The Germans ignored restrictions on submarine warfare in their determination to starve Britain of aid and supplies. The Allies imposed their own naval blockade to starve Germany and Austria of supplies—including food for civilians. World War II was still worse. Disregarding interwar agreements that sought to revive limits on submarine warfare, the American and British navies adopted a policy of unrestricted submarine warfare against Japanese merchant shipping. Disregarding agreements on the protection of civilians, British and American bombers devastated the cities of Germany and Japan from the air, with little pretense of focusing on "military" as opposed to "civilian" targets. Hundreds of thousands of civilians died, even before the culmination of these efforts at Hiroshima and Nagasaki. Such ferocity could be defended as lawful reprisal for enemy aggression or for treaty violations by the enemy, releasing the Allies from their own commitments. But the truth is that Western governments were not much concerned about legal niceties in the midst of all-out war.

The hallowed idea of neutrality just barely survived World War II. In a war that was seen so clearly as a battle of good against evil, nobody expressed admiration for states that had remained neutral. For several years the Soviets objected to admitting Ireland to the United Nations; members were required to be "peace-loving" and the Irish refusal to join the war against Hitler showed, said the Soviets, that Ireland was not reliably in favor of peace. Traditionally neutral states that had been overrun without serious resistance—Holland, Norway, and Denmark—were chastened by the experience and readily joined the Atlantic Alliance after the war to efface it. Even Switzerland was condemned for trading with the Nazis rather than admired for holding itself aloof, a judgment that over time has acquired quite a firm empirical basis. (No doubt attention will one day alight on Sweden, and not unjustifiably so.)

And yet some laws of war did survive, notably those covering the treatment of prisoners of war. Neither Stalin's Soviet Union nor the Japanese warlords professed to be bound by the 1929 Geneva Convention and neither expected any mercy from their enemies. But Germany remained a signatory and did honor its obligations toward fellow signatories—though not out of any sense of reverence for international legality. American and British (including British Commonwealth) prisoners were, with some exceptions, reasonably well treated by the Germans, even as their non-"Anglo" prisoners—and all prisoners of the Japanese—were horribly abused (or simply murdered). The reason for the restraint in the case of the Anglo-American war with Germany was a sense of reciprocal obligation and thus mutual deterrence. General Alfred Jodl testified at Nuremberg that Hitler had demanded the execution of captured Allied airmen in 1943 in retaliation for the devastating incendiary bombing of German cities. But Hitler's military staff evaded and finally buried this directive, fearing that it would trigger retaliation in kind against German prisoners in Allied hands.

Thanks to this history, it did not seem altogether hopeless to restore the Geneva Conventions after World War II. Indeed, it seemed only prudent. These conventions were not honored by the North Koreans and Red Chinese in the Korean War, nor by the Hanoi government in the Vietnam conflict. But even in these wars, communist authorities did not massacre American prisoners en masse. If they held them as bargaining chips, rather than vessels of sacred humanity, communist governments still saw mutual restraint as being in their interest, much as the Nazis had recognized during World War II.

The same logic of reciprocity and restraint pertains today, but do circumstances allow that logic to function? It is certainly in America's interest to adhere to these conventions when others also do so, but where does that leave us in a war on terrorist organizations and states that nurture them? Can humanitarian laws of war function with enemies who disdain the very idea of humanitarian restraint?

From Contract to Faith

The official position of the U.S. government is that prisoners at Guantanamo are not "prisoners of war" in the sense of the Geneva Convention, and they are not therefore entitled to claim the protection of every provision in the convention. The International Committee of the Red Cross and leading human rights groups, however, insist that they are prisoners of war or should at least have the presumption of such status, with individual denials of such status to be determined on the basis of individual trials. Since the U.S. government insists that it will treat the prisoners humanely—and the ICRC has confirmed that it is doing so—this dispute may seem a pointless quibble.

But it is not pointless, and it is more than a quibble. The designation of being a prisoner of war carries a certain sense of respectability. The prisoner of war is not a criminal, because soldiering is not inherently criminal. We may not want to say the same about terrorist forces, and there is clear precedent for this concern. The Western Allies treated soldiers of the Wehrmacht as men who were simply doing their duty, while SS troops were treated as members of what was designated a "criminal organization"—and thousands were sentenced to postwar imprisonment on that basis or detained much longer than ordinary German POWs.[2]

Apart from the moral or symbolic issue, serious practical issues are at stake as well in the current war. Among the most important are the implications for interrogation of prisoners. As everyone recalls from old war movies, prisoners of war are only required to give "name, rank and serial number"—or, as the 1949 convention adds (as an alternate means of identification), "date of birth." Human Rights Watch insists that this limitation does not prevent prisoners from volunteering more information, nor prohibit prison officials from seeking more. But the convention expressly stipulates that prisoners of war may not be "threatened, insulted or exposed to any unpleasant or disadvantageous treatment of any kind." The convention goes into considerable detail in trying to exclude unnecessarily "unpleasant or disadvantageous treatment."

Prisoners of war, for example, are supposed to have access to "canteens" where they "may procure foodstuffs, soap and tobacco and ordinary articles in daily use." They must be allowed to retain or receive money to buy such things, even if the money has to be provided by the detaining power as an advance on regular pay. Prisoners must also be allowed cooking facilities of their own to make use of little extras they may acquire. No such facilities exist in Guantanamo, and this is objectively helpful. It makes the job of interrogators easier if such comforts are not provided as of right but can instead be used as bargaining chips to induce cooperation.

Similarly, the convention envisions that prisoners will be housed together and be allowed to participate as a group in recreational, cultural and religious activities. Prisoners who want to lead prayer services with fellow prisoners are guaranteed the right to do so. At Guantanamo, the prisoners have been isolated in individual cells and the U.S. Army supplies its own Muslim chaplains for individual prayer sessions. When a prisoner is being questioned, it is useful for interrogators to suggest that others have already talked. For the prisoner, on the other hand, it may make a big difference (both for psychological and practical reasons) to know whether this is so. There is a good reason that social scientists often invoke the "prisoner's dilemma" as a model for decision-making under conditions of uncertainty. As a matter of security, moreover, it is much harder to plot an uprising or a mass escape if you cannot communicate easily with fellow prisoners. In the makeshift cells initially constructed at Guantanamo, it has not been possible to keep prisoners from communicating with each other by calling out from their open-air enclosures. But more permanent facilities may make fuller isolation more feasible. It thus remains a serious issue whether respect for the Geneva Convention should be understood as a legal obstacle to such procedures on the part of the prison administration.

Perhaps most important of all, the Geneva Convention requires that prisoners be "released and repatriated without delay after the cessation of active hostilities." It will not be easy to say when "active hostilities" have ceased when the opposing "power" is a non-state terrorist organization. Nor will it be a simple matter to say when it may be safe to return members of an international terrorist network to roam free again. The convention does allow for individual prisoners to be tried and punished for war crimes they may have committed prior to capture, such as direct participation in terror attacks on civilians. But it is very hard to assemble information about the past activities of individual prisoners captured with a terrorist force.

The ICRC and its human rights group allies insist that the convention requires individualized hearings to determine whether a particular detainee can be held as a war criminal or should be classified as a "lawful combatant," subject to the full protections of the convention. But again, this is hard to do before a great deal more information has been assembled—and a premature designation (enabling an individual to retreat to name, rank and serial number) will make it that much harder to obtain such information. All such practical considerations are dismissed by the ICRC and most human rights groups, however. They argue that if the United States says it is making "war," then the prisoners it takes should be considered, at least presumptively, prisoners of war until an individual can be shown by a competent judicial tribunal to be a terrorist. It should not matter, they argue, whether Al-Qaeda or Taliban forces adhere to all requirements of the Geneva Conventions so long as they are organized participants in what the United States itself regards as a "war." To pick and choose among the protections we offer, they contend, will "provide cover to other governments to ignore human rights standards," as Amnesty International argues, and, as Human Rights Watch warns, "put soldiers around the world at risk."

From Contract to Folly

The underlying premise of such arguments is that the "humanitarian laws of war" are now part of general human rights law. In the mid-1990s, the United Nations published the Geneva Conventions in the same volume with the Covenant on Civil and Political Rights, the Convention Against Torture, and some ninety other general human rights treaties adopted since World War II. No one says that these other protections can be suspended just because some signatories fail to uphold them. The ICRC insists, therefore, that the requirements of the Geneva Convention are "unilaterally binding."

This sounds sensible enough, but it makes the text and history of the conventions unintelligible. Each of the four conventions is proclaimed in the name of "the High Contracting Parties"—that is, the states that subscribe—and the provisions are expressly limited to "parties" on the understanding that the conventions are "contracts." So if "one of the Powers" engaged in a war is not a party to the convention, others in the war who are "parties" to the convention "remain bound by it in their mutual relations"—but not bound to it in relation to the non-party unless "the latter accepts and applies the provisions thereof."

This is the original idea of a treaty. A treaty, as the *Federalist* 64 explained in 1788, "is only another name for a bargain." At the heart of the Geneva Conventions is this bargain: fight according to these professional rules and we will treat you with professional respect.

The main rules for defining combatant status go back to The Hague Convention of 1899. They are not based on ancient ideas of rank and courtesy. Rather, the rules were drawn up at conferences at which military men were not merely present as observers, but constantly at the elbow of the diplomats and lawyers as full participants for what they could provide by way of practical advice. The rules thus rest pre-eminently on practical considerations. The rules allow even "militias" or "other volunteer corps" to qualify for POW status—if they belong to a "party to the conflict"—even if not part of regular armies. But to qualify as a lawful combatant, an individual fighter must be "commanded by a person responsible for his subordinates." One obvious reason for this is that the opposing army, if it is going to treat a captive with all the courtesies of a prisoner of war, must be sure that the captive will behave like a prisoner rather than an infiltrator ready to attack his guards the moment they turn their backs. Surrender is reliable only when those claiming to give up actually answer to the command of a superior who has ordered them to lay down their arms.

So, too, a "lawful combatant" must "carry arms openly" and also carry a "fixed distinctive sign recognizable at a distance" (that is, a uniform or insignia). An opposing army cannot respect the claims of non-combatants if it cannot discern who they are. The other criteria are encompassed in the final requirement that all lawful combatants must "fulfill the conditions" of "conducting their operations in accordance with the laws and customs of war." Armies are not required to respect the "laws and customs of war" against enemies seeking special advantage by exempting themselves from those laws.

Historically, the most common categories denied the protections of POW status (apart from pirates and robber bands) were spies and saboteurs operating out of uniform. The U.S. Supreme Court hastily approved the conviction of German saboteurs by secret military commission in 1942. Death sentences were imposed, even though the half-hearted efforts of these saboteurs, landed by submarine on Long Island, did no damage in the United States. No one thought it strange that the two Germans who cooperated with investigators were spared from execution as a reward for their cooperation. By the same token, postwar American war crimes tribunals dismissed charges against German officers who had executed Yugoslav partisans for sabotage efforts. It was held that because the partisans did not have clearly marked insignia, indicating their status as lawful combatants, killing them was not a war crime. Military courts were not willing to endorse the notion that saboteurs and secret partisans had the same status as lawful combatants.

The underlying bargain here rests most of all on the assumption that an organized army can be neutralized by its surrender. Valuable information might be gained by closely questioning surrendered troops, but armies have been willing to forego the right to pressure POWs into talking in order to assure respectful treatment when their own troops are taken prisoner. The calculus always looked different for bands of spies, saboteurs or secret agents operating behind enemy lines, where pressing for information seemed absolutely crucial because secrecy, more than massed formation, was the essential precondition for such enemy activity.

Now, to say that these requirements are no longer a matter of strict reciprocity between opposing forces—so that they may apply or not in individual cases regardless of the general practice of terrorist organizations—is only plausible if one thinks of them as categorical human rights norms, guaranteeing basic rights to all individuals regardless of context. But this was clearly *not* the premise under which the 1949 Geneva Conventions were drawn.

The idea of universal human rights norms was certainly known to the diplomats and generals who gathered in Geneva in 1949. The year before, the United Nations General Assembly had, with much fanfare, proclaimed a "Universal Declaration of Human Rights" premised on the idea that the world recognized basic rights for all human beings. Most of the governments negotiating the 1949 Geneva Conventions no doubt regarded universal human rights as a fine idea. No doubt, they also wished well to the machinery established in the UN Charter to "save succeeding generations from the scourge of war." But they did not regard these new ideals as sufficient reason to sacrifice the more tangible benefits of the traditional rules of war. To this day, UN human rights norms have no means of enforcement. But the laws of war always had some means of enforcement through the natural and logical operation of reciprocity.

If the protections of the Geneva Convention are regarded as reciprocal concessions by the "contracting parties"—the states sponsoring the forces in conflict—then systematic violations by one side should release the other side from its obligations. The opposing side might actually claim to be strengthening international standards by denying legitimacy to forces that systematically violate the laws of war. If the convention is seen as a statement of universal human rights standards, however, then every individual prisoner has some claim to these protections, unless it can be shown that he was personally operating in violation of the rules.

That is, of course, precisely where the ICRC and human rights groups position themselves. As the president of the ICRC put it, "the basic principles underlying [international humanitarian] law—humanity, impartiality and neutrality—are as valid as ever and certainly still of the utmost relevance."[3] That brings us to the deepest issues in the war on terrorism.

Moral Gravity and the Lightness of Neutrals

Today, human rights groups demand a neutral forum for adjudicating abuses, an international criminal court where the decision to press charges will be left entirely to an independent international prosecutor. Actually, it will not be left entirely to the prosecutor, for new procedural rules allow "victims" to appeal the decision of the prosecutor not to seek an indictment. This means that advocacy groups, mobilizing on behalf of victims, will have legal as well as political forums to press their views. As it happens, violations of the laws of war, including mistreatment of prisoners, are very much in the jurisdiction of the new court, so disputes like the one over the Guantanamo detainees may one day be pursued by a prosecutor at The Hague. The court would also have jurisdiction over crimes of "aggression" and broadly defined "war crimes," so American decisions to strike at terrorist bases or the countries harboring them could also trigger indictments.

Nobody imagined such a thing in the late 1940s when the current Geneva Conventions were negotiated. Certainly, nobody imagined that the ICRC would play a prominent role in arraigning offenders against the laws of war. The ICRC had never done that sort of thing before, and its wartime record did not suggest that it had either the inclination or the capacity to do so. During the war, the ICRC performed with reasonable efficiency in its traditional role, discreetly conveying inspectors' reports from prison camps to the opposing European powers. To win the trust of both sides, it reported abuses to home states of the prisoners, but it did not trumpet its findings to the world. And it said precisely nothing during the war about the Nazi extermination camps, though it had considerable information about them. Much has been made in recent years about the failure of the Vatican to protest against the Nazi Holocaust. But the ICRC's conduct was no better and in some ways worse. Whatever may be said about Pope Pius XII, at least he did not voice public praise for the SS. From its headquarters in Geneva—a much safer place than Rome—the International Red Cross published commendations of the work of the German Red Cross, even when the German chapter was directed by an SS doctor who conducted ghoulish experiments on concentration camp victims.

No doubt, the ICRC had its reasons. It did not want to compromise its role as a discreet go-between in the monitoring of prisoner-of-war camps. The Swiss government, with which the ICRC had always been closely associated, was itself eager to maintain good relations with Germany, and was fearful of being "swamped" by a "flood" of Jewish refugees. But whatever the reasons, the ICRC did not emerge from the war as inspiring example of humanitarian achievement.[4] The Geneva Conventions acknowledge in passing the ICRC's role as a monitor, but they do not make cooperation with it mandatory and they certainly do not establish the ICRC as the definitive arbiter of compliance with the conventions.

Partly because the ICRC remained cautious about its own role until relatively recently, a new set of conflict monitors arose in the 1970s and 1980s and quickly achieved much more prominence. Amnesty International, Human Rights Watch, and Médecins sans Frontières were much louder and more insistent in their denunciations of abuses because they were willing to provoke the hostility of governments. The ICRC has tried to reclaim leadership with public denunciations of its own in recent years, as in its very public and premature denunciation of American practices at Guantanamo. But the high prestige of Amnesty International and Human Rights Watch owes much to the period in which they arose. During the late 1960s and early 1970s, much Western opinion inclined to the view that the United States was acting the role of a bully in Southeast Asia. During the 1980s, much Western opinion inclined to the same view regarding American involvement in the nasty guerrilla wars of Central America. In the 1990s, the collapse of communism in Europe seemed to leave much scope for reform and improvement, but no enemy deeply threatened the United States or the West as a whole. In such a world it was easy for human rights groups to maintain a lofty detachment and retain their prestige as neutral moral arbiters.

For most Americans, September 11 changed all that. President Bush speaks of terrorist networks and the regimes that sponsor or harbor them as "evil." Countries that are not "with us" are to be regarded as "against us." There is not much patience for neutrality in these formulations. But that is almost beside the point. In truth, those who planned the attacks on the World Trade Center and those who nurtured them have no interest in "humanitarian law." Islamist radicals do not think of war as a conflict between states from which ordinary humanity should, as much as possible, be spared. They think of war as an all-out contest between peoples, so that American civilians (or, in the counterpart struggle in the Middle East, Israeli civilians) are no less legitimate targets than uniformed soldiers. Neither age nor sex nor disability makes any difference. The aim is simply to punish a whole society for its sins. The preconditions for reciprocal restraint are wholly absent.

The United States must not sink to the level of its adversaries, of course. Regardless of whether our restraint is reciprocated, the United States will need to observe some restraints for the sake of its own self-respect. Nobody, for example, suggests that the prisoners at Guantanamo should simply be executed without trial. But in a war against barbarism, it is hard to operate at all times within the gentlemanly code of the Victorian peace conferences that codified the modern law of war. We know this from precedent. In World War II, when the United States conceived itself at war with total barbarism, American bombers reigned merciless destruction on the cities of Germany and Japan. Michael Walzer argued decades later that this tactic was morally indefensible, and a serious case can be made for his claim—though a strong case can also be made for the answering claim that, in the final analysis, American bombing (including the use of atomic bombs on Japan) hastened the enemy's surrender and so saved lives overall.[5] There is room for legitimate debate about the restraints that should be observed even in a war with a very dangerous and unrestrained enemy. But imagine how Americans would have reacted during World War II if "neutral" advocates of humanitarian restraint had set themselves up as official arbiters of American war policy. Indeed, during the Battle of Britain, the ICRC did offer to monitor civilian damage inflicted by British and German bombers. Churchill rejected any such neutral monitoring role:

> It would simply result in a Committee under German influence or fear, reporting at the very best that it was six of one and half-a-dozen of the other. It is even very likely they would report that we had committed the major breaches. Anyhow, we do not want these people thrusting themselves in, as even if Germany offered to stop the bombing now, we should not consent to it. Bombing of military objectives, increasingly widely interpreted, seems at present our main road home.

Today's ICRC would deny that it is neutral in quite the way it was during the war against Nazi Germany. The ICRC and other advocacy groups were certainly quick to denounce the bombing of the World Trade Center last fall. But they are also eager to maintain credibility with Islamic opinion and with the larger trend of leftist opinion that instinctively sides with "oppressed people" and assumes Western wrongdoing in every conflict with non-Western peoples. So, for example, both Amnesty International and Human Rights Watch insist that "international law" requires that all Palestinians be assured the right to return to the places where their grandparents or great-grandparents may have lived in what is now Israel—a demand that even governments in Europe, which are very sympathetic to Palestinian claims, do not make. The ICRC has for decades allowed Islamic medical services to affiliate as "Red Crescent" rather than "Red Cross" services but refuses to acknowledge Israel's "Red Star of David" service because it lacks an authorized insignia. Meanwhile, during the recent fighting on the West Bank, the ICRC repeatedly condemned Israel for interfering with Palestinian Red Crescent ambulances—before finally warning the Palestinians not to use these vehicles to sneak weapons and fighters past Israeli checkpoints as they have been wont to do. Indeed, the ICRC is so receptive to Islamist opinion that last fall a staff officer in Geneva circulated within the organization a report that the attack on the World Trade Center had probably been organized by Israeli intelligence because Jews working at the WTC had stayed home from work on that day.

But the feelings of individuals in these organizations are not the point. In a war on shadowy terror networks, human rights advocates simply cannot provide even-handed monitoring on both sides. One of the attractions of terror as a strategic weapon is that actual attacks involve very small groups whose support structure can be disguised: states that sponsor or cooperate with these networks can deny their involvement. Human rights groups do not have intelligence services allowing them to shed light on these connections. But they can publicize what they regard as American abuses, because the United States is much more open about most of its operations. Similarly, advocacy groups can hope to affect American opinion, while their influence on dictatorial states like Iraq is effectively nil.

What is true for monitoring the activities of such groups is even more true for the International Criminal Court that these groups eagerly champion. Having received strong support from European governments, the 1998 treaty for the Court has now received sufficient ratifications to take effect. It will start operations in July. The Court will not be able to apprehend any terrorist or anyone else on its own, and terrorists will obviously find it much easier to hide than traveling American (or Israeli) officials. Moreover, the moral onus of an indictment will surely have more political weight—to say the least—against democratic states. After all, would Saddam Hussein be more dismayed by an ICC indictment than by a Security Council condemnation? Would Al-Qaeda leaders care in the least?

Another problem is that the Court can only deal with those proven guilty of precise crimes. What if a leader of a terrorist operation is acquitted of the precise charges before the court because concrete evidence is insufficient for legal standards of proof? Will the terrorist then be released? Will his comrades and followers also be released on the same ground? It will not be easy to disarm terror networks if the detention of their operatives can only be continued when a judge in The Hague finds them guilty of precise crimes. But, like it or not, the ICC is now a fact, and it is likely to reinforce trends in European opinion that complicate American policy. Among other things, the existence of the ICC will strengthen the notion that there really is a higher law of humanity, binding on everyone, and that supposedly unbiased, neutral judges have the moral authority to enforce this law.

Meanwhile, the active role of advocacy groups is also a fact. In Western Europe in particular, criticism of American policy from Amnesty International and the ICRC immediately won an attentive hearing. The United States must expect to be criticized. It has reason to cooperate with the ICRC, as it has in Guantanamo, to dispel slanders against actual American policy. But the United States also needs to remind Europeans that wars cannot always be fought by gentlemanly rules—not when the enemy disdains all civilized restraint. Europeans may need reminding on this point because, the British excepted, most of them did not do much fighting in the last great war against barbarism—or they did their fighting on the side of barbarism—and now regard actual war as something done only by other, less ennobled people. Contemporary Europe has reverted in many ways to the moral complacency characteristic of neutral Holland before each of the world wars.

Apart from Britain and Turkey, European states are unlikely to be serious military allies for the United States. But to retain a place in the community of civilized states, European nations still need to remember those very important security obligations that they still must honor. In their enthusiasm for unilateral and decontextualized standards of human rights, European states are in danger of letting terrorist operatives slip through their own police controls. Most of those directly involved in the September 11 attacks had spent much time planning, consulting and training for their missions in European cities. And European governments have been reluctant to undertake arrests and investigations on the scale required to stop future terrorists from refitting and regrouping in Europe.[6]

Yes, constitutional states must respect certain limits. But as Justice Robert Jackson famously put it, a "constitutional bill of rights" cannot be interpreted as "a suicide pact."[7] He wrote that only a few years after his return from service as chief U.S. prosecutor at the Nuremberg war crimes trials, which perhaps helped to clarify his perspective on what a constitutional state cannot do and what it must do. Yes, the United States owes "a decent respect to the opinions of mankind," as the American Declaration of Independence puts it. But the U.S. government remains responsible to its own people to make its own decisions about how to defend the American people. That is also in the Declaration of Independence.

We should do everything we can to encourage European cooperation in the struggle against terrorism. But we cannot delegate our own decisions about national defense to prosecutors in The Hague or moral monitors in Geneva any more than we would give final word on these matters to the spiritual admonitions of the Pope in Rome. The dispute about our detention policies in Guantanamo is a harbinger of serious emerging differences with our European friends. It is important to clarify the moral and legal grounds of the American position in that dispute. It is unlikely to be the last time in this war when we will have to assert our right to an independent policy.

Notes

1. The State Department cautioned American delegates in these terms: "The expediency of restraining the inventive genius of our people in the direction of devising means of defense is by no means clear and considering the temptations to which men and nations may be exposed in a time of conflict, it is doubtful if an international agreement to this end would prove effective." See Calvin DeArmond David, *The United States and the First Hague Peace Conference* (Ithaca, NY: Cornell University Press, 1962).
2. Even those who advocate broader protections still want to make certain moral distinctions. In 1977, many governments agreed to an additional protocol to the Geneva conventions (called Protocol I), extending protections to fighters in national liberation struggles, even when not connected to a recognized state. At the insistence of Castro's Cuba, then assisting such struggles in Africa, "mercenary" troops were excluded from any coverage. The Cubans wanted these soldiers of fortune, hired by the South African government, excluded from any protection, and the Cubans got their way. It is not easy to understand why professional soldiers fighting for pay are less worthy of protection than soldiers who volunteer out of fanatical commitment to a cause or out of fanatical hatred for a common enemy, but even the communists wanted to make moral distinctions among soldiers. The United States has never ratified this protocol and, despite arguments advanced by some human rights advocates, cannot plausibly be bound by it—so it has no relevance to American policy toward "volunteers" in international terror campaigns.
3. Yves Sandoz, *The International Committee of the Red Cross as guardian of international humanitarian law* (Geneva: ICRC, 1998), p. 12.
4. The record of the ICRC in World War II is reviewed in Caroline Moorehead, *Dunant's Dream, War, Switzerland and the History of the Red Cross* (London: HarperCollins, 1998).
5. Walzer's views appear in *Just and Unjust Wars* (New York: Basic Books, 1977), which argues that bombing of German civilians might have been justified, if at all, only in the early stages of the war to stave off Allied defeat but not after 1942. For defense of the strategic value of Allied bombing, see Richard Overy, *Why the Allies Won* (New York: W.W. Norton, 1995), which encapsulates the basic argument that the war was considerably shortened by bombing into 1945 and might not have been won at all without it.
6. See Michael Radu, "The Problem of 'Londonistan': Europe, Human Rights and Terrorists," Foreign Policy Research Institute, April 12, 2002.
7. *Terminiello v. Chicago*, 337 U.S. 1 (1949) at 37.

7

Seven Tests: Between Concert and Unilateralism

*Joseph S. Nye**

American foreign policy has changed dramatically since September 11, 2001. Priorities have been altered, several importance bilateral relationships recast and, not least, the general tone of the still-new Bush Administration toward multilateral diplomacy has softened. In the words of President George H. W. Bush, "Just as Pearl Harbor awakened this country from the notion that we could somehow avoid the call of duty and defend freedom in Europe and Asia in World War II, so, too, should this most recent surprise attack erase the concept in some quarters that America can somehow go it alone in the fight against terrorism or in anything else for that matter."[1] This new tone goes well beyond the White House. The State and Defense Departments, each in their own way, recognize the need to build coalitions. The Treasury, which had earlier rejected international cooperation on money laundering tax havens, rapidly became a proponent of cooperation. The Congress, meanwhile, quickly approved a big dues payment and confirmed a new U.S. ambassador to the United Nations—neither of which were on its front-burner before September 11.

It would be misleading to suggest, however, that the U.S. government has become, literally over a single night, wedded to full-fledged multilateralism. Some officials and observers, for example, have expressed concern that too wide a coalition against terrorism would shackle the United States, and that invoking the international authority of the UN or NATO would set a bad precedent.[2] In the Congress, at the same time that our closest ally, Great Britain, was

---

*Joseph S. Nye is dean of the John F. Kennedy School of Government and served as Assistant Secretary of Defense for International Affairs in the first Clinton Administration.

This essay first appeared in *The National Interest*, no. 66 (Winter 2001/02).

ratifying the treaty creating an international criminal court, Senator Jesse Helms was pressing legislation that would authorize "any necessary action to free U.S. soldiers improperly handed over to the court, a provision dubbed by some as 'the Hague invasion clause.'"[3]

Despite the new emphasis on coalitions against terrorism, Americans remain divided on how to engage the world. This division is well appreciated abroad. Internal debates about how to implement the Bush Doctrine of eliminating terrorism has clearly raised concerns in other countries that the United States would appoint itself the unilateral judge of whether a country is supporting terrorism, and the appropriate methods of responding to that support.[4] The U.S. rhetoric of coalition building has not assuaged these concerns, and in some instances may have deepened them.

There are three main approaches to this issue: isolation, unilateralism and multilateralism. Isolationism persists in public opinion, but it is not a genuine strategic option for American foreign policy today. While some people have responded to the terrorist attacks by suggesting that we cut back on foreign involvements, most realize that such a policy would not curtail U.S. vulnerability and could even exacerbate it. The main battle lines are drawn between two kinds of internationalists: those who advocate unilateral tactics and those who prefer multilateral ones. In William Safire's phrase, "uni is not iso-. In our reluctance to appear imperious, we could all too quickly abdicate leadership by catering to the envious crowd." [5]

Of course, the differences between these schools come down to a matter of degree, for there are few pure unilateralists or multilateralists. When the early actions of the Bush Administration led to cries of outrage about unilateralism, the President disclaimed the label and State Department officials described the administration's posture as one of selective multilateralism. But the two ends of the spectrum do anchor different views of the degree of choice that grows out of America's position in the world today. I suggest some rules here for defining a practical middle ground, but first we need to review the debate and its consequences as they now stand.

Some unilateralists advocate an assertive damn-the-torpedoes approach to promoting American values worldwide. They see the "present danger" as a flagging of our internal will and a confusion about our goals which, in their view, should be to turn a unipolar moment into a unipolar era. Robert Kagan and William Kristol have argued that a principal aim of U.S. foreign policy should be to bring about a change of regime in undemocratic countries such as Iraq, North Korea and China.[6] Our intentions are good, American hegemony is benevolent, and that should end the discussion. Charles Krauthammer has urged "a new unilateralism" and argues that multilateralism would mean "submerging American will in a mush of collective decision-making—you have sentenced yourself to reacting to events or passing the buck to multilingual committees with fancy acronyms."[7] Kagan and Kristol believe that "the main issue of contention between the United States and those who express opposition to its hegemony is not American 'arrogance.' It is the inescapable reality of American power in its many forms. Those who suggest that these international resentments could somehow be eliminated by a more restrained American foreign policy are engaging in pleasant delusions."[8]

But Americans are not immune from hubris, nor do we have all the answers. In Robert W. Tucker's view, "new unilateralism" advocacy is dangerous, *even if* its premises happen to be true: "For if we were truly acting in the interests of others as well as our own, we would presumably accord to others a substantive role and, by doing so, end up embracing some form of multilateralism. Others, after all, must be supposed to know their interests better than we can know them."[9] As one sympathetic European correctly observed, "from the law of the seas to the Kyoto Protocol, from the biodiversity convention, from the extraterritorial application of the trade embargo against Cuba or Iran, from the brusque calls for reform of the World Bank and the International Monetary Fund to the International Criminal Court; American unilateralism appears as an omnipresent syndrome pervading world politics."[10] When Congress legislated heavy penalties on foreign companies that did business with countries that the United States did not like, the Canadian Foreign Minister complained, "this is bullying, but in America, you call it 'global leadership.'"[11]

Other unilateralists, sometimes called "sovereigntists," focus less on the promotion than on the protection of American values, and they sometimes gain support from the significant minority of isolationist opinion that still exists in this country. As one put it, the strongest and richest country in the world can afford to safeguard its sovereignty: "An America that stands aloof from various international undertakings will not find that it is thereby shut out from the rest of the world. On the contrary, we have every reason to expect that other nations, eager for access to American markets and eager for other cooperative arrangements with the United States, will often adapt themselves to American preferences." [12] Americans should resist the encroachment of the new international humanitarian law with its claims of universal jurisdiction. Instead, as David Rivkin and Lee Carey argued in these pages, "the United States should strongly espouse national sovereignty, the bedrock upon which democracy and self-government are built, as the fundamental organizing principle of the international system." [13] Or as Senator Jesse Helms warned, the United Nations can be a useful instrument for America's world role, but if it "aspires to establish itself as the central moral authority of a new international order . . . then it begs for confrontation and, more important, eventual U. S. withdrawal." [14]

Multilateralists and unilateralists often dismiss each other's views with no little derision. We would be wiser to take a more dispassionate analytical view, because this debate has serious consequences; namely, a kind of schizophrenia in American foreign policy that is often but not only played out in a struggle between the president and Congress. We must remember that the Executive Branch took a prominent role in promoting such multilateral projects as the Law of the Seas Treaty, the Comprehensive Test Ban Treaty, the Land Mines Treaty, the International Criminal Court, the Kyoto Protocol on climate change and others, but the United States government as a whole has failed to follow through with Congressional ratification on any of them. In some instances, this schizophrenia has given rise to what *The Economist* calls "parallel unilateralism—a willingness to go along with international accords, but only so far as they suit America, which is prepared to conduct policy outside their constraints."[15] For instance, the United States asserts the jurisdictional limits of the unratified Law of the Seas Treaty. It has pledged not to resume testing nuclear weapons but, because of the unilateral nature of the decision, it does not gain the benefits of verification and the ability to bind others. In other instances, such as proposals to ban anti-personnel landmines, the United States has argued that it needs them to defend against tanks in Korea, but it has undertaken research on a new type of mines that might allow it to join by 2006.[16] In still other cases, such as the Kyoto Protocol, President Bush refused to negotiate and peremptorily pronounced it "dead." The result was frustration and anger abroad that undermined U.S. soft power, and that galvanized others to do things they might not otherwise have done.[17] In the words of one observer, at the start of his administration President Bush "contrived to prove his own theory that arrogance provokes resentment for a country that, long before his arrival, was already the world's most conspicuous and convenient target."[18]

During the 2000 presidential campaign, candidate Bush aptly described the situation. "Our nation stands alone right now in the world in terms of power. And that's why we've got to be humble and yet project strength in a way that promotes freedom. . . . If we are an arrogant nation, they'll view us that way, but if we're a humble nation, they'll respect us."[19] Yet, of course, our allies and other foreign nations considered the early practice of his administration arrogantly unilateral. Within a few months, America's European allies joined other countries in refusing to re-elect the United States to the UN Human Rights Commission for the first time. Secretary of Defense Donald Rumsfeld said that "gratitude is gone," [20] while Secretary of State Colin Powell explained that "the 'sole superpower' charge is always out there and that may have influenced some." [21] In the less temperate words of television commentator Morton Kondracke, "we're the most powerful country in the world by far, and a lot of pipsqueak wannabees like France resent the hell out of it. . . . When they have a chance to stick it to us, they try."[22] The House of Representatives responded by voting to withhold funds from the United Nations.

But things are more complicated than such responses acknowledged. It is true that America is resented by some just because it is so powerful and wealthy. But it is also true that American behavior affects the extent of resentment and the ways in which it is expressed. Candidate Bush was right, and so was Teddy Roosevelt. As we all know, at the beginning of the last century as America rose to world power, Roosevelt advised that we should speak softly but carry a big stick. Now that we have the stick, we need to pay more attention to the first part of his admonition—and we need not only to speak more softly, but also to listen more carefully, for we do not hold a monopoly on either truth or virtue.

That is why the United States should aim to work with other nations on global problems in a multilateral manner whenever possible. It is plainly in our national interest to do so, most of the time. The recent bipartisan commission on U.S. national security chaired by former Senators Gary Hart and Warren Rudman, was right to conclude that "emerging powers—either singly or in coalition—will increasingly constrain U.S. options regionally and limit its strategic influence. As a result we will remain limited in our ability to impose our will, and we will be vulnerable to an increasing range of threats." Borders will become more porous, rapid advances in information and biotechnologies will create new vulnerabilities, the United States will become "increasingly vulnerable to hostile attack on the American homeland, and the U.S. military superiority will not entirely protect us."[23] This means we must develop multilateral institutions that constrain others and provide a framework for cooperation. In the words of the Hart-Rudman Commission, "America cannot secure and advance its own interests in isolation." [24]

But again, that does not mean—or at any rate should not mean— that multilateralism is always appropriate. Multilateralism can be used as a strategy by smaller states to tie the United States down like Gulliver among the Lilliputians. It is not surprising that France prefers a multipolar and multilateral world.[25] Nor is it difficult to understand why less developed countries see multilateralism as being in their interests, because it gives them some leverage on the United States. But multilateralism is still generally in American interests. As Joshua Muravchik put it: "By resting our actions on a legal basis (and accepting the correlative constraints), we can make the continued exercise of our disproportionate power easier for others to accept." [26]

Multilateralism does involve costs, but in the larger picture such costs are outweighed by the benefits. International rules bind the United States and limit its freedom of action in the short term, but they also serve U.S. interest by binding others as well. The United States should use its power now to shape institutions that will serve its long-term national interest in promoting international order. Thus Robert Tucker: "Since there is little reason for believing that the means of policy will be increased, we are left to rely on the greater cooperation of others. But the greater cooperation of others will mean that our freedom of action is narrowed." [27]

It is not just that excessive unilateralism can hurt us: multilateralism is often the best way to achieve our long run objectives. Action to shape multilateralism now is a good investment for the future. Today, as we have seen, "worried states are making small adjustments, creating alternatives to alliance with the United States. These small steps may not look important today, but eventually the ground will shift and the U.S.-led postwar order will fragment and disappear."[28] These tendencies are countered by the very openness of the American system. The pluralistic and regularized way in which foreign policy is made reduces surprises. Opportunities for foreigners to raise their voice and influence the American political and governmental system are not only plentiful, but constitute and important incentive for alliance.[29] Ever since Athens transformed the Delian League into an empire, smaller allies have been torn between anxieties over abandonment or entrapment. The fact that American allies are able to voice their concerns helps to explain why American alliances have persisted so long after Cold War threats receded.

The other element of the American order that reduces worry about power asymmetries is U.S. membership in a web of multilateral institutions ranging from the UN to NATO. Some call it an institutional bargain. The price for the United States was a reduction in Washington's policy autonomy, in that institutional rules and joint decision-making reduced U.S. unilateralist capacities. But what Washington got in return was worth the price. America's partners also had their autonomy constrained, but were able to operate in a world in which U.S. power was more restrained and reliable.[30] Seen as a sort of a constitutional bargain, the multilateralism of American preeminence is a key to its longevity, because it reduces the incentives for constructing alliances against us. And to the extent that the EU is the major potential challenger in terms of capacity, the idea of a loose constitutional framework between the United States and the societies with which we share the most values makes sense.

Of course, as we have suggested, not all multilateral arrangements are good or are in the U.S. national interest, and the United States should employ unilateral tactics in certain situations. A presumption in favor of multilateralism need not be a straightjacket. Almost everyone knows and understands this; as we have said, there are almost no pure unilateralists or multilateralists among us. But unless we have before us some general guidelines to determine when unilateralism makes sense and when it does not, we run the risk of oscillating unpredictably between one inclination and the other, moved this way and that by the vicissitudes of political fortune and the surprises of the world.

Fortunately, it is possible to devise such guidelines. Here are seven tests to consider.

First, in cases that involve vital survival interests, we should not rule out unilateral action, though when possible we should seek international support for these actions. The starkest case in the last half century was the 1962 Cuban missile crisis. American leaders felt obliged to consider the unilateral use of force, though it is important to note that President Kennedy also sought the legitimacy of opinion expressed in multilateral forums such as the United Nations and the Organization of American States. The campaign against terrorists and those who harbor them is a case in point, though again coalition support provides both help and added legitimacy.

Second, we should be cautious about multilateral arrangements that interfere with our ability to produce stable peace in volatile areas. Because of our global military role, the United States sometimes has interests and vulnerabilities that differ qualitatively from those of smaller states with more limited interests—as with, for example, the role of landmines in preventing North Korean tanks from crossing the demilitarized zone into South Korea. The multilateral treaty banning landmines was easy for other countries to sign because it had little or no practical significance for them—not so, obviously, in the U.S. case. Similarly, given the global role of American military forces, if the procedures of the International Criminal Court (ICC) cannot be clarified to assure protection of American troops from unjustified charges of war crimes, they might deter the United States from contributing to the public good of peacekeeping. The ICC procedures currently proposed give primary jurisdiction over alleged war crimes by American servicemen to the United States, but there is still a danger of overzealous prosecutors egged on by hostile NGOs in instances where the United States finds no case. We should seek further assurances on such points, such as clarifying declarations by the UN Security Council. While the ICC has problems, helping to shape its procedures would be a better policy than abetting the current trends toward national claims of universal legal jurisdiction that are evolving in *ad hoc* fashion beyond our control.[31]

Third, unilateral tactics sometimes help lead others to compromises that advance multilateral interests. The multilateralism of free trade and the international gold standard in the 19th century were not achieved by multilateral means but by Britain's unilaterally opening its markets and maintaining the stability of its currency. [32] America's relative openness after 1945, and more recently, trade legislation that threatened unilateral sanctions if others did not negotiate, helped create conditions that prodded other countries to move forward with the WTO dispute settlements mechanism. Sometimes the United States is big enough to set high standards and get away with it—witness our more stringent regulations for financial markets. Such actions can lead to a "race to the top" in creating higher international standards. The key, however, is that the unilateral action be designed to promote a global public good.

The Kyoto Protocol that caused President Bush such trouble at the beginning of his presidency could have been another case in point had it been handled differently. Many who accept the reality of global warming and support the Framework Convention on Climate Change (the "Rio Agreement" signed by the first President Bush and ratified by the Senate in 1992) believed that the Kyoto agreement was badly flawed because it did not include developing countries in its target for emission cuts and, according to *The Economist,* "could not be done except at ruinous cost, and perhaps not even then." A longer term plan based on milder reductions at the start, followed by more demanding targets farther out, would provide time for capital stocks to adjust and market based instruments such as tradable permits to lower the costs of emissions reductions, and reduce the trade-off with economic growth (which benefits a wide range of nations including the poor).[33] If, instead of resisting the science and abruptly pronouncing the protocol dead on grounds of domestic interest, the Bush Administration had said "we will work on a domestic energy policy that cuts emissions and at the same time negotiate with you for a better treaty," his initial unilateralism would arguably have advanced multilateral interests. [34]

Fourth, the United States should reject multilateral initiatives that are recipes for inaction, that cater disproportionately to the self-interest of others, or that are contrary to our values. [35] The "New International Information Order" proposed in the UN Educational, Scientific and Cultural Organization in the 1970s would have helped authoritarian governments restrict freedom of the press. Similarly, the "New International Economic Order" fostered by the General Assembly at the same time would have interfered with the public good of open markets. Sometimes multilateral procedures are obstructive, for example, Russia and China's efforts to prevent Security Council authorization of intervention to stop human rights violations in Kosovo in 1999. Ultimately the United States decided to go ahead without Security Council approval, but even then the American intervention was not purely unilateral, but was rather taken with strong support of our NATO allies.

Fifth, multilateralism is essential on intrinsically cooperative issues that cannot be managed by the United States without the help of other countries. Climate change is a perfect example. Global warming will be costly to us, but it cannot be prevented by the United States alone cutting emissions of carbon dioxide, methane and particulates. The United States is the largest source of such warming agents, but three quarters of the sources originate outside our borders. Without cooperation, the problem is beyond our control. The same is true of a long list of items: the spread of infectious diseases, the stability of global financial markets, the international trade system, the proliferation of weapons of mass destruction, narcotics trafficking, international crime syndicates, and transnational terrorism All these problems have major effects on Americans and their control ranks as an important national interest, but one that cannot be achieved except by multilateral means.

Sixth, multilateralism should be sought as a means to get others to share the burden and buy into the idea of providing public goods. Sharing helps foster commitment to common values. Even militarily, the United States should usually intervene with others. Not only does this comport with the preferences of the American public, but it has practical implications. The United States pays a minority share of UN and NATO peacekeeping operations, and the legitimacy of a multilateral umbrella reduces collateral political costs to our soft power.

Seventh, in choosing between multilateral and unilateral tactics, we must consider the effects of the decision on our soft or attractive power. If we continue to define U.S. power too heavily in military terms, we may fail to understand the need to invest in other instruments. Soft power is becoming increasingly important in a global information age, but soft power is fragile, and can be destroyed by excessive unilateralism and arrogance. In balancing whether to use multilateral or unilateral tactics, or to adhere or refuse to go along with particular multilateral initiatives, we have to consider how we explain it to others and what the effects will be on our soft power.

In short, American foreign policy in a global information age should have a general preference for multilateralism, but not all multilateralism. At times, we will have to go it alone. When we do so in pursuit of public goods, the nature of our ends may substitute for the means in legitimizing our power in the eyes of others. As the editor of this magazine has put it, "Sometimes, as a matter of discrete policy choices, the United States will, and should, find itself isolated. . . . But auto-isolation as a tenet of strategy is harmful to American primacy at a time when, strange though it may sound, we cannot act selfishly without the cooperation of others."[36] If, on the other hand, the "new unilateralists" succeed in elevating unilateralism from an occasional temporary tactic to a full fledged strategy, they are likely to fail for three reasons: (1) the intrinsically multilateral nature of a number of important transnational issues in a global age; (2) the costly effects on our soft power, and (3) the changing nature of sovereignty. The September 11 attacks dramatically illustrated the importance of all three of these factors. How well the lessons will take remain to be seen.

Notes

1. Bush quoted in the *New York Times*, September 19, 2001, p.1.
2. See, for example, the comment of Richard Perle on NATO's invocation of Article V in U.S. support, in "After September 11: A Conversation," *The National Interest*, Thanksgiving 2001, p. 13?
3. Associated Press, "Britain Ratifies Treaty Creating Criminal Court," *International Herald Tribune*,, October 5, 2001.
4. Karen DeYoung, "Allies Are Cautious on Bush Doctrine," *Washington Post*, October 16, 2001, p.1.
5. William Safire, "The Purloined Treaty," *New York Times*, April 9, 2001, p. A21.
6. Robert Kagan and William Kristol, "The Present Danger," *The National Interest*, (Spring 2000) pp. 58, 64, 67.
7. Charles Krauthammer, "The New Unilateralism," *Washington Post*, June 8, 2001, p. A29.
8. Kagan and Kristol, p.67.
9. Robert W. Tucker, "American Power—For What?" *Commentary* (January 2000), p. 46.
10. Harald Muller quoted in Franz Nuscheler, *Multilateralism vs. Unilateralism* (Bonn: Development and Peace Foundation, 2001), p. 5.

11. Lloyd Axworthy quoted in Stewart Patrick, "Lead, Follow, Or Get Out of the Way: America's Retreat from Multilateralism," *Current History* (December 2000), p. 433.
12. Quoted in Peter Spiro , "The New Sovereigntists," *Foreign Affairs* (November/ December 2000), pp. 12–3.
13. David B. Rivkin Jr and Lee A Casey, "The Rocky Shoals of International Law," *The National Interest* (Winter 2000–01), p. 42.
14. Jesse Helms, "American Sovereignty and the UN," *The National Interest* (Winter 2000–01), p. 34.
15. "Working Out the World," *The Economist*, March 31, 2001, p. 24.
16 James Glanz, "Study Optimistic on Safer Land Mines, but Says Push is Needed," *New York Times*, March 22, 2001, p. A18.
17. Daniel Bodansky, "Bonn Voyage: Kyoto's Uncertain Revival," *The National Interest* (Fall 2001).
18. See"Roger Cohen, " Arrogant or Humble? Bush Encounters Europeans' Hostility," *International Herald Tribune*, May 8, 2001, p. 1, and Thom Shanker, "White House Says U.S. Is Not A Loner, Just Choosy," *New York Times*, July 31, 2001, p. 1.
19. "2nd Presidential Debate Between Gov. Bush and Vice President Gore," *New York Times*, October 12, 2000, p. A20.
20. Brian Knowlton, "Bush Aide Calls UN Vote an Outrage," *International Herald Tribune*, May 7, 2001, available at http://www.iht.com/articles/19081.html.
21. David Sanger, "House Threatens to Hold U.N. Dues in Loss of a Seat," *New York Times*, May 9, 2001, p. A1.
22. Quoted in *The Hotline: National Journal's Daily Briefing on Politics*, May 8, 2001, p. 4.
23. *New World Coming: American Security in the 21st Century* (Washington, DC: U.S. Commission on National Security/21st Century, 1999), p.4.
24. *Roadmap for National Security: Imperative for Change, Phase III Report* (Washington, DC: United States Commission on National Security/ 21st Century, 2001), pp. 2, 5.
25. Dominique Moisi, "The Right Argument, but the Wrong Tone," *Financial Times*, November 22, 1999, p. 13.
26. Joshua Muravchik in *Commentary,* January 2000, p. 41.
27. Robert W. Tucker, in *Commentary*, January 2000, p. 46.
28. G. John Ikenberry, "Getting Hegemony Right," *The National Interest* (Spring 2001), p. 19.
29. Robert O'Neill, "Working with the U.S.: An Allied Perspective," lecture, All Souls Foreign Policy Studies Program, May 10, 2001.
30. Ikenberry, pp. 21–2.
31. The problems stem not only from foreign courts, but from a new trend in lawsuits brought in U.S. courts to challenge human rights abuses around the world. American lawyers who boast about unilaterally exporting our conception of law, and who argue that "the post-cold war paradigm is the United States as global attorney," fail to reckon the costs of the doctrine of universal jurisdiction for the United States. William Glaberson, "U.S. Courts Become Arbiters of Global Rights and Wrongs," *New York Times*, June 21, 2001, p. 1. See also Henry A. Kissinger, "The Pitfalls of Universal Jurisdiction," *Foreign Affairs* (July/August 2001), pp. 86–96.
32. John Ruggie, *Constructing the World Polity* (London: Routledge, 1998), p. 118. Britain's unilateral willingness to bear the costs (and benefits) encouraged free-riding. American actions have been conditioned on reciprocity.
33. "Rage Over Global Warming," *The Economist*, April 7, 2001, p 18. For a careful study of Kyoto's flaws, see David Victor, *The Collapse of the Kyoto Protocol and*

the Struggle to Slow Global Warming (Princeton: Princeton University Press, 2001). See also Robert N. Stavins, "Give Bush Time on Climate Issues," *Boston Globe*, April 4, 2001, p. A21, and Bodansky, "Bonn Voyage."

34. Andrew Revkin, "After Rejecting Climate Treaty, Bush Calls in Tutors to Give Courses and Help Set One," *New York Times*, April 28, 2001, p. A9.
35. I am indebted to Robert Keohane for help on this point.
36. Adam Garfinkle, "The Present Opportunity," *The National Interest* (Fall 2001).

8

American Sovereignty and the UN

*Jesse Helms**

Earlier this year, UN Secretary-General Kofi Annan delivered an address to the General Assembly in which he declared that "the last right of states cannot and must not be the right to enslave, persecute or torture their own citizens." The peoples of the world, he said, have "rights beyond borders." He is surely correct.

The sovereignty of nations must, of course, be respected. But, properly understood, nations derive their sovereignty—their legitimacy—from the consent of the governed. Thus, Slobodan Milosevic can hardly claim sovereignty over Kosovo when he has murdered Kosovars and piled their bodies into mass graves. Nor can Fidel Castro or Saddam Hussein hide behind phony claims of sovereignty while they oppress their peoples.

As they watch the UN struggle with the question of sovereignty, however, many Americans are left exceedingly puzzled. Intervening in cases of widespread oppression and massive human rights abuses is not a new concept for the United States. The American people have a long history of doing so. During the 1980s, this policy was called "the Reagan Doctrine." In some cases, America assisted freedom fighters around the world who were seeking to overthrow corrupt regimes, providing them with weaponry, training and intelligence. In other cases, the United States intervened directly. In still others, such as in Central and Eastern Europe, America supported peaceful opposition movements with moral, financial and covert assistance. In each case, it was America's intention to help bring down oppressive regimes. The dramatic

---

*Jesse Helms was first elected to the United States Senate in 1972, serving four terms. During his tenure he served on the Senate Foreign Relations Committee, rising to become its chairman (and ranking minority member). He retired from the Senate in 2002.

This essay originally appeared in *The National Interest*, no. 62 (Winter 2000/01).

expansion of freedom in the last decade of the twentieth century has been a direct result of these policies.

In none of these instances, however, did the United States ask for or receive the approval of the United Nations to "legitimize" its actions. And yet the secretary-general now declares that approval by the United Nations Security Council is the "sole source of legitimacy on the use of force" in the world. It is a fanciful notion that free peoples need to seek the approval of an international body (a quarter of whose members are totalitarian dictatorships, according to Freedom House's 1999/2000 *Freedom in the World*) to lend support to nations struggling to break the chains of tyranny. The United Nations has no power to grant or decline legitimacy to such actions. They are inherently legitimate.

What the United Nations can do is help. The Security Council can, where appropriate, be an instrument to facilitate action by "coalitions of the willing," it can implement sanctions regimes, and it can provide logistical support to states undertaking collective action. As it stands, however, the Security Council has an exceedingly mixed record in being such a facilitator. In the case of Iraq's aggression against Kuwait in the early 1990s, it performed admirably; in the more recent case of Kosovo, it was paralyzed. The initial UN peacekeeping mission in Bosnia was a disaster, and its failure to protect the Bosnian people from Serb depredations is well documented in a recent report issued by the UN itself.[1] And, despite its initial success in repelling Iraqi aggression, in the years since the Gulf War the Security Council has utterly failed to stop Saddam Hussein's drive to build instruments of mass murder. It has repeatedly allowed him to play a game of expelling UNSCOM inspection teams, and has left him completely free for the past two years to fashion nuclear, chemical and biological weapons of mass destruction.

The American people will never accept the secretary-general's claim that the United Nations is the "sole source of legitimacy on the use of force" in the world. True, the U.S. Senate ratified the UN Charter fifty years ago. Yet in so doing, America did not cede one syllable of its sovereignty to the United Nations. Under the American system, when international treaties are ratified they simply become domestic U.S. law. As such, they carry no greater or lesser weight than any other domestic U.S. law. Treaty obligations can be superseded by a simple act of Congress. This was the intentional design of America's Founding Fathers, who cautioned against entering into "entangling alliances." This is why Americans look with alarm upon the UN's claim to a monopoly on international moral legitimacy. They see this as a threat to the freedoms of the American people, a claim of political authority over America and its elected leaders.

The effort to establish a United Nations International Criminal Court (ICC) is a case in point. Consider: the Rome treaty purports to hold American citizens under its jurisdiction—even though the United States has neither signed nor ratified the treaty. Put another way, it claims sovereign authority over American citizens without their consent. The Court's supporters argue that Americans should be willing to sacrifice some of their sovereignty for the noble cause of international justice. This, frankly, is laughable. International law did not defeat Hitler, nor did it win the Cold War. What stopped the Nazi march across Europe, and the communist march across the world, was the principled projection of power by the world's great democracies. And that principled projection of force is the only thing that will ensure peace and security on the international scene in the future.

Indeed, more often than not, "international law" has been used as a make-believe justification for hindering the advance of freedom. When Ronald Reagan sent American servicemen to liberate Grenada from the hands of a communist dictatorship, the UN General Assembly responded by voting to condemn the action of the President of the United States as a violation of international law—and did so by a larger majority than that which condemned the Soviet invasion of Afghanistan. Similarly, the U.S. effort to overthrow Nicaragua's communist dictatorship (by supporting the country's freedom fighters and mining its harbors) was declared by the World Court to be a violation of international law. Most recently, we learned that the chief prosecutor of the Yugoslav war crimes tribunal, Carla del Ponte of Switzerland, conducted an eleven-month investigation of alleged NATO war crimes during the Kosovo campaign. She declared that it is fully within the scope of her authority to indict NATO pilots and commanders. In the end, she chose not to prosecute President Clinton or NATO commanders and servicemen, but the very fact that she entertained the idea brings to light all that is wrong with the UN's conception of global justice, which proposes a system in which independent prosecutors and judges, answering to no state or institution, wield unfettered power to sit in judgment of the foreign policy decisions of Western democracies.

No UN institution—not the Security Council, not the Yugoslav tribunal, not a future ICC—is competent to judge the foreign policy and national security decisions of the United States. American courts themselves routinely refuse cases where they are asked to sit in judgment of our government's national security decisions, stating that they are not competent for the task. Why would Americans submit such matters to the judgment of an International Criminal Court, comprised of mostly foreign judges elected by an international body made up of the membership of the UN General Assembly?

Americans distrust concepts like the International Criminal Court and claims by the UN to be the "sole source of legitimacy on the use of force," because we have a profound distrust of accumulated power. Our Founding Fathers created a government founded on the dispersal of power and a system of checks and balances. In his 1962 classic, *Capitalism and Freedom*, the Nobel Prize-winning economist Milton Friedman rightly declared,

> Government power must be dispersed. If government is to exercise power, better in the county than in the state, better in the state than in Washington. [Because] if I do not like what my local community does, I can move to another local community . . . [and] if I do not like what my state does, I can move to another. [But] if I do not like what Washington imposes, I have few alternatives in this world of jealous nations.

Today, as the UN seeks to impose its utopian vision of "international law" on Americans, we can add this question: Where do we go when we do not like the impositions of the world? Today, while America's friends in Europe cede more and more power to supranational institutions like the European Union, Americans are heading in precisely the opposite direction. The United States is in a process of reducing centralized power by taking more and more authority that has been amassed by the federal government and delegating it to the individual states, where it rightly belongs. There is only one source of legitimacy of the U.S. government's policies—and that is the consent of the American people.

If the United Nations is to survive into the twenty-first century, it must recognize its limitations. The demands of the United States have not changed much since Henry Cabot Lodge laid out a set of conditions for joining the League of Nations eighty years ago: We want to ensure that the United States of America remains the sole judge of its own internal affairs, that the United Nations is not allowed to restrict the individual rights of U.S. citizens, and that the United States retains sole authority over the deployment of U.S. forces around the world. This is what Americans ask of the United Nations; it is what Americans expect of the United Nations.

The American people know instinctively that the UN lives and breathes on the hard-earned money of U.S. taxpayers. According to the U.S. General Accounting Office, in 1999 the United States contributed a total of more than $1.4 billion to the UN system in assessments and voluntary contributions. That is pretty generous, but it is only the tip of the iceberg. American taxpayers also spent about $8.8 billion of the U.S. military budget to support various UN resolutions and peacekeeping operations around the world. Thus the United States spent over $10 billion in one year alone to support the work of the United Nations. No other nation on earth comes close to matching that singular investment.

The money America spends on the UN is not charity. On the contrary, it is an investment—an investment from which the American people rightly expect a return. They expect a reformed UN that respects the sovereignty of the United States. The American people want the UN to serve the purposes for which it was designed: to help sovereign states coordinate collective action by "coalitions of the willing" (where the political will for such action exists); to provide a forum where diplomats can meet and keep open channels of communication in times of crisis; to provide to the peoples of the world important services, such as peacekeeping, weapons inspections and humanitarian relief.

This is important work. It is the core of what the UN can offer to the United States and the world. If, in the coming century, the UN focuses on doing these core tasks well, it can thrive and deservedly earn the support of the American people. But if the UN seeks to move beyond these tasks, if it seeks to impose its presumed power and authority over nation-states, I guarantee that it will meet stiff resistance from the American people.

Today, many Americans sense that the UN entertains greater ambitions than the efficient delivery of humanitarian aid, more effective peacekeeping, better weapons inspection, and the enhancement of great power diplomacy. They conclude from the secretary-general's declarations that the UN believes that only it can grant legitimacy to the use of force, and from the efforts to impose the ICC on America that the UN aspires to establish itself as the central moral authority of a new international order. It is an order the American people will not countenance. If the United Nations does not respect American sovereignty, if it seeks to impose its presumed authority over the American people without their consent, then it begs for confrontation and, more important, eventual U.S. withdrawal.

Note

1. "Report of the Secretary-General Pursuant to the General Assembly Res. 53-35 of November 1998: The Fall of Srebrenica," November 15, 1999.

9

Courting Danger: What's Wrong with the International Criminal Court

*John R. Bolton**

Advocates of a permanent international court to try perpetrators of war crimes and other "crimes against humanity" achieved a major success in July 1997, with the adoption of a multilateral agreement called "the Statute of Rome." This treaty will enter into force after ratification by sixty states (which is expected to occur in 1999 or soon thereafter), creating the first new global juridical institution since the International Court of Justice (ICJ) in 1945. In the eyes of its supporters, the nascent International Criminal Court (ICC) is simply an overdue addition to the family of international organizations, an evolutionary step up from the Nuremberg tribunal, and the next logical institutional development over the ad hoc war crimes courts in Bosnia and Rwanda.

On the surface, this logic is straightforward. Through the Genocide Convention of 1948, the four Geneva Conventions of 1949,[1] and subsequent agreements, many of the "principles" of Nuremberg have been adopted in international treaties. The Cold War, however, essentially froze any prospect that the United Nations could serve as a useful vehicle for the creation of new institutions to "enforce" these conventions. Until the Security Council created the Bosnia tribunal in 1993, and a copy for Rwanda shortly thereafter, there were no international war crimes courts. Only the sporadic use of national judicial mechanisms existed, and more often than not these legal systems were either unavailable to the victims of war crimes and crimes against humanity, or were deemed inadequate afterthoughts. The ICJ, although popu-

---

*John R. Bolton was senior vice president of the American Enterprise Institute and is serving in the George W. Bush Administration as undersecretary of state for arms control and international security affairs.

This essay initially appeared in *The National Interest*, no. 54 (Winter 1998/99)

larly known as "the World Court," has jurisdiction only over disputes between states, not the adjudication of individual guilt or innocence for violations of international codes of conduct.[2]

With the fading of the Cold War, and particularly with the inauguration of the Clinton administration, however, the International Law Commission[3] resumed serious discussions about the creation of a permanent international criminal court, moving in 1994 to a Preparatory Committee established by the General Assembly. This Committee (essentially a committee of the whole General Assembly) made the final preparations for the Rome Conference in the summer of 1998. The product of the Conference—the Statute of Rome—establishes both substantive principles of international law and creates new institutions and procedures to adjudicate these principles. Substantively, the Statute confers jurisdiction on the ICC over four crimes: genocide, crimes against humanity, war crimes, and the crime of aggression.

"Genocide" is defined essentially as in the original Genocide Convention of 1948, and prohibits acts intended to destroy national or ethnic groups (Article 6 of the Rome Statute). "Crimes against humanity" are broadly defined to prohibit "widespread or systematic" attacks against civilians that result in murder, enslavement, torture, rape, persecution, enforced disappearances, apartheid, and other enumerated offenses (Article 7). Prohibited "war crimes" include acts "committed as a part of a plan or policy" such as: violations of the four Geneva Conventions; attacks against civilian populations and objects or humanitarian personnel or installations; using weapons that cause superfluous injury or unnecessary suffering; outrages upon personal dignity; starvation as a method of warfare; using civilians as human shields; and a variety of other offenses (Article 8). The "crime of aggression," although declared criminal, is not defined, and the ICC's jurisdiction will not actually attach until the states party to the Statute of Rome agree on a definition pursuant to the Statute's amendatory articles.

Organizationally, the Statute creates an International Criminal Court of eighteen justices to be selected by the treaty parties, and elaborates the Court's structures and procedures. Judges on the Court must reflect "the principal legal systems of the world" and an "equitable geographical representation." Unlike the ICJ, the Court's jurisdiction is "automatic," applicable to individuals accused of crimes under the Statute, in many cases regardless of whether their governments have ratified it (Article 25). Moreover, the Court's jurisdiction includes not only those who actually commit offenses, but also commanders or persons who ordered their actions; who knew or should have known that crimes were about to be committed; or who failed to exercise proper control over subordinates, including heads of state or government and members of parliaments (Articles 27 and 28). Those convicted are subject to imprisonment and fines, but there is no provision for the death penalty (Article 77).

A particularly important new institution is the Office of the Prosecutor, which "shall act independently as a separate organ of the Court" (Article 42). The Prosecutor, elected on a secret ballot by an absolute majority of the parties, is responsible for conducting investigations and prosecutions before the Court; no member of the Prosecutor's staff may accept instructions from any outside source. The Prosecutor may initiate investigations based on referrals by those states party to the Statute, or on the basis of information which he or she otherwise obtains. Although the Security Council may refer a matter to the ICC, or may order it to cease a pending investigation, there is no requirement that the Council play any role at all in the ICC's work (Article 16).

Described in these terms, one might assume that the ICC is simply a further step in the orderly march toward the international rule of law and the peaceful settlement of international disputes, sought since time immemorial. Why, then, did the Clinton administration—a principal moving force to create a permanent war crimes court in the five years before the Rome Conference—find itself, to its dismay, unable even to sign the Statute, let alone propose its ratification by the Senate? Why was the United States so isolated from its European allies? What are the prospects for an ICC to which the United States does not belong?

But Whom Will the Hammer Strike?

What happened in Rome is the completely unintended consequence of the administration's own basic policies, starting in its first days in office. Security Council Resolution 808, creating an international criminal tribunal for Yugoslavia, was adopted on February 22, 1993, just a month after the inauguration. The Rwanda tribunal followed in Security Council Resolution 935 in July 1994. The administration declared these tribunals justifiable on their own merits, and also saw them as building blocks for the ICC. Over two years ago, David J. Scheffer, a confidante of Secretary of State Albright and chief American negotiator on the ICC, wrote:

> The ultimate weapon of international judicial intervention would be a permanent international criminal court (ICC).... The ad hoc war crimes tribunals and the proposal for a permanent international criminal court are significant steps toward creating the capacity for international judicial intervention. In the civilized world's box of foreign policy tools, this will be a shiny new hammer to swing in the years ahead.[4]

But this new hammer—the Court and the Prosecutor—has serious problems of legitimacy. The ICC's principal difficulty is that its components do not fit into a coherent "constitutional" structure that clearly delineates how laws are made, adjudicated, and enforced, subject to popular accountability and structured to protect liberty. Instead, the Court and the Prosecutor are simply "out there" in the international system, ready to start functioning when the

Statute of Rome comes into effect. This approach is inconsistent with American standards of constitutional order, and is, in fact, a stealth approach to eroding constitutionalism.

This difficulty stems from the authority purportedly vested in the ICC to create authority outside of (and superior to) the U.S. Constitution, and to inhibit the full constitutional autonomy of all three branches of the U.S. government—and, indeed, of all states party to the Statute. ICC advocates rarely assert publicly that this result is central to their stated goals, but it must be for the Court and Prosecutor to be completely effective. And it is for this reason that, whether strong or weak in its actual operations, the ICC has unacceptable consequences for the United States.

The Court's legitimacy problems are two-fold, substantive and structural. As to the former, the ICC's authority is vague and excessively elastic. This is, most emphatically, not a court of limited jurisdiction. Even the meaning of genocide, the oldest codified among the three crimes specified in the Statute of Rome, is not clear. The ICC's creation shows graphically all of the inadequacies of how "international law" is created.

The U.S. Senate, for example, could not accept the Statute's definition of genocide unless it is prepared to reverse the position it took in February 1986 in approving the Genocide Convention, when it attached two reservations, five understandings, and one declaration. One understanding, intended to protect American servicemen and women, provides that ." . . acts in the course of armed conflicts committed without the specific intent [required by the Convention] are not sufficient to constitute genocide as defined by this Convention." Another provides that:

> . . . with regard to the reference to an international penal tribunal in article VI of the Convention, the United States declares that it reserves the right to effect its participation in any such tribunal only by a treaty entered into specifically for that purpose with the advice and consent of the Senate.[5]

By contrast, Article 120 of the Statute of Rome provides explicitly that "No reservations may be made to this Statute." Thus confronted with a definition of "genocide" that ignores existing American reservations to the underlying Genocide Convention, the Senate could not attach these reservations (or others) to its ratification of the Statute. Stripped of the reservation power, the United States would risk expansive and mischievous definitional interpretations by a politically motivated Court. Indeed, the "no reservations" clause appears obviously directed against the U.S. Senate, and it is a treaty provision we should never agree to. Much of the media attention to the American negotiating position on the ICC concentrated on the Pentagon's fears for American peacekeepers stationed around the world. As real as those risks may be, however, the main concern is not that the Prosecutor will indict the isolated U.S. soldiers who may violate our own laws and values, and their own military training and doctrine, by allegedly committing a war crime. The main concern should be for the president, the cabinet officers who comprise the National Security Council, and other senior civilian and military leaders responsible for our defense and foreign policy. They are the potential targets of the politically unaccountable Prosecutor created in Rome.

The Statute of Rome's other two offenses (war crimes and crimes against humanity) are even more vaguely defined, to the point that an activist Court and Prosecutor can broaden the Statute's language essentially without limit. For example, the ICC Statute's definition of "war crimes" includes:

> intentionally directing attacks against the civilian population as such or against individual civilians not taking direct part in hostilities; [and] intentionally launching an attack in the knowledge that such attack will cause incidental loss of life or injury to civilians or damage to civilian objects or widespread, long-term and severe damage to the natural environment which would be clearly excessive in relation to the concrete and direct overall military advantage anticipated. . . .[6]

A fair reading of these provisions leaves one unable to answer with confidence whether the United States was guilty of war crimes for its aerial bombing campaigns over Germany and Japan in World War II. Indeed, if anything, a straightforward reading of the language probably indicates that the Court would find the United States guilty. A fortiori, these provisions seem to imply that the United States would have been guilty of a war crime for dropping atomic bombs on Hiroshima and Nagasaki.[7]

It is precisely this kind of risk that has led the U.S. Supreme Court to invalidate criminal statutes that fail to define exactly what they prohibit under the "void for vagueness" doctrine. "Void for vagueness" is a peculiarly American invention, which is unfortunate because the ICC's list of ambiguities goes on and on. Perhaps the most intriguing is the prohibition in subparagraph (p) against "committing outrages upon personal dignity, in particular humiliating and degrading treatment." Were the problems with the Statute of Rome not so gravely serious, one could imagine this provision as the subject of endless efforts at humor. The definition of "crimes against humanity" includes the catch-all phrase "other inhumane acts of a similar character intentionally causing great suffering, or serious injury to body or to mental or physical health." How will this phrase be interpreted? Who will advise our president that he is unambiguously safe from the retroactive imposition of criminal liability if he guesses wrong on "inhumane acts"? Is even a defensive use of nuclear weapons an "inhumane act"?

We are nowhere near the end of the list of prospective "crimes" that can be added to the Statute. Many were suggested at Rome and commanded wide support from participating nations. Most popular was the crime of "aggression," which, as noted, was included in the Statute but not defined. Although frequently easy to identify, "aggression" can at times be something in the eye of the beholder. Thus, Israel justifiably feared in Rome that its pre-emptive strike in the Six-Day War almost certainly would have provoked a proceeding against top Israeli officials had the Statute been in effect in June 1967. Moreover, there is no doubt that Israel will be the target of complaint concerning conditions and practices by the Israeli military in the West Bank and Gaza. The United States, with continuous bipartisan support for many years, has attempted to minimize the disruptive role that the United Nations has all too often played in the Middle East peace process. As if that were not difficult enough, we now face the prospect of the Prosecutor and the Court interjecting themselves into extremely delicate matters at inappropriate times. Israel, therefore, was one of the few governments that voted with the United States against the Statute.[8]

Coincidentally, the United States has had its own considerable experience in the past two decades with the concept of "independent counsels." It is an experience that strongly argues against repetition in an international treaty. Simply launching massive criminal investigations can have an enormous political impact. Although subsequent indictments and convictions are unquestionably more serious still, a zealous independent prosecutor can have a dramatic impact just by calling witnesses and gathering documents, without ever bringing formal charges.

The fundamental problem, however, with the latitude of the Court's interpretative authority stems from the decentralized and unaccountable way in which "international law," and particularly customary international law, evolves. Thus, Japan's Permanent UN Representative said approvingly,

> The war crimes which are considered to have become part of customary international law should also be included, while crimes which cannot be considered as having been crystallized into part of customary international law should be outside the scope of the Court.[9]

This statement expresses cogently the notion that customary international law evolves, or "crystallizes." It is another of those international law phenomena that just happens "out there," among academics and NGO activists. While the historical understanding of customary international law was that it evolved from the practices of nation-states over long years of development, today theorists write approvingly of "spontaneous customary international law" that the cognoscenti discover almost overnight. If this is where the ICC moves us, there is serious danger ahead.

But even beyond this risk is the larger agenda of many ICC supporters, invoking the nearly endless articulation of "international law" that continues inexorably to reduce the international discretion and flexibility of nation-states, and the United States in particular. In judging the Statute of Rome, we should not be misled by examining simply the substantive crimes contained in the final document. We have been put on very clear notice that this list is illustrative only, and just a start.

As troubling as the ICC's substantive and jurisdictional problems are, the problems raised by the Statute's main structures—the Court and the Prosecutor—are still worse. We are not considering a relatively passive court such as the ICJ, which can adjudicate only with the consent of the parties, or when the Security Council or the General Assembly asks for an advisory opinion. The Prosecutor is a powerful element of executive power, namely, the power of law enforcement. Never before has the United States been asked to place any of that power outside of the complete control of our national government.

Indeed, the supposed "independence" of the Prosecutor and the Court from "political" pressures (such as the Security Council) should be more a source of concern for the United States than an element of protection. "Independent" bodies in the UN system have often demonstrated themselves to be more highly politicized than some of the explicitly political organs, UNESCO and the ILO being cases in point. Political accountability, by contrast, which is almost totally absent from the ICC scheme, would have been a real protection. Instead, we now face the prospect, as "public choice" analysis would predict, that the ICC will be "captured" not by governments but by NGOs and others with narrow special interests, and the time to pursue them.

The American concept of the separation of powers reflects the settled belief that liberty is best protected when, to the maximum extent possible, the various authorities legitimately exercised by government are placed in separate branches. So structuring the national government, the Framers believed, would prevent the excessive accumulation of power in a limited number of hands, thus providing the greatest protection for individual liberty. Continental European constitutional structures do not, by and large, reflect a similar set of beliefs. They do not so thoroughly separate judicial from executive powers, just as their parliamentary systems do not so thoroughly separate executive from legislative powers. That, of course, is entirely their prerogative, and substantially explains why they are more comfortable with the ICC's structure, which so closely melds prosecutorial and judicial functions. They may be able to support such an approach, but we should not.

In addition, our Constitution provides that the exercise of executive power is rendered accountable to the citizenry in two ways. First, the law enforcement power is exercised only through an elected president. The president is constitutionally charged (Article II, Section 3) with the responsibility to "take Care that the Laws be faithfully executed," and the constitutional authority of the actual law enforcers stems directly from the only elected executive official. Second, Congress, all of whose members are popularly elected, exercises significant influence and oversight, both through its statute-making authority and through the appropriations process.

In European parliamentary systems, these sorts of political checks are either greatly attenuated or entirely absent, just as with structures such as the Court and Prosecutor created in Rome. They are accountable to no one. The

Prosecutor will answer to no superior executive power, elected or unelected. Nor is there any legislature anywhere in sight, elected or unelected, in the Statute of Rome. The Prosecutor, and his or her as yet undefined investigatory, arresting, and detaining apparatus, is answerable only to the Court, and then only partially. The Europeans may be comfortable with such a system, but that is one reason why they are Europeans and we are not.

By long-standing American principles, the ICC's structure utterly fails to provide sufficient accountability to warrant vesting the Prosecutor with the Statute's enormous power of law enforcement. Political accountability is utterly different from "politicization," which all agree should form no part of the decisions of either the Prosecutor or the Court. Today, however, the ICC has almost no political accountability and carries an enormous risk of politicization. This condition has little to do with our fears of isolated prosecutions of individual American military personnel around the world. It has everything to do with the American fear of unchecked, unaccountable power, and explains why America properly stood apart in Rome from Europe and Canada.

The Real International Interests at Stake

Beyond the particular American interests adversely affected by the ICC, we can and should worry about the more general errors of the ICC's supporters that will affect all nations. Thus, although the gravest danger from the American perspective is that the ICC will be overbearing and unaccountable, there is an at least equally likely possibility that, in the world at large, the new institution will be powerless and ineffectual. While this may sound contradictory, the ICC is ironically one of those rare creations that may be simultaneously dangerous and weak because its intellectual underpinnings are so erroneous or inadequate in so many respects.

The most basic error is the belief that the ICC will have a substantial, indeed decisive, deterrent effect against the possible perpetration of heinous crimes against humanity. Ironically, ICC proponents now criticize Nuremberg as an inadequate, ex post facto response to such crimes, and argue instead for the deterrent value of a permanent Court and Prosecutor.

Rarely if ever has so sweeping a legal proposal had so little empirical evidence to support it. The evidence demonstrates instead that the Court and the Prosecutor will not achieve their central goal because they do not, cannot, and should not have sufficient authority in the real world.

Behind the optimistic rhetoric, ICC proponents have not a shred of evidence supporting their deterrence theories. In fact, they fundamentally confuse the appropriate roles of political and economic power, diplomatic efforts, military force, and legal procedures. No one seriously disputes that the barbarous actions about which ICC supporters complain are unacceptable, but those supporters make a fundamental error in trying to transform matters of power and force into matters of law. Misunderstanding the appropriate roles of force, diplomacy, and power in the world is not just bad analysis, but bad and potentially dangerous policy. Recent history is filled with cases where even strong military force or the threat of force failed to deter aggression or gross abuses of human rights. ICC proponents concede as much when they cite cases where the "world community" failed to pay adequate attention, or failed to intervene in a sufficiently timely fashion to prevent genocide or other crimes against humanity. The new Court and Prosecutor, it is said, will now guarantee against similar failures.

But this is fanciful. Deterrence ultimately depends on perceived effectiveness, and the ICC is most unlikely to have that. Even if administratively competent, the ICC's authority is likely to be far too attenuated to make the slightest bit of difference either to the war criminals or to the outside world. In cases where the West in particular has been unwilling to intervene militarily to prevent crimes against humanity as they were happening, why will a potential perpetrator be deterred by the mere possibility of future legal action? A weak and distant Court will have no deterrent effect on the hard men like Pol Pot most likely to commit crimes against humanity. Why should anyone imagine that bewigged judges in The Hague will succeed where cold steel has failed? Holding out the prospect of ICC deterrence to the truly weak and vulnerable is a cruel joke.

Beyond the predictive issue of deterrence, it is by no means clear that "justice" is everywhere and always consistent with the attainable political resolution of serious disputes, whether between or within states. It may be, or it may not be. Unfortunately for moralists and legal theoreticians, human conflict teaches that policymakers must often make trade-offs among inconsistent objectives. This can be a painful realization, confronting us as it does with the irritating facts of human complexity, contradiction, and imperfection. Some elect to ignore these troubling intrusions of reality, but those who would ponder the ICC's practical merits do not have that option.

The existing international record of adjudication is hardly encouraging. The ICC's framers tacitly recognize this problem because, with virtually no debate in Rome, and with the full endorsement of the Clinton administration, they created the ICC outside of the United Nations system. So visibly separating the ICC from the International Court of Justice tacitly acknowledges that the ICJ has failed to garner the legitimacy sought by its founders in 1945.[10] In some respects, this is more than ironic, because much of what was said then about the ICJ anticipates recent claims by ICC supporters. These touching sentiments were not borne out in practice for the ICJ, which has been largely ineffective when invoked and more often ignored in significant international disputes. Indeed, the United States withdrew from the mandatory jurisdiction of the ICJ after its erroneous Nicaragua decisions, and it has even lower public legitimacy here than the rest of the UN.[11]

Among the several reasons why the ICJ is held in such low repute, and what is admitted privately in international circles, is the highly politicized nature of its decisions. Although ICJ judges supposedly function independently of their governments, their election by the UN General Assembly is highly politicized, involving horse trading among and within the UN's several political groupings. Once elected, the judges typically vote along predictable national lines except in the most innocuous of cases. Thus, the ICJ's failure to generate widespread international respect and legitimacy on "civil" matters may well provide the best explanation of why the new "criminal" court was established outside the UN.

The ICJ's failure is a continuing sore point for ICC supporters, one of whom, Kenneth Roth, recently acknowledged that much will depend "on the character and professionalism of the ICC prosecutor and judges." Roth cites the skill and integrity of several jurists serving on the Bosnia and Rwanda tribunals, and concludes that "there is every reason to believe that the ICC will be run by jurists of comparable statute."[12] Utterly absent from Roth's justification is even a mention of the judges of the ICJ during more than fifty years of existence, though it is surely an institution more comparable to a permanent ICC than are the ad hoc Bosnia and Rwanda courts. Roth's silence speaks for itself.

Although supposedly a protection for the ICC's independence, the provisions for the "automatic jurisdiction" of the Court and the Prosecutor are unacceptably broad. They constitute a clear break from the basic premise of the ICJ that there is no jurisdiction without the consent of the state parties. Because parties to the ICC may refer alleged crimes to the Prosecutor, we can virtually guarantee that some will, from the very outset, seek to use the Court for political purposes. In fact, the Rome Conference substantially minimized the Security Council's role in ICC affairs. The limited remaining role for the Security Council in the ICC is found in Article 16 of the Statute of Rome. Under that article, the Prosecutor is free to investigate, indict, and try before the Court completely at will, unless and until the Security Council acts to stop him. In requiring an affirmative vote of the Council to stop a case, the Statute shifts the balance of authority from the Council to the ICC. Moreover, a veto by a Permanent Member of such a restraining Council resolution leaves the ICC completely unsupervised. It seriously undercuts the role of the five Permanent Members of the Council, and radically dilutes their veto power. This was precisely the objective of the ICC's proponents.

Since the UN Charter charges the Council with "primary responsibility for the maintenance of international peace and security," it is more than passing strange that the Council and the ICC are now to operate almost independently of one another. Strange, that is, only if one is unfamiliar with the agenda of many governments and non-governmental organizations supporting the ICC, whose agenda has for years included a downgrading of the Security Council and especially the weakening of the veto power of its five Permanent Members.

This attempted marginalization of the Security Council is a fundamental new problem created by the ICC that will have a tangible and highly detrimental impact on the conduct of U.S. foreign policy. The Council now risks having the ICC interfere in its ongoing work, with all of the attendant confusion between the appropriate roles of law, politics, and power in settling international disputes.

Accumulated experience strongly favors a case-by-case approach, politically and legally, rather than the inevitable resort to adjudication contemplated by the ICC. One contemporary alternative is South Africa's Truth and Reconciliation Commission. In the aftermath of apartheid, the new government faced the difficult task of establishing and legitimizing truly democratic governmental institutions while dealing simultaneously with earlier crimes. One option would have been widespread prosecutions against those who perpetrated human rights abuses, but the new government chose a different model. Under the Commission's charter, those who committed human rights abuses could come before it to confess past misdeeds. Assuming they confessed truthfully, the Commission could in effect pardon them from prosecution. This approach was intended to make public more of the truth of the apartheid regime in the most credible fashion, to elicit thereby admissions of guilt, and then to permit society to move ahead without the continual opening of old wounds that trials, appeals, and endless recriminations might bring.

I do not argue that the South African approach should be followed everywhere, or even necessarily that it is the correct solution for South Africa. But it is radically different from that contemplated by the ICC, which seeks vindication, punishment, and retribution as its goals, as is the case for most criminal law enforcement institutions. The clear point is that, in some disputes, neither retribution nor complete truth-telling is the best objective. In many former communist countries, for example, citizens are still wrestling with the handling of secret police activities of the now defunct regimes. So extensive was the informing, spying, and compromising in some societies that a tacit decision has been made that the complete opening of secret police and Communist Party files will either not occur, or will happen with exquisite slowness over a very long period. In effect, these societies have chosen "amnesia" because it is simply too difficult for them to sort out relative degrees of past wrongs, and because of their desire to move ahead.

One need not agree with these decisions to have at least some respect for the complexity of the moral and political problems these societies face. Only those completely certain of their own moral standing, and utterly confident in their ability to judge the conduct of others in difficult circumstances, can reject the amnesia alternative out of hand. Our experience should counsel for a prudent approach that does not insist on international adjudication even over a course that the parties to a dispute might themselves agree upon. Indeed, with a permanent ICC, one can predict that one or more disputants might well invoke its jurisdiction at a selfishly opportune moment, and thus, ironically, make an ultimate settlement of their dispute more complicated or less likely.

The recent experience of Chile's General Pinochet compellingly demonstrates this possibility. Chile made painful choices to restore democracy in 1990 after seventeen years of military rule. Many, in Chile and elsewhere, felt that the general was treated too leniently. This is a legitimate view, but so too is its opposite, which asserts the primacy of returning the military to its barracks. Chileans made their choice and have lived with it. But for a self-selected Spanish official, it was not good enough. He sought to extradite Pinochet (during a visit for medical treatment, and under diplomatic status) from the United Kingdom for a trial in Spain on charges of, among other things, genocide. However this particular affair ends, it demonstrates the moral and political arrogance that will likely permeate the ICC, contributing materially to its potential for damage.

Another alternative, of course, is for the parties themselves to try their own alleged war criminals. ICC proponents usually ignore or overlook this possibility, either because it is inconvenient to their objectives, or because it utilizes national judicial systems and agreements among (or within) nation-states to implement effectively. One important example involves Cambodia. Although Khmer Rouge genocide is frequently offered as an example of why the ICC is needed, its proponents never explain why the Cambodians should not themselves adjudicate alleged war crimes.

Cambodia is again split by intense political differences. As before, the factions seek to internationalize their dispute, each hoping that external political intervention, including the idea of an international war crimes tribunal, will tip the domestic political scales in its favor. Instead, Cambodians should judge their own criminals. There is a strong argument that to obtain the full cathartic benefit of war crimes trials, a nation must be willing to take on the responsibility of judging its own. To create an international tribunal for the task implies immaturity on the part of Cambodians and paternalism on the part of the international community. Repeated interventions by global powers are no substitute for the Cambodians coming to terms with themselves.

ICC proponents frequently assert that the histories of the Bosnia and Rwanda tribunals established by the Security Council demonstrate why a permanent ICC is necessary. The actual evidence proves precisely the contrary: it is wildly premature to extrapolate from the limited and highly unsatisfactory experience with ad hoc tribunals to a permanent Court and Prosecutor.

For Bosnia, as noted above, the ad hoc court was established before the Dayton Agreement, and serves as an example of how a decision to detach war crimes from the underlying political reality advances neither the political resolution of a crisis nor the goal of punishing war criminals. Even today, after Dayton, the tribunal cannot achieve its declared objectives. ICC proponents complain about the lack of NATO resolve in apprehending alleged war criminals. But if not in Bosnia, where? If the political will to risk the lives of troops to apprehend indicted war criminals there does not exist, where will it suddenly spring to life on behalf of the ICC?

It is by no means clear that even the tribunal's "success" would complement or advance the political goals of a free and independent Bosnia, the expiation of wartime hostilities, or reconciliation among the Bosnian factions. In Bosnia, there are no clear communal winners or losers. Indeed, in many respects the war in Bosnia is no more over than it is in the rest of the former Yugoslavia, such as Kosovo. Thus, there is no agreement, either among the Bosnian factions or among the external intervening powers, about how the war crimes tribunal fits into the overall political dispute or its potential resolution. Bosnia shows that insisting on legal process as a higher priority than a basic political resolution can adversely affect both the legal and political sides of the equation.

In short, and very much unlike Nuremberg, much of the Yugoslav war crimes process seems to be about score settling rather than a more disinterested search for justice that will contribute to political reconciliation. If one side—most likely the Serbs—believes strongly that it is being unfairly treated, then the "search for justice" will have harmed Bosnian national reconciliation. This is a case where it only takes one to tango. Outside observers might disagree with this assessment, but outside observers do not live in Bosnia.

And again, the option of Bosnians trying their own war criminals is not even seriously discussed. One reason, of course, is that at the time of Dayton the Hague tribunal was already a fact of life that some parties did not want to modify. More troubling is that Dayton did not really accomplish much more than a de facto partition of Bosnia. Bluntly stated, if Bosnian Serbs, Croats, and Muslims had reached a true meeting of minds at Dayton, they would have resolved the question of war crimes allegations. That they did not is a straightforward admission that Dayton simply papered over, and almost certainly only temporarily, the underlying causes of past and future conflicts.

The experience of the Rwanda war crimes tribunal is even more discouraging. Widespread corruption and mismanagement in that tribunal's affairs have led many simply to hope that it expires quietly before doing more damage. At least as troubling, however, is the clear impression many have that score settling among Hutus and Tutsis—war by other means—is the principal focus of the Rwanda tribunal. Of course it is.

Consider also Iraq. Its August 1990 invasion of Kuwait unquestionably qualifies as an act of aggression, and there is little debate that the Iraqis committed any number of acts against Kuwaitis and others that would be illegal under the Statute of Rome. Yet, by conscious decision, neither the United

States nor any other power, including Kuwait, has seriously sought to create a war crimes tribunal for the Persian Gulf War, and the reasons are clear: this is a case to abjure war crimes prosecutions because the appropriate circumstances are not yet present.

In the first place, the victorious Gulf coalition never had as a goal the unconditional surrender of Iraq or Saddam Hussein's removal from power. Moreover, the key defendants from Saddam on down are not in custody, nor is potentially dispositive documentary and physical evidence, which is still in the hands of the Iraqi government and military. Prosecuting the alleged war criminals in absentia is therefore the only possibility, and this approach raises enormous potential risks. Specifically, in absentia prosecutions could give rise to "Versailles syndrome" feelings of injustice and persecution by the West, both among Iraqis and generally throughout the Arab world. What Iraq really needs is a new government that can decide on justice for Saddam and his henchmen as an element of that country's own internal political maturation.

ICC advocates defend the Statute of Rome by pointing to the doctrine of "complementarity" (deference to national judicial systems) embodied in the Statute. "Complementarity," like so much else connected with the ICC, is simply an assertion, utterly unproven and untested. If complementarity has any real substance, it argues against creating the ICC in the first place. If most national judicial systems are capable of addressing the substantive crimes the Statute proscribes, then that demonstrates why, at most, ad hoc international tribunals are necessary. Indeed, it is precisely the judicial systems that the ICC would likely supplant (such as in Bosnia or, possibly, in Cambodia) where the international effort should be to encourage the warring parties to resolve questions of criminality as part of a comprehensive solution to their disagreements. Removing key elements of the dispute, especially the emotional and contentious issues of war crimes and crimes against humanity, undercuts the very progress that these peoples, victims and perpetrators alike, must make if they are ever to live peacefully together.

Next Steps

Rather than walk away from the wreckage of its policy in Rome, the Clinton administration is actively working to recreate its shattered strategy to bring the United States into the ICC. It does so because its commitment to the ICC resides at the core of its foreign policy, and because of the intense criticism from the administration's erstwhile supporters, which may shock those unfamiliar with the Byzantine politics of international human rights. Those scorned demand that Clinton sign the Statute of Rome so that it will "put America back in the camp of the friends, rather than the enemies, of human rights."[13] This is true Puritanism: failure to support the ICC is proof of apostasy on human rights generally.

In response, the administration will likely take several steps. First, it will continue to negotiate with signatories in hope of obtaining sufficient amendments to allow the United States to sign on. Second, it will probably support transferring the work of the Bosnia and Rwanda tribunals to the ICC, thus triggering financial support from the UN (and therefore from its principal funder, the United States). Third, the administration will attempt to have the Security Council refer other matters (such as Cambodia) to the ICC, rather than have them come from state referrals or from the Prosecutor, thus also triggering the UN funding obligation. Fourth, they will seek to provide "temporary" or "transitional" assistance to the ICC, which, in the ways of all bureaucracies, may endure forever.

Given that we face two years before having even a prospect of a president who would resolutely oppose the ICC, we can only assume that the Statute of Rome will enter into force before then. Nonetheless, we should not assume that others, especially those who will pay the bills in our absence, will rush to make it fully functioning. Having done the "right thing" in creating the ICC, many European governments, which have more than a passing acquaintance with cynicism, may not rush to make it fully operational. Nor will they necessarily hasten to risk the catastrophic consequences of attempting to assert jurisdiction over an American citizen, interfere in Security Council matters, or otherwise obstruct U.S. foreign policy.

In fact, whether the ICC survives and flourishes depends in large measure on the United States. We should therefore ignore it in our official posture, and attempt to isolate it through our diplomacy, in order to prevent it from acquiring any further legitimacy or resources. U.S. policy toward the ICC should be, in a phrase familiar to President Clinton, "Three No's": no financial support, directly or indirectly; no collaboration; and no further negotiations with other governments to "improve" it. Such a policy cannot entirely eliminate the risks posed by the ICC, but it can go a long way in that direction. Certainly, members of Congress should press this view on the Clinton administration.

The plain fact is that additional "fixes" over time to the ICC will not alter its multiple inherent defects. The United States has many alternative foreign policy instruments to utilize that are fully consistent with our national interests, leaving the ICC to the obscurity it so richly deserves. Signatories of the Statute of Rome have created an ICC to their liking, and they should live with it. We should not.

Notes

1. The four Geneva Conventions cover the proper treatment of woUNded and sick members of the armed forces on land and at sea (and those who are shipwrecked), prisoners of war, and the treatment of civilians in times of war in occupied territories.
2. ICJ Statute, Article 34(1). The ICJ can also give advisory opinions to the UNited Nations. UN Charter, Article 96.

3. The International Law Commission is a UN body created by the General Assembly in 1947 composed of thirty-four "independent" experts, sitting in their personal capacities, charged with responsibility for "the progressive development of international law and its codification."
4. David J. Scheffer, "International Judicial Intervention," *Foreign Policy* (Spring 1996), pp. 48, 51.
5. See American Society of International Law, *International Legal Materials*, vol. 28, no. 3 (May 1989), p. 782.
6. Statute of Rome, Article 8.2(b)(i) and (iv).
7. Some governments and NGOs proposed in Rome that the use of nuclear weapons be specifically prohibited. While these proposals were not accepted, the Statute's actual language can certainly support arguments about the "criminal" effects of nuclear weapons for those seeking to outlaw them.
8. Israel also objected to a provision (Article 8.2.(b)(viii)) that makes it a war crime to effect "the transfer, directly or indirectly, by the Occupying Power of parts of its own civilian population into the territory it occupies, or the deportation or transfer of all parts of the population of the occupied territory within or outside this territory." The inclusion of Article 8.2.(b)(viii) is an excellent example of the politicization of what is masquerading as a purely legal process. We can expect no end to this kind of effort to gain political advantage by manipulating the Statute, the Court, and the Prosecutor.
9. Statement of Ambassador Hisashi Owada, head of the delegation of Japan, June 15, 1998.
10. Although the ICJ has its own Statute, it is expressly created by Chapter XIV of the UN Charter, and is thus one of the "principal organs" authorized thereunder.
11. The Nicaragua decisions are discussed at length in Robert Bork's "The Limits of 'International Law'," *The National Interest* (Winter 1988/89).
12. Kenneth Roth, "The Court the U.S. Doesn't Want," *New York Review of Books*, November 19, 1998, p. 45.
13. Roth, p. 47.

10

Dayton, Bosnia, and the Limits of Law

*Alfred P. Rubin**

In an attempt to create an American-style, multi-ethnic democracy in the Bosnia-Herzegovinian rump of the formerly multi-ethnic dictatorship of Yugoslavia, American negotiators brokered a complex series of formal undertakings known collectively as the Dayton Accord. This Accord was initialed by representatives of the Muslim-dominated Republic of Bosnia-Herzegovina—whose authority is rejected by its Serbian minority; by the Serb-dominated Federal Republic of Yugoslavia, which denies that it is involved in the Serb resistance to the nominal government of Bosnia-Herzegovina, but which was authorized by the leaders of that resistance to speak for them; by the Republic of Croatia; by a representative of the European Union; by the United States; and—apparently redundantly since they are members of the European Union—by France and the United Kingdom as well. This great abundance of initialing occurred on November 20, 1995, at Wright-Patterson Air Force Base near Dayton, Ohio, and was later rendered legally binding by a formal signing in Paris on December 14 of that year.

As written, the Accord presumes that a legal authority resides in the United Nations Security Council to act in cases of internal conflict. It assumes further that enforcement of the international laws of war by the community of nations is consistent with the current international legal order of separate states. Both bases for supposing the Dayton Accord to be legally binding are dubious.

Under the United Nations Charter, itself a binding treaty, the Security Council can require action from the members of the United Nations in accordance with judgments rendered by the International Court of Justice (Article 94.2), as well as in reaction to a "threat to the peace, breach of the peace, or act of aggres-

*Alfred P. Rubin is distinguished professor of international law at the Fletcher School of Law and Diplomacy at Tufts University.

This essay originally appeared in *The National Interest*, no. 46 (Winter 1996/97).

sion" (Article 39). But the war crimes tribunal at The Hague is not the International Court of Justice (ICJ). Aside from a preliminary judgment in July 1996 accepting jurisdiction in a case against the Federal Republic of Yugoslavia by the Republic of Bosnia and Herzegovina, not to be argued in substance until 1997, the ICJ has uttered no judgment whose implementation in the Balkan area is in question. Moreover, unless the Security Council itself makes a determination relevant to international peace and security, no organ of the United Nations is authorized by the Charter to "intervene in matters which are essentially within the domestic jurisdiction of any state" (Article 2.7).

Suppose the military struggle within the Bosnian "state" were legally a "civil war," as indeed seems to be the case. To assert that a civil war is by its nature a threat to international peace and security—however distasteful its rationales might seem to those standing outside the struggle, and however much governed it may (or may not) be by the laws of war observed internationally—is to try to make revolution illegal. If all states were well-governed today, or if stability were the overriding aim of international politics, such a proposition might be desirable. But as things are, that seems ill-based. Certainly, the Bosnian armed struggle itself cannot be called "international" by those who argue that a Bosnia-Herzegovina that incorporates its former Serb population with its designated territory preserves a historical unity. Nor, except in an inconsistent attempt to gain legal control over it, have the parties to the Dayton Accord accepted the international personality of the "Republika Srpska," the Serb organization fighting for independence in the territory of Bosnia-Herzegovina; and that organization is not represented in the United Nations, except by the very government against which it is rebelling. The government of the Serb-dominated Federal Republic of Yugoslavia denied that it represents the Bosnian Serbs in the United Nations, and says that it does not want to expand at the further expense of Bosnia-Herzegovina.

Nonetheless, the Security Council acted. It determined that the conflict in Bosnia was a threat to "international" peace and security.

If the Security Council, by its own vote, can categorize events in such ways as to avoid limits on its own authority placed there by those submitting to that authority, a radical change in the structure of the United Nations will have been achieved. It is a change that few members of the United Nations would agree to, other than the five great powers that have the protection provided by vetoes in the Security Council. If the Security Council were to use the case of former Yugoslavia as a precedent, defections from the United Nations might well result, threatening collapse of the organization as a whole. The alternative—regarding the case of the former Yugoslavia as unique—undermines the universality of the rule of law and the notion of the sovereign equality of states on which the organization is based (UN Charter, Articles 1.1 and 2.1). It is very difficult to understand how the authority of the Security Council to determine that a civil war constitutes a threat to international peace can be supported by people interested in the rule of law.

The War Crimes Issue

Meanwhile, the Security Council authorized a complex new organization centered in The Hague whose function is to bring "war criminals" of the military struggle in Bosnia-Herzegovina to "justice" (Resolution 827 of May 25, 1993). Why it did so is unclear. There is no evidence that holding "war crimes" trials will limit existing threats to international peace and security; making "war" less atrocious (even if that were possible) is not likely to limit the causes of or impetus to "war"—if anything, the opposite would more likely be the case. Instead, the creation of a war crimes tribunal seems to have been aimed at making lawyers the "guardians" of a violent society, in which war is all right as long as it is played by rules to which the concerned lawyers can agree.

Since lawyers are not elected and represent only their clients, and since the selection of judges is subject to the same political pitfalls that line the route to all elected legislative and political positions, it is hard to understand why setting up the tribunal would be a step toward a future less threatened by violence. Indeed, it seems obvious that the politically chosen members of the Security Council regarded their action in authorizing The Hague tribunal for Bosnia as a strictly political act. They made sure that only atrocities by participants in the actual struggle in the former Yugoslavia would be within the tribunal's purview; their own activities, even as armed "peacekeepers" there, are not. It is likely to the point of certainty that the political leadership of none of the permanent members of the Security Council—the United States, United Kingdom, France, Russia, and China—would submit its own political-military decisions, including possible atrocities committed by members of its armed forces, to the judgment of outsiders. Would Russia agree to allow a "neutral" tribunal to judge the conformity to an asserted international law of the acts of individual Russians relating to Chechnya? Chinese to Tibet? United Kingdom officials to Northern Ireland? U.S. officials to the Branch Davidian compound in Texas?

Does the international legal order then leave us helpless to ameliorate the evils wrought by the participants in a civil war? The answer is clearly no. But the ameliorations cannot be wrought by third party intervention, even if they are called "community" action.

In using the Security Council to erect a war crimes tribunal at The Hague, the U.S. government not only agreed that the authority of the Security Council extended to "war crimes" committed in a civil war, but also that "war crimes" were direct violations of "international law," and could be tried by an international tribunal set up by international authority. The parties to the Dayton Accord agreed "to cooperate in the investigation and prosecution of war crimes and other violations of international humanitarian law" not only in the traditional ways that law is applied, but as "otherwise authorized by the United Nations Security Council" (General Framework Agreement, Article IX). As noted above, the Bosnian Serbs, now calling themselves the Republika Srpska, are not parties to the Framework Agreement; their supposed commitment to it is derived from a separate agreement dated August 29, 1995, under which the Federal Republic of Yugoslavia was reportedly authorized to sign on behalf of the Republika Srpska those parts of the peace plan concerning the Bosnian Serbs. Since the Republika Srpska is not considered an international person by any of the parties to the Framework Agreement, it is not at all clear why anybody regards that Republika as legally bound by anything concluded internationally, or why an internal document of the Federal Republic of Yugoslavia, if that is what the "agreement" is, is regarded as governed by international law. What the U.S. negotiators wanted is clear; whether the law would permit them to achieve it in this way is more than doubtful.

But things get worse. In annexes to the Framework Agreement, too, cooperation with the Security Council's efforts was promised, "including the International Tribunal for the Former Yugoslavia" (Annex I, Article X): "All competent authorities in Bosnia and Herzegovina" must "cooperate and provide unrestricted access to . . . the International Tribunal for the Former Yugoslavia; and any other organization authorized by the UN Security Council with a mandate concerning human rights or humanitarian law" (Annex 6, Article XIII.4).

Presumably, the annexes' expression "Bosnia and Herzegovina" was intended as a geographical expression, not a political one, so the undertaking should be binding on whoever (other than United Nations forces) controls the territory. The parties to the annexes quoted are the Republic of Bosnia-Herzegovina, the Federation of Bosnia and Herzegovina (the Muslim-Croat part of the Republic), and the Republika Srpska (the Serbian organization regarded by the framers of the Dayton Accord as part of Bosnia-Herzegovina). Of those, only the first is a party to the Framework Agreement. The Federal Republic of Yugoslavia (the existing Serbian state) is an "endorser," a term left undefined in the published documents.

The agreement as a whole was apparently intended to bring the political leadership in Bosnia-Herzegovina under the authority of the tribunal at The Hague, thus establishing a "community" authority on war crimes superior to a nation's traditional authority to define and administer criminal law under its own constitution. But it is legally unclear that the parties to the Framework Agreement, who have no rights or obligations under the annexes, can claim any special role in their implementation. Moreover, the failure of a party to an annex to fulfill its apparent commitment is not a "crime" under international law; it is only a possible "breach of contract." As in our own domestic law, the remedy for a breach of contract lies with the party injured by the breach; that party can bring suit. It does not, and cannot, lie with a non-party who would like to supervise the performance of a contract to which it is itself not bound.

The attempt to use the forms of law to bring peace to the Balkans has apparently seized the imagination of experienced and superbly competent statesmen like Cedric Thornberry, a British lawyer, former assistant secretary-general of the United Nations, and deputy head of mission of UNPROFOR in the former Yugoslavia during 1992-94. In his recent Foreign Policy article "Saving the War Crimes Tribunal," Thornberry notes some of the weaknesses of the process, such as targeting some Bosnian Serb leaders—but not the equivalent Croat and Muslim leaders whose followers have committed atrocities. He argues nonetheless that the process itself is sound. But it is doubtful that the process is sound, and he seems unaware that the legal order provides more effective alternatives.

A Failed Precedent

There is a frequently cited precedent for using a legal tribunal and the notion of war crimes to bring "justice" to a legal order that seems incapable of enforcing the rules outsiders regard as vital: Nuremberg. But the precedent fails because the two situations are not analogous.

Nuremberg was a victors' tribunal; there were no "neutrals" involved in the prosecution or on the judges' bench. The Hague tribunal is supposed to be "neutral."

Nuremberg was in the middle of Germany and its greatest success was in exposing to the German people themselves the atrocities that had been done in their name by their government; it was part of a course of education that has had an enormous impact on German society. Contrarily, the Hague tribunal is about 750 miles from the scene of the atrocities and is widely viewed in the former Yugoslavia as a game being played by outsiders lacking a firm grip on local reality.

At Nuremberg, the Nazi archives were open to the defense as well as to the prosecution, and the need for Allied secrecy barely inhibited the ability of the defense to present evidence; indeed, some acquittals were based on that evidence. At The Hague, the documents and testimony needed for an effective defense are hard to expose and bring to the tribunal; there is no reason to expect the Bosnian Serbs to publish their internal records, and no reason to think that the Serbian Serbs would want those records, or their own Cabinet minutes that might reflect those records, exposed. Nor is there any reason to expect the Bosnian Muslims or Croatians to volunteer their own records, which might exculpate some low-level defendants by incriminating higher-level officials.

It is also frequently forgotten that a series of trials equivalent to Nuremberg was held in Tokyo, resulting in a major dissent (by the Indian judge), partial dissents (by the Dutch and French judges), and a separate opinion (by the Philippine judge). For fifty years now, the Nuremberg "precedent" has not been followed. Before the precedent is revived, it would be wise for those arguing for it to check the reasons why it was not deemed persuasive to some at Tokyo, or to many people for fifty years afterwards. The weakness of the Nuremberg precedent was certainly seen by the defendants at The Hague, even if not perceived by the prosecution.

The defendants' first line of defense was an attack directly on the authority of the Security Council to establish the tribunal, which was predictably rejected by the judges of the tribunal itself, who based their opinion on the presumed authority of the Security Council. It is hard to imagine anybody being surprised by the judges' attitude.

On a deeper level, one may question the assumption that the atrocities committed in the former Yugoslavia are violations of "international law," which by treaty and custom requires belligerents to forbid and punish defined military atrocities, but does not directly apply to individuals or authorize third-party tribunals to pass judgment on them unless submission to such tribunals is agreed by the belligerents themselves. The point is that international law is not directly enforced by criminal process, but international law can be said to require national criminal law to forbid and punish some particularly atrocious acts by individuals acting for a political purpose as part of an organized military force.

The international laws of war derive from state practice and from treaties. Until now those laws have been enforced only by tainted victors' tribunals and national or factional tribunals conducted by the belligerents themselves. The U.S. trial of Lieutenant William Calley over the My Lai massacre also treated some violations of internationally agreed rules as crimes under American military law. His immediate superior in the Army, Captain Ernest L. Medina, was acquitted. No third party tribunal was considered competent to hear any aspect of either case. The "international community" might be disgusted by the facts in the former Yugoslavia (or might not—most members have atrocities in their own recent history that they prefer be ignored). But disgust is not a basis for "jurisdiction to enforce" or "jurisdiction to adjudicate" in criminal matters in any country or in the international community.

"Jurisdiction to enforce" is a legal concept that requires that arrests be made within the territory or ship or aircraft or other similar place that can be assimilated to the territory of the arresting state. That is why, when U.S. agents "arrested" Fawaz Yunis, a Middle Eastern "terrorist," on board a Cypriot vessel, the agents first dragged him off the vessel, performed the formal "arrest" in an American ship, and then claimed that he had been apprehended on the high seas, as if clinging to a driftwood raft.

"Jurisdiction to adjudicate" means that there must be some national interest in the trial to support a state's application of its own criminal process to the facts: either the nationality of a victim, the location of the offense, the nationality of the accused, a substantial impact within the territory of the state purporting to run the trial, or some similar link. It was by this principle that the United States strongly protested West Germany's refusal to extradite Mohammed Ali Hamadei to the United States in 1987 to face trial for the 1985 murder of an American in a hijacked, American-registered aircraft on the ground in Beirut. Although Germany asserted that his offense was "universal" and a trial there would be legally proper, no particular German interest had been involved in Hamadei's offenses.

The analogy between war atrocities and "universal offenses" such as "piracy" or the slave trade does not relate to jurisdiction to enforce or to adjudicate, but only to the applicability of national criminal legislation: the reach of so-called "jurisdiction to prescribe." And, even there, the extension of a national jurisdiction to make criminal the acts of some foreigners outside the territory of the prescribing state has been much exaggerated by scholars unfamiliar with the actual cases and equally unaware of the dismal record of failed attempts to codify the supposed international criminal law relating to "piracy" or the international slave trade.

The tribunal at The Hague seems to translate the laws of war into a universal criminal law system. The reasons why this is unprecedented have nothing to do with lack of desire on the part of the powerful to impose their views of law on others. The reasons are related to the structure of international society, namely to the refusal of any state to submit its own troubles to the judgment of outsiders who refuse to apply the same processes to themselves.

A Better Way: Four Suggestions

So what should be done by civilized humanity when it is faced by atrocities perpetrated in a foreign civil war?

There are at least four alternatives. The first is to bring our notion of the existing international legal order closer to the realities of the existing international system. If, for any reason, international tribunals are not acceptable or not feasible, then policy can still be influenced by exposure. Exposure, through "truth commissions," if properly constituted and publicized, can provoke outrage. Outrage can trigger moral suasion and economic sanctions of the sort that reformed Germany and changed the constitution of South Africa. The Dayton Accord can be better attuned to reality by dropping its insistence on punishing war crimes under a hypothesized but non-existent international criminal law, and reconstituting it to be persuasive in the international moral order. The impact of this approach on the accused "war criminals" is not to submit them to a misconceived "criminal" process, but to confine them to territory controlled by their constituents; the "Kurt Waldheim" solution—by which the former secretary-general of the United Nations and president of

Austria, a possible but not proven war criminal, is effectively confined to the territory of Austria—works not because he is threatened with arrest and prosecution, but because nobody he respects will grant him a visa.

Second, erect a criminal law tribunal that can be supported by the belligerents and can supply the safeguards necessary to assure the "human rights" of the accused, including their right of access to whatever evidence is necessary to mount a rational defense. That can be done within the existing legal order, although not by the Security Council of the United Nations. To establish such a tribunal, the cooperation of the Bosnian Serbs would be necessary. Rather than including only the leaders of the Bosnian Serbs and the lower-level villains of Croatia and the Bosnian Muslims, the cooperation of all should be sought so as to make possible the indictment of the equivalent leaders of the Serbian Serbs, the Bosnian Muslims, and the Croatians. It might be very distasteful to deal with people whom our negotiators regard as villains, but a consistent effort stands a better chance of ameliorating the miseries of the former Yugoslavia than the current hypocritical attempt to criminalize the acts of some but not all of them.

Third, reinstitute the traditional legal remedies for atrocities in war: hand over accused "war criminals" to one or another of the parties concerned in the struggle, those whose legal orders clearly have "jurisdiction to adjudicate." Each side should, in its own moral and legal interest, punish its own villains. Each side has an interest in observing human rights safeguards when trying accused villains of an opposing faction. Provision can be made in accordance with the 1949 Geneva Conventions to "hand over" an accused villain to one of the belligerent powers and to assure that human rights safeguards, "protecting power" observers, Red Cross visitations, and other humanitarian institutions are put and kept in place.

Fourth, do nothing. It is just possible that some of the parties necessary to effect any real settlement in the former Yugoslavia are not yet ready for peace. If that is so, then any "peace" that we impose can be no more than a facade. In the meantime, humanitarian aid can continue to be rendered to the victims of the conflict and other pressures maintained to encourage a stable settlement.

The insistence on using the tragedy of the former Yugoslavia as a reason for establishing an international court seems to rest on the assumption that peace is impossible without justice. But "justice" is itself not assured by any human tribunal. It might be useful to remember that Plato wrote in Book I of The Republic that good people would not want to be "guardians," that they would rather have to be compelled to perform such a role (although by whom and how are not made clear). Those who believe that a legal tribunal is useful to assure justice, and that justice is a prerequisite to peace, would do well to ponder the alternatives and whether all those who speak publicly of the need for such one-sided "justice" really have in mind justice as seen by outsiders. The tribunal's role seems much more closely related to a struggle for authority over parts of the former Yugoslavia, or, indeed, control by Great Power or UN officials or lawyers over international affairs, in disregard of the imperatives and risks of representative democracy.

In sum, whatever one thinks of it in other respects, the Dayton Accord's emphasis on Security Council authority and an international tribunal to enforce a misunderstood version of the laws of war should not be supported. The tribunal in The Hague should be disbanded. It is time to move on to things that might really help develop peace and a sense of responsible order in the former Yugoslavia.

11

Retail Diplomacy: The Edifying Story of UN Dues Reform

*Suzanne Nossel**

Perhaps the broadest-based and most trenchant general criticism of the Bush Administration's foreign policy before September 11 was that it displayed an excessive and hurtful unilateralism. Whether one joined in that criticism or not, nearly everyone agrees that since September 11 the administration has been converted to a belief in at least some forms of multilateralism. But a tension remains: Can an administration whose core vision of international leadership is defined by go-it-alone options whenever possible really conduct an effective multilateral diplomacy? The question is not only whether the administration can keep a motley coalition together long enough to accomplish U.S. military and political goals in the war against terrorism. We need also to ask whether it will, and whether it should, maintain a commitment to multilateralism once the present crisis passes.

The answer is not simple; some mix of unilateral and multilateral methods surely makes sense. But the problem is clear. Despite (or perhaps because of) its superpower status, the United States has grown increasingly isolated in the United Nations and other international forums. In the past year, America has been reviled for sabotaging the Kyoto climate negotiations, bullied in the UN Security Council over Iraq and Israel, kicked off the Geneva-based Human Rights Commission for the first time in history, and provoked to walk out of the Durban racism conference in a huff. These setbacks generated not only dismay but also a reactive impulse in the Congress. As the first plane slammed into tower one of the World Trade Center, the post of U.S. ambassador to the UN had been stripped of its cabinet rank and left vacant for nearly eight months.

*Suzanne Nossel was Deputy to the Ambassador for UN Management and Reform at the U.S. Mission to the United Nations (1999-2001).

American arrears to the UN were at an historic high, with $582 million pledged in January mired in delay.

But as with choices between unilateral and multilateral means, the recent history of U.S. multilateral diplomacy is mixed. Despite the setbacks noted above, the United States has beaten the odds in several key recent multilateral battles. A year ago the United States kept Sudan, the duly anointed candidate of the African Group, off the UN Security Council. The United States ended Israel's 50-years of technical pariah status at the UN, winning our ally acceptance into a regional group. In late 2000 the Americans convinced the membership to accept Jesse Helms' UN finance formula, cutting its dues while forcing others to pay more.

On all of these issues, successes and failures, more was at stake than what was officially on the table. When the United States loses, both its pride and global standing are hurt. When it stands alone, even if it holds the line, it is vulnerable to accusations of high-handedness and double standards. When it succeeds by browbeating others, it triggers resentments. Every which way, it becomes harder to achieve American goals the next time around and, as we have learned this fall, one never knows when the "next time around" may be the time that really counts.

Both champions and critics of multilateral diplomatic forums have a stake in ensuring that as long as the United States is at the table in global forums, it is effective in promoting American interests and positioned to marshal global support when it needs to do so. Even critics of the United Nations have to concede that it plays an important role over an array of functions that serve U.S. interests: human rights and refugee protection, labor standards, international air traffic control and safety, and international public health among them. Likewise the UN's most enthusiastic supporters, who tend not to favor hawkish Republican administrations, would do well to restrain any impulse to partisan scolding, for that would not serve the goal of nurturing a U.S. leadership that is confident of its influence among the UN membership, and thus more willing to put trust in the organization. The old debate over whether multilateral institutions do America more harm than good is both tired and misleading. What is needed is a pragmatic discussion of the recent U.S. track record in the multilateral arena and what can be done to improve it. In a world where the interests of states and regional blocs differ, and in which the natural resentment of a preponderant power such as the United States makes it impossible for Washington to automatically have its own way, U.S. diplomacy must work hard to translate its general military and economic clout into effective and specific influence. Put another way, we need to focus better on the art of retail diplomacy.

A noteworthy recent example of successful retail diplomacy was the campaign to negotiate a reduction of America's UN dues. Like many examples of retail diplomacy, this effort was not particularly glamorous. But it worked, and it bears many lessons in diplomatic skill and stamina that American statesmen will need to learn in the months and years ahead.

Cutting U.S. Dues: A Case Study

In December 2000, after a 14-month campaign, the United States overcame nearly universal opposition at the UN to win an agreement to lower American dues to the organization. The victory fulfilled the terms of the 1999 "Helms-Biden" law, which provided for payment of nearly $1 billion in U.S. arrears to the UN, but only if the UN membership agreed to lower U.S. dues for the UN's regular budget and peacekeeping budgets by more than $170 million annually.

On the face of it, the U.S. position showed not a little chutzpah. The U.S. position was the equivalent of having Bill Gates, in response to an IRS enforcement action on back taxes owed, agree to pay up only if the IRS agreed to lower his tax bracket in future years, regardless of what he earned. When the UN membership signed onto the deal, Senators Helms and Biden were as stunned as anyone else, and led a historic standing ovation in the Senate Foreign Relations Committee for the triumph in what many saw as an era of waning American influence at the UN.

How did the United States convince 188 other countries to fork over more so that—during the longest period of prosperity in its history—the world's richest country could pay less? For starters, the United States wielded powerful leverage: nearly $1 billion in back dues that would be paid to the UN if the American demands were met. Beyond that, the charm, boldness and bravado of then- UN Ambassador Richard C. Holbrooke gave the advocacy effort unique momentum and profile.

But incentives and personalities, though valuable, were not enough. When "Helms-Biden" was passed in December 1999, dangling the promise of repayment in exchange for a dues reduction, a Canadian diplomat described the offer as "a lump of coal in the Christmas stocking"—and the Canadians are about the best friends the United States has at the UN. The UN membership was galled by the U.S attempt to attach strings to payments that it owed under the UN Charter, seeing the move as a bald-faced violation of international law and a dangerous precedent. What would stop the Japanese from withholding payments to protest their lack of a seat on the Security Council? And the Germans from following suit? Most of the membership was long on record opposing a U.S. dues reduction as inconsistent with the precept underlying the UN's financial system—that each country be assessed according to its "capacity to pay." This phrase became a mantra repeated in every accent known to humanity, the rallying cry of countries accusing the United States of foisting burdens onto the less fortunate.

By some accounts, this was all so much ritual howling before the inevitable concession to U.S. power and money. According to this view, the membership was bound to surrender because the United States was holding the organization to ransom; unless it gave in, the UN would risk bankruptcy. In forums like the UN, however, the best interests of the institution do not always dictate the course taken. For starters, there is an obvious point that Americans sometimes forget: decisions are not made by "the UN" but rather by 189 member states, each of which acts on its own self-interest. In this equation, the UN's financial needs often carry less weight than delegations' own financial interests, loyalties and vanities. Moreover, the organization had functioned under the weight of U.S. arrears for more than a decade, and there were plenty of governments that believed it would be better off holding firm by rejecting U.S. demands and reinforcing America's outcast image.

Perhaps the greatest obstacle to getting the UN to accept American terms was the zero-sum game of UN financing, where every dollar of reduced U.S. dues meant higher payments for another, usually poorer, country. Although virtually the entire UN membership privately agreed that, on the basis of their economic growth over the last decade, the Chinese could afford to pay more than their drastically discounted rate, virtually no one was willing to say so to Beijing. Developed and developing countries alike would sooner have left the UN insolvent than ask a poorer country—even a rising economic powerhouse—to pay more to enable a richer one to pay less. The ostensible imperative of giving in to U.S. power did not translate into the political will necessary to meet U.S. demands. So despite its financial leverage, a U.S. victory was hardly foreordained.

That power alone will not get the United States its way does not mean that America should avoid taking strong stands. In internal discussions, U.S. policymakers often propose that instead of taking aggressive public stances, the United States would do better to recruit other countries to front American views and thereby prevent a backlash against a "U.S. position." "Can't we get the Philippines to propose the dues cut?" some queried. While the intuition to recruit others to the U.S. cause is sound, America is far too big and visible to slink out the back door while others do its bidding. When an important U.S. goal is at stake, relying on the Philippines or Estonia to front for us is risky. There is no guarantee that our ally will make an effective case and, besides, U.S. silence rarely fools anyone in the midst of a contentious debate.

When important U.S. interests are at issue, then, the question is not whether to take a stand, but rather how—tactically—to win the fight without scorching the landscape. Success requires careful attention to the power dynamics at play in multilateral settings, the means and methods of persuasion, and the targeted use of U.S. bilateral power and influence.

The United States rarely wins arguments inside a multilateral meeting room. The impulse that leads college students to rise up against heavy-handed university administrators makes membership-wide meetings rallying points for resisting the powers that be. No country wants to be publicly seen to buckle under U.S. pressure. During the dues battle, formal meetings at the UN were bruising for the United States, with country after country taking the floor to demand that America pay its back dues "on time, in full, and without conditions." Even toward the end, as details of a compromise took shape in private meetings, the public rhetoric remained feverish. Open meetings make good theater, but deals are cut in back rooms. (For this reason, too, it was clear that by the time the U.S. delegation was winging its way to the Durban racism conference, the time to rally others to our cause had already passed.)

That the United States cannot saunter into a public meeting and expect others to fall into step behind it does not mean that official forums can be ignored. Moves to circumvent ordinary channels risk being labeled as power plays. Likewise, reciting U.S. proposals with a pompous "take it or leave it" approach may seem appropriate for a superpower, but it only undercuts our cause. By doing its homework and making convincing arguments in open meetings, the United States can gain some favor by showing that it knows it cannot rule by fiat and is willing to engage in give-and-take. In its public speeches during the dues debate, the U.S. delegation sought to disarm critics by conceding that the arrears were regrettable, and by pleading for help in solving a problem that was admittedly—in significant part, at least—an American creation. Success in these settings was measured in terms of diplomatic damage limitation.

But for every one diplomat in the U.S. seat, playing by the rules, ten others should be working the corridors, explaining the details of the American position one-on-one to foreign ambassadors. Instead of wholesale oratory, the cornerstone of multilateral advocacy efforts is retail persuasion tailored to influence individual constituencies.

Before starting the country-by-country approach, the United States must figure out how to frame its case in a way that others can freely adopt. Winning support hinges on making a coherent, persuasive argument that gives countries a way out from under their reluctance to accede to U.S. power. On the UN dues issue, everyone understood that if American demands were not met, Jesse Helms might never agree to pay a dime of U.S. arrears. But no country wanted to simply give in to an American *diktat* co-authored by the UN's number one public enemy. Even the Israeli delegation needed to present its foreign ministry with a face-saving justification for supporting the U.S. position. (The same impulse was at play when our closest allies asked to see U.S. evidence against Osama bin Laden before committing to the anti-terrorist effort. Even those that *want and intend* to side with us prefer to do it on their own terms.)

The United States set out early on to formulate the strongest possible argument for dues reform on its merits. Recognizing that talk of a U.S. dues cut prompted knee-jerk opposition, the U.S. delegation quickly retooled, dropping talk of a rate reduction in favor of a push for broad reform of the UN's entire financing system. Although the U.S. government did not care terribly about true "reform" of the UN's finance system, U.S. diplomats made this goal their rallying cry, recognizing that—unlike a stand-alone U.S. dues reduction—it was an agenda to which other nations could subscribe. Statistics were used to show that some countries were paying too little to the UN and others too much, and that the interests of fairness demanded reform. Ambassador Holbrooke presented unwitting foreign ministers with a laminated card listing every country's payment in order to drive home the point that a system, frozen in 1972, granting steep discounts to some of the richest countries in the world—including Singapore, Brunei and the United Arab Emirates—simply demanded overhaul.

At the UN, history counts for a lot; delegations often cite chapter and verse of past resolutions to support their points. Digging up quotations, speeches and proposals from days gone by enabled the U.S. delegation to frame an argument that let other delegations back away from their opposition gracefully. We reminded delegates of the dramatic days of 1946, when Senator Arthur Vandenburg—the Jesse Helms of his day (at least in some respects)—argued at the very first UN budget debate that the organization must cap the rate of its largest contributor, so that no country—not even the United States—could command excessive influence over decision-making.

Ambassador Holbrooke's arguments, laid out in charts and graphs, were pored over at countless meetings between the U.S. delegation and its counterparts. A diagram of a scale tilting precariously to one side was distributed in the capital cities of all UN member states to illustrate the imbalance in the organization's peacekeeping finance scheme. Over time, U.S. rhetoric on putting the UN on a "solid financial footing" by creating a "flatter, more equitable scale" echoed throughout the membership, finding its way into the speeches and statements of delegations from around the world. Eventually, Nigeria, Pakistan, Algeria and other unlikely allies could be seen button-holing regional colleagues in far corners of UN conference rooms, making the case that the finance system needed fixing. When delegates did meet *en masse*, having these countries repeat the merit-based arguments was infinitely more effective in turning around the remaining skeptics than U.S. pleas and threats.

Although everyone knew the United States was out to get its own rate cut and was making the UN an offer it could scarcely refuse, the reframing of the campaign into one for "reform" defused much antagonism. In the final weeks of the debate, when the momentum for change was unstoppable, the United States calmly but firmly reminded its fellow members that unless the final package met the American demands, even a reformed system would leave the UN in continuing financial crisis. At the tail end, when the majority of members had accepted U.S. logic but requested extra time to absorb the proposed rate increases, the American delegation quickly agreed, recognizing that this small concession would help achieve its goals with a minimum of resentment. This show of flexibility allowed the United States to come away with almost everything it originally wanted, as well as a reformed system that allowed many other participants in the debate to claim victory as well.

Entangling Alliances—Untangling Alliances

Like any survival contest, multilateral politics are dominated by alliances that complicate the task of persuading individual delegations to take the U.S. side. Recognizing the rationale and role of these coalitions and attacking them one by one is essential to building support. Most countries in the United Nations are small or poor or both. Casting lots with like-minded delegations gives weak nations a power base. Although the Cold War bipolarity that generated the Non-Aligned Movement (NAM) has long since collapsed, by acting under the 120-plus-member NAM umbrella, the developing world has a controlling bloc within the UN General Assembly. Smaller but still significant blocs include the European Union and its associate members, the Gulf Cooperation Council, the Rio Group, the Southern African Development Community and others. While these coalitions do not operate in all UN decision-making arenas, their influence is felt ever more widely.

The strength of such groups means that an American appeal to a bilateral relationship—for instance, with the United Kingdom or Mexico—may not lure the ally away from an opposing EU or Rio Group position. While many U.S. foreign policy-makers have long advocated a common European foreign policy—a single phone number to call, as Henry Kissinger once famously put it—at the UN the reality of European coordination is slow and cumbersome decision-making that often culminates in lowest common denominator positions dictated by Germany or France. On UN dues, as long as the French held the EU presidency and were determined to oppose the U.S. plan, private sympathy from the UK, Sweden, Portugal and others did little good. In the world of bloc politics, the United States must go beyond gaining the backing of friendly delegations to wrest them out of the grip of opposing group positions.

Unified political and regional groups cannot be attacked frontally. Since a major purpose of these alliances is to enable smaller countries to stand up to the United States, an open effort to divide and conquer these alliances usually just solidifies resistance. Nothing galled the French more than indications that the United States was trying "to divide the EU." Although the United States must respect group leadership, the key to changing a bloc's position is addressing the forces behind it. Alliances are generally made up of a large majority of countries that have no stake in the fight and may even privately disagree with the collective position, led by a handful of interested delegations that appeal to group unity to hold the others in thrall. Eroding a solid alliance entails both picking off the disinterested and turning around the core of hardliners.

The United States has yet to fully adapt its multilateral strategies to the reality of alliance politics. During the dues campaign, U.S. diplomats from the UN traveled the world to lobby delegations during key decision-making congresses of the Non-Aligned Movement and the Organization of African Unity. Through these efforts, the United States was able to influence group positions before they were finalized, a far easier task than attempting to reverse unfavorable positions after the fact. By recognizing that key turning points occur within the alliance structures long in advance of actual UN debates, the United States can get ahead of bloc politics, weighing in with key delegations before they have committed themselves to any particular line.

Because they rarely speak up in multilateral debates, the vast majority of delegations from small countries are often overlooked in advocacy efforts despite the voting power they wield. In the Human Rights Commission vote, for example, Andorra, Benin and Fiji held just as much sway over the final result—arrived at by secret ballot—as did China or Russia. Early on in the drive to lower U.S. dues, important delegations often asked why the United States bothered bringing its case to small delegations. Although the United States and other large countries often rue the "one country, one vote" system, the diffusion of power can be turned into an advantage. Harvesting the low-hanging fruit of small delegations can be relatively easy, and can help isolate more influential players in due course. Because of its size, resources and global presence, the United States is uniquely positioned to rally small delegations that others leave out of their lobbying efforts.

The value of soliciting backbench delegations is several-fold. When the United States first called for a debate on the dues issue, other countries resisted, claiming that the discussions would open up a Pandora's Box of irreconcilable differences, since no country would willingly pay a penny more under a revised system. By relying on its bilateral relationships to recruit Israel, Cyprus, Estonia, Latvia, Hungary and the Philippines to announce at the outset of the debate that they would "volunteer" to contribute more for UN peacekeeping, this argument fell away. Later on, when the United States needed proof that the General Assembly as a whole was ready to create an agenda item to discuss financial reform, eliciting dozens of letters of support from across the membership proved critical. At the UN, demonstrating the allegiance of fully half of the organization's 189 members—even if they are virtually all small countries with limited influence—causes opponents to cower.

Where delegations do not have a strong position, winning them over sometimes requires little more than some stroking. When small countries are lobbied personally by the U.S. ambassador to the UN, capitals take notice. During the dues campaign, the Ambassador Holbrooke paid countless visits to UN missions across New York City that had never before hosted any senior U.S. official. The Americans got to know each delegation and its issues: Oman was livid about the UN's peacekeeping failures and did not want to invest another dime in them; the Pakistanis would help, but wanted to ensure that their troop contributions to peacekeeping were properly recognized; the Germans could not discuss UN finances without bemoaning their exclusion from the Security Council. Hearing out these countries enabled the United States to see the dues issue from their perspective and craft effective appeals to them as a consequence. As importantly, the hours spent with each and every delegation helped build up the kind of close relationships that are indispensable in a crisis but that cannot be forged on the spot.

Bilateral Leverage Points

Power-point presentations and personal visits were not enough to sway staunch opponents to the dues reform agenda, however. Some delegations scoffed at what they deemed efforts to cloak a unilateral U.S. agenda in the guise of UN reforms. In these cases, the United States brought bilateral pressure to bear to persuade hostile delegations to moderate their opposition.

Although at a forum-wide level U.S. power can have a polarizing effect, American influence is a powerful weapon for persuading individual delegations. In *A Dangerous Place*, an account of his experience as U.S. Ambassador to the UN in the mid-1970s, Daniel Patrick Moynihan suggested that the United States use its bilateral ties to advance multilateral priorities. Absent other compelling bilateral goals, Moynihan argued, the U.S. Ambassador to Togo, for example, should make it his or her number one goal to secure that country's backing on key matters in the UN and other forums. By mobilizing support in this way, he suggested, the United States might have headed off the "Zionism Is Racism" resolution that sent U.S.-UN relations into a decades-long downward spiral.

Unfortunately, Moynihan's proposal went nowhere. Multilateral issues remain a sidebar to bilateral relationships. Ambassadors have no incentive to push remote and contentious multilateral issues that have little direct bearing on their day-to-day jobs. When the State Department asks that a typical UN issue be raised, embassies tend to simply fax off a background paper to the foreign ministry. When it is brought up at all, the issue is generally raised in isolation, rather than as something central to the give-and-take of the relationship. Even where embassies are willing to push, they rarely have sufficient information to persuade. Though the United States has unparalleled capacity to wage effective campaigns on the global stage via its network of diplomats, this machinery rarely kicks into gear.

On pressing issues, ambassadors need to be held accountable for delivering the support of their host countries and, in turn, they need to be equipped with the tools and incentives to do so. During the dues debate, the limitations of traditional channels, whereby only the State Department can "instruct" an embassy to raise an issue, became immediately apparent. Instruction cables, required to go through multiple "clearances" by various regional and functional bureaus, were too slow, formal and routine to elicit the necessary advocacy and energy. Instead, once the instructions were given, U.S. diplomats at the UN established direct relationships with their counterparts in various capitals, providing detailed, country-specific information in real time. Traditionally, when UN issues are raised in capitals, they are brought up only once, with the ambassador reporting back via cable whether the host country said "yes" or "no." On the dues issue, by contrast, since countries' initial reactions were invariably negative, the first approach needed to be supplemented by a campaign to turn "no" into "yes." U.S. diplomats at the UN implored their colleagues in embassies to press on in the face of opposition, and to raise the issue repeatedly whenever the country's relationship with the United States was discussed.

While the United States knows how to mount an aggressive diplomatic campaign when it needs to, the efforts tend to be confined to a handful of countries routinely judged as major players, irrespective of whether these nations are actually calling the shots on an individual issue. During the dues campaign, these stepped-up tactics were deployed around the world, with more than fifty embassies actively engaged. In this way, the United States was able to ferret out some unlikely ringleaders—Oman for the Gulf Cooperation Council, for example—who were ultimately behind unfavorable groups' positions.

Ledger Diplomacy?

The multifaceted relationships between the United States and most other countries make it possible to use both carrots and sticks to elicit cooperation. When a collective incentive such as the salvaging of the U.S.-UN relationship will not sway a country, a more targeted individual inducement may. Most nations count the United States among their most important relationships, a position that confers substantial leverage.

But links between bilateral and multilateral agendas are rare. The State Department strictly separates responsibility for multilateral and bilateral priorities, and the bureaucracy is deeply skittish about *quid pro quos*. While other countries routinely trade votes on candidates for election to international bodies, U.S. policy forbids it. As a result, on the Human Rights Committee vote we were deserted by some of our closest friends who had committed to trades with other countries in order to advance election campaigns they were waging. The conventional wisdom is that linking unrelated issues complicates bilateral relationships, risking charges of abuse of power.

The U.S. government also maintains no central ledger in which bilateral relationships are tracked. There is no place to turn to find out what the United States has done for a particular country lately, or what a country may want or fear. We do not keep formal track of which U.S. officials have trusted relationships with which foreign counterparts, of who in the business world might bring influence to bear, or even of what we have learned about how each government makes decisions. An ambassador or State Department desk officer will have part of the picture, but so will officials in Defense, Commerce and other departments and agencies. Likewise, no one tracks what the United States is seeking from others, so that just as one Executive Branch department is trying to curry favor on a top priority, another may be complaining about something petty. Because they are smaller, and their relations with the United States are of high priority, other countries' right hands are much more likely to know what their left hands are doing when it comes to relations with the United States. While they can play off a range of policy issues to get what they want out of the Americans, the United States is poorly organized to do the same.

During the UN dues negotiations, the U.S. delegation repeatedly learned after the fact of loans, debt forgiveness and other concessions made to countries that actively opposed the reform process. At the end of a long and contentious meeting with the Singaporean delegation, one of their diplomats pulled from his briefcase a press report announcing a U.S.-Singapore free trade agreement. "*This* is what matters", he said, dismissing the importance of the dues issue while steadfastly maintaining his country's refusal to pay more. Without a ledger, Singapore's recalcitrance at the UN had no impact on their favorable treatment at the hands of the U.S. Trade Representative. Had the matters simply been raised together, the free trade cooperation would have provided leverage on the dues issue even without an explicit *quid pro quo*. Allies and enemies alike know that the United States does not keep track of its bilateral relationships in this way, however, and thus rest assured that opposing the United States in multilateral forums will not trigger repercussions in the bilateral relationship.

The growing importance of multilateral decision-making demands steps to factor multilateral issues into bilateral relationships. Simply keeping closer track of countries' support in international forums—and making this information available to ambassadors and intermediaries—would signal other countries that their relationships with the United States cut across multilateral arenas. Before heading off to their posts, political officers stationed in U.S. embassies abroad should visit the UN for a briefing on their new host country's UN record, and a strategy session on how to promote better cooperation. While vote-swapping for international elections might bring more grief than gratification, on top priorities involving, for example, UN sanctions, countries should be told that their cooperation will be taken into account by officials with influence over the bilateral relationship.

This does not mean that the United States can or should demand lockstep support in multilateral forums from all aid recipients and trade partners, or disrupt important policy initiatives when involved countries fail to toe America's line on unrelated issues. Multilateral decisions with serious consequences are relatively few, and the scope of our bilateral relationships makes possible nuanced rewards and disincentives that do not compromise American principles or priorities. During the UN dues campaign, U.S. diplomats at the UN made a point of asking other countries whether there was anything that could be done for them bilaterally. While America's UN diplomats could not move mountains, small gestures—usually jostling a small favor loose from another area of the bureaucracy—often went a long way.

The multilateral context itself offers some opportunities for low-cost linkages. During the year of the dues debate, the U.S. delegation used support on that issue as a criterion for deciding which countries to support in contested elections to international bodies. While the United States would not back an inappropriate candidate simply because it backed the dues drive, positions on the dues issue were used to decide among qualified contenders.

This year, while the UN will focus heavily on terrorism, it will also debate and pass resolutions on other issues, ranging from combating AIDS, to nuclear proliferation, to small arms proliferation to global development. While these will pale in significance for the United States next to the anti-terrorism campaign, they will be of prime importance to certain countries. Our handling of their concerns—our level of engagement, flexibility and willingness to listen—will influence how others treat our priorities.

Another useful measure short of explicit *quid pro quo* is engaging cabinet secretaries, members of Congress and other U.S. officials to stump for support in key capitals. The Senate Foreign Relations Committee was heavily engaged in the dues campaign, visiting the UN, lobbying Washington embassies, and even writing to ask foreign leaders to agree to pay more. Near the end of the dues debate the U.S. Trade Representative and the Secretaries of the Treasury and Defense were enlisted to call ministers of finance, trade and defense in countries in which they had close ties. Although these officials were generally unfamiliar with the dues issue and were usually speaking to foreign colleagues equally remote from the UN negotiations, mobilizing these important interlocutors underscored the seriousness of the U.S. campaign and created a useful implicit link to other bilateral priorities.

Though targeted efforts can erode a solid group stance, there are invariably some delegations that cannot be won over. In the dues negotiation, these included Cuba, Libya and others who opposed initiatives simply because the United States had proposed them. But intractable nations can be isolated by convincing others that their opposition is politically motivated or based solely on narrow as opposed to enlightened self-interest. While delegations may be loath to criticize colleagues for ill-founded positions, the silent majority of moderates is willing to work quietly to prevent spoilers from blocking progress.

From December to September

The quest to lower America's dues and settle the arrears problem recedes in importance now that world peace and democracy are at stake. It is worth keeping in mind, however, that without the December 2000 deal the United States would be undertaking its delicate coalition-building from the position of the UN's biggest debtor, on the verge of losing its General Assembly vote. To get out of this awkward corner, the administration and Congress would have had to voluntarily pay the back dues, notwithstanding the proposed Helms-Biden bargain having been spurned. Likewise the UN membership would have faced a quandary: either refuse the United States in its hour of need, or put aside the dues issue, leaving UN finances in ruin and resentment toward the United States on the rise.

Though that crisis was averted, another very nearly flared. Although the Senate acted in January 2001 to approve payment of the promised arrears on the basis of Ambassador Holbrooke's deal, the House leadership sat on its hands for months, even proposing to attach new conditions to the promised payment. In early September, as the annual opening of the UN General Assembly approached, delegations concluded grimly that, nine months after the deal was reached, President Bush intended to arrive in New York empty-handed. Those who had supported the United States felt sheepish if not betrayed, and our opponents patted themselves on the back for having predicted U.S. faithlessness.

After September 11, the Congress moved swiftly to discharge payment, and the frustration dissipated, though it did not disappear. Rather than riding off the momentum reached in U.S.-UN relations when the December deal was announced, the administration was faced with a risky standing start, having to first put a new ambassador in the driver's seat of a rapidly moving vehicle. In the first few weeks it appeared as though we had pulled it off, but we must avert such situations in the future. Our multilateral behavior should be aimed to ensure that, whatever befalls us, we will be able to approach the UN free of baggage, as a trusted, respected leader able to mobilize support from around the world.

Whether it ever truly existed or not, the era of the United States as unchallenged global agenda-setter is over. In a globalized setting with competing centers of power, the United States must learn how to maximize its influence by bringing others on board, rather than trying to shove them off to the side as we press ahead. The surest way to dissolve the fragile international coalition we have assembled for the fight against terrorism is to take it for granted. Impatience or arrogance toward the UN will signal the world that the newfound U.S. focus on multilateralism is a passing fancy that will last only as long as the current crisis. Now is the time for a genuine change of course, built on the understanding that to win in the multilateral arena, the United States must rely not on power alone but on hard work—patient persuasion, alliance politics and targeted leverage. A failure to sharpen these tools may mean that an increasingly interdependent world hews less and less to American interests.

12

Fixing the United Nations

*Alan L. Keyes**

Americans have become increasingly skeptical about the importance and effectiveness of the United Nations. Serious doubts about the worth of the organization have emerged in editorial comment, public opinion polls, and congressional speeches. This skepticism has resulted in a spate of federal legislation on the growth of UN budgets. Other elements of it respond to the abuse of the United Nations by some member states for espionage purposes. Many Americans see the United Nations as an anti-American bastion, dominated by enemies of the United States, a place where America's views are ignored, her friends and allies unfairly attacked, and her precious democratic values corrupted or destroyed. After a few days in the General Assembly the question that occurs to many first-time U. S. delegates is: Why do we continue to belong? The question is no longer shocking, the idea of U.S. withdrawal no longer unthinkable. Yet despite this growing disaffection, opinion polls show that a majority of the American public believes that the United States should remain in the organization.

Given the mostly negative perception of the organization, the public's continued attachment to the idea of the United Nations requires some explanation. To be sure, something remains of the days when, to many Americans, the United Nations meant UNICEF, greeting cards, and neighborly help to the world's needy children and mothers. There remains too, a visceral attachment to the possibility of a forum where states can meet to talk rather than fight. Yet with a plethora of organizations devoted to international humanitarian aid, and with the UN's shortcomings as a peacemaking instrument now well known,

---

*Alan L. Keyes is a syndicated talk show host and columnist who served as the U. S. representative to the UN's economic and social council and as Assistant Secretary of State for International Organization Affairs during the Reagan Administration.

This essay first appeared in *The National Interest* no. 4 (Summer 1986).

neither image suffices to explain the public's persistent belief in the importance of continued U.S. membership in the UN.

The public's belief may reflect the affinity between what America is and what the United Nations is supposed to be. The United States is a community composed of many nationalities, peacefully cooperating under the aegis of a democratic charter of free government. America's success seems to validate the idea that respect for the rule of law and a basic charter of representative, democratic institutions can tame the tendency toward violence among people from diverse nations. Because they cannot escape their own historical destiny, Americans cannot simply eschew the idea of a successful international confederation.

It was an American president, Woodrow Wilson, who dreamt that some form of all-embracing democratic constitutionalism could be the basis for an international order. The hellish cauldron of World War II convinced Americans that the world could ill afford to ignore the lessons of his League's failure. In the United Nations they hoped to see Wilson's dream fulfilled.

Unfortunately, the reformed league repeated the fundamental flaw of its predecessor: it relied upon purely external means to discipline the behavior of its member states. Superficial critics often fasten upon the lack of proper enforcement mechanisms as the weakness of both the League of Nations and the United Nations. They contrast this with the existence of duly constituted courts of law and police forces within nation-states. Yet without proper education for the citizens, domestic law enforcement institutions would be overwhelmed by the violent tendencies of human nature. Domestic order ultimately depends upon the existence within each citizen of a principle of self-discipline. To this extent, most of an open, democratic society's members must share a certain common character, a certain minimal sense of moral value.

The Charter of the United Nations recognizes this necessity in theory. It prescribes minimal standards of character and moral value its member states are supposed to share. All are pledged to renounce aggressive war and to respect the self-determination of others. Yet in the actual composition of the organization no attention was given to the internal principles of its member states. Tyrannies and free democracies alike were admitted to membership, regardless of the fact that regimes based on tyrannical principles have no inherent reason to respect the underlying constitutional and democratic values of the organization and the international order it implies. Realists hoped that the great powers' interest in preserving order would take the place of this inherent respect. Idealists felt that the common interest of people in social and economic progress would act as a substitute for it. Experience has disappointed both.

Were such views simply naive? Were expectations too high? The more sophisticated apologists for the United Nations frequently base their arguments on these premises. They imply that Americans should never have expected significant results from the organization. America's early dominance of the organization fueled our unrealistic expectations. Had American hopes for the United Nations been more sober and moderate, they say, we would now be better able to appreciate its real achievements. We would not overreact to its shortcomings. As American influence diminished, these critics conclude, resentment reinforced our reaction to the inevitable problems and complexities of multilateral politics.

The conclusions that logically follow from this type of analysis pass for wisdom these days in the circles that quietly despised the serious, assertive style of such U.S. ambassadors to the UN as Daniel Patrick Moynihan and Jeane Kirkpatrick. Americans, it is said, should lower their expectations about the UN (while of course continuing to pay lip service to its ideals). They should accommodate themselves to the reality of America's loss of power in the organization, realizing that this decline is not mainly the result of Soviet influence or manipulation, but the inevitable effect of the proliferation of independent countries in the developing world. They should use the United Nations mainly as a forum for cultivating goodwill with the developing countries. This, the argument continues, means paying less attention to responding to what is said or done against the United States (especially as these actions are often just symbolic gestures intended chiefly for home consumption.) It means being more willing to accept the compromises that would enable the United States to purchase a better image with its European and developing country colleagues (not to mention pragmatic opinion makers in the U. S.) at little cost to any important American interests.

According to this view, U.S. participation in the United Nations is important mainly as an opportunity to work for better relations with other member countries. Of course, its proponents also claim to recognize the dangers of Soviet influence in the organization, and the need to counter it. The annual General Assembly resolutions on the situations in Afghanistan and Kampuchea are roundly applauded as worthy victories, and steps to curb the use of the UN Secretariat for espionage purposes are soberly encouraged. This time serving approach to the UN has a superficial appeal. However, it is based on an understanding of the United Nations that neglects both its fundamental flaw and its essential promise. As noted above, the flaw lies in the fact that the composition of the organization abstracts from differences in intemal principle among the member states. States based on tyrannical principles are accorded the same status and respect as those founded on democratic principles. In fact, over time, control of the organization has come to rest in the hands of a majority that includes a large number of unfree, undemocratic states. By simply accommodating itself to the power of this majority, the United States, and the free democracies in general, would compromise essential democratic principles. Notions of limited government, of individual choice as the foundation of lawful authority, of respect for the civil, political, and property rights of minorities—all these pillars of free democratic societies would have to be diluted, corrupted, or abandoned outright. The outwardly democratic and parliamentary forms of the United Nations would simply be a cover for the destruction of free democratic ideas. Its American founders wanted the United Nations to democratize international politics. The time serving approach would instead legitimize the influence of the de facto coalition of unfree regimes that makes up the UN majority.

Herein lies the kernel of truth in the views of those who believe the Soviet Union dominates the United Nations. For just as there is an affinity between democratic constitutionalism and the democratic form of UN institutions, so there is a strong affinity between the basically tyrannical principle that characterizes the Soviet regime and the principles on which many developing country governments are based. For them, mouthing the liberal democratic language of individual rights, popular government, and the rule of law is a bit of time serving hypocrisy. Though they speak of peace, security, and education in the United Nations, they rely upon violence, fear, and indoctrination in their own affairs. We can see evidence of this hypocrisy in every aspect of the UN's life.

In the political field Western democracies, and in particular the United States, come in for frequent condemnation by name. The tyrannies of the East bloc, though guilty of far more explicit crimes, are criticized only by implication, in mild, anonymous resolutions. The tyrannies of the developing world are almost never criticized, unless their relations with the United States make them exceptional targets. This is especially true with regard to human rights. El Salvador, a functioning democracy despite all the ravages of a relentless guerrilla war, merits a Special Rapporteur on human rights abuses, yet efforts to investigate the brutality of despotism in Ethiopia are vigorously resisted. Annually hundreds of thou sands of dollars are spent minutely monitoring the situation in Chile, yet only a few thousand went to document the suppression of Solidarity in Poland. The UN majority does not relish the thought of balanced, objective human rights inquiries, for very few countries in that majority would escape serious indictment.

Majority hypocrisy takes its toll as well in the area of economic and social development. The representatives of despotic governments fill the halls with rhetoric about the problems of development and the need for urgent action to address them. Their proposals for action, however, focus almost exclusively on statist, government dominated approaches to development. Such approaches have uniformly failed to produce results. They sacrifice development potential in order to consolidate power in the hands of the ruling political group. More decentralized market-oriented approaches to development have achieved notable successes. These, however, imply a diffusion of power beyond the urban, bureaucratic, and military political elite, into the hands of rural agriculturalists and small and middle-sized private entrepreneurs. Such power-sharing is incompatible with the tyrannical principles of most developing country governments. Therefore representatives of the coalition of unfree states that controls UN affairs resist serious discussion of the successful development models.

As a result of the same syndrome, UN representatives from developing countries are preoccupied with the issue of resource transfers from developed countries to governments in the developing countries. Whether discussion centers on financial assistance or mounting indebtedness, the underlying concern is always the same. The UN agenda dictated by the majority chiefly deals with the welfare and resources of governments. Thus, rather than aiming to improve the lives of people in developing countries, the agenda aims to promote the power and dominance of governments. In fact, by encouraging government dominated, statist approaches, it sacrifices the development interests of people everywhere to the narrow political interests of the governments that rule over them.

One consequence of this attitude is the majority's willingness to see the UN's development oriented forums preoccupied by a few highly divisive political issues. The subjects of disarmament, apartheid, and Palestinian rights constantly recur, no matter how much the agenda must be twisted to accommodate them.

Gatherings of experts on postal cooperation, telecommunications, population, or women's issues are confronted with demands for major decisions about fundamental political questions. Those who seek serious international cooperation for development are asked to purchase it at the price of political concessions in areas far outside their interest or expertise. If they resist, the ensuing controversy consumes a large chunk of time and attention, paralyzing and disrupting the proceedings, and at times bringing them to the brink of collapse.

The United Nations Educational, Scientific and Cultural Organization (Unesco) is the largest and best known casualty of this process of politicization. Its history exemplifies the subordination of development purposes to political goals. In particular, the progress of the New International Information Order (NIIO) clearly demonstrates the community of interest among the tyrannical regimes of the voting majority. Unesco is pledged by its charter to promote free communication in the interest of improving international understanding. Through the NIJO, however, the majority states seek to legitimize and extend internationally the control over communication and information they themselves impose at the national level. The minority of free democratic states are called upon not only to tolerate, but actively to cooperate in extending such control. The democratic principle of majority rule is thus abused by a tyrannical majority to achieve the destruction of an essential democratic freedom. The United States and a handful of the other free democratic members of the organization have rightly resisted this and other efforts to divert Unesco from its original goals. The result has been a deep and debilitating controversy, which has now led to the withdrawal of the U. S., the UK, and Singapore. Here again the chief losers are clearly the people of the developing countries. Their governments abuse UN organizations and processes in a quest for greater political power and control. As a consequence they deprive the developing world's needy peoples of the benefits they might enjoy as the result of effective international cooperation.

It would be unfair, however, to blame the failures of the UN system exclusively on the power of the de facto coalition of unfree states. The free democratic minority, which consists primarily of the United States and the other Western democracies, has been remarkably timid and inefficient in resisting the corruption of the Charter's basic norms and principles. They have routinely engaged in a strategy of self-censorship and preemptive concession that leaves not only the results but even the proposed agenda for discussion entirely to majority whim.

A prime example of this occurred during the 1986 session of the UN Human Rights Commission. Despite increasingly disturbing reports of human rights abuses connected with the Ethiopian government's program of forced resettlement, in which thousands of people may have perished, several of the free democracies refused to work in support of U.S. efforts to secure a resolution establishing a Special Rapporteur to investigate the situation. In fact some countries actively colluded with the representatives of Ethiopia to torpedo the U.S. effort. Given this kind of fecklessness in the face of massive and palpable disregard for free democratic principles, is it any wonder that the corruption of other basic norms of the UN Charter proceeds unabated?

It means nothing that the Charter is based upon free democratic values when the free, democratic member states of the United Nations are unwilling to offend or embarrass the unfree majority by vigorously asserting positions that oppose tyranny and promote free democracy. Other examples of the free minority's fecklessness abound, particularly with regard to economic issues.

In such UN exercises as the New International Economic Order (NIEO), Global Negotiations, and the International Development Strategy, free democratic states have accommodated themselves to concepts that promote statist and socialist approaches on an international scale. Yet these approaches have blasted the development prospects of every country unfortunate enough to try them. UN regulatory schemes, whether for infant formula or germ plasma production, are not only supported but initiated by free democratic states. This despite the fact that such schemes impose restrictions upon free markets and private initiative that would severely damage, if not destroy, the operations of free economic institutions in the international economic arena. Schemes derived from the "Common Heritage of Mankind" concept, such as the seabed mining provisions of the Law of the Sea Treaty, take regulation one fateful step further. They remove economic activity entirely from private hands in order to establish on the international level large, bureaucratic state enterprises. Like the disastrous white elephants in many developing countries, these schemes would wastefully absorb capital and human talents while becoming a net burden on the international economy.

All of these pernicious concepts and schemes have arisen, progressed, and triumphed with the cooperation of the free democracies. The world they imply, however, is one in which freedom would survive only in the narrow interstices of the over- whelming machinery of state power. The welfare state socialism of some European states cooperates unwittingly with the tyrannically oriented statism of many developing countries. The cynicism of an elitist diplomacy cooperates with the despotic cynicism of the Soviet bloc. The vested interest of a bloated secretariat cooperates with the petty ambitions and aimless restlessness of individual representatives and delegates. The result is a viciously self-centered game, a closed system disguised in the open vesture of parliamentary diplomacy. It is a world of easy trade-offs and accommodations where most lack the political courage and clarity of purpose needed to remember, much less defend, the meaning of free democratic principles.

The world-weary moral relativism that has become second nature in many free democracies sits all too well with the resentful moral hypocrisy of the unfree UN majority. The time-servers join the lip-servers in a tacit conspiracy against any who seriously assert that the free democratic values of the UN's Charter should be truly and universally respected. It is against this conspiracy, among those known to be the enemies of freedom and those too weak or decadent to be its friends, that the United States must develop the strategy of its participation in the United Nations system.

In the UN system words, arguments, and ideas are the principal mediums of exchange—the tools with which to shape an environment for cooperation, or the weapons of ideological conflict. Of course, the words are not ends in themselves. They are intended to influence opinion, to legitimize or delegitimize the actions and policies or even the existence of states, groups, and individuals. For many of its member states the UN is therefore principally an arena for propaganda in the broadest sense, an arena in which concepts for propaganda can be articulated and legitimized. Thus, the UN itself may not be the instrument through which the equation of Zionism with racism reaches as school child in Rwanda (though through Unesco educational materials it might be), but it provides the process through which that absurd and anti-Semitic notion was made to seem a legitimate slogan of international opinion. The UN itself may not be the instrument with which to fasten misguided statist policies upon aspiring peoples in developing countries, but it provides the process through which the NIEO's statist ideology of development took on the air of a triumphant worldview. The UN itself may not practice tyranny, brutality, and aggression against innocent people, but it provides the process through which political slavery can be disguised as independence, barbarism as progress, aggression, terrorism, and subversion as liberation movements.

President Reagan has clearly understood the importance of fighting against the insidious use of the UN as an anti-American propaganda weapon. As his representative at the United Nations, Ambassador Jeane Kirkpatrick recognized that it is dangerous for free democracies to allow a tyrannical UN majority, purporting to represent the voice of international conscience and opinion, to go unchallenged in its abuse of the essential concepts of democratic freedom.

She clearly established the principle that attacks on the United States or on its close allies and friends (for instance, attempts, contrary to the terms of the UN Charter, to deprive Israel of its membership in the General Assembly and other UN organizations) would have adverse consequences, either for individual member states or for the organization itself. The Reagan Administration gave notice that the U.S. would no longer patiently be victimized by double standards of conduct and judgment. States that wanted to enjoy American friendship outside the UN were made to realize that they could no longer securely enjoy its benefits if they ganged up with our enemies inside the UN. We also stopped considering it a victory when we were less harshly criticized, but still by name, for purported misdemeanors, while the crimes of the Soviet Union or of other aggressive tyrannies were condemned anonymously or simply ignored.

The Kirkpatrick years also involved a determination to stop efforts at typecasting the U. S. as the hapless scapegoat in the UN's ritual melodramas. This meant mastering the Byzantine features of the UN's wars of political maneuver in order to prevent the United States from being blamed for the fatal weakness of such schemes as "Global Negotiations," the NIEO, or projects for total disarmament. The Kirkpatrick team knew how to be effective in opposition. They also knew that, in the UN not being too obvious in one's opposition is sometimes the most effective way to defeat bad idea masquerading as a good cause.

As the result of Jeane Kirkpatrick's thoughtful, principled leadership the United States rediscovered its capacity for effective action in the forums of the United Nations This hard-won improvement in the U.S. position is not, however, identical with improvement in the UN itself. Though we have learned to combat and reduce the political damage to our interests, there remain the ideological, systemic, and institutional biases that make such damage inevitable. We now face the challenge of building on the position the U.S. has established over the past several years in order, if possible, to correct those biases. From the bast of a determined defense of U.S. interests, the United States can pursue an assertive effort to renew the original principles and purposes of the United Nations Charter.

As we plan such an effort we must remember that the United States possesses important assets even in the negative environment of today's United

Nations. The form and basic principles of the organization reflect our free democratic values. The UN stage can therefore still be the setting for us to articulate and dramatize their strength, and their superior relevance to the needs and aspirations of the world's people. Though we are not part of any bloc within the UN's party structure, we wield considerable power and influence outside it. By forging appropriate links between our relations in the outside world and our efforts in the UN, we may be able to identify a network of friends who will support us on key issues whenever such support does not contradict their own real interests. We do not control a voting majority within the system, but our financial and political support is critical to its existence. We may be able to promote needed institutional reforms by suspending the certainty of our support while negotiating appropriate reforms in exchange for reinstating it.

A policy for developing these assets might aim to: reassert the Charter's commitment to free democratic values, institutions, and practices; build effective coalitions of political support for U.S. efforts to promote those values; and restore or defend the integrity and effectiveness of the UN's permanent institutions.

Reasserting the Charter's commitment to free democratic principles and institutions will require a determined willingness to insist that the standards articulated in the Charter and the Universal Declaration of Human Rights be respected and applied consistently to all. In light of those standards, the United States should be willing to focus attention on the dramatic differences between its own basic respect for and adherence to those values and the persistent lack of respect often shown for them by the influential bloc of antidemocratic states in the UN.

Seriously distorted or manipulated international public opinion is a threat to U.S. interests. At best it can encourage indifference among traditional allies and consequent erosion of mutual support. At worst it can increase tension in various regions of the world contributing to passionate or even violent opposition. Policies that shape an opinion environment more hospitable to U.S. interests are therefore a critical element of U.S. foreign policy. The United Nations has useful potential as a setting for pursuing such policies. The Soviet Union and Third World blocs have long exploited international organizations for their propaganda value. In recent years we have successfully limited the damage from their campaigns. Such "damage limiting" efforts continue to deserve high priority, particularly on issues for which the UN's role has discouraged responsible solutions. However, the U.S. position established over the last several years presents an opportunity to assume a more assertive posture. We can do so on political issues to a degree, but particularly in the areas of human rights and economic and social affairs.

To pursue this assertive approach, though, we must first jettison the notion that victory or defeat is measured simply by the votes cast in favor of our point of view. In the UN environment there are often opportunities to dramatize our principles, and to highlight the transgressions of our opponents. If we fail to exploit those opportunities because we are afraid to lose or stand alone on a vote, then we are beaten even before the issue is joined. The consequence of such preemptive surrender is the gradual disappearance of our viewpoint from the UN scene. A good example of this can be seen in the human rights area. Property rights have traditionally been an important, indeed fundamental part of the canon of human rights in the free democratic tradition. Yet in UN human rights discussions today, no attention is given to these basic rights. The free democracies make not the slightest effort to assert their importance. Given the socialist rhetoric paraded by the majority of states, such assertions would probably find little support among them. To surrender the legitimacy of these basic rights for lack of majority support, however, denies their transcendent importance, which derives not from majority whim or government power, but from principles inherent in the concept of humanity itself. Such examples teach us that, win or lose, we must be willing to assert our principles, to appeal to a standard of legitimacy beyond the purview of majority whim. We must make clear that we are willing to assert the ideals embodied in the UN Charter and its basic declarations even if the majority of states decides to abandon them. Only by having the courage and determination to lose well will we create opportunities for meaningful victories.

In the economic and social areas the United States, and the free democracies in general, enjoy natural advantages. We have the best record of success and can offer the most practical cooperation to developing countries sincerely interested in improving the lives of their people. Rather than reacting to an agenda set entirely by others, in these areas we can and should put forward an agenda that appeals to the widespread desire for the advantages of economic and social progress. This agenda should stress the connection between progress and the spread of free democratic values. It should seek practical means to promote the establishment of political and social institutions that guarantee individual freedom. It should encourage economic policies that respect the human capacity for initiative and choice. We should promote this agenda not only in our speeches, but in resolutions we propose and in the UN development and technical assistance projects and programs we encourage with our support. In pursuing our goals in the UN, we should be willing to lose if that will effectively dramatize and promote our views. That does not mean, however, that we simply "go it alone." Thanks largely to the efforts of Ambassadors Moynihan and Kirkpatrick it is now understood that the UN political system functions as a set of voting coalitions or "blocs" which fundamentally influence the political dynamics of the organization and are the keys to diverse outcomes throughout the organization. In this system the United

States has come to be a country without a "bloc," and indeed without any truly reliable friends. To be effective in the UN, the United States must master the dynamics of the bloc system, and overcome the isolation currently imposed upon it by that system.

U.S. isolation within the system results from the unwillingness of those who should be our allies and friends to stand up and be counted in our support. Yet there are many countries in the UN whose values or interests should incline them toward support of the United States. In the first circle of these lie the free democracies, including above all the members of the Western group. In the second lie those developing countries whose political institutions or economic interests should imply a strong affinity for U. S. views. In the third are those countries, particularly among the less developed countries, whose prospects for economic growth and development depend heavily on their ties with the United States and the free democracies of the West. We must use the influence and leverage we have in the outside world to build support among these countries, adjusting our approach to suit the characteristics of that particular circle of countries we are working with. In particular we must give attention to making appropriate and effective linkages between behavior within multilateral forums and our bilateral relations with individual nations. We should make clear in suitable ways our belief that the principles of reciprocity and respect for common or mutual interests apply within the United Nations as well as without.

Enunciating such a linkage policy is rather easier than carrying it out effectively. Such implementation involves systematic keeping track of and evaluating the voting records and behavior of individual countries and their representatives in the various forums of the UN. It involves effective representation of the multilateral perspective decisions within the U. S. government that affect important aspects of our bilateral relations. We would not want UN behavior itself to be the determining factor in our relations with any given country. However we should consider a country's multilateral record along with other factors as key decisions are made in the areas of assistance, trade, etc. Those responsible for developing bilateral policies will not necessarily be receptive even to this degree of policy linkage. Its success will ultimately depend on the level of interest in effective U.S. participation in the United Nations.

Critical to the long-term prospects of the United Nations are the health and effectiveness of its secretariat: and of the international civil service system. Unfortunately, like so much else in the life of the organization these critical elements have been affected detrimentally by the dominance of the bloc political system. Bloc political factors, as well as the interests and ambitions of particular member states, have largely determined hiring, placement, evaluation, and promotion within the secretariats. Oversight by governing bodies, such as the General Assembly or the general conferences or assemblies of the specialized agencies, has been relatively ineffectual. This ineffectiveness has many contributing elements, some of them common to most legislative bodies struggling to maintain influence over expansionary public sector bureaucracies.

The UN has had a special problem, however. The certainty of ever-expanding resources in the assessed budget greatly reduced the necessity for responsible decision-making in the deliberative bodies or strict accountability for results in the secretariats. No irate electorates were involved, that would eventually take revenge at the polls for wasteful budgetary expansion financed at their expense. Ironically, this means political factors, particularly those of the majority developing country groups, dominate the budget process in the UN, rather than budgetary considerations. Because the developing country groups require nearly unanimous consensus in order to reach decisions, budgets expand to accommodate the largest common denominator of group interests. So long as competing interests are accommodated, choices among competing priorities are unnecessary. In fact such choices expose intra-group fissures and are politically inconvenient. It is therefore expedient not even to formulate them clearly.

The decision-making process in the UN General Assembly reflects this expediency. Program choices and budget choices are compartmentalized, with financial implications considered by a separate budget committee only after basic program choices have already been made in the program committees. Thus budgetary considerations may have a marginal, after-the-fact effect on choices of pro- gram priorities, but they are not allowed to exert a formative influence. This arrangement is completely subservient to the governing majority's need to maintain political cohesion, and concedes little to the interests of the small minority of states who contribute the overwhelming bulk of the UN's budget. In fact it relegates their concerns and influence to the status of marginalia.

The countries that pay most don't have the votes. The budget decision-making process itself is arranged to prevent the minority countries from raising their budget concerns before program choices are fixed. Since the influence of the financing minority is isolated and ineffective, the deliberative process on the UN budget encourages little or no concern for budgetary efficiency, i.e., the quality of results achieved per unit of resources expended. Not only do major contributors suffer, as budgets expand to no good end, the goals and people UN activities should serve suffer, as quality succumbs to political expediency. Member states and their people do not secure from the UN the benefits membership is supposed to provide.

When the UN was founded, the idea of an assessed budget to which members were obliged to contribute was intended precisely to prevent the erosion of benefits from the organization that has in fact occurred. Because the major contributors have by and large faithfully fulfilled their obligations, a system has evolved that isolates and neglects their interests, thereby harming the interests of the organization. This is entirely contrary to the Charter's intention, clearly stated in Article 2, Section 2:

> All Members, in order to ensure to all of them the rights and benefits resulting from membership, shall fulfill in good faith the obligations assumed by them in accordance with the present Charter.

Under the present budgetary system, the faithful fulfillment of obligations by some has been manipulated, to their detriment and that of the organization, in order to guarantee the political advantage of the governing majority. The reciprocal connection between obligation and benefit envisaged by the Charter has been disregarded. As a consequence the members' sense of obligation has eroded, with more states willing to adopt the cynical self-serving attitude taken by the Soviet Union and the Eastern bloc since the organization began. The current financial problems of the United Nations must be viewed in the context of this breakdown of reciprocity. Acting the part of the indignant electorate, the United States Congress has raised serious doubts about the United States' continued willingness to pay for the operation of a system whose structure and results seem stacked against it. The Kassebaum amendment reflects the Congress's understanding of the structural bias in the present budget process. The absence of any exemption for the UN from the Gramm-Rudman process merely reciprocates the UN majority's marginal regard for the interests and concerns of major contributors. By forcibly restricting the horizon of the UN's budget expansion, these measures introduce the necessity for budget discipline thus far absent from the UN's history. By linking this restriction in part to a requirement for fundamental structural reform, the congressional action compels attention to the root cause of the UN's budgetary inefficiency, i.e., the systemic imbalance between power and responsibility, voting majorities and financial contributions, benefits and obligations. In implementing the laws affecting the U.S. contribution to the United Nations, the United States government can strive to achieve several short and longer-term goals. First, we can try to assure that the system's response to the need for greater budget discipline results in greater quality and effectiveness, not just in numerical cutbacks that disregard issues of basic program priorities and efficient resource use. Second, we can encourage and cooperate in processes aimed at achieving structural reforms that address the systemic imbalances outlined above.

Third, we can take steps to encourage greater effectiveness in the UN's secretariat. As we pursue the first two objectives we must keep in mind that the UN is not a monolithic organization. Though all parts are affected to some degree by the serious problems we have been discussing, some are healthier than others. Since our cutbacks aim at achieving a constructive purpose, they should be implemented in a fashion consistent with this purpose. Our approach should allow us to differentiate to some degree between qualitatively different parts of the system, while reinforcing incentives for the improvement of the system as a whole.

The third of these objectives is particularly critical over the long term. The UN is a service organization. The quality of its people and their dedication to its principles and purposes are crucial to its success. Absent courageous leadership, however, neither quality nor dedication can be sustained.

The United States government should therefore pay close attention to UN personnel questions, particularly where leadership positions are concerned. We should recruit vigorously and put forward qualified Americans for appropriate roles. We should fight against the cynical double-standard that has allowed the Soviet Union to ignore the concept of an independent international civil service, making Soviet nationals in the secretariats strictly disciplined instruments of their government's overt or clandestine purposes. No matter how assiduously the United States pursues the goals and objectives we have discussed, there can be no unilateral guarantee of eventual improvement in the United Nations. The process of change, if it occurs, will certainly have all of the slowness and frustration characteristic of multilateral negotiations. The pressure we put on the system can only assure that problems will no longer be swept under the rug. It cannot force solutions if other member states, or vested interests within the secretariats, are determined to forestall constructive change. We must be patient, persistent, and capable of maintaining an unpopular stand over a period of years. This is not an easy challenge for a free democratic government, especially in an area where the stakes often seem less than critical. In a sense, however, the stakes are as large as the best hopes of mankind. Should the UN's role in those hopes eventually fail, it will be good for us to know that the United States did all that it could to impel the organization toward a better destiny.

Part 3

Law Enforcement and Foreign Policy

13

Law in Order: Reconstructing U. S. National Security

*William Wechsler**

Few tools of U.S. foreign policy are as vitally important *and* as consistently overlooked as law enforcement. Terrorism, organized crime, drug trafficking, arms smuggling, sanctions busting and foreign corruption are serious challenges confronting American policymakers, and law enforcement has an important—sometimes central—role in combating each of these threats. That role suffers, however, from two fatal flaws. First, differences in bureaucratic culture and viewpoints between the law enforcement and national security communities make coordination difficult. Law enforcement agencies generally refuse to see themselves as components of U.S. foreign policy. Nor does the traditional foreign policy establishment adequately appreciate the distinct culture, capabilities and constraints that characterize U.S. law enforcement agencies. Second, there are structural impediments to effective coordination, both among the various law enforcement agencies and between such bodies and the traditional national security agencies. Federal law enforcement agencies, themselves riven by turf battles, lack proper civilian oversight and are organizationally ill suited for integration into the wider foreign policy community.

Previous administrations have tried, but failed, to address these problems. Too many important actors prefer things, as they are, most significantly the various Federal law enforcement agencies themselves. In the past, the need to fix the systematic inefficiencies bedeviling Federal law enforcement seemed less pressing. But the world has changed, and U.S. law enforcement must

---

*During the Clinton Administration, William F. Wechsler held positions as Special Advisor to the Secretary of the Treasury, Director for Transnational Threats at the National Security Council, and Special Assistant to the Chairman of the Joint Chiefs of Staff.

This essay first appeared in *The National Interest* no. 67 (Spring 2002).

change with it. Just as war is too important to be left to the generals, law enforcement reform is too important to be left to FBI directors and Customs commissioners.

International Crime: A Threat to U.S. National Security

For most of American history, there has been a bright line on the Federal level between national security threats on the one hand and criminal threats on the other. The former were international, the latter domestic. The international side was the purview of the military and intelligence agencies; the domestic side that of the law enforcement agencies. This separation was primarily intended to prevent military encroachments on civilian authorities and civil liberties. The fear of militarism in American civil society remains deeply embedded in the national consciousness and has long been incorporated into American governance. U.S. government actions are still defined by the *Posse Comitatus* Act, passed in 1878 to prohibit the military from performing certain domestic police functions.

In recent decades this bright line has blurred. Traditional crimes in the United States have increasingly been found to have links to criminal networks overseas. Narcotics trafficking, most obviously, cannot possibly be combated by domestic law enforcement operations alone. A bipartisan consensus also has emerged that the threat from foreign narcotics trafficking is not just a law enforcement concern but also a matter of national security. Thus in 1987 did President Reagan overrule his Secretary of Defense and instruct the military to go abroad to help fight the war on drugs.

As technology advanced and borders became increasingly porous after the Cold War, it became evident, too, that international crime in *all* of its various forms threatened U.S. national security interests. Sometimes the threats were direct. Terrorists groups like Al-Qaeda, no longer as dependent on state sponsorship, began targeting Americans at home and abroad. They also engaged in a host of criminal activities apart from terrorism, from arms trafficking to people smuggling to securities fraud. Vast networks of criminals based in Russia, Nigeria, Latin America, East Asia and elsewhere went global, infiltrating the United States as one of the world's most lucrative targets. Hackers halfway around the world broke into U.S. computer systems, including sensitive systems belonging to the military and intelligence agencies.

International crime also poses indirect threats to U.S. national security. Criminal syndicates have corrupted government officials, undermined democratic governance, and hindered economic development in many countries. This has been well documented in post-communist states like Russia, developing countries like Nigeria, post-conflict societies like Bosnia and countries of particular concern to the United States like Mexico. In Colombia, groups engaged in drug trafficking, terrorist activity and other serious crimes even challenge the government itself for control over territory and the population just as communist insurgencies did a few decades ago.

Criminal syndicates have also helped to undermine regional stability. In Sierra Leone, for instance, the illegal smuggling of "conflict" diamonds helped finance a brutal civil war. Elsewhere in Africa and around the world, arms trafficking by organized criminal networks has stoked regional conflicts that might otherwise have died down. Criminal syndicates have been instrumental in violating U.S. and international sanctions regimes in such places as Iraq and Serbia. Russian criminal organizations are reportedly involved in smuggling materials for weapons of mass destruction—chemical, biological and nuclear. In other places, such as in Albania, criminal organizations have driven regime change, as when the collapse of a pyramid scheme precipitated anarchy and flooded next-door Kosovo with small weapons. Financial crimes such as money laundering and counterfeiting have the potential to undermine national banking systems and contribute to instability in the global financial system. Economic crimes such as piracy—both physical and intellectual—affect U.S. companies' competitiveness in foreign markets.

What We Have Here is a Failure to Communicate

Given the stakes, all appropriate foreign policy tools should be employed to combat criminal threats to U.S. security interests, and employed in a coordinated process according to a comprehensive strategy. Unfortunately, this commonsense view is far too uncommon in Federal law enforcement agencies today.

As to the direct threats to this country, for example, nobody denies that Federal law enforcement has a critical and even a predominant role to play in combating threats like terrorism, drug trafficking and international organized crime. But other tools of U.S. foreign policy also need to come into play to combat international crime, including diplomacy, cooperation in multilateral forums, financial sanctions, and in some cases covert operations and overt military campaigns. In these cases, obviously, law enforcement activities must be coordinated into the overall strategies, even in those instances when law enforcement has the lead. Sometimes this works well. When it comes to the rendition of terrorists from abroad, for instance, U.S. law enforcement agencies have developed excellent working relationships with the military and intelligence agencies. But law enforcement officials who have become accustomed to the considerable freedom of action and limited civilian oversight that domestic operations afford often chafe when confronted with the need to coordinate with others when operating abroad.

Americans are proud that nobody in the United States, not even the president, is above the law. This principle is drilled into the consciousness of every law enforcement officer. Since the abuses of Federal law enforcement by the Nixon Administration, Federal agents have taken refuge in the axiom that criminal trails should be followed to their conclusion by non-political technical experts, no matter what the wider consequences. Law enforcement officers remain suspicious that requests for "coordination" with other government agencies are subterfuges for political interference, even on matters of foreign policy. Even worse from the point of view of many Federal law enforcement agents, others argue that law enforcement objectives—putting an individual criminal behind bars—should sometimes be subordinate to other objectives, such as disrupting a terrorist network, winning a military campaign, or "merely" maintaining positive bilateral relations with certain other countries. Some law enforcement agencies have become especially adept at using the media and the Congress to draw attention to allegations of "political interference" in such cases.

This viewpoint is extremely shortsighted. First, the isolation of law enforcement agencies from other agencies and from the interagency process harms the effectiveness of law enforcement operations themselves. U.S. diplomacy is too often unable to assist law enforcement efforts because ambassadors are not informed about specific cases or are not asked to secure cooperation from foreign governments. Yet such diplomatic efforts could be extremely valuable, because many foreign governments are more comfortable speaking with U.S. diplomatic (or intelligence) agencies than with U.S. law enforcement agencies, and because diplomats sometimes possess additional leverage to use on behalf of the national interest.

One example: for years U.S. law enforcement strained hard and usually failed to trace criminal money trails overseas to countries with strict bank secrecy laws. Then, in 2000, a multilateral diplomatic initiative to "name and shame" certain money laundering havens successfully coerced several countries to change their laws and adopt stronger international anti-money laundering standards.[1] Now, U.S. law enforcement can track money in ways it never could before. In recent months, Liechtenstein and the Bahamas—two countries "named and shamed"—have provided important information to the United States about elements of Al-Qaeda's financial network. It is inconceivable that the United States would have had access to this same information two years ago, before diplomacy was brought to bear on this problem.

Second, the lack of coordination with law enforcement agencies can harm U.S. foreign policy. Sometimes U.S. foreign law enforcement operations anger foreign heads of government when they are kept out of the loop. Not that foreign governments should be allowed to halt or hinder U.S. investigations; their anger and irritation is often a price we must pay to enforce U.S. laws. But law enforcement objectives can often be achieved without harming bilateral diplomatic relations—if only law enforcement personnel would stop intentionally hiding their activities from the State Department and the National Security Council.

Information as well as activities relevant to U.S. national security that come from law enforcement sources also often go unshared with the national security community. There are complicated, painstaking and heavily scrutinized methods for disseminating intelligence information to law enforcement agencies, always scrubbed so it can be used in court without revealing intelligence sources and methods. But there are no similar procedures for law enforcement information to routinely make its way into intelligence agencies and thereby into the wider national security community. It is up to law enforcement officials to decide when information they have is relevant to national security, but such decisions normally go beyond their area of expertise. For many years during the Clinton Administration, the Justice Department and the associated law enforcement agencies refused to agree to a basic memorandum of understanding to establish even first principles as to how information should be shared.

The problems that arose from this state of affairs were not merely hypothetical. Former CIA Director James Woolsey has publicly complained that he was unable to obtain terrorist-related information once the Justice Department decided to bring the 1993 World Trade Center bombing case to court. In another situation during the Clinton Administration, the FBI discovered that the wife of the former Russian delegate to the International Monetary Fund might have been involved in illegally moving $7 billion in Russian money of unknown origin through the Bank of New York. Not until this case was reported in the *New York Times* did the Justice Department and the FBI think to brief the National Security Advisor or the Secretary of State on the matter.

Third, law enforcement objectives often differ from wider U.S. objectives, and that is natural. The FBI's job is to arrest criminals in such a way that a court case against them will result in a conviction that can stand the test of an appeal. But law enforcement goals should not be presumed preeminent by definition. Even when U.S. laws have clearly been broken, other objectives may be more important to the nation. One such case is President Bush's wise decision to treat Al-Qaeda primarily as a military adversary rather than a law enforcement concern. Another example: During the Clinton Administration, the Justice Department repeatedly objected to the use of economic sanctions against foreign drug cartels as proposed by the national security agencies, preferring that efforts be restricted to building cases in U.S. courts. This view was held by the law enforcement agencies despite the success of President Clinton's 1995 order, under the International Emergency Economic Powers Act, to disrupt the Cali cartel's financial network. Not until 1999 were additional sanctions imposed, and then only after the Congress, frustrated by the lack of similar actions against other cartels, passed the Foreign Drug Kingpin Designation Act.

Problems of the Indirect

When it comes to direct threats to the United States from international crime, U.S. law enforcement agencies generally object to the involvement of national security agencies, believing that the latter may curtail or otherwise interfere with their operations. But this dynamic is reversed when it comes to indirect threats. In these cases, law enforcement agencies generally refuse to become substantially involved, notwithstanding pleas from the State Department. The reason is that many in U.S. law enforcement simply do not care if foreign countries and their governments are being harmed by international crime, unless there is a clear connection to a case that can be brought to trial in U.S. courts. As they see it, it is not their job to worry about damage to U.S. national security interests or regional stability abroad. State Department officials are therefore left more or less on their own to deal with international arms trafficking, sanctions busting, alien smuggling, trafficking in women, corruption and all the rest of the dark side of globalization. That is also why law enforcement agencies give low priority to foreign law enforcement training and technical assistance efforts, administration of justice development programs, post-conflict governance initiatives, and the civilian policing components of UN peacekeeping operations. This reluctance has even carried over with respect to places like the Balkans and Haiti, where conditions had previously deteriorated to the point that U.S. military forces had to be called into action.

But the stakes of this abnegation are even larger than that. The transformation of Russia into a functioning, market democracy was one of the primary objectives of U.S. foreign policy in the 1990s. Yet U.S. law enforcement had no overall strategy to combat Russian organized crime unless it set foot on U.S. soil. Moreover, Russian organized crime gained strength and influence in Hungary, a new NATO member and an important ally for U.S. efforts in the Balkans. This was of great concern to Hungary's President and had been identified as one of the primary threats to Hungary's economic and political development by the U.S. ambassador. Yet the FBI refused for years to assign even one agent to the U.S. embassy in Budapest, much less actively assist the Hungarian National Police in combating Russian organized crime. It took a meeting between President Clinton and the Hungarian President, and a personal request from the National Security Advisor to the FBI Director, before even this small step could be taken.

The traditional national security agencies also share blame for the lack of integration of the law enforcement agencies into U.S. foreign policy. Most foreign policy experts know little and care less about the capabilities and limitations of U.S. law enforcement. As a result sometimes unfair expectations are set or improper requests are made. International law enforcement issues are too often a secondary concern of the foreign policy establishment, and sometimes they are ignored entirely. Particularly when foreign governments themselves are implicated in crimes, U.S. diplomats can be reflexively unwilling to press issues that may result in a deterioration of bilateral relations. The State Department's Bureau of International Narcotics and Law Enforcement Affairs, despite relatively strong leadership in recent years, is still considered a bureaucratic backwater. It only rarely attracts the most capable civil servants and foreign service officers, and has historically been marginalized by the leadership of the department.

Structural Impediments

Some of these problems might be solved by changes in leadership, but structural changes will be necessary as well. In 1995, President Clinton issued Presidential Decision Directive 42 which, for the first time, defined international crime as a national security threat. A NSC-chaired interagency working group was established to coordinate the government's efforts to combat this threat. And in 1998 President Clinton released the first-ever International Crime Control Strategy, describing the goals and objectives of this new effort.

This effort paid off. Its achievements include the aforementioned "naming and shaming" effort against money laundering havens, a series of multilateral treaties negotiated by the State Department on subjects such as small arms trafficking, a series of bilateral Mutual Legal Assistance Treaties negotiated by the Justice Department, greater efforts to combat trafficking in women, and the financial sanctions on the Cali drug cartel (the first time this tool was used against a non-state actor). There were also some successes in the wars on drugs and terrorism, and new initiatives to protect critical infrastructures from information warfare and cyber crime. But overall, despite President Clinton's personal interest and strong pushes from the National Security Council and the State Department, the effort left too much undone. Part of the problem flowed from the differing viewpoints and failures of coordination between law enforcement agencies and national security agencies, but other difficulties stemmed from structural failings in the law enforcement community. These failings deserve special attention, and remediation.

The very structure of the Justice Department illustrates the low priority assigned to curtailing international crime. Its international training, technical assistance, counter-intelligence and criminal programs are spread out over several different offices and report to a multitude of different Justice Department officials. Most regrettably, a single assistant attorney general oversees both international and domestic criminal investigations. One person who held that post during the Clinton Administration told me that, before he took the job, he had not spent even ten minutes thinking about international crime. While the State Department, Pentagon and CIA are all organized geographically, no one in the Justice Department is responsible for what the department and its subordinate agencies are doing with regard to, say, Russia.

Even if there were such a position, the Justice Department would *still* suffer from its institutional inability to oversee its subordinate law enforcement agencies. During the Clinton Administration FBI Director Louis Freeh was rarely if ever held accountable by Attorney General Janet Reno. In keeping with the legacy of J. Edgar Hoover, Freeh functioned without effective civilian oversight, a pattern that was replicated down the chain of authority. The law enforcement agencies that fall under the Treasury Department, too, operate more or less independently from the civilians to whom they are allegedly accountable. This became evident in 1997 when Ray Kelly, then the Under Secretary of the Treasury for Enforcement, took what seemed to be a demotion to become the Commissioner of the U.S. Customs Service—one of many law enforcement agencies that he *already supposedly oversaw*. The move only made sense upon recognition that Customs operates with little effective civilian oversight.

Even if the problem of civilian oversight was somehow fixed, the massive problems stemming from the sheer number of Federal law enforcement agencies would still exist, as would the lack of coordination among them, the lack of cooperation with state and local authorities, and the vast operational inefficiencies that result. In 1991 the General Accounting Office identified an astonishing 148 different Federal agencies with some law enforcement functions.[2] On far too many issues jurisdictional confusion hampers investigations. The various law enforcement agencies are notoriously turf-conscious, regularly refusing to share information with each other, always focused on securing "credit" for convictions.

The mission statements of many law enforcement agencies reflect this focus; to an outsider (and even to many insiders) they seem oddly centered on ensuring institutional primacy with regard to specific crimes, particularly ones where legal jurisdictions are unclear. Databases are rarely combined between agencies and equipment is often not interoperable. "Interagency" offices and task forces are established to great fanfare, and then become ineffective because key law enforcement agencies refuse to join, fearing that they would then become "subordinate" to another. Basic data on the number and types of crimes are often incomplete, and are tracked according to differing methodologies in different agencies. Standardized procedures do not even exist across the law enforcement community in such areas as recruitment, selection and training; surveillance; rules of engagement; forensic laboratory management and classification and use of forensic data. In the course of virtually every high-profile case, state and local law enforcement officials complain that Federal law enforcement agencies refuse to share information, making it harder for them to function.

These are not new insights. Every decade or so another outside group of experts examines the structure of Federal law enforcement, and they all come to virtually the same conclusion: it's a dysfunctional mess. Sadly, these conclusions have all also been ignored. In 1996, for instance, after public outcry over law enforcement actions in Waco and Ruby Ridge, the Congress asked Judge William H. Webster, a former director of both the FBI and the CIA, to chair a commission to examine the state of Federal law enforcement. Its admirable final report was published four years later and, alas, promptly shelved. This was a shame. The Webster report is as comprehensive and critical a review of the structure of Federal law enforcement as has ever been written, and includes a number of far-reaching recommendations. It is not too late to adopt them.[3]

Time for Change

The Webster report's overall conclusion was that "the current organization of Federal law enforcement needs to be changed." While that call went unheeded during the final year of the Clinton Administration, the Bush Administration can and should take up the challenge now, and if it does it has reason to expect success. The reason is that a rare confluence of events has pushed Federal law enforcement to a crisis.

First, a string of high profile debacles have recently embarrassed the FBI, puncturing its public image and finally allowing criticisms to be voiced in public. Consecutive episodes such as the Robert Hanssen spy case, the botched investigation of Wen Ho Lee, the media leaks attacking Richard Jewell, the cover-up of deficiencies in its crime lab, its improper withholding of documents in the Timothy McVeigh case, and the intelligence and operational failures in the domestic war on terrorism have finally put many in the Congress in the mood to ask some hard questions.

Second, there is a growing consensus, too, that simply ponying up more resources will not solve the problem. After all, the Clinton Administration tripled the FBI's counterterrorism budget and the number of its agents, and the FBI still failed utterly to detect the events of September 11 being planned on American soil. Nor had they any knowledge that Al-Qaeda was planning to attack Los Angeles International Airport during the millennium celebrations, something that came to light only after an alert Customs agent caught a terrorist with explosives at the border.

And third, now that President Bush has declared a war on terrorism, questions about law enforcement reform have taken on a new urgency. The continuing investigation into Al Qaeda's operations in the United States make clear how much was missed and has highlighted the need for various law enforcement agencies to better share information concerning suspected terrorists. On September 11, as the public has now learned, the FBI had no computer system to centralize its intelligence and share it with other agencies. And Tom Ridge, the director of the new White House Office of Homeland Security, is undoubtedly confronting the same coordination problems that beset the Clinton Administration after 1998, when it issued Presidential Decision Directives 62 and 63 and first established government-wide initiatives to defend against cyber- and bioterrorism. The Bush Administration—wisely, in my opinion—batted down suggestions that Ridge's office be made a separate agency;

its real challenge will be to find ways to make the other agencies of government, including the law enforcement agencies, do their own jobs better.

Attorney General John Ashcroft and FBI Director Robert Mueller have already taken initial steps that show cognizance of the need for structural change. Mueller has overhauled the bureau's top management to place more emphasis on counterterrorism and cybercrime. Ashcroft has rightly taken control of the terrorism investigation from the Southern District of New York, begun to separate the service and enforcement functions of the Immigration and Naturalization Service, and, at long last, given the Justice Department's inspector general jurisdiction over allegations of FBI misconduct—a fundamental step if the FBI is to be accountable to civilian oversight. In recent months, too, Congress has passed laws to encourage law enforcement to share more of their information with national security agencies.

President Bush should now take the next step and call for a comprehensive review of law enforcement, with the intention of producing lasting, systemic reform. Politically, such an effort is more likely to succeed if sponsored by a Republican administration, because the GOP has stronger traditional ties to law enforcement. President Bush will also benefit from the absence of the adversarial relationship that existed between some law enforcement agency heads and the Clinton White House, in part due to the several investigations of the President.

A New Vision for Federal Law Enforcement

Before the administration sets forth to fix this problem, it would do well to recognize that the structural deficiencies facing law enforcement are not without precedent. The reform of U.S. military structure that began after World War II and led ultimately to the Goldwater-Nichols Act in 1986 is a salutary model for study. This is not the place to review what has already been widely analyzed and well appreciated, except to stress three principle lessons. The first and most important lesson that should be drawn is that the incrementalist approach does not work; the entrenched interests that oppose reform can be overcome only when leaders at the highest levels of the Executive and Legislative Branches work in a bipartisan spirit to seek comprehensive changes. The second lesson is that unification is the goal, "jointness" is the means, and clear lines of authority are the prerequisite. And the third lesson is that it is possible to ensure a high order of professionalism and even degrees of independence among career officers while still guaranteeing effective civilian oversight and wider integration into the foreign policymaking process.

So, then, what would a reformed Federal law enforcement community look like? There are four necessary components of reform: *consolidation* of proliferating law enforcement agencies; *coordination* among the remaining agencies; *centralization* of both civilian and agency accountability; and *integration* into the wider foreign policy community.

First, consolidation. If the Federal law enforcement community were organized functionally as the military services are, the multitude of its agencies could be consolidated into three.

(1) A *Federal Investigative Agency* would have as its primary mission the investigation of Federal crimes, both at home and abroad. It would combine the law enforcement functions of the FBI, the Drug Enforcement Administration (DEA), the Bureau of Alcohol, Tobacco and Firearms (ATF), the Criminal Investigation Division of the Internal Revenue Service (IRS-CI), the Financial Crimes Enforcement Network, and the investigatory elements of the Secret Service (USSS). This step alone would eliminate much friction among existing agencies, eliminate duplicative efforts, remove barriers to coordination, and save money in the long run. This idea is not new, and leaders of both parties have supported it in the past. In the 1980s, then-Associate Attorney General Rudolph Guliani oversaw a study that proposed combining the DEA and the FBI. In 1993 Vice President Al Gore's "reinventing government" initiative recommended that the DEA, ATF and FBI be merged.[4] And the Webster Commission also recommended that ATF and DEA become part of a larger FBI.

(2) A *Border Enforcement Agency* would be constituted of uniformed federal officers and focus on defending the borders of the United States. It would combine the U.S. Customs Service, the U.S. Coast Guard, and the planned Bureau of Immigration Enforcement, including the U.S. Border Patrol, the uniformed arm of the Immigration and Naturalization Service. Neither is this a new idea. The Hart-Rudman Commission, which at the start of the Bush Administration—*before* September 11, 2001—called for a new effort to defend the U.S. homeland against terrorist threats, also recommended the combination of the Customs Service, the Border Patrol and the Coast Guard.[5] And shortly after taking office, Tom Ridge called a series of cabinet-level meetings to push this idea, which he intended to make a centerpiece of President Bush's most recent State of the Union address. Unfortunately, he soon learned how difficult it is in Washington to overcome bureaucracies intent on defending their turf, so the plan was sent back for "further study." In the end, President Bush followed the same path as his predecessors: He called for increased budgets, but no serious reorganization.

(3) A *Federal Protective Agency* would be charged with protecting the physical security of U.S. government officials, buildings, properties and persons under government control. It would combine the protective division and uniformed service of the Secret Service with the Bureau of Diplomatic Security, the Federal Protective Service (the law enforcement and security arm of the General Services Administration), the U.S. Marshall Service, the Federal Bureau of Prisons (with one-third of all Federal personnel authorized to carry firearms), newly federalized airport security personnel, and the U.S. Park Police. It would be operationally efficient, though perhaps political unrealistic, to also include the numerous independent federal police forces that primarily

operate in and around Washington, DC. (Most Americans have no idea, of course, that the Congress, the Supreme Court and the Library of Congress, which are located right next to one another, each have their own police forces.)

Why not go all the way and create just one law enforcement super-agency? Three reasons. Some degree of competition is healthy. Distinct functional missions—investigations, border enforcement, physical protection—may require distinct institutional cultures. Perhaps most important, though, is the traditional and sensible American reluctance to put all police powers in the hands of one person or institution. The protection of our civil rights requires strong law enforcement; the protection of our civil liberties requires separated law enforcement institutions.

Second, coordination. As with the military, all three of these agencies would coordinate their planning and operations across all levels, starting with the top. A joint committee of agency directors, modeled after the Joint Chiefs of Staff, would be established, and a joint staff made up of some of the strongest law enforcement officers would be created to aid its work. Similarly designed joint organizations would be placed in the field to manage at the local level. Special Federal law enforcement regional agents would be responsible for coordinating the local operations of the special agents in charge from all three Federal law enforcement agencies in any given geographic area.

Third, centralization of accountability. Reform of law enforcement should avoid the mistakes made in 1947 by military reformers. A chairman of the joint committee of agency directors should be named, and that person should be made the principal career law enforcement advisor to the president and attorney general. To promote professionalism, the practice of installing political appointees at the top of law enforcement agencies should end. Career law enforcement officials should be promoted to lead their agencies, as is done in the military. To promote civilian control, the military model should again be followed: the chairman should hold office for a two-year term, renewable by the president only once. Similar term limits should be put on the directors of the various law enforcement agencies.

Centralization should also take place on the civilian side. Only by an accident of American history does the U.S. Treasury Department have significant law enforcement responsibilities. No other modern state has placed bodies like Customs, ATF and the Secret Service in its finance ministry. As argued above, these functions should be removed from the Treasury, leaving it with its primary missions intact. (No president has chosen his secretary of the treasury on the basis of his knowledge of law enforcement issues.) Similarly, the Coast Guard, as a military and law enforcement agency, does not belong in the Transportation Department, whose secretary cannot be expected to have expertise on either military or law enforcement matters.

All of these agencies, in their new structure as described above, should come under the civilian authority of an expanded Department of Justice, where they belong. The Webster Commission usefully pointed out Executive Order No. 11396, signed by President Lyndon Johnson in February 1968, which charged the attorney general with coordinating the law enforcement and crime prevention activities of all Federal departments and agencies. Now, more than thirty years after the order was issued, it is high time to implement it.

Admittedly, this will not be easy. Historically, the attorney general has been unable to effectively oversee even the FBI, much less a host of other Federal agencies. A new position should be established, therefore, with a title perhaps of deputy attorney general for law enforcement, the holder of which will focus only on the oversight of law enforcement programs, plans and operations. The Justice Department staff will need to be augmented as well, with civilians with experience in law enforcement—which DOJ's present cadre of predominantly civilian lawyers lacks. A stronger Justice Department committed to effective oversight could also centrally administer the sixty different Offices of the Inspector General, which have in recent decades taken on wider law enforcement functions. Most importantly, the Justice Department should directly oversee the inspectors general of the law enforcement agencies. Strengthened oversight by Congress is also necessary to guard against abuse. Arrangements that ensure the General Accounting Office access to information on the one hand, and congressional oversight committees on the other, are essential to ensure that structural reform efforts produce true operational reforms.

Fourth, integration. The attorney general should formally be made part of the National Security Council through a change in law, and the chairman of the joint committee of agency directors should hold the same formal observer position at the NSC as does the chairman of the Joint Chiefs of Staff. They should each have a top official—an assistant attorney general at Justice—whose responsibilities are focused solely on international and national security affairs. Those officials, and their subordinates responsible for foreign geographic regions, should participate in all the relevant interagency working groups to develop and implement U.S. foreign policy. A new international division of the Department of Justice would oversee all international law enforcement investigations and prosecutions, ending the dangerous near-autonomy that some Federal law enforcement officials now wield when they are in the field overseas.

At present, despite the placement of more than 2,000 U.S. law enforcement agents and support personnel abroad, law enforcement agencies' foreign staffing planning documents are not well coordinated, either within the law enforcement community or with other Federal agencies. Furthermore, foreign law enforcement activities too often take place without the full knowledge of the embassy chief of mission, the local representative of the president. Agents stationed in the same embassy that represent different law enforcement agencies bring their habits with them, competing for foreign sources, often refusing to share information. Once again, the model should be that of the U.S. military, where different Services rotate in the role of embassy military liaison officers, and report to the chief of mission.

This vision of a reformed Federal law enforcement will not be realized anytime soon. But it can be done more quickly than the decades it took to reform the military. The key question is, will President Bush take advantage of the rare opportunity to push reform?

Perhaps he will. The President certainly understands the importance of terrorism and other international criminal threats to U.S. national security. His national security team is undoubtedly confronting the lack of integration between the law enforcement and the foreign policy communities. His homeland security director has already made important—albeit stillborn—proposals on law enforcement reform. He may find that, in the current environment, there are members of Congress on both sides of the aisle who are ready to tackle the tough issues if the President is willing to lead the way. President Bush has clearly proven that he can lead. Let us, then, hope for the best.

Notes

1. See my "Follow the Money", *Foreign Affairs* (July/August 2001).
2. Federal Criminal Justice System—A Model to Estimate System Workload, U.S. General Accounting Office, April 1991.
3. *Law Enforcement in a New Century and a Changing World: Improving the Administration of Federal Law Enforcement, Report of the Commission on the Advancement of Federal Law Enforcement* (January 2000).
4. Report of the National Performance Review, *From Red Tape to Results: Creating a Government that Works Better and Costs Less*, September 7, 1993.
5. United States Commission on National Security/21st Century, *Imperative for Change*, February 2001.

14

The Law at War: How Osama Slipped Away

*Ruth Wedgwood**

In the spring of 1996, the White House was preoccupied with Bosnia—implementing the Dayton Agreement, ferrying American troops across the Sava River, building facilities at Tuzla, attempting to install an unworkable three-headed government in Sarajevo, hoping to persuade Muslim, Croat, and Serb factions to let refugees return to their burnt-out homes. Bosnia may have been important to the confidence of Europe and the credibility of NATO—but everything is relative. On the same White House watch, a far more important war was left unattended by Richard Holbrooke and Bill Clinton. We let Osama bin Laden escape our clutches.

Bob Woodward's astonishing account of White House decision-making, featured in the October 3 *Washington Post*, laid out a sad Clintonian story of too little, too late. It is a story that bears important lessons for the conduct of the present campaign against terrorism. Well studied, it is a lesson that can teach us to avoid the dangerous confusion between war and peace, and between adjudicative fact-finding and the conduct of a serious foreign and national security policy. It is a lesson that, despite the shock of September 11, we still need to learn.

In February 1996, Ali Othman Taba, Sudan's Foreign Minister, asked the U.S. ambassador in Khartoum what the Sudanese government could do to redeem its heretofore indulgent record on terrorism. Ambassador Tim Carney and State Department official David Shinn laid out a series of sensible demands, including the expulsion of a group of Egyptian nationals conspiring to assassinate President Hosni Mubarak, and the closure and dismantling of

*Ruth Wedgwood is professor of law at the Yale University Law School. In 2001-02 she was a visiting scholar at the Paul H. Nitze School of Advanced International Studies, Johns Hopkins University.

This essay first appeared in *The National Interest* no. 66 (Winter 2001/02).

Hamas training facilities that readied young men for Palestinian terrorist operations. At the top of the list, however, was the request to put an end to the swaggering presence in Khartoum of Osama bin Laden, who even then was notorious for bankrolling a number of Islamic terrorist groups around the world.

Indeed, by 1995 there was already compelling evidence that bin Laden was financing and training Egyptian and Algerian Islamist groups. He funded a group called Muhammad's Army (*Jaish Muhammed*) that was responsible for terror attacks in Jordan. Bin Laden's farm outside Khartoum had been turned into a camp reserved for the use of Hamas in training new recruits. He bankrolled a December 1992 bombing in Aden that killed two tourists and nearly missed killing or injuring almost 100 U.S. servicemen en route to Somalia for famine relief operations. Bin Laden's brother-in-law, Mohammed Jamal Khalifah, financed Ramzi Yousef in organizing the 1993 World Trade Center bombing designed to topple one of the twin towers upon the other, and funded terrorist groups in the Philippines. In November 1995, a U.S. military training center for the Saudi National Guard based in Riyadh was blown up by a van loaded with explosives, killing five Americans, with the tentacles again leading back to bin Laden's network.

The U.S. government therefore had strong motivation to pursue negotiations with Sudan over bin Laden's future. These negotiations continued in earnest when Major-General Elfatih Erwa, Sudan's Defense Minister, visited the United States in March 1996. During that visit, Erwa stated that the Sudanese government was prepared to offer two solutions to the bin Laden problem. One was to place bin Laden under strict surveillance, with Sudan reporting regularly to American officials about his activities and movements. The other was to deliver bin Laden into the custody of a third party acceptable to both Khartoum and Washington.

No one seems to have taken Erwa's first proposal seriously. With regard to the second, however, the White House thought to explore whether Saudi Arabia would be willing to jail bin Laden. As it turned out, they were not, and the Clinton Administration declined to press them. Bin Laden was the son of a powerful family of Saudi industrialists with business connections to major U.S. and European firms, and with other forms of influence built up through the family's large bequests to major American universities. So, predictably enough, the Riyadh connection struck out and, in the end, the White House nonchalantly decided to let bin Laden go about his business.

Bin Laden departed Khartoum by plane in May to return to his old haunts in Afghanistan where he had financed and trained *mujaheddin* for the war against the Soviet Union in the 1980s. Before long, bin Laden's particular business began to thrive. Just five weeks after bin Laden was turned loose in Afghanistan, Al-Qaeda attacked another American target. On June 25, 1996, a truck with several hundred pounds of TNT drove up to the perimeter of the

Khobar Towers military barracks in Saudi Arabia, where hundreds of American GI's were housed. Without any adequate alarm system to alert the residents, American sentries spotting the truck were stymied, and 19 servicemen were killed in the massive explosion. (In a twisted turn of fate, the contract for reconstructing the American barracks was awarded to the Saudi construction company run by bin Laden's brothers.)

As bin Laden's plane lifted off from Khartoum, no one in a position of responsibility in Washington was able to convince a distractible President to intercept or divert bin Laden's airplane, and evidently none tried to do so. One of the reasons turned on the administration's reading of the law. Terrorist financier and clear and present danger as he was, bin Laden had never been "linked to a dead American" by the measure of strict juridical standards. Thus, when the opportunity arose to capture bin Laden, FBI director Louis Freeh opposed it. He did so out of worry that the Justice Department would not be able to make a successful criminal case against him in an American courtroom. The White House deferred to this fatal misjudgment. (Secondhand reports suggest that former President Clinton is now aware of this error, and considers it perhaps the worst mistake of his presidency.)

Why was Mr. Freeh so reluctant to get his hands on bin Laden in 1996? The trouble is that information obtained from terrorism suspects in interrogations or confessions is not admissible in domestic American criminal trials unless the informant is willing to testify directly. It is possible, therefore, for the government to have reliable information obtained through intelligence channels and still not be able to use it as evidence in an American court of law. On the surface, Freeh's worries were justifiable. It would have been disastrous to have snatched bin Laden only to have had to set him free again because a conviction against him could not be obtained.

But Freeh's worries were justifiable only on the surface. The responsible officials at that time read the law in a narrow and needlessly self-constraining fashion. The fact is that the law of war permits anticipatory self-defense. It is anticipatory self-defense, for example, to cut off the bankroll that underwrites and replenishes terrorist networks. Even domestic law condemns individuals who aid and abet crimes, as well as those who "induce" criminal activities. Under the law of conspiracy, a sponsor is liable for ongoing criminal acts, whether or not he knows of a particular target, so long as he knows the general nature of the criminal enterprise. In March 1996, bin Laden clearly fulfilled these requirements.

The notion of anticipatory self-defense is hardly a new idea. In the 19th century, for example, Daniel Webster recognized the right of the British under "anticipatory self-defense" to stop an expedition of Irish Fenian revolutionaries from crossing the Niagara river into Canada, even if the revolutionaries had not yet committed any specific crimes on Canadian soil. The point, however, is that to apply this concept it is necessary for U.S. officials to recognize that the law of war is appropriate to the situation at hand. There has been a great deal of confusion about this—less since September 11 than before it, but much confusion nonetheless. Terrorism has to do with attacks on civilians for any number of political purposes. It is a criminal activity although, raised to the level of mass-casualty results, it can also be construed sensibly as an act of war, particularly if states have been complicit in the activity. But attacks against uniformed military personnel operating on foreign soil—even if they are American military personnel—are not, strictly speaking, acts of terrorism. No matter how unconventional they may be, these are acts of war. The October 1993 attack on the U.S. Marine compound in Lebanon, the attack on Khobar Towers, the bombing of the U.S.S. *Cole*, all fall into this category. In that light, it is a stretch *not* to apply the law of war to such cases.

Clearly, it has been—and it still is—a very dangerous intellectual failure to confuse what the proper role of criminal law in the realm of national security should be. Our inability to satisfy artificial rules of trial evidence does not mean that an international fugitive should be left to roam around with TNT and willing accomplices. Even if bin Laden's activities before May 1996 did not carry the point home, the East African embassy bombings of August 1998 surely should have. Those bombings, which not only destroyed our embassies in Dar-es-Salaam and Nairobi but also killed 200 people and wounded 4,500, were a major escalation in bin Laden's campaign against the United States. But for Washington, gripped in the midst of the Monica maelstrom, these attacks failed to pass the threshold of seriousness.

As may be recalled, the Clinton Administration responded two weeks later with Tomahawk missiles launched against targets in Sudan and Afghanistan. However, the only serious target was a rumored meeting of bin Laden and his lieutenants in one of his Afghan training camps. The targeting of sites in Khartoum proved especially problematic. The main plant suspected of chemical weapons manufacture was dropped from the list because of the possibility of collateral damage. The second proposed target, the al-Shifa pharmaceutical plant, was not known to be anything more than a transshipment point. (In trying to justify the selection of al-Shifa as a target for U.S. strikes, the principals of the Clinton foreign policy team boggled the basic facts about the plant in their press briefings, which detracted from the credibility of U.S. strikes.) But the more serious issue was timing. To avoid any collateral damage, the dispatch of the Tomahawks was delayed (until 7:30 PM in Sudan and 10:00 PM in Afghanistan). By that point, the meeting of bin Laden's lieutenants had broken up. Foes and allies alike dismissed "Operation Infinite Reach" as a botched job.

The Clinton Administration, however, felt that its approach to terrorism—treating individual perpetrators as criminals rather than conceiving their collective efforts as acts of war—was vindicated by the successful prosecutions which unfolded in the Federal courthouse in lower Manhattan. Sixteen defendants were found guilty of the 1993 World Trade Center bombing in trials conducted from 1994 to 1996. Carrying over efforts from the Clinton tenure, the Bush Justice Department managed to convict four conspirators of the East African embassy bombings in May 2001. Officials in both the past and current administration judged these results to be significant successes.

And then, three months later, within just six blocks of the same courthouse, the World Trade Center collapsed and nearly 5,000 lives were lost.

In a real war against terrorists, each cell member counts as a combatant. Under the law of war and legitimate rules of engagement, each can be targeted as a member of a hostile force. If he should surrender, he can be detained as an unprivileged combatant while the conflict is underway. Authorities need not wait for each conspirator to complete a terror attack before rounding up each member of the network. Terrorists are illegal combatants, to be sure—they do not rise to the dignity of prisoners of war because they fail to carry arms openly and deliberately use terror against civilians as an illicit instrument of intimidation. But the law of war is still applicable.

Indeed, the law of war has a separate quiver of criminal tools appropriate to the exigencies of international terrorism. Bin Laden and his cohort can be tried by a military commission just as legitimately as a civilian court. President Franklin Roosevelt convened such a commission to try the German saboteurs who plotted to blow up U.S. facilities during World War II. President Lincoln used military commissions during the Civil War to try agents who took over civilian vessels for the Confederate Navy. Military commissions can be carefully structured to ensure fair process. Moreover, unlike civil courts, where proceedings become a matter of public record, military commissions can prevent the disclosure of sensitive intelligence information.

Osama bin Laden enjoys no right to be a para-American. He has no right to demand a domestic civilian trial in the O.J. fashion of "anything-goes" due process. In his 1998 *fatwa*, he declared war against the United States, and he has launched terrorist paramilitary operations here and abroad. Thus, if he and his lieutenants should be caught before they are killed, they can be tried under the laws of war.

Treating terrorism as if it were simply another form of crime to be handled by law enforcement agencies also has had negative repercussions overseas. Part of the rationale for treating all unconventional attacks against the United States and U.S. forces and assets abroad is that we can secure better cooperation with others through legal means than through a diplomacy unaided by reciprocal legal obligations. Unfortunately, practice has generally betrayed theory. Washington has gone repeatedly to its Arab allies, asking them for help in apprehending terrorists, putting members of local terrorist networks on trial, restricting their travel, or expelling known members from the country. Time and again, we have been disappointed, unwilling to accept that that many governments are intimidated by the terror networks. A number of regimes have struck Faustian bargains with the terrorists, allowing them free rein to operate in return for protection against attack. For too long, the United States has chosen to ignore the reality that it must undertake its own defense, and that it simply cannot delegate this responsibility to others. We cannot achieve through legal arrangements that which we are manifestly unprepared to achieve by other means.

It is now five years since bin Laden's escape to Afghanistan, and it took the tragedy of the September 11 bombings to finally cure our political attention deficit to the terrorist war against the United States. Now, at long last, we must get serious and understand that self-defense sometimes requires acting unilaterally and before the fact, without deferring to the sensibility of nominal allies in the region and, most importantly, without tripping unnecessarily over our own legal system. As Alice's Queen of Hearts might say, it is madness to have criminal trials first, and self-defense only later.

15

The Reach of American Law

*Robert H. Bork**

The Supreme Court made a great many headlines last term. The abortion and high school commencement prayer decisions aside, few attracted more press attention and scandalized commentary, both at home and abroad, than the holding that our courts can try a Mexican citizen whom the United States kidnapped from his own country.

The *New York Times* editorial page called the decision "astonishing" and agreed with the three dissenting justices that it was "monstrous." Senator Daniel Patrick Moynihan, who frequently sees violations of international law in American actions abroad, said, "The decision is manifestly wrong." In the *Los Angeles Times,* under the headline "The Supreme Court's Insult to Law-Abiding Countries," a law professor denounced the "moral shabbiness of both our nation's conduct and the court's approval" of it, the "intellectual poverty" of Chief Justice Rehnquist's majority opinion, and an "intense and extreme ... right-wing activism" that is "against individual rights." Canada, Switzerland, and nations all over Latin America protested.

The excitement is misplaced, for the decision is undoubtedly correct. It does, however, raise in a dramatic context the vexed issue of the respective duties of courts and the executive branch with respect to the reach of U.S. law abroad.

Pursuant to a joint effort to stop or lessen international drug trafficking, Mexico allows agents of the U. S. Drug Enforcement Agency to operate on its territory. Enrique ("Kiki") Camarena-Salazar, one such American agent, was kidnapped by Mexican drug traffickers and tortured with a red hot pipe to make him reveal what information law enforcement officials had. He was then

---

*Robert H. Bork is a senior fellow at the American Enterprise Institute.

This essay was originally published in *The National Interest*, no. 29 (Fall 1992).

killed. The DEA had reason to believe that one Humberto Alvarez-Machain, a physician and citizen of Mexico, assisted in this grisly proceeding by prolonging Camarena's life, so that his torture and interrogation could be extended.

Lower level DEA officials, determined to bring Alvarez to justice, offered a reward for his delivery to this country. Alvarez was seized in his office in Guadalajara, taken by private plane to El Paso, Texas, and arrested there by DEA officers.

Alvarez was indicted for several crimes, including conspiracy to kidnap and kidnapping a federal agent, and the felony murder of a federal agent. These are crimes under U.S. law wherever they occur. The district court, however, held that it lacked jurisdiction because Alvarez's abduction at the insistence of the U.S. government violated the extradition treaty with Mexico. The court of appeals affirmed, but the Supreme Court reversed and remanded the case for trial.

The Opinions

Of the three types of issues the Alvarez abduction raises—legal, diplomatic, and moral—the Supreme Court was properly concerned only with the first. Much of the criticism of the Court's decision, however, is made on grounds of morality. Quite aside from the fact that the decision can also be defended on moral grounds, such criticism rests on the increasingly popular supposition that it is the function of the Court to decide on the general "rightness" of matters brought before it—i.e., to decide as the critic would decide if he had combined judicial, legislative, and executive power. Our perception of the Court's role is less and less that of a group of lawyers striving to arrive at the better view of the meaning of law in ambiguous contexts than that of a body of philosophers seeking universal principles of natural justice. It must be admitted that the Court has often accepted just such an inflated view of its function, but in *Alvarez* it did not.

Both the majority opinion by Chief Justice Rehnquist and the dissent by Justice Stevens, joined by Justices Blackmun and O'Connor, engaged in close readings of the extradition treaty to determine whether it forbade the abduction. The dissent found additional support for its conclusion in customary international law, which the majority sloughed off rather quickly. A treaty is, of course, a form of international law, but a form far more definite than many branches of that subject. Customary international law, said to be derived from observation of the actual practices of nations, is frequently vague and internally inconsistent. But a treaty is a legal document rather than commentators' summaries of international practice or a statement of moral principle. The Court majority, therefore, set itself the mundane legal task of interpreting a contract between the United States and Mexico to determine whether the parties had ruled out such a kidnapping.

The terms of the treaty with Mexico, as the chief justice's opinion observed, do not purport to specify the only means by which either country may gain custody of a national of the other in order to prosecute him. The jurisdiction of the trial court had, therefore, to be determined by examination of other legal materials which might give meaning to the silence of the treaty.

There had never been a case quite like this one; it was, in legal parlance, a case of first impression. There were, however, precedents that shed some light. The most prominent were two cases decided on the same day in 1886, *United States v. Rauscher and Ker v. Illinois. Rauscher* held that a person extradited to the United States under a treaty with England could not be prosecuted here for a crime other than the one for which he had been extradited. *Ker* held that a fugitive abducted from Peru by a private person, a Pinkerton agent, could be tried in this country. In the latter case, the Court rejected the argument that the abductee had a right under the existing extradition treaty to be brought here for prosecution only according to the treaty's terms.

It might be thought that *Rauscher should* govern Alvarez's case since the United States was there forbidden to prosecute except in accordance with the treaty. But *Rauscher,* unlike Alvarez, rose out of the cooperation of two governments in law enforcement. It was proper that the United States be confined to the terms of the very treaty it had invoked to obtain the defendant's presence. One cannot demand and receive performance under a contract and simultaneously refuse to be bound by it. There was, moreover, an act of Congress that seemed to confirm this under- standing of the treaty.

The difference between the kidnapping from Peru and *Alvarez,* of course, was that there was no American government involvement in the former case and the Peruvian government had not protested as Mexico did. Still, the principle is much the same. In the absence of a specific law whose protection the defendant is entitled to claim, it does not matter to an American court how the defendant was brought within its jurisdiction. This is perfectly sensible. The kidnapping of Alvarez undoubtedly violated Mexican law, and Mexico asked for the extradition of those it thought responsible for trial in its courts. But U.S. courts do not apply Mexico's criminal code. The request for extradition, moreover, was necessarily addressed to the executive branch; the judiciary would become involved only if the executive complied and the person to be returned appealed to the courts on the ground that his was not an extraditable offense.

The chief justice noted that the *Ker* decision, as well as the position of the United States that the case applied to forcible abductions made outside the United States-Mexico treaty, had been brought to the attention of the Mexican government as early as 1906. Nevertheless, in negotiating the current version of the treaty, Mexico did not attempt to limit the effect of *Ker.* This omission is relevant because the treaty did adopt the principle of the other 1886 decision, *Rauscher, that* an extradited person may be tried only for the offense which was the cause of extradition, even though that principle was already embodied in U.S. law.

Justice Stevens' dissent argued from the comprehensiveness of the treaty that it must be read to govern all methods of obtaining the presence of a foreign national for prosecution here. But his reasoning from the treaty's provisions seems less than airtight:

> Article 9 expressly provides that neither Contracting Party is bound to deliver up its own nationals, although it may do so in its discretion, but if it does not do so, it "shall submit the case to its competent authorities for purposes of prosecution. "

This certainly seems, as the dissent says, to cover the subject of extradition comprehensively, but it does not address the question of one nation's allowable actions if the other neither grants extradition nor initiates a prosecution. Though it is clear that Mexico, if asked, would not extradite Alvarez, it would be unfair to conclude that Mexico would not prosecute him. That nation had already prosecuted, convicted, and given the maximum sentence of forty years to others involved in Camerena's torture-murder. The Court did not address the question of Mexico's intention, which, for reasons to be developed, was a proper omission.

The dissent's citation of other treaty provisions—requiring "sufficient" evidence to grant extradition, withholding extradition for political, military offenses or when the person has already been tried, and the like—do not clarify what happens when these requirements have been satisfied but the country whose national is sought will neither extradite nor prosecute. Thus, it is not entirely true, as the dissent charges, that the majority "concludes that the Treaty merely creates an optional method of obtaining jurisdiction over alleged offenders, and that the parties silently reserved the right to resort to self help whenever they deem force more expeditious than legal process." It would fit the facts of *Alvarez* more accurately to say that the Court concluded, albeit tacitly, that the option of self-help is available when the executive branch thinks the requested state has not complied with Article 9. Again, we have no way of knowing what the executive branch thought, and the Court did well not to inquire.

Alvarez claimed as well that he had been denied due process of law. The *Ker* Court rejected the defendant's argument that his kidnapping violated due process of law, a ruling reaffirmed in 1952 when the Court, in the case of a man kidnapped in Illinois by Michigan officers, held that

> due process of law is satisfied when one present in court is convicted of a crime after having been fairly apprized of the charges against him and after a fair trial in accordance with constitutional procedural safeguards. There is nothing in the Constitution that requires a court to permit a guilty person rightfully convicted to escape justice because he has been brought to trial against his will.

Finally, Alvarez invoked customary international law in an effort to defeat the jurisdiction of the U.S. courts, arguing not that international law applied directly but rather that international kidnappings are so clearly condemned by such law that its principles should guide the interpretation of the treaty. The Court found no principles, other than the most general and unspecific, that justified adding a term to the parties had not adopted.

Conflicting Principles

Actually, there is a fairly specific international law principle relevant to Alvarez's case. A nation's territorial integrity is considered a basic attribute of sovereignty, and that integrity, commentators generally agree, is violated when agents of a foreign nation enter the country to seize persons for trial in the foreign nation. Though it is commonly said that the principles of international law are embodied in the law of the United States, in fact violations are commonly handled not by courts but by the executive branch. Persons abducted abroad and brought here for trial have, upon the protest of the foreign government whose territory was invaded, often been returned.

Moreover, as is common in law, perhaps most particularly in international law, one seemingly firm principle is immediately countered by another. Here, the principle of Mexico's territorial integrity is countered by the right of self-defense of the United States. Even forcible abductions have been justified on that ground. Alvarez's abduction may be justified on a similar principle of self-defense, a principle which would not seem to be affected by whether there was a protest by the nation in which the abduction took place. Abraham Sofaer, then the legal adviser to the State Department, testified to Congress in 1989 that among the factors to be considered are 44 the seriousness of the offense for which the apprehended person is arrested; the citizenship of the offender; whether the foreign government itself had tried to bring the offenders to justice or would have consented to the apprehension had it been asked; and the general tenor of bilateral relations with the United States." These are obviously not factors for consideration by courts but by the political branches of our government.

Drug traffickers, with whom Alvarez was allegedly working, constitute a major threat to this country, which in itself may justify unconsented action against such persons by the American government. Alvarez's specific offense, using his medical skills to keep an American agent alive for additional torture, is among the most heinous that can be imagined.

Whatever the validity of the self-defense argument, which seems tenuous to some, it seems clear that courts should not employ customary international law to limit the president's powers. In 1980, the Department's Office of legal Counsel (OLC) took up the question of the Federal Bureau of Investigation's authority under U. S. law to arrest a fugitive in a foreign country without that country's consent. The 1980 opinion concluded that the principles of customary international law deprived the FBI of any such power under domestic law. The 1980 opinion reasoned that the authority of the United States is limited by the sovereignty of other nations so that the president and Congress could not legally authorize action in a foreign country that ran counter to customary international law, and, it was thought, extraterritorial arrests by the FBI would violate such customary law.

In any event, whether or not the United States was free to depart from customary international law, the FBI itself was subject to its general enabling statutes, and these, while they do not themselves restrict the agency's authority in this regard, must be interpreted to prevent the FBI from departing from the principles of customary international law. The first argument was that the United States itself could never lawfully violate those principles; the second was that even if the United States could, our own statutes must be read not to allow extraterritorial arrests, though the statutes could be changed.

Since these conclusions would place our government under an absolute prohibition against bringing criminals such as terrorists to book under all circumstances, the subject was reexamined by Reagan's OLC, then headed by William Barr, who is now President Bush's attorney general. The conclusions were rather different. Barr's opinion did not quibble about the content of customary international law, but went directly to the issue of the power of the United States to violate or, as he put it, "depart from" those norms. Under our constitutional structure, Barr said, the legislative and executive branches are free to take or direct actions that are not in accord with principles of customary international law. That conclusion found support in an 1814 opinion by Chief Justice John Marshall which described the rule of customary international law as

> a guide which the sovereign follows or abandons at his will. The rule, like other precepts of morality, of humanity, and even of wisdom, is addressed to the judgment of the sovereign; and although it cannot be disregarded by him without obloquy, yet it may be disregarded.

The rule may also be one which cannot be disregarded without incurring not only obloquy but sanctions, challenges in the International Court of justice, suits against the United States in the foreign nation whose law was violated, deterioration of relations with the country in which the abduction took place, and reduced law enforcement cooperation by other nations. But these consequences, however much they should count in making a decision to conduct an abduction abroad, are legally irrelevant to the authority of the United States under its own law to seize foreigners abroad for trial here. All these considerations properly fall within the discretion of the executive branch and Congress and are not properly the subject of judicial determination.

The Barr opinion also rejected the conclusion of the 1980 opinion with respect to the limitations customary international law places upon the FBI's enabling statutes. The Bureau is given authority to make arrests without any specification of a territorial limitation. Because the president has constitutional authority to act contrary to customary international law, the restrictions of that law should not be attached to general statutes in a way that prevents the president from exercising his authority. Barr's 1989 opinion seems correct. International law, including customary international law, should not affect our constitutional arrangements, however desirable it may be that the executive branch make every effort to act in conformity with internationally recognized principles.

The chief justice's opinion did not discuss the firmness of Mexico's determination to try Alvarez, the various principles and counter-principles of international law that might be brought into play, or the opposed views of OLC in 1980 and 1989. At first sight, this may seem cavalier, but it was probably deliberate and undoubtedly wise. Had the Court entered upon these subjects, it would have had to discuss such matters as Mexico's law enforcement. Assuming, as seems entirely likely, that judicial inquiry would have found that Mexico would prosecute and punish Alvarez, the Court would have committed itself to engage in such inquiries with regard to other countries in future cases. The mere fact of such an inquiry would be resented and an adverse determination would certainly heighten the strain on our relations with the country in question. Rehnquist's opinion closed, perhaps for that reason, with the observation that there are benefits in allowing these matters to be resolved by diplomacy.

The Executive's Call

Alvarez is best seen, therefore, as a sound separation of powers decision. That is the meaning of the Court's observation that "[Alvarez] and his *amici* may be correct that [his] abduction was 'shocking' . . . and that it may be in violation of general international law principles. Mexico has protested the abduction of [Alvarez] through diplomatic notes ... and the decision of whether [he] should be returned to Mexico, as a matter outside of the Treaty, is a matter for the Executive Branch."

One of the difficulties with the case is that the decision to kidnap Alvarez was not made by executive branch officials with no responsibility for our foreign affairs. That difficulty was cured in this instance because the abduction was ratified when the United States refused either to return the abducted Mexican or to amend the extradition treaty between the two countries to prohibit such kidnappings. It is now U.S. policy that such abductions may be made only with the agreement of the president and the Departments of State and justice. The refusal to amend the treaty to ban kidnapping may reflect the judgment that this would require amending all extradition treaties to which the United States is a party. Our government could not very well pick and choose on the ground that some governments are trustworthy and some are not. The decision not to eschew kidnapping in all cases undoubtedly reflects a further judgment that this tactic must be held in reserve in an era with a rising incidence of terrorism and international drug trafficking that threatens Americans abroad and at home.

There are, of course, very good reasons why the United States may resort to the forcible removal of a suspect in violation of foreign law and in opposition to the wishes of the foreign government involved. Some governments actively sponsor terrorism directed at Americans or have officials who are themselves heavily involved in drug trafficking; some display high degrees of corruption in law enforcement; some would find it politically unpopular to turn over their nationals to the United States for trial; some, having found on their own soil terrorists or drug traffickers of other nations, are afraid of violence against their own citizens in retaliation. Unless the United States is willing to render its citizens even more vulnerable, there will be occasions when it must seize foreigners on foreign soil or on ships or airplanes registered in or owned by other countries. There are more U.S. laws that apply to actions taken abroad by foreign nationals than most people realize. Reacting to specific acts of terrorism, Congress has gradually expanded the list of crimes abroad that are punishable here. Initially, airline hijacking was covered; then, after the assassinations of President John F. Kennedy and Senator Robert Kennedy, Congress enacted a criminal prohibition on the murder of a president or vice president anywhere in the world. After the murder of a diplomat, Congress gave criminal jurisdiction to U. S. courts to try those who killed or assaulted designated diplomatic employees, and moved on a few years later to outlaw assaults, murders, and kidnappings of members of the Cabinet, the Supreme Court, and Congress. When terrorists began attacking or seizing Americans who held no government positions, Congress first provided criminal penalties for those who took American hostages, and finally went the whole route by providing criminal jurisdiction here over those who kill or assault Americans anywhere in the world in acts of terrorism. There is no real doubt concerning the legality of these exercises of jurisdiction. There is also no real doubt that if an American president were assassinated in Algeria by a citizen of that country, Americans would support the assassin's abduction—even those who now denounce the seizure of the accomplice to Camarena's assassination.

The separation of powers problems inherent in the extraterritorial application of U.S. law are not always so easily resolved as in *Alvarez.* Matters are clearest when a decision is made at the highest levels of the executive branch. Whatever one thinks of the wisdom of the attorney general's recent statement of his intention to apply U.S. antitrust laws to Japanese firms acting in Japan, there is no doubt that American relations with Japan were taken into account by those to whom the Constitution delegates that task.

Unfortunately, precisely those considerations of international relations which the separation of powers delegates to the political branches are brought into court for adjudication when a state or a private party invokes the extraterritorial jurisdiction of the court. The recent indictment of Saudi Sheik Kamal Adham, obtained by New York State in the BCCI scandal, shows the potential for state embarrassment of our foreign relations. But the most frequent complications arise in private antitrust actions.

The Sherman Act applies to both the domestic and foreign commerce of the United States and actions taken abroad by citizens of other nations can have the requisite jurisdictional impact on either form of commerce. A price-fixing cartel consisting of foreign companies that sell worldwide can obviously affect the amount of imports flowing into the United States as well as prices in our domestic market. Such effects have been held to be sufficient to support antitrust jurisdiction in American courts. It hardly needs saying that such jurisdiction, and the resultant demand for documents, testimony, and the possible imposition of damage awards frequently leads to angry responses by foreign governments. Some governments have enacted blocking statutes to prevent the production of documents or testimony by their nationals.

There are doctrines intended to mitigate the extent to which U. S. courts can interfere with our foreign relations by assuming jurisdiction over actors in or policies of other countries. One is the principle of comity, which means that the U. S. court whose jurisdiction is invoked by a private party will make a judgment about which state has the paramount interest in the matter and defer to its law. Another is the act of state doctrine, which holds that our courts will not question acts required to be done on its own soil by a foreign nation. Neither of these doctrines has provided a satisfactory resolution of the conflicts between our courts' assertions of extraterritorial jurisdiction and the desire of other nations not to have their policies hampered or their citizens harassed by our courts.

Our Antitrust Law Abroad

In the late 1970s, for example, private antitrust actions were brought in a number of federal and state courts against firms involved in an international uranium cartel. The Canadian, Australian, British, and South African governments filed briefs in many of those actions stating that the cartel had been formed according to the affirmative policies of those governments, and U.S. antitrust laws should not be applied to the uranium producers involved. Our courts were signally unimpressed. In one case, a federal court of appeals published an opinion criticizing the subservience of the foreign governments to the uranium companies. There was not the slightest justification for that remark and it was bitterly resented. Our State Department wrote to the court, asking that such language not be used.

For one American defendant, I argued the act of state doctrine as a defense in four different courts, with uniform and complete lack of success. The results say a good deal about the deficiencies of court-evolved principles to deal with foreign relations problems raised by assertions of extraterritorial jurisdiction. My argument was straightforward: foreign nations stated that they had required participation in the cartel as a condition of mining uranium in their territories; the act of state doctrine both insulated the cartelists from the Sherman Act and prohibited our courts from doubting the word of the foreign nations involved. Each court seemed to take the argument seriously, deliberated at some length, but then ruled that the act of state doctrine was no defense—without a word of explanation.

Though the argument seemed airtight, I think I understand why we lost and why no judge wrote an opinion: the argument was too airtight—it could not be refuted and it also could not be accepted. If the word of the United Kingdom about its policies had to be accepted, then, in the next case, the court might find itself urged to accept the word of a Muammar Qadaffi or a Leonid Brezhnev. There are duplicitous as well as reliable foreign governments. To accept the act of state argument in the uranium cartel case would place the court in the future position of leaving American plaintiffs at the mercy of corrupt foreign governments, or of having to decide which governments were trustworthy and which were not. The first alternative is difficult, perhaps impossible, to accept, while the second involves an even greater interference with the relations between the United States and other nations than the exercise of extraterritorial jurisdiction.

It may seem that the solution to such dilemmas is to have the executive branch, through the State Department, inform the court whether the exercise of jurisdiction is appropriate in such cases; but that, too, has serious problems. It is one thing for the executive branch to limit its own invocation of a court's jurisdiction for reasons of state; it is quite another for the executive branch to urge the courts to deny relief to an American citizen who has an otherwise valid claim. Fairness aside, there are apt to be domestic political repercussions. In the uranium cartel cases, repeated, but always unsuccessful, efforts were made to get the State Department to make representations to the courts about the impropriety of doubting the word and ignoring the policies of the foreign governments.

The State Department lawyers recognized the problems with the act of state doctrine, but even if there had been no doctrinal difficulties, for the Department to file on the side of the cartelists would have meant spending scarce political capital. Members of the Senate had expressed their outrage that the Department of Justice, recognizing the foreign relations problems, had let the companies off with a slap on the wrist.

Scholarly debate has swirled and will continue to swirl around exercises of extraterritorial jurisdiction by the United States. Given the nature of the problem, no entirely satisfactory resolution seems possible, at least where such jurisdiction is invoked by states or private parties. The indictment in August of fugitive Columbian drug trafficker Pablo Escobar by a New York federal court, and the announcement by the U.S. government of a $2 million reward for information leading to his capture, show how timely this issue remains. It is encouraging, however, that the Rehnquist Court, in the context of extraterritorial executive action, has resisted the impulse to insert the courts into what is best seen as a foreign policy question entrusted to the political branches.

16

Law in the Service of Terror

*Douglas J. Feith**

Were there nothing more to it than destruction and brutality, terrorism would not command the world's attention as it does. It is gripping because its purpose is grand: the getting (or keeping) of political power. To fail to recognize terrorism as political method—more than simple madness or simple crime—is to preclude appreciation of why terrorist organizations do much of what they do.

Such organizations devote a great deal of effort to participating in international conferences, cultivating relations with governments, and capitalizing on their own earnest invocations of international law as the source and the sign of their struggles' legitimacy. It seems bizarre that a group willing to murder children as a means of conveying a message would concern itself with what people think of its legal or moral grounding. But such is the case.

That terrorist organizations take international law seriously (which is not at all to say that they comply with it) is evident from the history of the Geneva Diplomatic Conference on the Reaffirmation and Development of International Humanitarian Law Applicable in Armed Conflict—hereafter the Diplomatic Conference—which met from 1974 to 1977 under the auspices of the International Committee for the Red Cross (ICRC).

The record of the Diplomatic Conference sheds light on how terrorism, law, and politics tie together. It calls attention to the gulf that divides Western liberal political culture from that of totalitarian and most Third World powers with respect to conceptions of law and of human rights. It reveals the pitfalls of dialogue in the absence of common values, common interests, and common usage of words. And it opens for examination the negotiating techniques West-

---

*Douglas J. Feith serves as the Undersecretary of Defense for Policy in the George W. Bush Administration and, at the time this article was written, was serving as the deputy assistant secretary of defense for negotiations policy.

This essay originally appeared in *The National Interest*, no. 1 (Fall 1985).

erners routinely employ in international forums, techniques rooted in the conviction that consensus is more important than principle.

Humanitarian Law

The law of armed conflict has traditionally been divided into "Hague rules," which limit the means and methods of allowable warfare (e.g., what may be targeted, what weapons and techniques may be used), and "Geneva rules," which mandate humane treatment of war victims. The four Geneva Conventions of 1949 form the crux of inter- national humanitarian law.

In the years after 1949, the sporadic efforts to promote conferences to modify the Geneva Conventions bore little fruit. But by 1974, the ground had become amply fertile, largely by means of United Nations General Assembly resolutions that supported "national liberation movements" and thereby highlighted the Geneva Conventions' failure to sanction the kind of warfare such movements usually wage. Interest in creating rights for irregular forces combined with other interests—for example, that of the ICRC in increasing protection for its medical personnel and that of the United States in pressing North Vietnam for an accounting of U.S. prisoners of war and the remains of fallen U.S. soldiers—to draw 126 states in February 1974 to participate in the first session of the Diplomatic Conference.

Notwithstanding its humanitarian subject matter and the legal nature of its mission, the Diplomatic Conference from its inception operated as most United Nations forums then did (and do), as a theater for harshly expounded, highly ideological politics. The major international events and circumstances of the period—the successful wars against Portuguese rule in southern Africa; the North Vietnamese conquest of South Vietnam; the assertion of power by Third World oil exporting states, in particular Arab states; the PLO's inspirational alchemic accomplishment in converting terrorism into broadly based diplomatic stature; the Soviet Union's rapidly increasing military power and its growing role in "wars of national liberation" far outside Russia's historical sphere of activity; and the traumas inflicted on the United States by Vietnam and Watergate—tended to embolden many non-Western conference participants and proved unconducive to disinterestedness and to deference to traditional principles of international order.

Liberation Law Promoted

The Diplomatic Conference's work on updating the 1949 Conventions was based on two draft protocols, the first covering "international" and the second "non- international" armed conflicts. How to categorize "wars of national liberation" was a heated issue with weighty legal and diplomatic ramifications, and it arose at the outset.

So the Diplomatic Conference lost little time in adopting a resolution that invited the participation of "national liberation movements" from around the world. The following groups accepted and, though they lacked entitlement to vote, participated in rewriting the international community's humanitarian law: African National Congress (South Africa); African National Council of Zimbabwe (Rhodesia); Angola National Liberation Front (FNLA); Mozambique Liberation Front; Palestine Liberation Organization; Panafricanist Congress (South Africa); People's Movement for the Liberation of Angola (MPLA); Seychelles People's United Party; South West Africa People's Organization; Zimbabwe African National Union; and Zimbabwe African People's Union.

The original working draft stated simply that Protocol I applies to those situations that the 1949 Geneva Conventions classified as international conflicts. At the Diplomatic Conference, amendments were proposed to specify that such situations include wars of national liberation, defined with reference to the struggles of "peoples" against "colonial domination," "alien occupation," and "racist regimes."[1] Most struggles of that kind, entailing the direct involvement of only one sovereign state, had for years commonly been deemed internal or non-international matters. Declaring such struggles to be international, however, would legitimate the many foreign interventions, diplomatic and material, made on behalf of the various "national liberation movements." As the East German representative explained:

> [T]he General Assembly ... [has] declared that "armed conflicts involving the struggle of peoples against colonial and alien domination and racist regimes are to be regarded as international armed conflicts in the sense of the 1949 Geneva Conventions". That resolution was extremely important because it confirmed that the colonial Power had no rights of sovereignty over colonial territories and peoples, [and] that assistance by foreign States to the liberation struggle of colonial peoples did not constitute interference in the domestic affairs of the colonial Power....

Proponents of applying Protocol I to "national liberation" conflicts contended that the treaty should affirm both "the right of peoples to self-determination," and the "lawfulness" of armed conflict to realize that right. The characterization of self-determination as a right was repeatedly attributed to the United Nations Charter. Wars fought to achieve that right were often referred to as "just" or "legitimate." The failure of the Diplomatic Conference to consecrate such wars, it was said, would amount to a denial of both political reality and current law. According to the USSR representative, the "sole object" of the proposed national-liberation-war language was to "embody in humanitarian law a rule which was already in existence and which took into account the realities of the times." Opposition to such language could be attributed only to mean self-interest on the part of Western imperialists. The Tanzanian representative declared that his delegation "was not prepared to accept a humanitarian law drawn up solely in the interest of the imperialist powers." The Nigerian representative later added that "if the Conference did not agree that the national liberation struggles were governed by draft Protocol 1, his delegation's fears would be confirmed: the problems would be dealt with solely from the point of view of the western Powers, in defiance of the principles of international law...."

The Senegalese representative warned that a wrong decision on this issue by the Diplomatic Conference could aggravate the problem of terrorism:

> It was the feeling of injustice so engendered which was mainly responsible for what was described as "international terrorism." When thousands of innocent people were daily being slaughtered in many parts of the world, it was difficult for people to be shocked at the few dozen innocent victims of the hijacking or sabotage of airliners. Without justice, humanitarian law was merely an empty word.

Liberation Law Dispraised

Opponents of the amendments on "wars of national liberation" denounced them as destructive not only of humanitarian law, but of the prohibition against war promulgated in Article 2(4) of the United Nations Charter, the first principle of international law since World War II. They argued that the amendments would legally sanction the resurrection of the medieval "just war" doctrine[2] and effectively abolish the distinction between international and non-international conflicts. Furthermore, the most important terms in the amendments lacked definition, so the application of humanitarian law would depend on subjective judgments rooted in politics.

The British representative expressed "surprise" at the text of the amendments:

> The various arguments had presented no convincing case for considering an internal struggle as an international one. Moreover, it was a basic principle of the Geneva Conventions, The Hague Regulations and other instruments that legal and humanitarian protection should never vary according to the motives of those engaged in a particular armed struggle. Deviation from that principle would mean damaging the structure of The Hague and Geneva Conventions and would involve the need to reconstruct the whole of humanitarian law. Moreover, to discriminate between the motives of those engaged in the struggle would violate essential principles of human rights.
>
> It was true that self-determination was mentioned in the Charter of the United Nations, but as principle, not as a right. Nowhere in the Charter did the right to engage in armed struggle appear. No resolution of the United Nations could amend the Charter, which would remain inviolate until amended in the proper manner. Terms like "struggle for the self-determination of peoples" were all too vague. What is a "people"? Such terms were elastic, as Biafra and Bangladesh had shown. They could not be used as a basis for law-making.

The Swiss delegate elaborated further on the distinction between law and politics:

> [The amendments] tended to establish a particular category of conflicts on the basis of subjective criteria stemming from the causes of those conflicts and the aims of the parties. That entailed a move from the field *jus in bello* to a zone which held dangers for the Conference, namely, *jus ad bellum*.... [I]t would be very dangerous, and against the spirit of humanitarian law, to classify armed conflicts on the basis of non-objective and non-legal criteria.

States like Iraq, Nigeria, the Soviet Union, and Yugoslavia, which can be (and have been) charged with denying the right of self-determination to certain of their national and ethnic groups, supported the national-liberation-war amendments without evincing concern that such groups would derive any aid or comfort from them. The amendments' opponents pointed out that there existed no objective standards for judging whether a group qualified as a national liberation movement. "Any separatist band of armed criminals in a colonial territory might claim to be engaged in an armed struggle in furtherance of their people's right to self-determination," observed the Irish representative. The amendments' supporters, however, saw the matter not primarily as one of definitive standards but of international recognition; the prevailing view was that a national liberation movement is any group recognized as such by "the regional intergovernmental organizations concerned"—for example, by the League of Arab States or the Organization of African Unity. Indeed, it was on that basis that the movements listed above were invited to participate in the Diplomatic Conference. Given the nature and record of those regional bodies, one could confidently predict whether a given armed group would obtain recognition as an authentic national liberation movement or whether, for reasons of its unprogressiveness or the inadvisability of crossing its antagonist, it would be denied the protections of Protocol I.

Several states objected that extending Protocol I to wars of national liberation would discriminate invidiously against sovereign states in favor of irregular forces fighting them in their own territory. The problem would arise because the irregular force and its state-enemy would both enjoy rights under Protocol I and the 1949 Geneva Conventions, but only the latter would command the kind of resources (e.g., law courts and medical facilities) required for the fulfillment of the corresponding obligations. The Italian representative commented:

> [T]he word "Powers" used in the ... Geneva Conventions could only mean States and not authorities other than States. That fact was borne out not only by the letter and spirit of the Conventions, but also by the circumstances that application of many provisions of the Geneva Conventions called for complicated machinery which was, generally speaking, available only to States.

The United States representative later added:

> Liberation movements could not fulfill all their obligations under the Conventions and would thus be branded as being in violation of those Conventions. The only benefit which those movements would receive from labeling their struggle as international would be enhanced political status, but nothing on the humanitarian plane.

The representatives of the Mozambique Liberation Front and the PLO dismissed this objection, treating the issue as one of good intentions, respect for law, and willingness to do all one can do, rather than as a matter of objective capability to perform an extensive list of specified duties.

The last major argument against extending Protocol I to wars of national liberation invoked the practical principle that humanitarian law should be crafted to encourage compliance. If the law's applicability to a group of fighters hinged on their cause's legitimacy, a state battling a "national liberation" group would refuse to apply the law, lest it make a fatal political concession. In the words of the Israeli representative:

> Protocol I's national-liberation-war provision] had within it a built-in non-applicability clause, since a party would have to admit that it was either racist, alien or colonial .... [S]uch language . . .ensured that no State by its own volition would ever apply that article.

Ends and Means

A very large portion of the Diplomatic Conference, which ran for over three years, was spent in this debate over the status of "wars of national liberation." Though it generated its share of heat, the debate is remarkable for the dearth of actual engagement between the sides. They generally talked past one another.

The participants who adhered to the traditional concepts underlying the 1949 Geneva Conventions, who for ease of reference and with general accuracy may be labeled "Western," distinguished between considerations appropriate for a political body, such as the United Nations General Assembly, and those suitable for either a humanitarian organization like the ICRC or a treaty-drafting body like the Diplomatic Conference. Accordingly, as we have seen, they made their case against the national- liberation-war amendments with legal arguments.

Their concept of law derived from that body of philosophy, the pride of Western civilization, whose appendages include the Magna Carta, the United States Constitution, and the *Declaration of the Rights of Man.* In brief, it is law as impartial principle, expressed in objective phraseology, duly defined, to be applied to specific cases by disinterested judges. Its essence is fair procedure—due process of law—which binds all elements of society, including the government. Its purpose is to safeguard the rights of individuals from the depredations of other private actors and of the government. Where this conception prevails, law imposes limitations on all political activity within the state, even that of the party in power, which is held accountable for any violations. In such circumstances, the notion of a common good is derived from the ground up—that is, from the protection of the rights of individuals. This Western view of law does not allow for a group to invoke "the people's interest" to justify depriving an individual, without due process of law, of his life, liberty, or property. Nor does it allow for action in the name of the people in the absence of their express consent.

The Western representatives' legal arguments made no apparent impression on their interlocutors from the "Socialist" camp and from much of the Third World. In most of the world outside the West, law does not constrain governments; indeed, it often serves merely as a device by which ruling parties suppress their opponents. Adherents to the view that collective interests—described as those of the ruling party, the state, the people, or whatever—necessarily outweigh the interests of individuals have understandable difficulty in conceiving of law as it is known in the West. As the record of the Diplomatic Conference makes plain, the idea of law as separate from and above politics is the light and delight of a small minority of nations.

This helps account for much of the ships- passing-in-the-night nature of the Article I debate. The Western representatives wanted to weigh the merits of competing legal formulations. The non-Westerners wanted to use the Protocol to strengthen approved "national liberation movements." The Westerners argued that such a political aim may be legitimate for a political resolution of the United Nations, but not for a legal document. The non-Westerners rejected the distinction and continually made erroneous reference to General Assembly resolution as international law.[3] The Westerners warned that vague and subjective wording would make humanitarian law a tool of politics. The non-Westerners already viewed it as such and evidently considered the circumstance desirable; none expressed qualms about making the applicability of the law to irregulars a matter for decision by the Arab League, the OAU, and other such political forums.

The Westerners defended the merit of the political neutrality of the UN Charter and the 1949 Geneva Conventions. They explained that amending and reinterpreting so as to politicize those treaties would negate the advance (rare and valuable, albeit largely theoretical) that they effected in the direction of world peace and respect for human rights. Certain states and causes, to be sure, could reap quick benefits from such mischief, but these would likely prove fleeting in a world where international law, having lost its neutrality, lost its moral force and therefore much of its sway over those states that heed it.

This cut little ice with the "Socialist" and Third World delegates, many of whom denied that existing international law was neutral and described it as pro-imperialist or pro-Western. Moreover, a number spoke as if there were no such thing as a neutral principle of law. They seemed to view international law as a zero-sum game: if a provision is supported by the West, it must be undesirable for the Third World.

Liberation Law Ascendant

The debate, in short, produced no meeting of minds on fundamentals. The Westerners presented their case force- fully and generally emphasized the points that most deserved emphasis-that the proposed national-liberation-war language would legitimate certain types of war, license belligerent foreign meddling in the sovereign domain of certain states, politicize humanitarian law, and thereby render that law even less sturdy a shield for its intended beneficiaries.

Given this critique, it may surprise the reader to learn that the relevant part of Article I of Protocol 1, as ultimately adopted by the Diplomatic Conference with but one negative vote, reads (in relevant part) as follows:

> The situations [to which Protocol I applies] include armed conflicts in which peoples are fighting against colonial domination and alien occupation and against racist regimes in the exercise of their right of self-determination, as enshrined in the Charter of the United Nations and the Declaration of Principles of International Law concerning Friendly Relations and Co-operation among States in accordance with the Charter of the United Nations.

The March 1974 vote in committee on that paragraph was 70 votes in favor and 21 against (Belgium, Canada, Denmark, Federal Republic of Germany, France, Israel, Italy, Japan, Liechtenstein, Luxembourg, Monaco, Netherlands, New Zealand, Portugal, Republic of Korea, South Africa, Spain, Switzerland, United Kingdom, United States, Uruguay), with 13 abstentions (Australia, Austria, Brazil, Burma, Chile, Colombia, Greece, Guatemala, Holy See, Ireland, Philippines, Sweden, and Turkey).

Ultimately, however, the vote in plenary on Article 1, in May 1977, was 87 in favor and one against (Israel), with II abstentions (Canada, Federal Republic of Germany, France, Guatemala, Ireland, Italy, Japan, Monaco, Spain, United Kingdom, and the United States).

The PLO representative was gratified:

> [He expressed] deep satisfaction at the result of the vote, by which the international community had re-confirmed the legitimacy of the struggles of peoples exercising their right to self-determination.... The overwhelming majority against the single vote cast by the Zionist representative was a source of deep satisfaction and would also be an encouragement to the peoples of southern Africa waging a just struggle for self-determination.
>
> The Arab people of Palestine fell within all three of the categories mentioned in paragraph 4: they were under colonial domination; their territory was under foreign occupation, despite the assertions of the terrorist Begin; and they were suffering under

> a racist regime, since Zionism had been recognized in a United Nations resolution as a form of racism. He wished to express his gratitude to the justice- and peace-loving peoples who had given their support to the struggles of all peoples fighting for self-determination.

The record of the Diplomatic Conference is silent on why many of the no-voters became abstainers three years later. In fact, several, in explaining their plenary abstentions, cited the very objections to Article I on which they had justified their earlier "no" votes. The British representative recalled that "the main reason for [UK] opposition ... was that [paragraph 41 introduced the regrettable innovation of making the motives behind a conflict a criterion for the application of humanitarian law." He stated that his delegation has "not wish[ed] to see the Protocol founder on that difference of opinion" and, because "the cardinal principle of equality of application to all participants had been respected," his delegation felt "relieved." The relief seems, however, to flow from begging the question, for the determination as to which fighting group qualifies as a "participant" remains under Protocol I a political judgment.

The United States offered no formal explanation of its plenary vote. It is noteworthy that certain U.S. government lawyers involved in the negotiations recommended, in a 1977 "working group review and analysis," that the U. S. government sign and ratify Protocol 1, refrain from making any reservation regarding Article 1(4), and mitigate the problems inherent in that provision through a strict construction. They observed that "[t]he kinds of conflict that nations deemed covered by the general phrase wars of national liberation were those fought against the foreign element in Vietnam, Guinea-Bissau, Angola, Palestine, southern Africa, and Mozambique," and concluded: "The narrow interpretation suggested above appears to be one that is in the United States interest."

The Uniform and the Irregular

From the point of view of the "Socialist" and Third World delegations, establishing the international character of "national liberation struggles" was a necessary step toward exempting the participants therein from the municipal law of their sovereign enemies. Under the 1949 Geneva Convention on Prisoners of War (GPW), combatants in international conflicts are deemed entitled to commit acts of belligerency that would be punishable if committed by an ordinary individual. And such combatants, if captured by their enemy, have a right to special treatment as prisoners of war. But the GPW does not bestow combatant status on just any fighter, guerrilla, terrorist, or irregular engaged in an international conflict. The conditions for qualification set forth in the GPW favor the interests of non-combatants above those of irregular forces.

Article 4 of the GPW affords combatant status to regular uniformed soldiers (whether or not the power for which they fight is recognized by its enemy as a party to the conflict) and, in subparagraph A(2), to:

> Members of other militias and members of volunteer corps, including those of organized resistance movements, belonging to a Party to the conflict ... provided that such militias or volunteer corps, including such resistance movements, fulfill the following conditions:
>
> (a) that of being commanded by a person responsible for his subordinates;
> (b) that of having a fixed distinctive sign recognizable at a distance;
> (c) that of carrying arms openly;
> (d) that of conducting their operations in accordance with the laws and customs of war.

These conditions have roots in the laws of war that reach back at least to The Hague Conventions of 1907 and 1899, the Brussels Declaration of 1874, and the American Civil War. They effectively preclude non-uniformed paramilitary bands, like the typical terrorist group or national liberation movement, from qualifying for combatant/POW status. Such a force ordinarily is not recognized as a party to the conflict. Unless it has a secure base in a region beyond the writ of the government it is fighting, wearing uniforms and carrying arms openly would be suicidal. And, as previously discussed, such forces usually lack the facilities needed to fulfill the formidable obligations the Geneva Conventions impose on parties. In attempting to explain the stringency of the GPW's standards, some commentators have alleged that the drafters were largely oblivious to guerrilla warfare. The evidence is abundantly to the contrary, however. The irregular exploits of the partisan and resistance movements in World War 11 were too celebrated to have faded from the drafters' memories by 1949.

The rationale for the conditions, especially the "openness" requirements in subsections (b) and (c), is to be found in the traditional solicitude for civilians that is the primary *raison d'être* of international humanitarian law. If one had to render all of humanitarian law while standing on one leg, one might well proclaim: combat- ants are to be distinguished from noncombatants; the rest is commentary. In a war in which the participants appear openly as soldiers, each soldier may reasonably assume that people who look like civilians *are* civilians and that they pose no threat and may safely be spared attack. On the other hand, as G.I.A.D. Draper has noted:

> Once the ... man with the bomb who is a civilian in all outward appearances but can blow you to smithereens as you pass him by, once you bring such a person within the frame- work of the protection given to regular armed combatants under article 4 of the Geneva Prisoners-of-War Convention, you make life for every single civilian hang upon a thread....

At the Diplomatic Conference, however, traditional considerations of the rights and interests of individuals, however, conflicted with the conception of humanitarian law dominant among the "Socialist"/Third World majority. In that conception, humanitarian law is not about individuals, but causes. If a rule that protects innocent bystanders impedes the success of a humanitarian cause-one aimed at liberating a territory from "colonialists," "aliens," or "racists"—it is not a humanitarian rule.

It was clear to all that the respective interests of the civilian and the irregular fighter conflict. "Openness" requirements are invaluable to the former and dangerous for the latter. Whereas the drafters of the GPW interpreted their charter in conformity with traditional individualist ideas of human rights, the majority at the Diplomatic Conference was intent on shifting the balance of the law in favor of the non-uniformed fighter.

Articles 43 and 44 of Protocol I, as adopted by the Diplomatic Conference (see box) make this radical shift. The final plenary vote on Article 44, in April 1977, was 66 in favor (including the U.S.), 2 against (Brazil and Israel), and 18 abstentions.

The Protocol I standards for irregular forces deviate from the long-standing rules in several respects. Among the most important are: (1) There is no requirement for a "fixed distinctive sign—that is, a uniform. (As this exemption applies only to irregulars, Article 44 actually makes it easier for irregulars to obtain combatant/POW status than for a regular soldier to do so.) (2) The general requirement to carry arms openly has been dropped; one must do so only during certain military operations. And (3) a combatant forfeits his right to be a prisoner-of-war only if he violates the narrow "openness" rule of the second sentence of Article 44(3), but even then he retains all the POW protections afforded by the GPW.

It is not difficult to grasp why the PLO representative declared Article 44's adoption in committee "encouraging" and "an important step forward in the growing recognition, through international instruments, of the legitimacy of the struggle of national liberation movements and the need to guarantee their fighters adequate protection"; and one easily comprehends his statement, following its adoption in plenary, that "national liberation movements ... could not fail to welcome the protection accorded to their combatants by [Article 44] ...... What may be less obvious is why the United States, breaking ranks with a number of its allies and other states, voted in favor of the Article and praised it as "an important advance in the law."

Love and the Law You Get

Early on at the Diplomatic Conference, the United States co-sponsored a draft article that would have granted POW status to captured members of irregular forces only if they "distinguished themselves from the civilian population in their military operations by carrying arms openly or by a distinctive sign recognizable at a distance or by any other equally effective means" and otherwise complied with the laws of war. The draft article would have denied POW status to an individual irregular only if he failed to fulfill the broad "openness" conditions. The failure of individual irregulars to fulfill the two conditions would not have deprived other members of their irregular force of POW status upon capture.

That proposed article would have relaxed the GPW "openness" requirements by allowing irregular forces to choose their own means of distinguishing themselves from civilians, but, as a U.S. representative explained, "[t]he single important issue is that combatants be distinguished from civilians-how it is done is not so important as the fact that it is done." The unique importance of openness in all military operations would have been reflected in the provision that made violation of that requirement the sole exception to the rule in favor of POW status. In justification of the proposed exception, the U.S. representative, calling it "fundamental," "essential," and "basic," stated:

> In our view, a combatant who deliberately fails to distinguish himself from other civilians while engaging in combat operations has committed such an extraordinary violation of the laws of war and so prejudices the protection for civilians that he loses his entitlement to be a prisoner of war. . . . The desire and urgency to protect the civilians is no different today than it was in 1907—or 1949—and the lives of civilians are no less important today than they were then.

The gap between this initial U.S. stand on the POW issue and the provisions of Protocol I is difficult to bridge. Article 44, after all, does not condition POW status for irregulars on their distinguishing themselves from civilians during all military operations, and Article 43 fails to make an irregular force's compliance with the laws of war a condition for combatant status.

In explaining his delegation's support for Articles 43 and 44, U.S. Ambassador George A. Aldrich attributed much weight to the first sentence in Article 44(3), which he described as a "basic rule" that "meant that throughout their military operations combatants must distinguish themselves in a clearly recognized manner." The paramount justification, however, was the belief that Protocol I might induce groups like the PLO, SWAPO, and other "movements" participating in the Diplomatic Conference to comply with the laws of war:

> [Article 44] conferred no protection on terrorists. It did not authorize soldiers to conduct military operations while disguised as civilians. However, it did give members of the armed forces who were operating in occupied territory an incentive to distinguish themselves from the civilian population when preparing for and carrying out an attack.

Ambiguous Oaths

Commentators who think the Diplomatic Conference robbed civilian Peter to terrorist Paul are unimpressed with the several admirable provisions in Articles 43 and 44 that Ambassador Aldrich and other Protocol I proponents prefer to highlight. Notwithstanding the first sentence of Article 44(3), the skeptics see the new law as less kind to civilians and more generous to irregulars—guerrillas and terrorists—than is the old law of the GPW. They note that the first sentence of Article 44(3) is less precise than the corresponding provisions in the GPW and in any event is merely hortatory; no rights or privileges hinge on adherence to it. In contrast, fulfillment by irregulars of the "openness" requirements of the GPW is a condition of POW status thereunder. Moreover, the principle embodied in Article 44(3)'s first sentence is vitiated by the next sentence, which actually grants POW status to combatants who do not distinguish themselves from non-combatants during all military operations.

Under Protocol I, whatever protection non-combatants retain against the danger of combatants operating in civilian garb derives from this same, hotly debated second sentence of Article 44(3). Failure to satisfy the "open-ness" obligation it sets forth is the only offense that would cause a combatant to forfeit his right to be a POW. Yet, as the commentators roundly have remarked, several of the provision's pivotal terms are undefined and subject to widely differing interpretation—for example, "deployment." Ambassador Aldrich, in a 1981 law review article, outlined the problem:

> [T]he term "deployment" is a critical one for guerrillas operating in occupied territory. The negotiating history reveals that there was no agreement on the meaning of that term. Some delegates asserted that any movement toward the place from which an attack was to be launched would be part of a "deployment." Certainly, the word is ambiguous....

For those who might wonder why such a "critical" term in so significant a provision was allowed to remain ambiguous, the ambassador volunteers that "its ambiguity was probably essential to agreement at the conference to the text." For those who might rudely query, "Who needs an agreement under such circumstances?" no answer is offered.

As a consequence of the ambiguity of "deployment," a state that captures in its territory a terrorist from one of the sanctioned "national liberation movements" and finds he is concealing a bomb would be required by Protocol I to grant him POW status unless it can establish that he was "engaged in a military deployment." Article 45 of Protocol I lays the burden of proof squarely on the state. If states targeted by terrorists were to adhere scrupulously to these provisions, it would be a boon for the terrorists. If, as is likelier, the states (even though parties to Protocol 1) prosecute and punish the terrorists as mere terrorists (not "combatants"), it will show disdain for Protocol 1, with inevitable collateral damage to other (and more estimable) treaties on the laws of war.

The Swiss representative offered a noteworthy condemnation of Article 44:

> [T]he article would only have the effect of doing away with the distinctions between combatants and civilians. The consequence would he that the adverse party could take draconian measures against civilians suspected of being combatants.

Like the praiseworthy first sentence of Article 44(3), the provision in Article 43(t) stating that the armed forces of a party to a conflict "shall be subject to an internal disciplinary system which . . . shall enforce compliance with the [laws of war]" lacks teeth. It states an obligation, but it does not state that a member of otherwise qualified armed forces forfeits his combatant status if those forces violate that obligation. The contention has been made that compliance with the laws of war is a "condition" for POW status for guerrillas, but such an inference appears ill-grounded. Where the drafters wanted to make POW rights conditional—e.g., in Article 44(3)—they did so expressly, and the thrust of Articles 43 through 46 is to create an overwhelming presumption in favor of granting such rights in any doubtful case.

Where does this leave the contention—the chief justification offered by the U.S. delegation for its support of Article 43 and 44—that dropping the broad "openness" requirements for irregulars creates an incentive for irregulars to comply with the laws of war? Need irregulars comply with the law to obtain combatant/POW status under Protocol I? For individual members of irregular forces, the answer is an almost unqualified negative. As noted earlier, the only violation of the law that strips an individual combatant of "his right to be a prisoner of war" is his failure to fulfill the narrow and opaque "openness" requirements of Article 44(3)(a) and (b), and even in that case he "shall ... be given protections equivalent in all respects to those accorded to prisoners of war by the [GPW] and by this Protocol." If there is an incentive here, it is pretty feeble, for it is hard to see the penalty for non-compliance.[4]

As for compliance by armed forces collectively, even a policy of violating the laws of war would not, under the express provisions of Articles 43 and 44, deprive a member of his entitlement to combatant/POW status. One could look for the elusive incentive in Article 96(3), which allows any so-called national liberation movement, by filing a unilateral declaration in which it undertakes to apply the laws of war to its struggle, to become, in effect, a party to the Protocol. But once such a movement successfully files its declaration, no provision of Protocol I can deny its members POW status on the grounds of collective non-observance of the rules. Hence, no incentive there either.

All in all, the humanitarian benefits of Articles 43 and 44, measured as a function of the putative incentive for irregulars to comply with the law, fall far short of the costs entailed in blurring (not to say erasing for all practical purposes) the distinction between combatants and non-combatants.

Slowly over centuries, humanitarian law strove to mitigate war's harm to civilians through demanding discrimination between combatants and non-combatants. Now comes the Diplomatic Conference and, in the name of "developing" humanitarian law, through a single subordinate clause, lays waste the legal and moral achievement of ages. That clause, of course, is in Article 44(3): "Recognizing, how- ever, that there are situations in armed conflicts where, owing to the nature of the hostilities an armed combatant *cannot* so distinguish himself ..." (emphasis added). The "cannot" is a masterstroke of amoral draftsmanship.

Notwithstanding the exegeses of Westerners straining to rationalize their complicity, the PLO representative quoted above correctly proclaimed the significance of this work of the Diplomatic Conference. It amounted to an endorsement, in the politically potent form of a legal instrument, of both the rhetoric and the anti-civilian practices of terrorist organizations that fly the banner of self-determination. One can find phrases and even whole sentences in Protocol I that repudiate bald terrorism and deprecate attacks on civilians, but they are not the gist of its operative provisions. They are a faint counterpoint to the booming "progressive," collectivist, ends-justify-the-means blare of the innovative elements of the document.

The Wages of Consensus-Mongering

There is much that is unconstructive in the goings-on of multilateral diplomatic forums around the world. But for truly malign perverseness, it would be hard to top the Diplomatic Conference. The Official Record tells a sinister and sad tale. What makes it sinister is the harm done to potential victims of war and terrorism through prostitution of the law. Beyond that, what makes it sad is the role played by the Westerners. The stakes were higher at the Diplomatic Conference than at a typical UN forum. The subject matter was no ordinary diplomatic resolution, but a treaty with actual potential for affecting the safety and well-being of war victims. The Westerners, from the outset, demonstrated appreciation of the stakes, astuteness in substantive analysis, and skills in pleading. But on issue after issue, when confronting the "Socialist" and Third World states' resolute attachment to patently harmful proposals, the Westerners backed down. They usually put up a good fight for a while, but then they either signed on or they slunk into the shadow of an abstention. At any of several junctures, they could have walked out and rendered the whole exercise academic (for without the major Western powers, no humanitarian agreement would have much standing in the world). But they stayed. Representatives of tyrannies upheld their convictions—stood on their principles, as it were—while the representatives of states where law really governs exalted the necessity for flexibility and compromise above all other principles. Thus with nary a negative vote, the assembly issued up a pro-terrorist treaty masquerading as humanitarian law.[5]

Notes

1. Quotations here are from the Official Records of the Diplomatic Conference—a summary account of the proceedings—as found in H. Levie, *Protection of War Victim: Protocol I to the 1949 Geneva Conventions* (1979). Uvie's four volumes reproduce much of the Official Records.

2. See generally John Norton Moore, “A Theoretical Overview of the Laws of War in a Post- Charter World, with Emphasis on the Challenge of Civil Wars, Wars of National Liberation, Mixed Civil-International Wars, and Terrorism,” *American University Law Review* 31 (1982): 841-842. (“Just war is dead in international law. The United Nations Charter killed it, and rightly so. Under the Charter, the use of force is lawful in defense, but not as affirmative conduct to seek resolution of issues by force, however just the cause is perceived to be.”).
3. The United Nations Charter provides that the Security Council has authority to make “decisions” and that the other UN members are bound “to accept and carry out” such decisions. Article 25; see generally UN Charter Chapters VI, VIl, VIII, and XIl. In contrast, the General Assembly’s functions and powers are explicitly non-legislative: “The General Assembly may *discuss* any questions ... [and) may make recommendations . . . .” Article 10 (emphasis added). In other words, the Security Council can make international law, but the General Assembly can make only non- binding declarations. The many contrary assertions of revisionist lawyers are simply not compatible with the plain language of the UN Charter.
4. Another key undefined term in Article 44(3) is “visible.” The PLO representative stated: “Contrary to the suggestions of certain delegations, his own delegation interpreted [“visible to”] to mean visible to the naked eye, since any recourse to electronic devices would divest the article of its value and undermine its very purpose.” 2 Levie 509.
5. The original article ended with the following postscript: “The United States signed Protocol I and Protocol II in December 1977. The decision on whether to submit either or both of the items to the Senate for advice and consent on ratification is currently under discussion within the administration. It will hinge on whether the unacceptable elements are remediable through U. S. reservations and clarifications.” As of the time this edited volume was assembled (2002), the United States has not ratified either protocol.

Part 4

The Debate Over Human Rights

17

Human Nature and Human Rights

*Robin Fox**

In the closing months of his presidency, Bill Clinton and some of his entourage have taken to using the buzzphrase "human and political rights" to replace the simpler "human rights." A call to the White House press office produced no explanation of the coinage, but assured me that "no policy change was implied." It's always nice to know that it is business as usual.

One would like to think that some sense of the paradoxes and complications of the term "human rights" had come home to the administration, and that in consequence it was on its way to even more qualifications: perhaps "human, political, economic, legal, cultural, national, sexual and domestic rights." This may be too much to hope for, but one gets the impression that President Clinton has meant to restrict "human" to "personal and family" and so needs to tack on "political" to cover all those "rights" that are to do with the wider society and participation in it. But what does this mean? That political rights are not human? That "human" has to do only with our persons and families? Whatever happened to "natural rights," which traditionally used to cover all of the above?

So much has now been written about "human rights" that, like President Clinton, we tend to lose our perspective and get confused. As with the classic issue of "natural rights" before it, the debate becomes so infused with passion that straight thinking is almost impossible. Argument about rights of one sort or another is both possible and desirable, particularly given the current penchant for using "human rights" as a basis for often quite brutal foreign policy decisions. But we have to recognize that putting "human" in front of "rights"—when, for example, talking of the "human right" of people to free elections—

---

*Robin Fox is University Professor of Social Theory at Rutgers University.

This essay originally appeared in *The National Interest*, no. 62 (Winter 2000/01). The responses originally appeared in *The National Interest*, no. 63 (Spring 2001) is simply to use a warm hurrah word as a rhetorical device. In the same way, wars of political suppression become "humanitarian interventions," and anything we do not currently happen to like becomes "unnatural," even if it is something as basically human as the hunting of game animals or investment in multiple spouses.

Both "human" and "natural" do have a real content, and we can identify that content. Given the all-too-free use of these terms, perhaps we should ask ourselves what that content might be. The trouble is that we have used them as hurrah words for so long, that we balk at any result that is not consonant with our current enlightened prejudices. We want to define what is natural; we do not want nature to do it for us, for the result might not be pretty.

Thus, if anyone were to make an argument, however logical, coherent and backed by evidence, that there was no natural or human right to vote, for example, he would not be answered so much as ridiculed and condemned as reactionary and anti-humanitarian. Yet a respectable argument could indeed be made that there is nothing in nature, or certainly in the nature of being human, that demands the right to vote as such. That right is not so much a natural or human right as one contingent on the fairly advanced economic and political development of certain civilizations. This is probably the sort of thing Clinton has in mind when he adds political to human in the rights catalogue.

The natural/human right might be phrased as "a right to a say in the affairs of one's group." How such participation in group decision-making is to be ensured, however, is not defined by anything in nature or humanity. Voting only becomes an issue at a certain sophisticated level of political development. It may be possible to argue that at such a level everyone has a right to vote (although exceptions will rapidly be listed—children, lunatics, felons, peers, exiles, non-residents, resident non-citizens, non-property owners, unregistered persons), but such a right is scarcely natural or human. It is more properly cultural, or social and political, deriving from the nature of government so achieved rather than from facts of nature or humanity.

On the other hand, a very good argument could be made, using basic kin selection theory, that there is a natural and human right to revenge. If someone kills my nephew or grandson, he robs me of a proportion of my inclusive fitness, that is, the strength of my personal gene pool. To redress this imbalance, it could be argued, I have the right to inflict a similar loss on him. I should be allowed to deprive him of someone related to him. This could be satisfied by killing two of his first cousins, or any such combination that would level the balance sheet. It is remarkable that many systems of vengeance in human society seem implicitly to observe the logic of inclusive fitness. They do not, for example, necessarily prescribe that I kill the person responsible: one of his kin or clan will do just as well.

This system of vengeance is less efficient as a redress than a system whereby I would get to impregnate one of the perpetrator's females, thus forcing him to raise to viability a person carrying my own genes. Actually, in the example cited this would amount to overcompensation, since I would gain by half to a loss of one-quarter. It would be more exact if my brother were allowed to make the impregnation, thus restoring the exact balance. Either method is of course impractical given intertribal or clan hostility, but note how ubiquitous is the practice of impregnating captive women or the women of defeated rivals. The advancing Russian forces in World War II made a massive effort to redress the imbalance caused by German depredations during Operation Barbarossa. Russian genes are now being nurtured by the Federal Republic's economic and welfare systems on a vast scale.

I probably do not have the right to demand that any superordinate entity carry out this vengeance for me (although I may call on supernatural agencies, and will commonly use sorcery to harm an offender). In strict fitness theory I am bound to redress my own wrongs and either succeed or fail, thus determining my own ultimate fitness in terms of the genes that I, and those who have genes in common with me through descent, contribute to the pool. Perhaps the most basic claim we have against a collective entity is that it leave us alone to settle our affairs. It is generally observed, however, that as human societies evolve, many of the self-help functions are delegated to some superordinate authority.

This is the essence of the social contract: for the sake of harmony within the group, certain basic rights to individual action are delegated to the group itself. Hence, compensation comes to substitute for vengeance. Again, this is often framed in reproductive terms: compensation for a murdered man is that which will enable his kin to raise another child to replace him. In many systems before the advent of the monopolistic state, there was no question of personal retribution through the execution of the murderer. Just compensation, which would enable the genetic replacement of the victim, was considered sufficient. This can be seen as a humanitarian advance in human morals, or as a retrograde step depriving individuals of the right of vengeance, but either way there is no question that it preserved the idea of redressing the genetic imbalance caused by a human-activated death. The monopolistic state, however, declares that there is no individual right to vengeance, and reserves that right to itself. Thus the state exacts retributive justice, but leaves the kin of the victim without compensation, and the imbalance permanent. It is not clear how this is an improvement on the older systems of self-help or compensation ("blood money").

The Woody Allen Question

It does, however, raise an interesting question: At a certain point of development in human social complexity, does the collectivity acquire "human rights" over the individual? This is important because so much of the above-mentioned writing on human rights assumes them to be by definition individual rights. This often goes to the length of seeing no rights as inhering in any collectivity—except, perhaps, the family—and even as seeing the collectivity as the automatic enemy of human rights. Such rights are almost by definition rights against the state. But there have always been human collectivities; we are, as F.H. Bradley observed, following Darwin, following Aristotle, a rootedly social animal. In fact, Bradley argued, we could show that individuals did not exist: the social was real and the individual the abstraction. Take away from any so-called individual everything contributed to his nature and person by society (starting with the genetic contribution of his parents, grandparents and so forth) and what is left? Nothing. The whole idea of rights being peculiar to individuals only becomes possible with self-conscious creatures, of which humans are the only example.

What sense does it make to attribute individual rights to ants? Woody Allen's neurotic worker, oppressed by the collective morality of the colony in the movie *Antz*, is only funny because it is impossible: an anthropomorphizing of the ant condition. But it is interesting because that is precisely what has happened in the human situation. A mammal living in socially complex colonies, like baboons or chimpanzees, suddenly (in evolutionary terms) became conscious of its own condition, probably by evolving powers of speech with which to talk about it. Baboons cannot have individual rights any more than ants. They simply do what they have to do to be baboons and produce more baboons. But once a primate is conscious of its condition, then it can start to ask the Woody Allen type of question: "Why must I always do the things the group wants to do? Why can't I decide for myself what is good for me?" In this way it can formulate the notion first of "individuals" and then of certain things owing to individuals: just as the group has a "right" to a territory, so an individual has a "right" to . . . the answer is pretty much anything it can think up. Once started on this delusional pathway there is ultimately no limit except that of the imagination.

The individual "rights" that a primitive, self-conscious, but of necessity group-living primate would claim would of course be based on its individual needs to feed and procreate successfully. But it is important to note that at this level the need to claim rights over the demands of the group would not arise, since the group would be the individual's inclusive kinship network. All individuals feed, struggle for dominance, mate and raise young. In this process, the existence of the group is a necessity like the existence of natural resources. Individuals will make altruistic sacrifices for the group since it is essentially a group of kin, and thus represents the repository of their inclusive fitness. There is no way in which the small group of relatives could be seen as somehow having different interests from those of the individuals composing it. In Bradleyan terms, there could be no distinction between the society and the individual.

A Profoundly Unfair Process

As levels of social complexity increased after the Neolithic revolution, some 10,000 years ago, organisms would increasingly be dealing with (relative) genetic strangers who made demands on them in the name of social units whose genes were not identical by descent with theirs. It is at this stage that true conflict would have occurred, as organisms started to feel the need to assert their "rights"; that is, the things they needed to do in order to ensure their fitness: the means of reproduction.

In a strict sense, this is the upper limit of the natural or human claims that an organism (read: individual) can have against any collectivity of genetic strangers. It is the area Clinton seems to have in mind when using "human." It is a claim based on the functional necessities of reproductive competition. It cannot be a claim to reproduce successfully, only a claim to be allowed to compete for reproductive success. It is not a claim for fairness: something that Rawlsians would like to write into the "original position." Natural selection is a profoundly unfair process; indeed, that is the point of it. Some start with a genetic advantage over others; all men are not created equal. But all have a right to play their hands to the best of their ability. The group has no obligation to level the playing field unnaturally, but it has an obligation to let the players play.

So we might say that the only basic human rights are those that allow individuals to compete in the reproductive struggle. These would be rights of access to potential mates, and to the resources needed to acquire, hold and breed with them; and the right to raise offspring to viability. (This would underline the claim that the right to "equality" refers to equality of opportunity, not equality of outcome. The outcome has to be unequal or natural selection would not take place.) We could speak of a "human right to procreate," although I would prefer to state it as the "right to engage in reproductive competition." For it is important that we recognize these basic human rights not as claims to some kind of benevolence or handouts from the collectivity (even though we may decide such benevolence is due for other reasons). They are claims to be allowed to take part in the reproductive struggle. Insofar as we fail, we fail, and as long as we were not artificially restricted in our attempt we have no cause for complaint.

To take a currently contentious issue: Is there a "human right" to free choice of one's marriage partner? (I am sure Clinton would regard this as a "human" and not a "political" right.) To those of us reared in a relentlessly individualistic society, such a right seems obvious and basic. But it is so only in such a society. In a society where the clan or extended family is the basic unit—and note that this itself is the basic "human" unit—then it is equally obvious that such a choice is too important to be left to individual whim. What is at stake is the continuing reproductive success of a group of genetically close individuals. The parents of any potential couple carefully monitor the match in light of the probability of a successful reproductive outcome. In doing so, they are acting not only in protection of their own inclusive fitness, but also, in terms of their greater experience and predictive ability, in protection of that of the young couple.

There is nothing either unnatural or inhuman here. On the contrary, our attitude of allowing whimsical affections and passions to decide the choice of partner, with the often subsequent consequences of divorce, step-parent abuse, one-parent family problems and the like, can be seen as inhuman, unnatural and reprehensible. But so high in our value system have we elevated individual choice that it appears to us simply "self-evident" that arranged marriage is unthinkable. It is an infringement of "human rights." It may be an infringement of something, and there may indeed be good moral arguments against it, but the "human rights" argument will not wash.

You might counter that I have just said that the group should not interfere with the right to compete for reproductive success. But in the case just cited it does not do so. Rather, it seeks to reinforce the chances of individual reproductive success, and we could forcefully argue that the group has the "human right" to do so. Societies with arranged marriages are easily out-reproducing those with free choice, despite the access to better medical care, sanitation and nutrition in the latter. There is nothing in the "laws of nature" that says the kin group (the pool of genes related by descent) should not seek to enhance the reproductive success of its members. On the contrary, it should seek to do so, since individuals—given imagination, intelligence and free will, and hence the capacity for delusion—as often as not act against their reproductive self-interest.

Thus, non-kin collectivities, while certainly often acting against the interests of their members, will also often move in to prevent at least self-destructive behavior that might injure individual reproductive success: drug misuse, suicide, child abuse, infanticide or abortion. More positively, they support those whose behavior has reduced their chances of raising children to viability. Monastic institutions in the Middle Ages, while manned by celibate "brothers and sisters," were homes for a staggering number of otherwise doomed infants deposited by those unable to support them. Social welfare systems operate on the same principle: although we have no natural right to their assistance, they have a natural right to assist us. Here non-kin collectivities are taking over the functions that originated, and have their logic, in the kin group. If we support them and they support us it is because of a natural extension of mutuality from the "original position" of kin support.

It is in the interest of a nation, for example, that it reproduce itself. It tends, in its delusional-ideological system, to pass itself off as a super kin group. At the primitive level of evolving humanity (99 percent of our existence as a species) there was no need for such pretense. The kin group was, in essence, the social collectivity. This is why I have argued above that at the most basic, and hence most "human," level there would be no "rights" issue. In promoting the success of near kin we are promoting the success of our own genes (or, more correctly, they are using us to promote their success).

Still within the purview of basic kin selection theory, we have another human right: the right to nepotistic assistance. We have the right both to assist close kin and to receive assistance from them in the pursuit of our own reproductive success. Until the advent of meritocratic bureaucracy, the world lived by this principle. It is what "kinship" is all about: all those gentes, clans, sibs, septs, moieties, phratries, lineages, houses, kindreds and extended families. There is no human society that does not map out, often in alarming detail, its universe of kin, the better to calculate the degree and kind of help and obligation expected. The term nepotism, from the Latin nepos (grandson, sister's son), was first invented to describe the hypocritical (but most certainly "natural") tendency of prelates either to favor their nephews or to hide their illegitimate sons under the nepotic title. In another stunning reversal of natural values, we have now made it one of the worst crimes against "equality"—which it most assuredly is. This does not prevent us, though, at all levels of society up to the very top, from wallowing in the hypocrisy. The most basic feature of social evolution is not so easily defined away.

The point of the above examples is to make us wary of a free and easy use of the terms "human" and "natural." It is not to say that there are no other rights than those that exist in some guttural, shambling, scavenging state of protohuman existence. Of course there are. But we should be more careful in the logical underpinning we choose to give to these rights, if for no other reason than that we render the terms meaningless and empty and rob them even of rhetorical value.

Also, as we have seen, human rights may be rights to all kinds of behaviors that our sophisticated and sensitive liberal natures may abhor. Hunting is a good example, given the current threat in England to ban fox hunting on "humanitarian" grounds, which seem to have more to do with puritanical objections to the hunters' enjoyment than with the supposed suffering of the fox. A very good case could be made that the "right to procreate" (which has now been established in U.S. common law) includes the right to polygamy (polygyny and polyandry) for those who can afford it and want it. Why should the state—on grounds that are always fuzzy and derive largely from religious prejudice—limit the number of spouses? The overwhelming majority of human societies (approximately 85 percent) have allowed or enjoined polygamy. Again, the "advanced" societies have reversed this tendency, which is wholly "natural" in a sexually competitive species of large land mammals with moderate sexual dimorphism and late-maturing young. As with the Romans, the argument for monogamy is egalitarian. But as we have seen, nature is not egalitarian: if some succeed and some fail in the polygamy stakes, then the same is in fact true of monogamy, where some will always outbreed others. And yet again, the monogamous societies, while banning multiple marriages as "unnatural," hypocritically allow all kinds of multiple mating—serial monogamy being the most common example in modern Western society.

It is a pretty safe bet that almost anything we have condemned as "unnatural" is something that we know will flourish if we leave it alone. For if something is natural we have no need to buttress it with sanctions; it will take care of itself.

Nature's Neutrality

What, then, should we call these rights that are not basic, natural or human, but which we "know" to be desirable? (Thus we may not know what human rights are, but we certainly know when we have lost them.) Surely, you say, we should not give in to relativism and suggest that they are simply local preferences without universal validity. At least I hope you are saying that, because that pernicious doctrine has achieved a sinister grip among the scribbling classes. It is perhaps strange that the triumph of relativism should come at the same time that the pursuit of "human rights issues" has come to dominate international affairs and foreign policies. Yet the two trends are not unrelated. In a world of relativistic morals, we would have no basis for attacking offenders against "rights" if these could be dismissed as mere cultural preferences. We therefore have to underpin certain rights as "human" to stress their universality. If they pertain to all humans—on what grounds is not always clear—then they are impervious to the relativist's objection. What is truly strange is that a good many theory-befuddled academics and activists hold both views at the same time, lauding relativism in defense of "multicultural" agendas while denouncing, say, female circumcision as contrary to "universal human rights." Logic is usually the first fatality in ideological warfare.

The cherished rights enshrined in the Constitution, the Declaration of the Rights of Man, the UN Charter and human rights declaration, and all the treaties and commissions up to the Helsinki Accords and the establishment of the International Criminal Court—all of these are highly evolved political and social rights that derive from the Western Enlightenment tradition, with its basic values of equality and universalism. Many of them are peculiar to the Christian tradition. Despite attempts to base these rights on "nature," in most cases they—by their very design—either run counter to nature or, at best, concern things about which nature is strictly neutral.

We have looked at some of the former. As examples of the latter we might suggest that "nature" gives us no clues about what form certain institutions might take, only about the rules of engagement, as it were. We should be able to accrue resources so as to take part in the reproductive struggle. But exactly how we should accrue those resources (whether they include that Enlightenment favorite, "property," for example), to what lengths we should go to prevent others (our reproductive rivals) from accruing them, and to what extent we should assist our close kin by passing resources to them—on all these matters nature is silent. The winners will be rewarded, but they will be rewarded if they cheat as well as if they play fair. They will be rewarded if they kill and torture, if that is what gets more of their genes into the pool. They will be rewarded if they cooperate, if that is what gets it done. We can see that some behaviors will be self-defeating—too many cheaters will leave too few suckers—and probably self-limiting as a strategy in the long run. But in the short run, a cheater can perfectly well manage a respectable score in the inclusive fitness stakes. We still celebrate the con man and the huckster, and especially deride the cuckold. The law may take one view, but popular opinion is not fooled.

Inclusive fitness theory—preserving and enlarging one's personal gene pool—is only one way into the issue of what is basically human. I have taken it here simply as an example. Take another approach, say, the findings of psychology into the basic list of human motivations. Certainly we shall find some that suit our warm and compassionate version of "human," but there will be a list of others that we would not want on any list of things to be fought for and protected and promoted.

Take again those things we have in common with our nearest animal relatives, the chimpanzees, whose genetic material is 98 percent our own. There is the warm and fuzzy list all right, but there is also, as Jane Goodall discovered to her warm-hearted horror, warfare, genocide, cannibalism, homicide, female beating, infanticide, violence, domination and more.

Take, say, those features that have been found common to all human societies by comparative ethnography. Once again, the list of saintly characteristics is overbalanced by the dark features that seem so inescapably human. It is a pure act of judgment to say that the dark features, all of which can be shown to have contributed to survival, are to be regarded as less "human" than the ones we have selected as worthy of promotion. And there will be yet others that have served survival purposes and are regarded as benign by even a majority—and have been so regarded throughout history—such that in our enlightened judgment they must be added to the list of the truly human.

Aspirations, Not Needs

So where are we left with our rights problem? Does it really matter if the term "human" is wrongly applied to rights? It does, because this is an area that is too important for us to indulge in systematic self-delusion. We are moving into a period when the pursuit of "human rights issues" is filling the vacuum in foreign policy left by the disappearance of clear-cut "national interest" issues (for example, Robin Cook's much-touted "ethical foreign policy" for the UK).

This has already been the excuse for us to break the rules of international behavior established in the "national interest" period, to bomb a sovereign nation into submission and kill at least one thousand people. This stance threatens to start another and more deadly war with China. It is moralistic, self-righteous and aggressive. It is dangerous as well as hypocritical in its selective action. Yugoslavia was in the end massively bombed to preserve "the credibility of NATO." How useful that "human rights" could be invoked as a cynical justification. (See also the human and "national" rights of Kuwaiti sheiks that were so gallantly protected in what otherwise might have seemed to be an old-fashioned war to protect our vital oil interests.) And given the moral state of our politicians, this is about all we can expect.

Robert Benchley was of the opinion that whenever a government began shouting "spies!" it was inevitably trying to divert attention from its own shady business. Perhaps we can be forgiven for suspecting something of the sort when we hear politicians chanting the mantra of "human rights"—usually to cover some hypocritical, and inevitably blundering, manipulation of the UN by the powers in the Security Council.

Given the inevitable skepticism about governmental honesty (or at least competence), we should at the very least insist on being clear about what we are doing and on what grounds we are doing it. We should not take action on the grounds that what we are supporting or suppressing is in some sense essentially "human," when it is no such thing. A great deal of what is human is in fact what is at the root of what we are opposing, suppressing, killing and destroying in the name of human rights. To achieve the kind of world envisioned in the treaties, charters and commissions, we must indeed suppress and destroy—or at the very least control—human nature. We are not acting for it, we are acting against it, or we are supplementing it in those cases where it gives us no guidance. As Katherine Hepburn said to Humphrey Bogart in *The African Queen*: "Human nature, Mr. Allnut, is what we are put on this earth to rise above."

Human rights theorists are often quite honest about this. They disclaim any attempt to base these rights on human nature or human needs and define them as "the best to which we can aspire," or as based on "a moral vision of a dignified human life." This is fine, but it is not then plausible to claim at the same time that these rights are "based on the very fact of being human." They are not; they are based on the fact of individuals being trapped in oppressive collectivities. This is why they must, by definition, be individual rights.

There is nothing wrong with defining rights in terms of high human aspirations, but they will then require a very different justification from rights based on human needs. They involve, in effect, a purely teleological justification: human rights become the rights we need in order to achieve a certain desired end state of society, not rights derived from the elusive state of true humanness. Thus rights involving inclusive fitness are more likely to be respected currently in fundamentalist Islamic societies than in Western democracies. But societies based on Islamic law are usually the ones most offensive to human rights activists.

It can be argued that human rights based on aspirations are no less human than those based on needs. But the problem is that we can aspire to virtually anything, and how do we choose between competing aspirations? Needs at least give us some criteria of arbitration, and very necessary ones, since many liberal-democratic-individualist aspirations, however laudable, have the quality we observed of running counter to basic needs and thus defeating their own objectives. Is there any point in aspiring to a state of affairs that is so inhuman that it is unsustainable, however ethically desirable? The true hair-splitters will want to argue that such impossible aspiration is also very human, and so it is; we are nothing if not a paradoxical animal.

Human Rights and the National Interest

One of the major paradoxes surrounding the human rights issue is that it became central to foreign policy as part of a deliberate strategy to protect the national interest. Human rights activists will not like this claim, of course. They prefer, as is their way, to think they are acting from nothing but the highest and purest moral considerations. But even they will admit that these explicit concerns—as opposed to a general U.S. urge to be the world's good guys—had a definite beginning in the Ford administration. They prefer, however, to forget that this stance was deliberately engineered by Daniel Patrick Moynihan to counter the hypocrisy of the Third World communist bloc.

Moynihan, as ambassador to the UN, was tired of just sitting there and taking it when the bloc used anti-capitalist moralizing as a basis for attacking the policies of the democracies at the behest of the USSR. So he developed the strategy of counterattacking (or even getting in the first punch) on the grounds of the abuse of "human rights" by these regimes. This brilliantly put the democracies on the attack, reversing their previously defensive stance of continual apology. It put the onus of explanation and justification on the totalitarian dictatorships and their bullyboy leaders. It was not, however, something that arose out of humanitarian concern for the benighted inhabitants of these Third World terror regimes, but out of the need to combat their governments' belligerence in the UN, and hence to curtail the influence of our major competitor.

I am not saying that anything Senator Moynihan did could have been totally cynical, but he was quite clear about the development of this as a strategy of foreign policy first and foremost. In *A Dangerous Place* (1978), he describes this as his "jujitsu principle": "to use the momentum of the majority against the majority." It was in the defense of the national interest and in the interest of the Western alliance. As one strategy among many to promote our collective ends, it had its place. As an excuse for foreign policy today—given the huge amount of post-Cold War military hardware available, and the compelling urge presidents and premiers seem to have to use that hardware—it deserves a close and skeptical scrutiny. This involves both a scrutiny of its practical dangers, best left to strategists, and of its theoretical underpinnings. With this latter enterprise, some otherwise useless academics can at least show that even if the emperor has new clothes, they are woven of dubious synthetic fibers.

Responses

It is hard to know whether Robin Fox has his tongue firmly planted in his cheek, particularly when he observes that "a very good case could be made . . . [for] the right to polygamy" in a magazine not noted for its licentiousness. On the assumption that he means what he says, however, his contention that the term "human" is wrongly applied to rights cries out for a response.

In a few respects Fox has it exactly right: there is massive confusion as to the philosophical basis for human rights and too often human rights advocates do frame their arguments in strictly moral terms, much to those arguments' occasional detriment. But instead of dispelling the confusion Fox adds to it by his conflation of the notions of "natural rights" and "human rights."

In the first place, while of course some human rights advocates base their defense of rights on natural law, this is far from the universal or even most common basis for understanding the nature of rights. A simple glance at the preamble to the Universal Declaration of Human Rights (the document that grounds most other human rights covenants and treaties) reveals the straw man Fox has tried to set on fire.

The first five "Whereas" clauses lay out the rationale for the list of rights to follow. The first clause refers to "the inherent dignity . . . of all members of the human family," a reference that might be ascribable to natural law doctrine, if it were not regarded merely as "poetry," but even this clause goes on to argue for recognition of that dignity on the pragmatic grounds that it leads to "freedom, justice and peace." The second "Whereas" notes that violations of rights have resulted in acts that have "outraged the conscience of mankind," a simple statement of fact following the Holocaust. The third advocates rights in order to obviate the need for revolution; the fourth in order to promote "friendly relations between nations"; and the fifth in order to "promote social progress." One can certainly disagree with any of these assertions but there is nary a natural law argument among them. Indeed, as Paul Gordon Lauren so ably lays out in his history of the writing of the Universal Declaration (The Evolution of International Human Rights: Visions Seen), the composers largely avoided basing the Declaration on either religious or natural law grounds exactly because they could come to no common agreement on these matters.

To challenge contemporary notions of human rights, then, because they may be at odds with various "theories" of what is "natural" (and it is exactly because basic kin selection theory and all the rest are no more than theories that natural law philosophy lies in such philosophical tatters when it comes to making it the grounds for any ethical system) is to elevate a chimera to the level of a debate that is not taking place. "Human rights" refers to "humans' rights," "the rights of humans," something human beings possess or can claim, but not necessarily something derived from the nature of the claimant any more than "Robin's article," an article written by Robin, requires that we come to an agreement about what kind of person he is. Rights are in fact often understood as providing the boundaries or limits to acceptable human behavior, be that behavior prompted by "human nature" or human choices.

Ultimately Fox even acknowledges as much by granting that "Human rights theorists . . . often . . . disclaim any attempt to base . . . rights on human nature or human needs and define them as 'the best to which we can aspire', or as based on 'a moral vision of a dignified human life.'" And that kind of philosophical pragmatism is exactly what most human rights advocates would claim. "But how do we choose between competing aspirations?," Fox asks. The answer is that the nations of the world, through the adoption of treaties or the decisions of international judicial bodies, articulate at different levels of consensus the evolving standards of what constitutes acceptable behavior. This may seem "squishy" but notions of acceptable behavior have always been subject to changing mores. Were they not, slavery would still be considered an acceptable form of social organization to vast majorities of the world's people, as it was 200 years ago. And even if one believes that slavery is somehow a "natural state," do we really want to say its abolition may be "unsustainable, however ethically desirable"?

Fox's major disservice to the cause of clarity, however, is that he leaps to indict his erroneously conceived notion of human rights for the deaths of 1,000 people in Serbia, a potential war with China and God knows what else. Even if one grants that the pursuit of human rights is responsible for these consequences—a dubious proposition—what are we to make of the fact that 150 million people have died in this century alone thanks to governments ignoring human rights claims and pursuing what they perceived to be in the "national interest"? Daniel Patrick Moynihan may have utilized human rights rhetoric in the pursuit of political advantage, but today his strategy appears a prescient one, for in as globally intertwined a world as this one, to ignore human rights claims is to jeopardize not only our national security but our economic, environmental and public health as well.

William F. Schulz
Executive Director
Amnesty International USA

Fox replies:

Mr. Schulz's letter seems like one of those hurriedly penned replies by those with an axe to grind and a turf to protect. I was simply trying to illustrate my contention that there was a lot more to the "human" in "human rights" than is granted in the prevalent philosophy. I added that the current lists are deliberately skewed in the direction of the features of human nature favored by those doing the listing. Mr. Schulz admits this, but proclaims it a virtue. That is his privilege. Human rights, he says, should not be derived from "natural rights" but from the prevailing consensus of the aspirants. I disagree for the reasons stated in the article. That is my privilege. He perfectly illustrates my point with his arrogant condemnation of the human millions engaged in polygamous marriages as "licentious." These law-abiding, hard-working, peaceful people, striving to do their best for spouses and children, thus know what to expect from the leading spokesman for "human rights." I rest my case.

18

Natural Rights and Human History

*Francis Fukuyama**

Terms like sanctity remind me of animal rights. Who gave a dog a right? This word right gets very dangerous. We have women's rights, children's rights; it goes on forever. And then there's the right of a salamander and a frog's rights. It's carried to the absurd.

I'd like to give up saying rights or sanctity. Instead, say that humans have needs, and we should try, as a social species, to respond to human needs—like food or education or health—and that's the way we should work. To try and give it more meaning than it deserves in some quasi-mystical way is for Steven Spielberg or somebody like that. It's just plain aura, up in the sky—I mean, it's crap.[1]

—James Watson

If James Watson, Nobel laureate, co-discoverer of the structure of DNA, and one of the towering figures of twentieth-century science, should become a bit impatient with the injection of the word "rights" into the discourse of his particular domain of genetics and molecular biology, we might well excuse him. Watson is famous both for his temper and for his often unguarded and politically incorrect remarks; he is, after all, a hardheaded scientist and not a scribbler on political and social matters. Moreover, he is correct in his central observation about contemporary rights discourse: it is a lot of crap. His remark is reminiscent of the utilitarian philosopher Jeremy Bentham, who famously commented that the French Declaration of the Rights of Man and the Citizen's assertion that rights were natural and imprescriptible was "nonsense upon stilts."

---

*Francis Fukuyama is Bernard Schwartz Professor of International Political Economy at the Paul H. Nitze School of Advanced International Studies, Johns Hopkins University.
This essay originally appeared in *The National Interest*, no. 64 (Summer 2001). The responses originally appeared in *The National Interest*, no. 65 (Fall 2001).

The problem, however, does not end there, because we cannot in the end dispense with serious discussion of rights and talk only of needs and interests. Rights are the basis of our liberal democratic political order and are key to contemporary thinking about moral and ethical issues. And any serious discussion of human rights must ultimately be based on some understanding of human ends or purposes, which in turn must almost always be based on a concept of human nature.

It is here that Watson's field, biology, becomes relevant, because the life sciences have been making important discoveries about human nature in recent years. So, much as natural scientists would like to maintain a wall of separation between the natural "is" that they study and the moral and political "ought" engendered by discourse on rights, this is ultimately a dodge. The more that science tells us about human nature, the more implications there are for human rights, and hence for the design of institutions and public policies that protect them. These findings suggest that contemporary capitalist liberal democratic institutions have been successful because they are grounded in assumptions about human nature that are far more realistic than those of their competitors.

Rights Talk

Over the past generation, the rights industry has grown faster than an Internet IPO in the late 1990s. In addition to the aforementioned animal, women's and children's rights, there are gay rights, the rights of the disabled and handicapped, indigenous people's rights, the right to life, the right to die, the rights of the accused, victims' rights, as well as the famous right to periodic vacations that is laid out in the Universal Declaration of Human Rights. The U.S. Bill of Rights is reasonably clear in enumerating a certain set of basic rights to be enjoyed by all American citizens, but in 1973 the U.S. Supreme Court in *Roe v. Wade* manufactured a new right out of whole cloth, based on Justice Douglas' finding in the earlier Griswold decision of an "emanation" from the "penumbra" of the similarly shadowy right to privacy. Constitutional scholar Ronald Dworkin comes up with an even more novel argument: Since having an abortion involves a major life decision on a par with making a religious commitment, the right to abortion turns out all along to have been protected by the First Amendment's guarantee of religious liberty.[2]

Rights on an international level are in no better shape. As Mary Ann Glendon has described in her book, *A World Made New*,[3] the Universal Declaration of Human Rights was hammered out in 1947 as the result of a heroic diplomatic effort that sought to bridge ultimately irreconcilable Western and Soviet views in the shadow of a deepening Cold War. Later international human rights documents added new layers of economic and social rights demanded by socialists and social democrats to the fundamental liberal rights favored by

Americans. If you want to amuse yourself, pick up a copy of the Brazilian constitution, ratified in 1988, and read through its enumeration of individual rights: the section is as long as the telephone book of a small city, and contains not just the right to the pursuit of happiness, but to happiness itself.

Given this monumental confusion, why do we not follow James Watson's advice, abandon talk of rights altogether, and simply speak of human "needs" or "interests"? Americans more than most peoples have tended to conflate rights and interests. By transforming every individual desire into a right unconstrained by community interests, one increases the inflexibility of political discourse. The debates in the United States over pornography and gun control would appear much less Manichaean if we spoke of the interests of pornographers rather than their fundamental First Amendment right to free speech, or the needs of assault weapon owners rather than their sacred Second Amendment right to bear arms.

Arguably, the same inflexibility appears when rights are invoked at an international level. A country that makes human rights a significant element of its foreign policy tends toward ineffectual moralizing at best, and unconstrained violence in pursuit of moral aims at worst. Countries that think of themselves as having only national interests, on the other hand, can pursue a policy of realpolitik that, it is said, is safer both for the country in question and for the international system as a whole. As Henry Kissinger might have explained in A World Restored, the reckless Alexander I was a proponent of rights, while the prudent Metternich, architect of the Congress of Vienna, proceeded in terms of interests.

The Necessity of Rights

So why not abandon what Glendon labels "rights talk" altogether? The reason we cannot do this, either as a theoretical or practical matter, is that the language of rights has become, in the modern world, the only shared and widely intelligible vocabulary we have for talking about ultimate human goods or ends, and, in particular, those collective goods or ends that are the stuff of politics. Classical political philosophers like Plato and Aristotle did not use the language of rights—they spoke of the human good, and of human happiness and the virtues and duties that were required to achieve it. The modern use of the term "rights" is more impoverished, because it does not encompass the range of higher human ends envisioned by the classics. But it is more democratic, universal and easily grasped. The great struggles over rights since the American and French revolutions are testimony to the political salience of this concept. The word "right" implies moral judgment (as in, "What is the right thing to do?") and is our principal gateway into a discussion of the nature of justice and of those ends we regard as essential to our humanity.

Watson is in effect advocating a utilitarian approach with his advice simply to try to satisfy human needs and interests without reference to rights. But it runs into the typical problem of utilitarianism: the question of priorities and justice when those needs and interests conflict. You are a powerful and important community leader in need of a new liver because of a drinking problem; I am an indigent, terminally ill patient in a public hospital, on life support but with a healthy liver. Any simple utilitarian calculation that seeks to maximize the satisfaction of human needs would dictate that I be involuntarily removed from life support so as to harvest my liver for the sake of the important leader and the people who depend on him. The fact that no liberal society permits this to happen reflects a view that innocent people have a right not to be involuntarily deprived of life, no matter how many important needs may be satisfied as a result.

Rights trump interests because they are invested with greater moral significance. Interests are fungible and can be traded off against one another in a marketplace; rights, while seldom absolute, are less flexible because it is hard to assign them an economic value. I may have an interest in a pleasant two-week vacation, but that cannot compete with another person's right not to be held as a chattel slave and work someone else's fields. The slave's right to freedom is not just a strong interest on the slave's part; a disinterested third party might say that the condition of servitude is unjust because it is an affront to the slave's dignity as a human being. The slave's freedom is somehow more basic and fundamental to his status as a human being than my interest in a pleasant vacation is to mine, even if I assert my interest more passionately than the slave does his.

Political systems enshrine certain kinds of rights over others, and thereby reflect the moral basis of their underlying societies. The United States was founded on the principle stated in the Declaration of Independence that "all men are created equal", and that "they are endowed by their Creator with certain unalienable rights." That principle, as Abraham Lincoln explained, was violated by the institution of slavery. The Emancipation Proclamation and passage of the Fourteenth Amendment corrected this grave inconsistency and laid the basis for subsequent American democracy.

So if rights prioritize human ends or goods and set some above others as the foundation of justice, where do they come from? The reason that there is a constant inflation in the scope of rights is precisely because everyone wants to raise the relative priority of certain interests over others. In the cacophony of rights talk, how do we decide what is genuinely a right and what is not?

There are in principle three possible sources of rights: divine rights, natural rights, and what one might call the contemporary positivistic view of rights as located in social law and custom. Rights, in other words, can emanate from God, Nature and Man himself.

Rights derived from revealed religion are not today the acknowledged basis of political rights in any liberal democracy. John Locke begins his Second Treatise on Government with an attack on Filmer and the doctrine of divine right; the very essence of modern liberalism was to eliminate religion as the explicit basis of political order. This was based on a practical observation that religiously based polities were constantly at war with one another because there was not sufficient consensus on religious first principles. The background for Hobbes' description of the state of nature as a war of "every man against every man" was the sectarian violence of his time.

None of this, of course, prevents private individuals in liberal societies from believing that Man is a creature created in God's image, and that basic human rights therefore come from God. Scientists like Watson or Richard Dawkins become extremely impatient when people with religious convictions talk about the "sanctity of life", but they need to learn to be more tolerant; such views are very deeply held, and are not going to go away as a result of greater education, rationality and the like. Such views become problematic only when rights presumed to derive from God are asserted as political rights, as in the abortion controversy. For they then run into the same problem recognized by Locke: It is extremely difficult to achieve social consensus on issues involving religion.

The second possible source of rights is nature, or, more precisely, human nature. Despite Jefferson's invocation of the Creator in the Declaration, he, like Locke and Hobbes, believed that rights needed to be grounded in a theory of human nature. A political principle like equality had to be based on empirical observation of what human beings were like "by nature"; since, as he said in a letter to Roger C. Weightman on June 24, 1826, it was not the case that some men were born with saddles on their backs, slavery was in principle contrary to nature and therefore unjust.[4]

It is this tradition of natural right that Robin Fox attacks in his recent article in this magazine.[5] Fox points out that the concept of human nature has undergone a major revival in recent years as a result of new research in the life sciences, and that it can now be given a "real content." The problem, he argues, is that much of that content is not very pleasant to behold, and would serve poorly as a basis for political rights. Evolutionary biology, for example, has given us the theory of kin selection or inclusive fitness, which asserts that human beings seek to maximize their reproductive fitness by favoring genetic relatives in proportion to their shared genes. This leads, in Fox's view, to implications like a natural or human right to revenge, or a right of a murder victim's family member to impregnate the perpetrator's females, since these are all behaviors that occur naturally in both human and animal societies.

Fox's argument, as stated in this piece, is reminiscent of what has been labeled the "naturalistic fallacy"[6], a tradition that stretches from David Hume to twentieth-century analytical philosophers like G.E. Moore, R.M. Hare and others. Particularly strong in the Anglo-Saxon world, the naturalistic fallacy argues that nature cannot provide a philosophically justifiable basis for rights, morality or ethics.

Since the philosophical school dominant in contemporary academia believes that any attempt to base rights on nature has long since been debunked, it is understandable that natural scientists are quick to invoke the "naturalistic fallacy" as a shield to protect their work from unpalatable political implications. Many of the findings of contemporary biology in areas like cognitive neuroscience, genetics and evolutionary theory would seem to have controversial political implications in such areas as the heritability of intelligence, criminal behavior, homosexuality or natural differences between the sexes. Many of these findings would seem to support conservative views, since they suggest that there are natural limits to social constructionism and therefore to human freedom. Evolutionary biologists in particular have run afoul of feminists, since they have argued that many sex differences are based on biology rather than socialization. Since most natural scientists are either apolitical or else bien pensant liberals, it is easy for them to evoke the naturalistic fallacy and argue, as Paul Ehrlich recently did in his book *Human Natures*,[7] that human nature gives us absolutely no guidance as to what human values should be.

It is my view that the common understanding of the naturalistic fallacy is itself fallacious, and that there is a desperate need for philosophy to return to the pre-Kantian tradition of grounding rights and morality in nature. But before I can state this argument more fully and explain why the post-Kantian dismissal of natural rights is misguided, we need to look at the third source of rights, which might be labeled "positivistic." The weaknesses of the third, positivistic approach to rights are indeed what necessitate the effort to resurrect the concept of natural rights.

The most readily available way of determining the source of rights is to look around and see what the society itself declares to be a right, through its basic laws and declarations. In his response to Fox in the Spring issue of this magazine, William F. Schulz, executive director of Amnesty International, argues that contemporary human rights advocates have long since dropped any notion that human rights can or should be based on nature or natural law. Instead, according to him, "'human rights' refer to 'humans' rights', 'the rights of humans', something that human beings possess or can claim, but not necessarily something derived from the nature of the claimant." Human rights are, in other words, whatever human beings determine they are.

As a political strategy for negotiating documents like the Universal Declaration of Human Rights, there is no doubt that Schulz is correct in saying that rights are whatever you can get people to agree they are, and that there will never be consensus on a set of natural rights. There can be procedural refinements to make sure a positive right actually reflects the will of the society that declares it, such as rules that require ratification of bills of rights by supermajorities (as in the case of the U.S. Constitution). The First Amendment rights to freedom of speech and religion may or may not be ordained by nature, but they are ratified as part of a constitutional process. But this approach means that rights are essentially procedural: if you can get a supermajority (or whatever) to agree that all people have a right to walk around in public in their underwear, then that becomes a fundamental human right along with freedom of association and freedom of speech.

So what is wrong with a purely positivistic approach to rights? The problem, as any human rights advocate will know in practice if not in theory, is that there are no positive rights that are also universal. When Western human rights groups criticize the Chinese government for jailing political dissidents, the Chinese government responds that for its society, collective and social rights outweigh individual rights. The emphasis of Western organizations on individual political rights is not an expression of a universal aspiration, but rather reflects the Western (or perhaps Christian) cultural biases of the human rights groups themselves. The Western human rights advocate might respond that the Chinese government has not followed the correct procedure, insofar as it has not consulted its own people in a democratic manner. But if there are no universal standards for political behavior, who is to say what the right procedure is?

And what does an advocate of a positivistic approach like Schulz have to say in response to another, culturally different society that follows the right procedures and yet promotes abhorrent practices like suttee or slavery or female circumcision? The answer is that no response is possible, since you have declared from the outset that there are no transcendent standards for determining right and wrong beyond whatever any particular culture declares to be a right.

Why the Naturalistic Fallacy is Fallacious

The problem of cultural relativism brings us back to reconsider whether we might have been premature in discarding an approach to human rights based on human nature, since the existence of a single human nature shared by all the peoples of the world can provide, at least in theory, a common ground on which we can base universal human rights. Belief in the naturalistic fallacy runs so deep in contemporary Western thought, however, that resurrection of a natural rights argument remains a formidable task.

The idea that rights cannot be grounded in nature rests on two separate, though often interrelated, arguments. The first is attributed to David Hume, one of the fathers of British empiricism, who is widely believed to have proven once and for all that it is impossible to derive an "ought" from an "is."[8] That is, a statement of moral obligation cannot be derived from an empirical observation about nature or the natural world. When natural scientists assert that their work has no political or policy implications, they usually have in mind the Humean "is-ought" dichotomy; because human beings are genetically inclined to behave in certain species-typical ways does not imply that they should behave in that manner. Moral obligation comes from some other shadowy, ill-defined realm distinct from the natural world.

The second strand of the naturalistic fallacy would argue that, even if we could derive an "ought" from an "is", the "is" is ugly, amoral or indeed immoral. Nietzsche put the idea much more forcefully than any bone-dry British analytical philosopher ever could in *Beyond Good and Evil*:

> 'According to nature' you want to live? O you noble Stoics, what deceptive words these are! Imagine a being like nature, wasteful beyond measure, indifferent beyond measure, without purposes and consideration, without mercy and justice, fertile and desolate and uncertain at the same time; imagine indifference itself as a power—how could you live according to this indifference?[9]

Robin Fox presents us with an up-to-date version of this line of thought based on contemporary sociobiology: nature commands that we get our genes into the next generation by killing off rival males and impregnating their mates.

To rebuild an argument in favor of natural right, we need to take on each of these arguments in turn, beginning with the "is-ought" distinction. More than forty years ago, Alasdair MacIntyre pointed out that Hume himself neither believed in nor abided by the rule commonly attributed to him that one could not derive an "ought" from an "is."[10] At most, what the famous passage from the Treatise said was that one could not deduce in a logically a priori way moral rules from empirical fact. But like every serious philosopher in the Western tradition before him since Aristotle, Hume believed that the "ought" and the "is" were bridged by concepts like "wanting, needing, desiring, pleasure, happiness, health"—that is, by the goals and ends that human beings set for themselves. He gives the following example of how one is derived from the other: "If I stick a knife in Smith, they will send me to jail; but I do not want to go to jail; so I ought not (had better not) stick a knife in him."

There are, of course, a huge variety of human wants, needs and desires that can produce an equal diversity of "oughts"; it is at this point that human nature enters the picture. For virtually every pre-Kantian philosopher had an implicit or explicit theory of human nature that set certain wants or needs above others as being more fundamental to our humanness than others. I may want my two-week vacation, but your desire to escape slavery is based on a more universal and more deeply felt longing for freedom, and therefore trumps my want. Hobbes' assertion of a basic right to life (which is the precursor to the right to life enshrined in the Declaration of Independence) is based on an explicit theory of human nature that posits that the fear of violent death is the strongest of human passions, and therefore produces a right more basic than, say, the assertion of religious orthodoxy.

The radical break in the Western tradition comes not with Hume but with Kant, who with the categorical imperative sought to detach morality in its entirety from any concept of nature.[11] It was Kant who argued that true moral choice implied freedom of the will, which meant in turn freedom from any form of natural causality: moral agents routinely defy the laws of physics by choosing not what their material bodies tell them they want, but what reason dictates to be right. Kant expressed in philosophical terms a view that was embedded in Protestantism: that human nature was sinful, and that moral behavior required rising above or suppressing our natural desires.

Much of subsequent Western philosophy has followed the Kantian route toward so-called "deontological" theories of right, i.e., theories that try to derive a system of ethics that is not dependent on any substantive assertions about human nature or human ends. Many deontological theories elevate moral autonomy to be the chief if not the only human good, a view that has become embedded in a good deal of contemporary U.S. constitutional law.

I believe that this broad turn away from human nature-based theories of right is flawed for a number of reasons that, due to space limitations, cannot be fully explicated in this article. Perhaps the most revealing weakness is the fact that virtually all philosophers who attempt to lay out a deontological theory of rights end up re-inserting various assumptions about human nature into their theories. The only difference is that they do it covertly and dishonestly, rather than explicitly, as in the earlier tradition from Aristotle to Hume.

An example of this is John Rawls, whose theory of justice explicitly sidesteps any discussion of human nature and seeks to establish a set of minimal moral rules that would apply to any group of rational agents based on the so-called "original position." As critics of Rawls have pointed out, the original position itself and the political implications Rawls draws from it in fact contain numerous assertions about human nature, in particular his assumption that human beings are risk-averse. William Galston has pointed out similar flaws in the thinking of post-Rawlsian legal theorists like Ronald Dworkin and Bruce Ackerman, who try to define the rules of a liberal society while eschewing any reference to priorities among human ends or, in more contemporary language, between possible lifestyles.[12]

What about the other leg of the naturalistic fallacy argument, which says that even if rights were derivable from nature, that nature is violent, aggressive, cruel or indifferent? Human nature at a minimum points in contradictory directions, toward competition and cooperation, toward individualism and sociability; how can any particular "natural" behavior be the basis of natural rights?

The answer, I believe, is that while there is no simple translation of human nature into human rights, the passage from one to the other is ultimately mediated by the rational discussion of human ends, that is, by philosophy. That discussion does not lead to a priori or mathematically provable truths;

indeed, it may not even yield substantial consensus among the discussants. It does, however, allow us to establish a hierarchy of rights, and it allows us to rule out certain solutions to the problem of rights that have been politically powerful in the course of human history.

Take for example the human propensity for violence and aggression. Few people would deny that this is somehow grounded in human nature; there are virtually no societies free of murder or that have not experienced armed violence in some form. But what we notice in the first instance is that random violence against other members of the community is prohibited in every known human cultural group. This is no less true among man's primate cousins: a troop of chimpanzees will occasionally experience violent aggression from a younger male that, like the Columbine High School shooters, is lonely, peripheral or otherwise seeking to make a point.[13] But the older members of the community will always take measures to control and neutralize that individual because community order cannot tolerate such violence.

Primate violence, including human violence, is legitimated primarily at higher social levels, that is, on the part of in-groups that compete with out-groups. Warriors are treated with respect and honor in a way that school shooters are not. Hobbes' war of "every man against every man" is in fact a war of every group against every group. In-group social order is driven by the need for competition against out-groups, both over evolutionary time (there is a great deal of evidence that human cognitive capabilities were shaped by these group-oriented competitive needs[14]) and in the course of human history.[15] There is a sad continuity from non-human primates to hunter-gatherer societies to contemporary ethnic and sectarian violence as (primarily) male-bonded groups compete against one another for dominance.[16]

This might be taken to be confirmation of the naturalistic fallacy, and thus the end of the story, but for the fact that human nature encompasses a great deal more than male-bonded violence. It also encompasses the desire for what Adam Smith called "gain", the accumulation of property and goods useful to life, as well as reason, the capacity for foresight and the rational ordering of priorities over the long term. When two human groups butt up against one another, they face a choice between engaging in a violent, zero-sum struggle for dominance, or else in a peaceful, positive-sum relationship of trade and exchange. Over time, the logic of this choice (what Robert Wright labels "non-zero-sumness"[17]) has driven the boundaries of human in-groups to ever larger communities of trust: from tiny kin groups to tribes or lineages, to states, nations, broad ethnolinguistic communities and eventually to what Samuel Huntington labels cultures, that is, communities of shared values encompassing many nation-states and hundreds of millions if not billions of people.

There remains a significant amount of violence at the boundaries of these ever- larger groups, made more deadly by the simultaneous advance of military technology. But there is a logic to human history that is ultimately driven by the priorities that exist among natural human desires, propensities and behaviors. Human violence over the past 100,000 years or so has become increasingly controlled and pushed to the outer boundaries of these ever-larger groups. Globalization—a world order in which mankind's largest in-groups no longer violently compete with one another for dominance but trade peaceably—can be seen as the logical culmination of a long-term series of decisions in favor of positive-sum competition.

Violence, in other words, may be natural to human beings, but so is the propensity to control and channel violence. These conflicting natural tendencies do not have equal status or priority; human beings reasoning about their situation can come to understand the need to create rules and institutions that constrain violence in favor of other natural ends, like the desire for property or gain, that are more fundamental.

Human nature is best at providing us with guidance as to what political orders will not work. Robin Fox makes fun of the idea that the contemporary evolutionary theory of kin selection or inclusive fitness could constitute the basis for rights. But a better understanding of this theory would have led us to predict the bankruptcy and ultimate failure of communism, due to its failure to respect natural inclinations to favor kin and private property.

Karl Marx argued that man is a species-being, that is, that human beings have altruistic feelings toward the human species as a whole. The policies and institutions of real-world communist states—like the abolition of private property, the subordination of the family to the party-state, and commitment to universal worker solidarity—were all predicated on this belief. (Visitors to Moscow in the days of the USSR may remember the statue there to Pavel Morozov, a little monster celebrated by Stalin for turning his parents in to the secret police.)

There was a time when evolutionary theorists like V.C. Wynne-Edwards postulated the existence of species-level altruism, but modern kin selection theory denies the existence of strong group-selection pressures.[18] It postulates instead that altruism arises primarily out of the need of individuals to get their genes passed on to successive generations. Human beings will by this account be altruistic primarily to family members and other kin; a political system that forces them to spend their Saturdays away from their families working on behalf of the "heroic Vietnamese people" will meet very deep resistance.

Human Nature and Politics

The preceding example demonstrates the ways in which human nature and politics are intertwined: kin selection indicates that a political system that respects the right of people to follow their own individual self-interests and attend to family and close friends before they attend to strangers halfway around the world will be more stable, workable and satisfying than one that does not. Human nature does not dictate a single, precise list of rights; it is both complex and flexible as it interacts with various technological environments. But it is not infinitely malleable, and our underlying shared humanity allows us to rule out certain forms of political order like tyranny as unjust. Those rights that speak to the most deeply felt and universal human drives, ambitions and behaviors will be a more solid foundation for political order than those that do not. This helps explain why there are a lot of capitalist liberal democracies around the world at the beginning of the twenty-first century, but very few socialist dictatorships.

Does this then mean that capitalist liberal democracy of the sort practiced in the United States is an ideal political system because it is optimally consistent with our underlying natures? And if so, does this further imply that we need to predicate our foreign policy on the extension of American-style rights to all peoples around the world? Here the answers become necessarily more nuanced and complex.

Robin Fox is on much firmer ground when he argues that there are many aspects of contemporary American society that are in some sense profoundly unnatural, such as our hyperindividualism, the impersonality of most of our social connections, and our imposition of anti-nepotistic rules that force us to hire qualified strangers before family members. There are many traditional, non- or pre-liberal societies that better respect group identity, face-to-face community and kinship than the United States. Rigid insistence on our part that all societies around the world respect human rights as we understand and institutionalize them risks being simultaneously arrogant, naive and politically imprudent.

But the kinds of political and economic institutions we now have are the by-product of the interaction of our underlying human desires and aspirations with the possibilities afforded us by science, technology and the economic horizon that the latter creates. Individualism and rules against nepotism are dictated by the requirements of a modern capitalist economy, whose economic benefits satisfy latent longings of our underlying natures. Most Americans are willing to give up a more natural kind of face-to-face community, where we are surrounded primarily by kin and close friends, for the more diverse, wealthy, entertaining, technological and necessarily impersonal world that constitutes modern urban life.

But the important point is, *so is virtually everyone else in the world*, because ultimately they are human beings with very similar sorts of underlying preferences. There are, of course, plenty of people who continue to live in a variety of traditional societies and seem to be quite contented doing so. But that is often the case because they cannot figure out how to transform their society into a more modern one, or else because they simply have not heard what modern societies are like. The moment they find out, they usually decide they like what they see, which explains why there is a massive flow of migrants or would-be migrants from less developed to developed countries, and virtually no one making the journey in the opposite direction.

Human rights as understood in contemporary liberal democracies, then, comes as part of a larger package. These rights express the moral aspirations and priorities of modern societies, that is, of societies based on the systematic employment of science and technology for the satisfaction of human needs. To seek to export only the human rights part of that package to societies that are either traditional, non-democratic or otherwise based on contrary political principles can often be counterproductive and, if the country in question is powerful, dangerous as well. Human rights can be said to be universal only in a developmental sense: they become explicit aspirations primarily of societies that are both economically and politically developed. They are, in other words, a by-product of History in the Hegelian-Marxist sense.

On the other hand, virtually everyone around the globe seeks development, and it is perfectly reasonable for the United States and other Western countries to embed a universalist human rights policy in a broader strategy designed to help them get there. American-style human rights may be foreign to traditional Chinese culture, but they are not necessarily foreign to educated and technologically inclined Chinese who hope to integrate their country more fully into the global economy. Communist China cannot be forced to respect human rights, but it is not unreasonable to help guide an economically modernizing and politically liberalizing China toward institutions that will protect and extend human rights over time.

Anyone seeking to prove today that the signers of the Declaration of Independence were right in believing that human rights are based on human nature faces an uphill battle. But advocates of universal human rights need to reflect carefully on the importance of human nature to their cause. For if human beings are not in the end fundamentally similar under the skin, despite obvious differences in race, ethnicity, culture, wealth and education, then on what grounds can we demand that all governments treat their citizens with equal consideration? So too for the beleaguered notion that we have reached the end of History: an end to the historical process makes sense only if human nature provides a constant standard by which we can measure the suitability of our political institutions under a given technological horizon. Constant, that is, until such time as biotechnology gives us the ability to create new beings born, in effect, with saddles on their backs, and a new human nature comes to dictate a new set of posthuman rights.

Responses

Francis Fukuyama has written his usual interesting piece, and he is right that we must clean up our moral assumptions before we translate them into policy. I agree with almost every word of his general argument. Indeed, many of his conclusions parallel some of my own: that the propensity to control violence is as strong as the propensity to violence itself, for example. This must seem odd since he has chosen to make me a whipping boy for his "discovery" that the naturalistic fallacy isn't fallacious. I find this odd, since for forty years I have been arguing that the philosophical world was wrong about Hume, who did nothing more than observe the facility with which men leap from is to ought. I have never been one of those scientists "quick to invoke the naturalistic fallacy as a shield to protect their work from unpalatable political implications": unequivocally and absolutely the opposite, often to my cost.

I don't say with Ehrlich that human nature gives us no guidance. In my article to which Fukuyama refers ("Human Nature and Human Rights", Winter 2000/2001, reprinted in this anthology as Chapter 17) I say it either gives direct guidance, or tells us what we might wish to avoid, or is neutral. I was simply concerned to point out that those who are trumpeting the "human" in human rights are mostly trampling on many human rights to promote the political rights they happen to favor. I am *agreeing* with Fukuyama; I certainly do not "dismiss natural rights." He does not happen to like some of the rights I derive, but that is another matter.

I would have thought that my analysis of the issue of the human rights of the collectivity versus those of the individual—an analysis very guilty of naturalism—would be music to a Hegelian! I think we could have a serious discussion here about naturalism, once Fukuyama figures out that we are on the same (naturalistic) side. The ground would then be cleared for some substantial disagreement over whether rights trump needs (a hierarchy of needs could perhaps solve that one), or over his notion that the economic benefits of a modern capitalist (liberal) economy satisfy "latent longings of our underlying natures." Maybe so, but how?

Consider that in an environment of evolutionary adaptation characterized by scarcity there was, for example, no need for endogenous curbs on our desire for sweet and salty things. Scarcity was its own curb. These "latent longings" however, once offered limitless satisfaction, lead to gorging, obesity, heart disease, alcoholism and addiction to opiates. The analogy holds with material goods, entertainment, violence, competition, information, power, sex and so forth. We are presented not with healthy satisfactions, but with an array of Niko Tinbergen's "supernormal stimuli" that overwhelm our scarcity-dependent controls. Socialism is not an alternative—I have always argued that it was simply another version of the industrial phase—but neither is what we've got. Fukuyama thinks that what is—in capitalism—is right because, in the historical short run, it beat out its opposition. This is a precarious principle, as is his assumption that people prefer the anonymity of modern cities to the traditional world of kin. People who flee to the cities of the capitalist world are not fleeing kinship but poverty. Of course, no one is going the other way, but not because they want to abandon kinship; they don't want to give up material prosperity. Individualism and anonymity are prices they have to pay, not wholesome choices they voluntarily make. Most immigrants immediately recreate their world of kin when they arrive here, and even our own internal migrants attempt to establish, via elaborate customs of friendship, that same particularistic world. (Note the popularity of *Seinfeld*, *Friends* and similar "non-family" sitcoms.) Now *this* is a debate worth having.

Robin Fox
University Professor of Social Theory
Rutgers University

Francis Fukuyama's provocative article, "Natural Rights and Human History", attempts to clarify the sources of rights in his three-fold distinction: divine rights, natural rights, and what one might call the contemporary positivistic view of rights as located in social law and custom." In short, the possible sources are "God, Nature and Man himself."

Fukuyama's argument for nature, "or, more precisely, human nature", leads him to the sticking point. He believes people must choose human nature-based thinking, because the only "positive rights" approach that he conceives of is, or leads necessarily to, cultural relativism, a conception in which "you have declared from the outset that there are no transcendent standards for determining right and wrong beyond whatever any particular culture declares to be a right."

Fukuyama is wrong to put things this way. It is possible to see the best answer to the question he poses—what are the justifiable or true sources of rights?—by combining positive rights with human nature-based rights thinking.

This is not some idea of compromise or vague splitting of a difference.

Why insist, as does Fukuyama, that everyone must choose for nature now? Why not a conception of rights that is simultaneously moral and historical? Why not posit that a human nature-based conception of rights is the correct or best version of rights, noting that the historical process—as Fukuyama himself is celebrated for arguing—is leading in an identifiable general direction, the direction of liberal democratic politics and morality? A gradual convergence of cultures, states, and nations on at least many of these rights (and thus also of wrongs) is, he himself argues, quite clear. And from Kant on, this view of rights as process as well as condition has been quite clear in our intellectual frameworks.

Is it so necessary or convincing to draw only a single line in the sand, rather than one full plus one dotted line? Truth is historical as well as logical. By insisting on the single true answer, by waving unnecessarily the red flag of cultural relativism, Fukuyama oversimplifies the question of the sources of rights and creates political divisions within what should be his own camp, which is otherwise much larger than he thinks.

Ronald Tiersky
Eastman Professor of Politics
Amherst College

Fukuyama writes: "Americans more than most peoples have tended to conflate rights and interests. By transforming every individual desire into a right unconstrained by community interests, one increases the inflexibility of political discourse. The debates in the United States over pornography and gun control would appear much less Manichaean if we spoke of the interests of pornographers rather than their fundamental First Amendment right to free speech, or the needs of assault weapon owners rather than their sacred Second Amendment right to bear arms. . . ." For someone who once wrote a book about the victory of classical liberal ideals this is a very strange declaration.

Natural rights, properly understood, are liberties, spheres of personal authority within which one does as one judges fit—even if it may be unwise, imprudent, or cowardly—and others must gain entrance by permission. If I wish to publish or read pornography, for example, this is my right and none may prohibit me from doing so. I am no child, they aren't my parents.

It is just this kind of liberty that distinguishes the American political tradition from that of Asia, Europe and other places around the globe. Yes, in some measure it leaves America to rely on its rhetorical skills to exert influence and limits it from charging in everywhere with force. But one would assume someone who understands, even champions, classical liberal ideals would find this just the way things ought to be. Other nations bully those who stand in the way of their interests but in America we respect—or should or hold out the ideal that we would—everyone's basic rights, even when these oppose our interests.

Tibor R. Machan
Silverado, CA

In "Natural Rights and Human History" Francis Fukuyama writes: "Anyone seeking to prove today that the signers of the Declaration of Independence were right in believing that human rights are based on human nature faces an uphill battle." I don't know where Fukuyama has been since I first began publishing my defense of Abraham Lincoln, and justifying his conviction that human rights were based upon human nature. In my recent book, *A New Birth of Freedom: Abraham Lincoln and the Coming of the Civil War*, Chapter 2, I systematically took up, and like Thomas Aquinas, replied to every objection to the thesis that the self-evident truths of the Declaration of Independence were the foundation of all political rights, and of all constitutional government. Fukuyama should review my book, and express his agreement or disagreement with the argument set forth therein. Perhaps we would end in reproducing the famed debate on fundamentally the same topic, between my teacher Leo Strauss, and his teacher, Alexander Kojève.

Harry V. Jaffa
Claremont McKenna College

Fukuyama replies:

I apologize to Prof. Fox if I made him out to be a proponent of the naturalistic fallacy, contrary to what he has argued at different points over a long and distinguished academic career. What I was going on was the article on human rights that he published in *The National Interest*, and there, beyond a doubt, he makes fun of the idea that contemporary sociobiological understandings of human nature can give us useful guidance with regard to human rights. He does not in this piece rise to the defense of transcendent human rights and in fact scorns the idea that they can be a basis for foreign policy. So we in fact appear to disagree, at least with respect to what he wrote for this magazine. Readers who want to understand his position more fully should look to his other works, as referenced.

The issue he raises at the end of his letter is an important one. It is clear that life in modern, technological capitalist liberal societies is in many ways highly unnatural, beginning with the ready availability of calories that he mentions, to the unlimited types of social, consumer and other kinds of choices available to people today. My point was not to argue that our world was the best of all possible worlds with respect to our natures, but rather that it was better than others that have been put into place in the past century, and that attention to human nature would have given us guidance in that regard. Liberal societies do better than socially engineered ones because they permit people to recreate things like kinship networks and social norms that come naturally to them. But there is no question that the absence of community and rules in modern societies can be highly alienating, because human beings were never adapted to live in that fashion.

With regard to Prof. Tiersky's comment that I shouldn't dichotomize natural and positive or historical rights, I don't think that I did so. I of course believe that there is such a thing as History in the Hegelian sense of human beings freely acting to shape their environment, ends and behavior. This can nonetheless coexist with a notion of nature. As Aristotle would have argued, the existence of nature and natural standards of right does not rigidly dictate one set of values, institutions or regime, nor does it rule out the possibility of historical progress. Aristotle noted that while man is a political animal by nature, the first *polis* had to be created in historical time by a lawgiver. Nature does however serve as a framework within which historical institutions emerge, one that allows us then to evaluate the possibilities History has created. And nature puts limits on our own self-modification. As both Plato and Aristotle understood, it is hard to know what nature is unless one listens to what people say about themselves. So positive rights are necessary to supplement our understanding of natural rights; but they are insufficient by themselves.

Mr. Machan's point is, as I understand it, that the United States was founded on what we would now label libertarian principles. This is simply not true: most of the American Founding Fathers believed that virtue was necessary for a successful democracy, to the extent that many believed that the states (though not the Federal government) had a right to establish religious belief. Most would almost certainly have disapproved of individuals consuming pornography in the privacy of their own homes. We have moved toward what Michael Sandel labels "procedural liberalism" in which the state takes no interest in virtue or individual ends only in the second half of the twentieth century. I am in fact a supporter of classical liberalism, at least of the Tocquevillian variety, which implies the need for certain values beyond the bare-bones procedural institutions to guarantee the possibility of ordered liberty.

With all due respect to Prof. Jaffa, his otherwise erudite book on Lincoln is but a slender reed standing in the gale of modern opinion that maintains that rights are only positive or culturally relative. Would that he has convinced *these* opponents as thoroughly as he thinks he has. His real argument is with them, not with me.

Notes

1. Quoted in Gregory Stock and John Campbell, *Engineering the Human Germline: An Exploration of the Science and Ethics of Altering the Genes We Pass on to Our Children* (New York: Oxford University Press, 2000), p. 85.
2. This argument is made in Dworkin, *Life's Dominion: An Argument about Abortion, Euthanasia, and Individual Freedom* (New York: Vintage Books, 1994).
3. Glendon, *A World Made New: Eleanor Roosevelt and the Universal Declaration of Human Rights* (New York: Random House, 2001).
4. Quoted in Adrienne Koch and Willam Peden, eds., *The Life and Selected Writings of Thomas Jefferson* (New York: Modern Library, 1944), pp. 729–30.
5. Fox, "Human Nature and Human Rights", *The National Interest* (Winter 2000/01).
6. Fox has noted to the author that in other of his writings, particularly *Conjectures and Confrontations: Science, Evolution, Social Concern* (New Brunswick, NJ: Transaction Publishers, 1997), he has explicitly argued against the naturalistic fallacy. I am seeking to respond to the argument he put forward in this journal; readers should consult other of his works for a fuller account of his views.
7. Ehrlich, *Human Natures: Genes, Cultures, and the Human Prospect* (Washington, DC: Island Press, 2000).
8. Hume's exact statement is: "In every system of morality which I have hitherto met with, I have always remark'd, that the author proceeds for some time in the ordinary way of reasoning, and establishes the being of a God, or makes observations concerning human affairs; when of a sudden I am surpriz'd to find, that instead of the

usual copulations of propositions, is, and is not, I meet with no proposition that is not connected with an ought, or an ought not. This change is imperceptible; but is, however, of the last consequence. For as this ought or ought not expresses some new relation or affirmation, 'tis necessary that it should be observ'd and explain'd; and at the same time that a reason should be given, for what seems altogether inconceivable, how this new relation can be a deduction from others, which are entirely different from it." Hume, *Treatise on Human Nature*, Book III, Part I, Section I (London: Penguin Books, 1985).

9. Friedrich Nietzsche, *Beyond Good and Evil* (New York: Vintage Books, 1966), Section 9, p. 15.
10. MacIntyre, "Hume on 'Is' and 'Ought'", *Philosophical Review* (October 1959).
11. Hume has been wrongly interpreted as a kind of proto-Kantian, but in fact he falls squarely in the older tradition of deriving rights from human nature.
12. See Galston, "Liberal Virtues", *American Political Science Review* (December 1988).
13. For numerous examples of this, see Frans De Waal, *Chimpanzee Politics: Power and Sex among Apes* (Baltimore, MD: Johns Hopkins University Press, 1989).
14. See my book, *The Great Disruption: Human Nature and the Reconstitution of Social Order* (New York: Free Press, 1999).
15. "Defensive modernization" describes a process whereby the requirements of external military competition drive internal sociopolitical organization and innovation. There are many examples of this, from reforms in post-Meiji Restoration Japan to the Internet.
16. See my "Women and the Evolution of World Politics", *Foreign Affairs* (September/October 1998).
17. Wright, *NonZero: The Logic of Human Destiny* (New York: Pantheon Books, 2000).
18. The intellectual landscape on the issue of group selection has changed somewhat recently with the work of biologists, for example, David Sloan Wilson, who have made the case for multi-level (that is, both individual and group) selection. See Wilson and Elliott Sober, *Unto Others: The Evolution and Psychology of Unselfish Behavior* (Cambridge, MA: Harvard University Press, 1998).

19

The Ground and Nature of Human Rights

*William F. Schulz, Robin Fox, and Francis Fukuyama**

Power, Principles and Human Rights

(William Schulz)

One of the factions in the early Christian Church, followers of the charismatic preacher Montanus, believed that only those who ate a steady diet of radishes would be saved. The women in the community who played an inordinately powerful role in the life of the movement especially promoted this healthy regimen. Had Montanism prevailed, Christians might eat vegetables at Holy Communion rather than wafers and the Roman Catholic Church might suffer today no shortage of priests. But, whether it was resentment of roots or of "rabble", the Church fathers of the day declared the Montanists enemies of the Church in AD 170 and that was, for all intents and purposes, the end of that. Why did the Montanists fade into history? Did God really have no taste for radishes? Was it somehow a violation of natural law for women to assume a leadership role in the Church? Or did the Montanists simply lack the capacity to build an adequate consensus for their views? Had they been operating in China, where a saying has it that "only those who appreciate root vegetables can know the true meaning of life", might the story have been different?

Whether it be a religion, a nation or the world at large, the norms that govern reflect either the views of those who are at the moment holding the

*William F. Schulz is Executive Director of Amnesty International USA. Robin Fox is University Professor of Social Theory at Rutgers. Francis Fukuyama is Bernard Schwartz Professor of International Political Economy at the Paul H. Nitze School of Advanced International Studies, Johns Hopkins University.

This symposium first appeared in *The National Interest*, no. 68 (Summer 2002).

power, or the principles that have managed to claim a consensus among enough people that the powerful dare not challenge them. This is true, too, of human rights.

From the standpoint of those of us active in the human rights movement, it would be wonderful if we could prove to the satisfaction of the world that some universally recognized deity had imbued human beings with a set of rights that happened to coincide with the thirty articles of the Universal Declaration of Human Rights (UDHR). But absent that unlikely scenario, we are left with two other options upon which to base the notion of human rights, one of which—the theory of natural rights—has been the subject of considerable debate in recent issues of *The National Interest*.

In the Winter 2000/01 issue (reprinted in this anthology as chapter 17), anthropologist Robin Fox warns that if we base human rights claims on our understanding of human nature, we may end up with some pretty distasteful maxims, such as a the "right" to impregnate females belonging to tribes whose members have killed my offspring, thus diminishing my gene pool. Most of what we call "human rights", Fox says, "either run counter to nature or, at best, concern things about which nature is strictly neutral." Francis Fukuyama takes a more sanguine approach to the doctrine of natural rights in the Summer 2001 issue (reprinted as chapter 18). Dismissing Hume's criticism of the "naturalistic fallacy" (the idea that we can derive moral imperatives from factual indicatives), Fukuyama claims that human nature "does . . . allow us to establish a hierarchy of rights, and it allows us to rule out certain solutions to the problem of rights that have been politically powerful in the course of human history."

This colloquy reflects a widespread confusion about the philosophical basis for human rights claims. This problem is not new. It is a confusion that, while it may not have plagued the authors of the Declaration of Independence, certainly nipped at the heels of those who composed the Universal Declaration of Human Rights (UDHR) in 1948—and has accompanied the struggle for human rights ever since. While proposals to ground the principles of the UDHR in explicit references to God and Nature were soundly rejected by its drafters, the Declaration does contain language that certainly implies acceptance of the doctrine of natural law (e. g., the first Whereas in the Preamble affirms the "*inherent* dignity . . . of all members of the human family"; Article 1 asserts that "all human beings are *born* free and equal in dignity and rights [and] *endowed* with reason and conscience", and Article 16 refers to the family as the "*natural* . . . group unit of society [emphases added]).[1] Other references imply a more pragmatic approach (e. g., the first Whereas endorses recognition of that inherent dignity as "the foundation of freedom, justice and peace in the world.")

Be the underpinnings of the UDHR as they may, the failings of natural law as a philosophical basis for human rights go well beyond Fox's imagination, which is why few human rights advocates cite that doctrine today in justifying human rights claims. Nor does Fukuyama successfully rehabilitate the posture; indeed, his argument illustrates exactly what is wrong with it. To get clear, then, about the grounds upon which human rights are staked, we must look again at both natural law and the third alternative source, what Fukuyama calls the "positivistic" view. We will soon see that both views do indeed, as Fukuyama argues, have profound implications for how the United States carries on its foreign policy.

"What is man", asked Isak Dinesen, "but an elaborate machine for turning red wine into urine?" The fundamental problem with natural law theory, even before we get to Hume's objection that an "ought" cannot be derived from an "is", is determining what characteristics of sufficient import to serve as a basis for the delineation of rights are common to all human beings, and who decides that they are? Dinesen's observation that human beings turn red wine into urine is factually true of every person, as far as we know, but her sardonic suggestion that this is the essence of being human is one that most sober people are likely to reject outright.

But on what grounds do we reject it? The history of natural law theory would suggest that conceptions of human nature have varied wildly throughout the ages, and that the ones that have predominated at any one time have done so far more for political than for philosophical or scientific reasons. In the Middle Ages, for instance, the law of Nature was interpreted by the Church to condemn usury. Most church property at the time was in the form of land, and landowners, because their wealth is illiquid, need to borrow money. So "naturally" they opposed usury and conveniently found Natural reasons to do so. But with the rise of Protestantism, whose adherents were drawn primarily from the middle class (i. e., the "lending class"), Nature suddenly had a change of heart and was understood to look with favor on usury. Or to take another example: the great champion of natural law, John Locke, famously believed that the rights derived from it only inhered in the propertied classes and hence that women and peasants could make no claim to them. And what do we do with the ancient Uro people of Peru, who did not believe they were human at all and hence would *a priori* reject any notion of human nature? We tell them they are wrong of course, just as we tell solipsists they are wrong, on the grounds that the vast majority of us say that they are.

Now comes Robin Fox with his claim that human nature does have a "real content" and "we"—by which he apparently means anthropologists—can tell us what it is. He cites kin selection theory and suggests a series of "rights" that it implies. But quite apart from the fact that some of those "rights" he derives, such as the right to avenge the killing of a grandchild by murdering two of the killers' first cousins, are abhorrent, the fact is that anthropological theories are notoriously subject to the whims of academic fashion. Unless we are prepared to supplement the End of History with the End of (Social) Science, we rest our rights, under this approach, on intellectual quicksand. And even if we do allot to the anthropologists responsibility for seeing to it that human rights are consistent with human nature, to which anthropologists do we assign this job—the Marxists, the feminists, a subcommittee of the American Anthropological Association or Robin Fox? All that we can say for sure is that whoever would land the task would be the one who at the moment is wielding the greatest power in the halls of academe.

If Fox is too specific in the rights he cites as derivative from natural law, Fukuyama is too general. To his credit he admits as much ("there is no *simple* translation of human nature into human rights"; "human nature does not dictate a single, precise list of rights"). But still he wants to maintain, almost nostalgically, it seems, the Nature-rights connection. He is reduced, therefore, to arguing that, while "violence . . . may be natural to human beings . . . so is the propensity to control and channel violence", and that

> our underlying shared humanity allows us to rule out certain forms of political order like tyranny as unjust. Those rights that speak to the most deeply felt and universal human drives, ambitions and behaviors will be a more solid foundation for political order than those that do not.

Leaving aside the questions as to whether human beings have chosen to "control and channel violence" for natural or pragmatic reasons and how we determine "our underlying shared humanity", the problem with Fukuyama's observations is not so much that they are wrong as that they are, in a philosophical sense, uninteresting. Take one of the most universally agreed upon human rights, the right not to be tortured. If all Fukuyama is arguing is that the prohibition against torture "speaks to the most deeply felt and universal human drive" to avoid pain, he is probably right (though even in this case the existence of genuine masochists who revel in pain may call into question the universality of the pain-avoidance "drive"). Certainly, it is not unreasonable to argue that the right not to be tortured is more consistent with "our underlying shared humanity" than would be a right to torture anybody at any time one feels like it. But, having said this, have we said anything very helpful? We have, at best, identified some lowest-common-denominator-type characteristic and argued that the rights we affirm ought not to be at odds with it.[2]

Without taking the complicated step of translating these broadly construed "natural" inclinations into a clear, defensible set of rights, we are reduced to confronting agony with abstraction. Once again, to his credit, Fukuyama knows this. In elaborating upon the struggle between our propensity for violence and our inclination to channel it constructively, Fukuyama says: "These conflicting natural tendencies do not have equal status or priority; human beings *reasoning* about their situation can come to understand the need to create *rules* and institutions that constrain violence in favor of other natural ends" [emphasis added]. But what are those "rules" if not rights? And who is doing that reasoning? Just Francis Fukuyama? Just the readers of *The National Interest*? Just a select group of philosophers? If we are really to capture what is most "shared" about our humanity, the best answer will be the widest possible number of responsible agents. Otherwise we risk having the rules set by a dictator, an elite or a cabal of power-mongers. The most efficient way to see that power is controlled and dispersed is to spread it around. But that leads us to that dread perspective that Fukuyama has labeled "positivism."

"Any serious discussion of human rights", Fukuyama says, "must ultimately be based on some common understanding of human ends or purposes." Depending on what he means by that, it is a tall order. While the Universal Declaration of Human Rights was being created, Unesco surveyed 150 intellectuals to determine the philosophical basis for human rights. Not surprisingly, those surveyed could not agree and the UN Commission on Human Rights voted not to distribute the UNESCO report.[3] Imagine how trying to get them to agree on the "ends or purposes" of life would have turned out!

But why should they need to come to consensus on such abstract matters in order to agree that torture is wrong? Any two people can both be against torture even if one believes that the purpose of life is to get into Heaven and the other believes it is to avoid being bored. Despite their differences, they can both very well agree that they would rather not live in a world in which torture is commonplace. That is because human rights are not dependent upon our sharing ontologies, teleologies or eschatologies; they are dependent upon our sharing a commitment to what makes for a civilized world, as "civilized" is defined at the moment by the vast majority of the international community. Human rights, as embodied in the UDHR, provide a set of norms or guidelines, "best practices", if you will, by which to set limits to tyranny and organize a decent society.

Perhaps all that Fukuyama means by a "common understanding of human ends or purposes" is agreement on the definition of a "decent society." But one suspects that this will not be enough for him because such a definition inevitably changes from generation to generation (just as our conceptions of natural law do) and Fukuyama wants something reliable forever. Otherwise, why criticize positivism by claiming that it allows for "no universal standards for political behavior" to which to appeal against the Chinese canard that collective rights trump individual? "Abhorrent practices like suttee or slavery or female circumcision" must be accepted, Fukuyama says, because positivism provides "no transcendent standards for determining right and wrong beyond what any particular culture declares to be a right." But these claims are wrong on several counts.

In the first place, though it is true that the values implicit in the UDHR derive from the Enlightenment tradition, virtually every country in the world has affirmed them. The UDHR was drafted by representatives from a wide variety of cultures, including Asian; voted on affirmatively by countries from every culture and corner of the world; agreed to implicitly by every country that has joined the United Nations; and is regarded today as customary international law by every international court on the globe. While its affirmation is not literally "universal" in the sense that one will, of course, find people who do not agree with it and many who violate it, the UDHR can claim far more "transcendence", and hence provides a far greater "universal standard for political behavior", than does Fukuyama's doctrine that violence is a result of human nature as opposed to Divine punishment, distraction from the Eight-Fold Path, unfortunate parenting or just plain bad judgment.

One of the results of the far-flung influence of the Declaration is that in many cases human rights abuses do not just violate universal standards; they violate the laws of the very countries in which those abuses are found. Torturing dissidents in China, for example, violates that country's constitution, no matter how loudly Chinese leaders proclaim that individual rights are subordinate to social. In that case we do not need to appeal to "universal standards;" we need only ask the Chinese to obey their own laws. Female genital mutilation, too, is against the law in almost every country in which it is found.

But what about countries whose laws or cultural practices *do* violate international human rights standards? What do we say to them? Do we really have no response to cultural relativism, as Fukuyama seems to think? Far from it. We have the best possible response: "Your practice violates the closest thing we have to agreement among the world's people as to what constitutes cruelty."

Are rights derived from such agreement apodictic? No. Like all laws and standards, they evolve. Human rights at the international level rely upon the same principle that the U.S. Supreme Court invokes when it determines that "evolving community standards", concerning what constitutes pornography or whether it is acceptable to execute the mentally retarded, influence the interpretation of justice. What if the arc of the universe does *not* bend toward justice and these standards become regressive? Theoretically that is possible, though experience seems to show that the more people involved in the standard setting (that is, the more widely the power to set standards is shared), the less likely the backsliding.

Wouldn't it be wiser to rely on *truth* rather than power, or consensus? Absolutely, but then deciding what is "true" between nations has rarely been as simple as Clemenceau made it out to be when he replied to a question as to what historians would say was the cause of the first World War: "I do not know what they will say was the cause of the war, but I do know that they will not say that France invaded Germany." (Had Clemenceau never heard of revisionism?) Rights that are grounded in international consensus—even "semisensus"—and elaborated in formal treaties and conventions are far more likely to be perceived as politically legitimate than notions of what Truth or Nature does or does not justify. Is the arrangement perfect? No, but then imperfection is only "natural."

The debate we have been carrying on in these pages is not just an esoteric one, though it may seem like it at times. Indeed, its practical implications may disclose something about why all comers take the positions they do. For if human rights are not grounded in some elite's definition of natural law but reflect what the UDHR labels "a common standard of achievement for all peoples and all nations", then the United States, like every other country in the world, must take the values and opinions of others into account as it formulates its policies. When it comes to matters that have implications for human rights, in other words, unilateralism has no place.

This is a hard pill for some foreign policy realists to swallow. As Condoleeza Rice wrote in *Foreign Affairs* magazine during the last presidential campaign: "Foreign policy in a Republican administration . . . will proceed from the firm ground of the national interest, not from the interests of an illusory international community." But if human rights are determined by the evolving standards of the international community, it is no wonder they play such a modest part in the foreign policy calculations of those who would regard that community as an illusion.

The problem is, however, that reality always threatens to confound the realists. Just as little more than a year after Dr. Rice wrote those words in *Foreign Affairs*, she and President Bush have been scrambling valiantly and for the most part successfully to enlist that "illusory international community" in pursuit of the common interest it shares with the United States in defeat of terrorism, so the United States has taken pains—in its conduct of the war, for example—to see that the human rights values of that community are not offended. And why should the United States care about those values? Because it knows that, far from being an "illusion", the opinions of our allies directly affect our national interest; the opinions of the fence-sitters will be swayed by any perception of hypocrisy; and the opinions (and actions) of our adversaries can be countered by, among other things, an appeal to world opinion.

Better, then, to hammer out the details of what counts as a human right in the halls of diplomacy than in the recesses of a professor's study. Neither place guarantees a harmonious discussion, but at least the former makes it far more likely that those whose lives are shaped by the decisions will at least have a place at the table.

Human Rights and Foreign Policy

(*Robin Fox*)

William Schulz is out once again on a turf-protecting mission. His organization is a major beneficiary of the international human rights conglomerate, and he wants to establish its privilege to be the sole definer and defender of said rights, as promulgated in the Universal Declaration (UDHR). Since many governments behave in a pretty beastly way to some of their people most of the time, it is a good idea to let them know that someone is watching and will tell. In the unlikely event that my government should decide to torture me, I would be glad that he was around to chastise them. I also agree that about some things there is a consensus among what we take to be "civilized" nations, and if he wants to call these things "human rights" that's fine.

The trouble is that one does not have to move far from torture, lack of due process and the like to find huge areas of disagreement, *despite* what governments might have signed by way of international agreements or even made into national laws. To please the Western governments that initiate these things, non-Western governments sign on to a list of values that their people do not know about, their preachers do not preach, and their jurists and scholars do not accept. If we add up China, North Korea, most of Southeast Asia, and the whole Muslim world from Morocco and Nigeria to Indonesia, we have a "substantial majority of the international community" that does *not* subscribe to the liberal, democratic, Enlightenment values of the UDHR, whatever documents their governments might have endorsed. (India officially subscribes to at least the democratic ideal, but again this is not something that sits easily with the majority of its people. The caste system, which embraces the bulk of the population, is the very opposite of democracy.) To appeal to a phantom "civilized majority" of the world community as a basis for human rights definition and enforcement could be a very dangerous illusion. I happen to like the UDHR list because I come from the tradition that created it. But I am not a Chinese communist bureaucrat, a Pashtun mullah in the Northwest Frontier Province, a Wahhabi in Saudi Arabia, a Brahmin in the Punjab, or an East African or Nigerian village chief. Their views on forced abortion, legal mutilation, due process, women's claustration, lower-caste impurity, and female circumcision, Mr. Schulz would no doubt find as "abhorrent" as he finds the law of talion. (This law, which seems to give squeamish critics such a problem, would be seen by any Afghan tribesman fighting as our ally to be a law of nature. And let us not forget the millions who give Charles Bronson and Clint Eastwood a standing ovation in our own cinemas, and vote regularly for the death penalty.)

In particular, we are faced with the alarmingly rapid population growth of an increasingly resentful, devoutly Muslim world; a world that fundamentally does not accept Mr. Schulz's "civilized consensus." Rather, most of the devout see it as propaganda from the infidel, imperialist West, out to inflict "humiliations" (their favorite word) on the only kind of society acceptable to God. There is no room for compromise here. Our way of life is, for them, a direct offense to God; it is an offense against everything the *umma* should be. As our President keeps saying, the Islamic fundamentalists hate "freedom and democracy" and "our way of life", but not only because of material or political resentment: they know they have the better, God-ordained, and therefore inevitable, alternative. What we see as the pursuit of "inalienable" individual rights, they see as godless materialist corruption. The time of their being tempted, like the latter-day Atatürks who rule them, to ape the secular West has passed almost without our notice. The time also has passed when we might hope that they would eventually see the light and morph into "moderate" pro-Western world citizens. The trend is entirely in the opposite direction. The terrorists may well be, as the President insists, a small minority of Muslims, but they enjoy widespread sympathy and support. The kind of society the devout want to live in, even if not as extreme as that of the Taliban, would have little time for most of Mr. Schulz's admirable list of consensus virtues. (Listen to our new ally, the chief justice of Afghanistan, for example, on that state's right to go on mutilating thieves.) Unless we grasp this point, we will continue to delude ourselves with the fantasy that these are simply "backward" societies that will someday catch up with the march of history; that is, with our secular, liberal-democratic, capitalist version of utopia. Francis Fukuyama used to think this "progress" was inevitable, and that the spectrum of human rights we endorse should prevail because they are the ones compatible with our kind of society, which itself must prevail, and so lead to "the end of history." I wonder if he still believes this?

Where, then, do we go for a definition of human rights? The issue is probably moot since, as Schulz correctly observes, those with the power to enforce their version will win anyway. God forbid it should be the American Anthropological Association, whose members, sunk in post-modern, deconstructionist, self-referential relativism, would be more likely to agree with him than with me. I simply wanted, in what has turned out to have been an unexpectedly contentious essay, to point out that there are certain basic human *needs and emotions* that even "natural rights" advocates, who pay lip service to "universalism", try to avoid.[4] And they avoid them precisely because these needs are not pretty when viewed from the lofty heights of the UDHR. But I also pointed out that some of these basic features (including the natural rights of the collectivity over the individual—a point that gets repeatedly missed) do find their closest expression in devout Muslim societies. And the "rights" derivable from these needs are among some of those that are most "abhorrent" to Schulz and other defenders of the UHDR.

This is of importance to our conduct in the world, and is not—as he rightly sees—just a recondite quarrel among professors. Not only is there no "universal majority consensus", but the version of human rights that so appalls us in our now major competitors may be more firmly grounded in human nature than is our own version. This is not a happy conclusion; but we must start to take our opponents at least as seriously as they take us. The recent polls of Muslim countries shocked us in our naivete by showing how strongly the majority in all of them, even the most Westernized, see themselves as being in relentless opposition to us. Above all we must make an imaginative attempt to shake off our obsessive concern with the individual, and hence individual rights, and try to understand the strength of the appeal to a collectivist, theocratic, kinship-oriented society. If we do not, Schulz and his Enlightenment friends may end up living under the universal-consensus Muslim DHR, which, on his theory, he would be bound to accept.

I do not want this to happen any more than he does, but we will not prevent it by pursuing a Clinton-style (or Blair-style) human-rights-based foreign policy. Tinkering with that policy to try to make the Muslim masses love us will not work. They will not love us, so we had better make sure they respect us enough to accept our accommodation. And we should try also to get over the false hope that alleviating poverty, in and of itself, will "cure" the problem. The most militant are not the poverty stricken; their quarrel with us is spiritual, not material. Our pursuit of a human-rights policy will not impress them, for they do not share our vision of individual human rights, and they do not trust such a policy to be disinterested—quite rightly. We must grasp, too, that they are increasing by the millions yearly, while we decline.

A realistic foreign policy may be occasionally hurtful to our liberal consciences, but it will be necessary if Mr. Schulz and his UDHR world are to survive. For one thing, we had better work hard to ensure that China is with us rather than against us, whatever its human rights record. A common fear of Muslim militancy may be the issue that will help to forge bonds between NATO, China, India and the former Soviet-bloc countries, especially Russia itself. Thus the NATO nations are belatedly coming to recognize publicly (they knew it all along) the deep, and still enduring links between Al-Qaeda, other Islamic terrorist groups, and the Muslim militias and "liberation armies" of the Balkans and the Caucasus. The NATO powers must surely now wish in their hearts that they had Osama bin Laden in the dock at the Hague, and not Slobodan Milosevic, however much he personally deserves to be there. Serbia, whose infrastructure the NATO powers destroyed and whose people they bombed into poverty in the name of human rights, had not attacked or even vaguely threatened any of them. There is at least the possibility that a judicious intervention at the right time to assist the legitimate government of Yugoslavia in dealing with dissident Islamic terrorists in Bosnia and Kosovo might have prevented some of the massacres and ethnic cleansing from all sides. What is more, if this intervention had done the job of subduing the *mujaheddin* and cleaning out the terrorist cells (instead of clandestinely arming and then overtly supporting them), it might even have prevented the horrific events of September 11th.

The paradox is that we may from time to time have to suspend *some* of our principles in order to protect *all* of them. (This is what we are pragmatically forced to do anyway, which is what makes an "ethical foreign policy" as such an exercise in pious hypocrisy.) The pursuit of morally elevated universal values is warming to our civilized consciences, but in the cold eye of history it is only survival that counts.

Truth Matters, and Universality Beckons

(*Francis Fukuyama*)

William Schulz fails to distinguish between the practical task of building a global consensus in favor of human rights and getting governments to observe them (which is what he and his organization do), and the *philosophical* question of where these rights come from and how they are grounded. The former project depends on consensus, log-rolling and negotiation, where the opinions of large numbers of people are critical. The latter, however, is related to something called *truth*. Philosophy and its modern offspring science are the rational quest for truth, which always was and always will be the province of what he dismisses as "elites." What these elites think, of course, will not matter in the short run to a government seeking to torture or jail its opponents. But in the long run, they serve to establish the broad framework of ideas that eventually gets translated into practical political programs. If people today, in contrast to Thomas Jefferson and his Enlightenment precursors, believe that the truth about rights is not "self-evident" or even humanly accessible, it is only because they have been taught a watered-down version of the thought of philosophers such as Nietzsche and Heidegger from a few generations back.

The philosophical truth about rights is important in another way, as well, that has do to with why William Schulz bothers to get out of bed in the morning. Surely he has not dedicated his life to the struggle for human rights simply because it is the majority opinion of people around the world, or even the opinion of the world's well-meaning people, that this struggle is important. If he were in the midst of an agitated crowd that suddenly decided to lynch someone who expressed an unpopular opinion, he would certainly not be content to consult majority opinion on what was right to do; he would look instead to his own internal moral compass. There must be some *principle* involved here to which one assigns a truth value. One could, of course, consult the opinions of the larger surrounding community that may make lynching a crime, but that simply begs the question of whether those laws and the regime that promulgates them are themselves just. Why indeed bother consulting global "consensus" or majority opinions at all? That already presupposes a certain moral truth about the value of consensus or democracy. And where do we get that opinion? It's turtles all the way down from there: at a certain point, we have to leave off consulting the opinions of people around us, and confront the essentially *philosophical* question of the inherent truth about principles of right and wrong.

Moreover, Schulz pretends that there is a universal consensus in favor of human rights, and that the task for us is simply to get nations to enforce the norms and laws to which they have subscribed. This is plainly not the case: from radical Islamists to promoters of Asian values to leftover communists and authoritarians, there are plenty of people around the world who would object in principle and most certainly in practice to the implementation of many of the human rights norms for which he is fighting. It is true that, with the defeat of communism and fascism in the 20th century, there is greater scope for agreement in the world now over what constitutes human rights. But even the most unreflective observer must recognize that what Amnesty International promotes as human rights arise out of values born in the individualistic Western Enlightenment, with deep roots in Christianity. They are not some syncretic mishmash of global values, but the clear historical products of the values of one particular part of the world.

If these values are now spreading to other parts of the world that do not share the cultural premises of the Western Enlightenment, the question arises as to *why* they are spreading. Is this simply the result of the power and prestige of the West? Is it a form of mass psychosis? If so, the promotion of human rights in non-Western societies would actually constitute a grave *injustice*, a crushing of genuine moral and cultural alternatives by the wealthy and powerful.

The alternative interpretation is that these values are spreading because they in fact have a universal appeal; that is, that they respond to deeply held aspirations of people around the world, regardless of their cultural background. These values would be comparable in this sense to the scientific method, which was born under certain specific cultural and historical conditions in Western Europe, but which then spread throughout the world because of their universal validity. And if this is the case, one must then wonder *why* they are universal. If we reject the mass psychosis interpretation, the answer can only be that there is indeed a commonly shared human essence which, despite differences in culture and environment, responds similarly to certain opportunities and injustices. And we thus arrive back at the issue of human nature, and the natural rights that arise from it.

Ironically, I agree more with Schulz than with Fox about the place of human rights in American foreign policy. It is, of course, possible to promote human rights in reckless or imprudent ways, or to let them trump other important national interests. But for the United States in particular, a moral grounding for foreign policy is essential to sustain democratic consensus behind American involvement in the world. And that moral concern, if exercised with judgment and moderation, will ultimately be of benefit to those people around the world who suffer from injustice as well.

Notes

1. See Johannes Morsink, *The Universal Declaration of Human Rights: Origins, Drafting & Intent,* (Philadelphia: University of Pennsylvania Press, 1999), chapter

8, for a discussion of the debates surrounding issues of natural law in the drafting of the UDHR.

2. Paradoxically enough, those "natural" qualities of human beings upon which it would be easiest to win universal consensus, such as the biological needs for food or shelter, would imply a whole series of social and economic rights that are recognized by the UDHR and the human rights community, but which Fukuyama and many Americans would probably disavow.
3. Morsink, pp. 301-02.
4. Robin Fox, "Human Nature and Human Rights," *The National Interest* (Winter 2000/01) This is reprinted in this anthology as chapter 17.

20

What Price Human Rights?

*William F. Schulz and John R. Bolton**

Dear John:

I have noted with interest your recent appointment to the Commission on International Religious Freedom, recently created to report on violations of religious rights around the world. You would not have accepted this assignment, I am sure, if you did not care about stopping human rights abuses. At the same time your bona fides as a conservative make you an exquisite interlocutor with whom to debate the state of U.S. human rights policy today.

As far as I am concerned, that policy is pretty much of a mess. I don't believe that human rights ought to be the sole consideration governing U.S. international relations or even always the primary one. But I do believe that they ought to be a serious factor in how we relate to other nations, and that violations ought to have real and consistent consequences. That is both because respect for human rights is endemic to America's understanding of itself and because ignoring human rights crimes often has profoundly deleterious effects upon our national interest. (One of the reasons we are now so tangled up in Bosnia and Kosovo is because two Presidents waited far too long to counter Milosevic's evil ambitions.)

Given this premise, then, it helps not at all for the United States to send China decidedly mixed signals on its abominable human rights record. It is

---

*William F. Schulz is executive director of Amnesty International USA. John R. Bolton was senior vice president of the American Enterprise Institute and is serving in the George W. Bush Administration as undersecretary of state for arms control and international security affairs.

This exchange of letters was originally printed in *The National Interest*, no. 56 (Summer 1999). This dialogue took place during the NATO air campaign against Yugoslavia. The letters are reprinted without editorial updating.

certainly confusing at best to trumpet our outrage at abuses in pariah states like Cuba and Libya while ignoring similar violations by allies like Saudi Arabia and Turkey, or trading partners like Nigeria and Indonesia. To waffle on the Land Mines Treaty or the International Criminal Court (ICC); to let Karadzic and Mladic go scot-free; to ignore Africa altogether—the policy is a mess.

But it is too easy just to blame the administration. For in my view far too many conservatives have also abandoned bedrock principles when it comes to human rights. After all, the protection of individual liberties against oppressive governments is supposed to be at the heart of conservative political theory. But as Jesse Helms points out in a recent article in Foreign Affairs, it is the conservative business community that has opposed economic sanctions designed to win those liberties. I personally believe sanctions to be of limited utility, and even then only in very circumscribed situations (and Amnesty itself takes no position on them); but they certainly ought to be included in our quiver. So should the possibility of military intervention. But it is too often conservative voices that most vociferously resist a U.S. peacekeeping role overseas to stop the slaughter of innocents.

It troubles me that a Republican Congress allows taxpayers' dollars to be wasted when U.S. security assistance is used to commit human rights violations in places like Colombia or Turkey, and when political asylum seekers, many of whom have stood up for American values in their home countries, are tossed into county jails with the general prison population.

I know from your recent article in these pages on the International Criminal Court ("Courting Danger: What's Wrong With the ICC," reprinted in this anthology as chapter 9) that part of your own criticism of the human rights movement has to do with your disdain for so-called "customary international law." But of course the basis for most customary law when it comes to human rights is the Universal Declaration of Human Rights and the Covenants that flow out of it. Such principles of international law were incorporated explicitly into the International Religious Freedom Act that established the commission on which you now sit because, without them, your impending criticism of other nations' treatment of religious minorities would risk sounding hollow, parochial, even xenophobic.

Elsewhere you have implied that General Pinochet should be tried, if at all, by his Chilean compatriots ("The Global Prosecutions," *Foreign Affairs*, January/February 1999). But given Pinochet's manipulation of the Chilean constitution before he stepped down—and his threats to cause mayhem ever since—that is like asking a jury to render a verdict while a defendant holds a gun to its head.

So I guess it comes down to this: while I am happy to skewer the Democratic administration whenever it deserves it, I am left wondering how do those conservatives who mistrust sanctions, resist military intervention, and pooh-pooh international law intend to stop human rights violations?

I certainly recognize that the human rights movement has made its own share of mistakes, both substantive and strategic. What I wonder is whether those of all political stripes can't find common ground to stop these tragic abuses. Perhaps our exchange will provide the beginnings of an answer.

Sincerely yours,
Bill

Dear Bill:

I agree with you that U.S. human rights policy today is "pretty much of a mess." But to understand why, we need to start well before any analysis of the appropriate role of "human rights" in foreign policy. We must first understand how freedom is best protected in individual nations, which is, after all, where we live.

We should really be debating individual liberty, not "human rights." Liberty is America's highest value, and what we offer by example to other nations ready to bear the heavy burden of sustaining it. By contrast, "human rights" stresses democratization more than liberty, and carries too much unrelated baggage, including values that are often at war with liberty. Isaiah Berlin captured the point well in his essay "Two Concepts of Liberty," explaining how Benjamin Constant

> asked why a man should deeply care whether he is crushed by a popular government or by a monarch, or even by a set of oppressive laws. He saw that the main problem for those who desire 'negative', individual freedom is not who wields this authority, but how much authority should be placed in any set of hands.

I start with an overall skepticism about all aspects of government, not just those few protected areas on the "human rights" honor roll. I note that your letter doesn't define "human rights." Perhaps you agree with me that continuing economic deregulation and lower taxes should currently be our highest political priorities in enhancing the liberty of individual Americans. Or, perhaps you prefer such things as mandating patients' "bills of rights," enforcing racial and gender employment quotas, and limiting political contributions and expenditures. Your view will certainly measure your commitment, and that of your "human rights" colleagues, to real liberty.

Next is the operational issue of how best to protect liberty. The Framers of our Constitution thought this their principal task, which is why they labored to create a national government of separated powers, and a division of authority between national and state governments. The Framers understood that it was the institutional clash among the different branches that would most effectively keep power from "one set of hands." Michael Novak has summed up the Framers' belief: "In God we trust. . . . For every one else, checks and balances."

Although even many Americans believe that the Bill of Rights is what protects their "human rights," this is a profoundly misguided view both of what the Framers intended, and of what, in practice, protects our liberty. Your letter mentions the Universal Declaration of Human Rights rather than the Bill of Rights, but James Madison's cogent assessment applies to both:

> experience proves the inefficacy of a bill of rights on those occasions when its control is most needed. Repeated violations of these parchment barriers have been committed by overbearing majorities in every State.

The Constitution protects liberty not just because it has the best list of rights, but because its daily operation prevents the concentration of power that would threaten those rights. Clearly Madison's approach was correct: history's pile of meaningless constitutions and declarations about "rights" could severely depress the market price of wallpaper.

Thus, my analysis, while libertarian in outcome, is Burkean in logic—to understand history's most successful defense of liberty before venturing abroad. This explains my concentration on matters you apparently think are "parochial, even xenophobic." I am nonetheless unshakably of the view that these preconditions to safeguarding liberty within our own nation must inform our foreign policy.

Let me, therefore, set out what I see as the basic propositions that follow from this experience:

First, American foreign policy decisionmakers should be responsible for and accountable to Americans, not to "world opinion" or "the international community," whatever those might be. For it is, of course, American national security we are discussing when we discuss foreign policy.

Second, our interests and our preferences may or may not be the same thing at the same time; no U.S. policy can succeed that does not comprehend and analyze these variables distinctly and dispassionately. To put it bluntly, the unswerving pursuit of preferences over interests may compromise the advancement and protection of both.

Third, reasoning from abstract principles alone does not resolve individual cases, and emotional self-satisfaction is not the same as policy. As *The New Republic* put it in 1914, "unless you build from the brutalities of earth, you step out into empty space." An adult foreign policy demands neither instant gratification nor conformity to one-size-fits-all prejudices.

The Clinton administration's failure to comprehend such prudential considerations—let alone follow them—substantially explains why not only our human rights policy, but our foreign policy as a whole, is a "mess." The real determinant of success internationally is judgment, the ability to discern conflicts among our preferences and assign priorities for our interests consistent with available resources. Exercising that judgment is not aided by slogans or buzz words, which evaporate when confronted with a complex and contradictory reality.

Sincerely,

John

Dear John:

Your letter is very helpful, although I suspect we live in two different worlds.

While liberty may be "America's highest value," it has never been the only one—life, happiness, property and a free conscience were the others the Founders derived from natural law—and its preservation is put in jeopardy if it stands in isolation from the others. Furthermore, as the conservative scholar Clinton Rossiter made clear in his classic study of the Founders' political thought, the purpose of government, in addition to protecting liberty, was to "secure [our] persons and property against violence, remove obstructions to [our] pursuit of happiness, help [us] to live virtuous, useful lives, and in general preserve the largest degree of natural equality."

Now you and I will certainly agree that democracy is the best form of government by which to obtain these goals, but where did you get the idea that "'human rights' stresses democratization more than liberty"? In fact it is just the opposite. Nothing in the international human rights framework precludes Jordan from having a King, though it certainly prohibits that King from imprisoning his nonviolent critics. Indeed, some of the world's purest democracies, including ours, are guilty of serious human rights violations.

You ask for a definition of "human rights" and I present it to you in the form of the Universal Declaration of Human Rights. You are correct of course when you disparage the power of parchment alone to secure rights . . . which is exactly why you should support some form of international enforcement mechanism like the International Criminal Court. Absent that, the question posed in my first letter becomes even more urgent: however do you propose to stop unfair trials, false imprisonment, torture and genocide?

Your answer seems to be that we should ruminate on the American experience and make the tough calls (whatever those are). But even your hero Burke taught that every nation has a place in a worldwide civilization, albeit one unfolding in accord with what he called "a divine tactic." Tell American business, or our soldiers stationed overseas, that we should ignore "world opinion"! It is exactly in order to secure American interests that we are forced to take others' interests into account in our decision making.

There are two reasons why human rights must not be peripheral to American foreign policy making. First, because they reflect those fundamental American values, including liberty, that Rossiter describes. If we would be the model you wish us to be, then our policies must conform to our values. Maybe an artist's model can get away with sitting pretty and passive, but we can't.

And when we do, as we did in 1994 while Rwanda was imploding, the consequences are enormous—for other people surely, but also for any sense of a moral order in the world, to say nothing of our own souls. This is in part, I presume, the motivation behind your work against religious persecution.

The second reason is because our own political and economic interests are so often implicated in assuring respect for other people's fundamental human rights. When foreign countries neglect labor standards, they tempt U.S. companies to transfer production and jobs overseas. When U.S. corporations invest internationally, they risk enormous losses caused by the instability and corruption that the denial of human rights so frequently fosters. Given increasing globalization—the fact, for example, that our pension funds are regularly invested in foreign markets—almost every American has a direct financial stake in encouraging respect for human rights. And, as we have seen all too clearly in the recent Chinese missile secrets scandal, a national security stake as well. For who can doubt that had the United States been more willing to stand on principle and engage China over its human rights abuses, so we would have been less inclined to overlook China's intelligence perfidy for fear of it jeopardizing a pocketful of gold?

Be it toxins that know no boundaries and are spread when a free press or independent monitoring groups are stifled; drug interdiction made more difficult when U.S. counter-narcotics assistance is diverted to commit political crimes; immigration flows caused by the denial of basic rights at home; or terrorists, their human rights abuses having failed to deter us from supplying them arms, turning those very same arms against us—in these ways and dozens more, taking human rights seriously is far from abstract and far from just a matter of preference.

This is the world I live in, John, and, whether you like it or not, you do too. So my question to you once again is simply this: what are we going to do about it?

Sincerely yours,
Bill

Dear Bill:

I must say I am somewhat confounded by your approach so far. I expected that you would describe why you (and the larger human rights community) believe that human rights should be central to American foreign policy. Instead, you have adopted a scattershot approach to what are in your view various mistaken foreign policy decisions, and thrown several miscellaneous punches at me personally. Flattered as I am by the personal attention, I want to stay on course to delineate the real differences between our respective positions. Let me try again.

First, U.S. foreign policy decisionmakers—as opposed to academics or pressure groups—have to make American policy. Is the United States the centerpiece of your foreign policy concerns, as it is for me, or is it something else? If it is a broad theory about the way the world should look, or "world opinion," or whatever else you think is valuable, I think you should say so unambiguously.

Second, abstractions and generalizations, whether about "human rights" or "geostrategic imperatives," mask often difficult, case-by-case choices among values and interests. Setting priorities and making choices (and understanding and accepting the consequences) is what policy is about, not simply talking about condemning this injustice or righting that wrong. Let's look at a catalogue of specific cases.

• China: You argue that "engaging" with the PRC about its human rights abuses would have made us "less inclined to overlook China's intelligence perfidy for fear of jeopardizing a pocketful of gold." I think you have this badly mixed up. In the political circles where I travel, we have been concerned about PRC efforts to proliferate the technology of weapons of mass destruction, its military adventurism in the South China Sea, and its repression of religious freedom and ethnic differences for some time. Let me allay any fears you have: real threats to U.S. national security easily trump commercial concerns.

I want to get in a word here about Taiwan as well. One of President Clinton's worst acts of appeasement was his remarks in China mouthing almost word for word the PRC's "Three Nos" policy (no independent Taiwan; no "two Chinas"; no Taiwan membership in international organizations requiring "statehood"). Although his much-touted speech about PRC human rights violations received more attention here, it was apparently broadcast unannounced and untranslated in China; by contrast, the President's implicit disparagement of the free society on Taiwan was flashed around like a Communist Party press release. I didn't notice that human rights groups sprang to Taiwan's defense; perhaps I missed it. The critical tone and substance concerning China in the State Department's annual human rights report doesn't redress the balance. Beijing believes that President Clinton speaks best for his administration, not the anonymous scriveners at State.

• Haiti: Deciding whether to intervene militarily in Haiti was a no-brainer, and President Clinton got it wrong. There was no strategic significance requiring intervention, which was justified almost entirely from a "human rights" perspective. We can all thank Providence that our casualties have been so light. And, on "human rights," what has been accomplished? Almost nothing, after over four years of U.S. occupation. Political assassinations of opposition leaders are back in style, parliament has expired, and Haiti is again ruled by presidential decree. What a mistake from start to finish.

• Somalia: This was the Clinton administration's first exercise in "assertive multilateralism" and "nation-building." It was one thing for President Bush to launch a massive humanitarian relief operation, which nonetheless had a limited mission and duration. It was quite another to turn Somalia, a place of no discernible interest to the United States, into a massive social experiment, which is what the administration did with relish. The tragic deaths of American soldiers in Mogadishu only underline how perilous it can be to pursue abstractions over interests.

• Chechnya: Press reports indicate that human rights abuses were probably committed by the military forces on both sides of the Chechnyan war of secession. Once again, however, I see no tangible American interests implicated by the fighting, whichever side was behaving most reprehensibly. My approach would have been to tell both sides privately through formal and informal channels to desist, but I would not have contemplated any military involvement to correct human rights abuses. Would you?

Obviously this list could go on and on; you or I could legitimately have picked different conflicts or problems. But all of them illustrate my central point: making policy involves trade-offs between interests and values that often speak in absolute terms. The human rights community has never admitted this dilemma, let alone come to terms with it.

Sincerely,
John

Dear John:

Of course we are talking about the role of human rights in American foreign policy. Where we differ is that I believe that making human rights concerns central to that policy—not making them the exclusive determinant or even always the pre-eminent one but always at least integral to it—is in our best interests. That, as I have said in both my letters, is for two reasons: because human rights mirror America's highest values (including liberty) and any nation that abandons its highest values betrays itself, and because nine times out of ten the pursuit of human rights is also in our best strategic interests. Furthermore, and not incidentally, the United States has undertaken a series of legal obligations with profound human rights consequences. You may not like it but the Senate has ratified the Convention Against Genocide, as well as many other human rights-related treaties and covenants, and to flout the rule of law by acting as if those obligations mean nothing is hardly the way to win friends for the democratic way of life around the world.

Where we also differ, I guess, is that I believe that there must be some consistency to our human rights policy based upon a coherent set of principles—philosophical and/or legal. Does this mean that we respond with the same degree of force or the same tactics to every human rights crisis? Of course not. I don't know a single human rights organization that advocated U.S. military intervention in Chechnya, where to do so might have gotten us into confrontation with another nuclear power. But when genocide was underway in Rwanda, the UN commander on the scene believed (correctly, as it turned out) that it could be short-circuited with the provision of just a few hundred more UN troops; and as the United States has legal obligations to prevent genocide, there is no excuse for our obstructing an international response.

You advocate "setting priorities and making choices" but you give no indication of the basis upon which you could do so, and if that basis is somehow contained in the four examples you discuss, it will take a keener mind than mine to tease it out. (Your observations on Haiti, by the way, are startling. You claim that U.S. intervention was based upon "no strategic significance" and that "almost nothing" in the way of human rights has been accomplished. But have you forgotten the thousands of Haitian refugees streaming toward our shores? And do you really believe that an end to three thousand political killings and who knows how many thousands of rapes is really nothing?)

As it makes foreign policy decisions about human rights, the United States should keep in mind such principles as these: that our criticism of other governments (be it China for religious persecution or Cuba for political prisoners) must rest upon more than American tradition or muscle if it is not to risk being dismissed as mere whim or prejudice; that therefore the United States must actively promote international standards on human rights and abide by them ourselves; that our commitment to those standards requires us to leverage our influence (sometimes diplomatically, sometimes economically, sometimes militarily) to advance human rights; and that there is rarely, if ever, a conflict between such advancement and our national security. On the contrary, in as complex and interdependent a world as this one, enforcing uniform human rights standards—establishing institutions of accountability through which to end impunity, for example—will in the last analysis make the world a far safer place for all of us.

We are in a shooting war in Kosovo today in part because we failed to abide by these principles, failed to be as tough on criminals overseas as we claim to be here at home. Regardless of one's position on the current military action, it is hard to dispute that, had we acted earlier in Bosnia to stop the slaughter there, and had we taken Karadzic and Mladic into custody after they were indicted in The Hague, the odds are better than even that Milosevic would not be playing the dangerous game he is today.

Certainly it is true that *realpolitik* requires a balancing of interests rather than a proclamation of absolutes. I would contend, however, that those interests are seriously compromised if we give short shrift to human rights. To base U.S. policy on no more than a narrow notion of today's profit is worse than shortsighted. It is positively hazardous. It is to end up walking blind through shifting sands.

Sincerely yours,
Bill

Dear Bill:

There is no subtle way to say that your policy is at best hopelessly incoherent and internally contradictory, and at worst perilously detached from tangible American interests. You say variously that human rights should be "central" to our foreign policy and not given "short shrift," that they must be "based on a coherent set of principles" (although not "a proclamation of absolutes"), and that we "must actively promote international standards on human rights." Even granting that you abjure "the same degree of force or the same tactics in every human rights crisis," your universalist rhetoric makes it impossible by definition to square your actions with your faith. You say that not "a single human rights organization . . . advocated U.S. military intervention in Chechnya," but you applaud the U.S. military interventions in Haiti and criticize our passivity in Rwanda. This menu simply confirms my point. It may not bother you, but it should bother any foreign policy practitioner in a democracy who must explain a complicated reality to a confused public.

Your very effort to lock away in the closet the true believers of the human rights movement shows exactly what I mean. You say I give no basis for my priorities and choices, but this shows you have either not read my previous letters, or that you do not understand or acknowledge what national interests are. The choices we face are among individually valuable but often competing interests, and it is precisely my point that there is no magic formula to know in advance how to behave in each diverse case. In Cap Weinberger's famous phrase, if I said any more here, I would only be repeating myself.

You may finally have acknowledged that we are talking about American foreign policy, but that reluctant admission cannot disguise that what you are really trying to do is construct a world order in which America is simply one more part of the food chain. I do not accept that future. You worry that our criticism of other governments "will be dismissed as whim or prejudice." If that is what others believe, so be it; the willfully ignorant are not worth our time or resources in any event. If any foreign leaders really think that the consistent advocacy of our basic interests is "whim or prejudice," I can only hope that they are the leaders of our enemies, because we will prevail easily against them.

Let's take Kosovo as the last case study, and an excellent one it is because it shows the results when human rights policy goes to war, this time in President Clinton's air campaign. What truly happened in Kosovo, not in the sunny world of human rights rhetoric but in the real world where idealistic but misguided policies actually take their toll? Hundreds of thousands of additional Kosovars, whose rights we were supposedly protecting, are now dead or have become refugees, separated from their families, never again to return to their homes. In Serbia, the human rights air war has achieved the unthinkable: increasing popular support for an authoritarian regime that denies democratic freedom to the very Serbs now rallying to its side. I see no gain for human rights here.

You say that "the odds are better than even" that earlier action in Bosnia and the arrest of key Bosnian Serb leaders would have deterred Slobodan Milosevic from his present conduct. This is utter nonsense. If there were ever a case where the deterrence theories so beloved by human rights advocates should have worked, it was Kosovo. Instead, they are exposed as unsupported by the evidence, and illusory in their protections.

There is a functioning war crimes tribunal for Bosnia, not to mention the International Criminal Court created last summer in Rome. It was the supposed success of the former that led to the creation of the latter; but neither has had the slightest impact. To the contrary, it is undisputed that the pace of ethnic cleansing dramatically increased after the NATO attacks began. Kosovo is thus a paradigm case where even with powerful weapons literally dropping from the skies on the war criminals, they are still at it. The Clinton administration's continued threats of war crimes prosecutions show that it is in a state of denial about the havoc its misguided policies have caused.

We do not know, as this letter is written, how Kosovo will ultimately turn out, but we cannot wait until historians decide. Responsibility for the incompetence of the Clinton administration's human rights war lies not only on the President and his top advisers, human rights devotees all, but also on those who press these policies politically without taking into account the failings of the leaders they elect and support. Kosovo is an example of a policy gone horribly wrong, but not because of insufficient attention to human rights by the administration. The opposite, coupled with what can only be described as a dreamy concept of real American interests, is more likely.

Under the two most recent Republican Presidents, who coupled idealism with a hard-headed view of America's interests, we won this century's third world war, and peacefully at that. Under their successor (not to mention their immediate predecessor), who professes that human rights are, as you wish, at the center of his policy, we have stumbled badly all around the world, squandering opportunities and interests without end.

I think the choice is easy, but as our letters reveal, we apparently disagree.

Sincerely,

John

21

"Exporting Democracy"—and Getting It Wrong

*Owen Harries**

When in May of this year (1988), a *New York Times* editorial spoke of "ugly police-state repression," it was not referring to Romania or Cuba. And when shortly afterwards that newspaper's magazine carried a cover-story about "a city of fear," the city in question was not Beirut or Belfast (or, as many Americans may have anticipated, New York itself. In each case the subject was Singapore. If you have recently been absorbed by the big issues-the Meaning of Glasnost, the End-of-the-Cold-War-As-We-Have-Known-It, How Dan Quayle got into the National Guard, etc.—it may have escaped your notice that the American press has been launching a sustained attack against Singapore. But as that attack illuminates some of the problems the United States has in dealing with friendly Third World countries that are less than perfectly liberal and democratic, it is a phenomenon that merits some attention.

The press's relegation of Singapore from a paragon of virtuous free enterprise to police state is a consequence of three interrelated issues: the detention by Lee Kuan Yew's government of a number of people allegedly involved in subversion; the expulsion of an American diplomat; and the restriction of the circulation of four American-owned newspapers and magazines. Each of these involves a clash between prevailing American views of what democratic rectitude demands and a small country's notion of what its security requires.

The Detentions

In the spring of 1987 the Singapore government used its powers under the Internal Security Act (inherited from the British) to detain without trial twenty-

---

*Owen Harries is editor emeritus of *The National Interest*.

This essay was originally published in *The National Interest*, no. 13 (Fall 1988).

two people accused of involvement in a Marxist conspiracy. All but one of these were released by the end of the year, the government having concluded that they were pawns manipulated by others rather than dangerous subversives. Eight of them, however, were rearrested in April 1988 after issuing a statement claiming that they had been mistreated while in captivity and that earlier self-incriminating statements they had made on television had involved coercion and distortion by editing. Two prominent lawyers were also detained at this time, one for allegedly instigating the recantation and the other for questioning about his relations with an American diplomat. Some of these have subsequently been released. At the moment, the total number of political detainees in the "city of fear" is six. Almost unanimously, American commentators have maintained that the detentions were unjustified, that they were the result of "panic" *(Wall Street Journal*, or of a "persecution complex" (*Journal of Commerce*), or, more pretentiously, of "a deep Conradian fear of being swallowed up by the jungle" (Ian Buruma in the *New York Times Magazine*). Others have interpreted the arrests in terms of the coming general election, seeing them as an attempt to perpetuate one-party rule by "intimidating into conformity various segments of the population" (Jerome Alan Cohen, writing in the *New York Times*).

Some or all of these characterizations may be right. But no serious grounds for believing them are provided in any of the pieces quoted. Indeed, evidence of any hard investigative reporting of the background and circumstances of the detentions is singularly lacking in the American press. We are told that the twenty-two people arrested last year were young and well educated, and that they included human rights lawyers, religious activists (mostly Catholics), and social workers. Buruma also reports that "these alleged revolutionaries were polite, even timid, neatly dressed ...." And that is about it.

The clear implication in many of the pieces is that it is absurd to maintain that such people could have been involved in any subversive activity. But, unfortunately, it is by no means absurd. Attempting to appropriate the human rights issue and using it to undermine the authority of governments is a common and often effective tactic of the extreme left, both in the Third World and the West. And since the advent of "liberation theology" and the conversion of the World Council of Churches into an instrument for the furthering of Third World radical causes, religious affiliation—particularly of an activist kind—no longer justifies a presumption of innocence. This is not to say, of course, that the twenty-two detainees in the Singapore case were necessarily involved in any subversive activity, but merely that the description of their backgrounds offered by American newspapers does not clarify the matter.

Ironically, an article published in *Asiaweek*, a Hong Kong based publication that subsequently had its circulation restricted by the Singapore government because of events flowing from that same article, gives a fuller and more balanced account of the detainees than any that have appeared in the American press.[1] The article maintains that "Associates of the detainees, by and large, do not deny the bare facts in the government's allegations. It is the interpretation of those facts that is in dispute." It then goes on to say that the accused clearly were critical of the governing party; that several of them had been members of a "study group" in England organized by an activist who had fled from Singapore after serving a jail sentence; that many of them were, "at least at one time, influenced by Marx and Mao;" and that they "did, in a sense, form a network" in Singapore. The supporters of the detainees put one interpretation on all this, the Singapore authorities another. In the eyes of the former, the people involved were "socially-oriented liberals committed to creating a more democratic and equitable country," according to *Asiaweek*. The government, on the other hand, while conceding that the detainees posed no immediate threat in themselves, maintained that over time their more ruthless manipulators could have transformed them into dangerous agents. Arguing that the government could not afford to wait for "a smoking gun or a blood-stained parang," Home Affairs Minister Jayakumar distinguished open opposition from the intolerable activities of those who "engage in subversion, purveying Marxism, infiltrating the legitimate organizations, hiding under cover of religious organizations and publications."

In television interviews, several of those detained made statements compromising themselves and others. One admitted that he foresaw peaceful protests leading to "disorder and maybe even rioting, bloodshed." Another said that Tan Wah Piow, the alleged leader of the study group in Britain, had links with the outlawed Communist party of Malaysia. But as these statements were made while in detention and have since been repudiated by some of the detainees, their value is limited. More significant, perhaps, is a remark that, according to *Asiaweek*, one of those detained made to a friend before she was arrested: "We are only *Ruching kurap* [small fry]." This, which amounts to less than a declaration of innocence, was precisely the conclusion reached by the Singapore authorities after interrogating the detainees.

Several of those arrested claimed to have been tortured. The Singapore government insists that no one was, though it acknowledges that a certain amount of psychological stress and disorientation is part of its interrogation process. Jerome A. Cohen, late of the Harvard Law School and acting on behalf of Asia Watch in this instance, rejects the distinction: "Mr. Cohen said he found deeply disturbing both the use of psychological torture and what he called a pervasive Singaporean, if not Asian view that 'if you haven't hit somebody, it isn't torture'" (NYT, May 12, 1988). What the detainees have specifically complained of is that in the course of their interrogation they were kept in very cold temperatures, made to stand for long periods while being questioned, deprived of sleep, held in solitary confinement, forced to wear prison clothes, and, in some cases, slapped on the face.

Such treatment is certainly repugnant. But is it really "torture"? If so, it will be necessary to find a new term to describe the much more extreme measures that have usually been described as torture (violent beatings, the application of electric currents to testicles, the tearing out of fingernails, massive doses of castor oil, the use of mind-destroying drugs, etc.). Moreover, we must recognize that every police force in the world (including those of the United States, at least until very recently) employs "torture" in the sense that is now ascribed to Singapore.

This semantic dispute could almost have been invented to illustrate a point recently made by Irving Kristol:

> One of the successes of the 'human rights' movement has been to broaden the definition of "torture" to include what would otherwise be classified as "police brutality." Americans would be disapproving of but not outraged by police brutality or the use of third-degree methods against prisoners in distant lands; we are, after all, familiar enough with this phenomenon at home, and would not be surprised to learn that it is far more common in "less civilized" (i.e. most other) countries. But torture, real torture, is an abomination to the bourgeois-liberal sensibility, a violation of that sense of human dignity which is at the very root of our liberal individualism. So a focus on torture is a brilliant bit of public relations (*The National Interest*, Winter 1986/7).

The Hendrickson Case

The second of the three questions at issue involves the request of the Singapore government that the United States withdraw a political officer, Mason Hendrickson, from the one hundred-strong U.S. Mission in Singapore, on the grounds that he had improperly interfered in the domestic affairs of the country. Under the Vienna Convention governing diplomatic relations, such interference is impermissible. The United States had no option but to comply. Subsequently it retaliated by requesting the withdrawal of one officer from the small Singaporean mission in Washington, though the officer in question was not accused of improper conduct. The government of Singapore based its charges against Hendrickson on the sworn testimony of the lawyer Patrick Seong, given when he was under detention, that the diplomat had, sometimes in the presence of more senior State Department officials, encouraged disgruntled Singaporeans in anti-government activities.

The dispute obviously turns largely on what Hendrickson actually said in his meetings with Singaporeans. But it also involves opposing interpretations of what is permissible and proper behavior on the part of diplomatic officers. Whatever happened in this particular case, there can be little doubt that—given the American concern to promote democracy in the world (something repeatedly stressed by President Reagan and Secretary of State Shultz), and the enormous dependence of many Third World countries on the United States—American diplomats often take a broad view of what they are entitled to do, indeed what they should do, in relation to the domestic politics of the countries in which they are stationed. (Does anyone believe that they respect the letter of the Vienna Convention in, say, Honduras, South Korea, or the Philippines?) The government of Singapore, on the other hand, being extremely sensitive about its domestic politics and feeling very vulnerable to subversion from sources other than the American embassy, interprets the Convention strictly.

In this instance, the ongoing criticism in the American press and the fact that the U.S. government had recently reneged on a deal to extend Singapore's eligibility for trade benefits under the Generalized System of Preferences (GSP) in return for the adoption of copyright legislation by Singapore, almost certainly influenced the decision to press the issue publicly, rather than deal with it discreetly. Discussing the Hendrickson episode in his speech to Parliament on June 1, Lee Kuan Yew made a point of saying that members of his government felt they "had been taken for a ride and treated shabbily" over GSP.

The Singaporeans have shown every confidence in the merits of their case. Lee has proposed a committee of three international experts to look into the facts and to decide whether Hendrickson and other State Department officials had or had not acted legitimately. If it found that they had, the Singapore government would apologize to the State Department. Lee offered the idea "as a fair way to put an end to the matter." Despite the traditional American fondness for conciliation and arbitration, the proposal has not been taken up by Washington.

Restricted Circulation

The third and most interesting quarrel between the American press and the government of Singapore involves the restriction of circulation of four foreign publications—all American owned and all reputable. These are *Time* magazine (whose circulation in Singapore was reduced from 18,000 to 2,000 in October 1986); the *Asian Wall Street Journal* (cut from 5,000 to 400 in February 1987); *Asiaweek* (11,000 to 500 in October 1987); and the *Far Eastern Economic Review* (9,000 to 500 in December 1987). The restrictions on all but *Time* magazine are still in force.

The dispute is the more interesting because, of all the 120 or so Third World countries, Singapore is probably the most hospitable to the foreign press. Any news addict given a choice of which Third World country to live in for a few months would do well to opt for the city-state, for his taste would be well catered to. Over three-and-a-half thousand foreign publications are available there, including such staple fare as the *Economist* and *the International Herald Tribune*, and the BBC World Service is received around the clock.

How then did the dispute arise? The first three cases listed above—*Time*, the *Asian Wall Street Journal*, and *Asiaweek*—are essentially the same. These publications ran articles about the internal politics of Singapore; the government of Singapore considered the articles unfair and inaccurate and responded with letters to the editor; the editors declined to publish the letters as received; the government reacted by "gazetting" the publications and restricting their circulations. Shortly after it was gazetted, *Time* published the original letter from the Prime Minister's press secretary and nine months later the restrictions on its circulation were lifted. *Asiaweek* also published the original letters a month after being gazetted, but eight months later the restrictions had not been lifted. The AWSJ did not subsequently print the letter in dispute and its proprietor (Dow Jones Publishing Company [Asia] Inc.) filed a motion in the Singapore High Court for leave to annul the restriction. The motion was heard and dismissed with costs in May of this year. A notice of appeal has been filed.

The *Far East Economic Review* case is somewhat different and developed against a background of long-standing acrimony between the magazine and the Singapore government. It involved an article quoting a Catholic priest's secondhand account of a meeting between Lee Kuan Yew and the Archbishop of Singapore, following the 1987 detentions. The Singapore government asserted that the account was false, defamatory (the Prime Minister has taken out a writ for libel), and that it interfered in domestic politics in a serious way by attempting to pit the Catholic Church against the Prime Minister. While the *Review* did publish the letters of the government spokesman, it claimed that it was under no obligation to check the facts in the article as it was merely reporting the priest's views and taking no position as to their veracity:

> Let us spell it out in the simplest possible terms. If Kim Jong Il, the son of the dictator of North Korea, should announce that his father is a reincarnation of the Buddha, we would possibly consider that noteworthy. If we printed the story, it would not mean in any sense that we believed it, or that we were presenting the dictator's reincarnation as a fact.

The Singapore government's response to that position:

> *FEER* is thus propounding the thesis that a newspaper can legitimately print anything it wishes, whether true, false, or even defamatory, so long as it is able to quote a source who actually made the statement. It claims it is under no obligation to check its facts, satisfy itself as to the truthfulness of its source, or verify the assertions against other witnesses, nor can it he held answerable for any lies and libels which may thereby be published. This is a preposterous thesis which will sanction journalistic mendacity.

The upshot was that the government restricted the magazine's circulation and the *Review* responded by ceasing all circulation and distribution in Singapore. The Prime Minister's libel action is still pending.

At various points in these controversies the State Department intervened to express regret at the actions of the Singapore government in restricting the circulations of the magazines and the hope that the issues would soon be resolved. These statements provoked furious protest from the Singaporeans on the grounds that they represented "an unprecedented interference in Singapore's internal affairs." The subsequent exchanges between the two governments cast light on the causes and nature of the dispute.

The State Department responded to Singapore's protest by claiming that the U.S. government took no sides regarding the specific claims of any party to the dispute, but that its statements reflected the government's "fundamental and long-standing commitment to the principles of a free and unrestricted press." It then went on to elaborate:

> "Free and unrestricted" in American usage means that within broad limits, set at the boundaries of other individual liberties (e.g. criminal libel), the press is free to publish or not publish what it chooses, however irresponsible or biased its actions may seem to be. Where the media are free, the marketplace of ideas sorts the irresponsible from the responsible and rewards the latter.

At various times, and depending on who is speaking, the Singapore government has responded to this position at two levels. On one—favored by Singapore's Ambassador Tommy Koh in Washington, among others—they have mounted a defense in terms that appeal to American notions of fairness. They point out that Singapore has not banned the publications in question but merely limited their circulation, that they are available in libraries and that articles may be photocopied. The object has been to punish the journals in question, not to deprive Singaporeans of information.

Further, they stress that at least in three of the four cases, the dispute turned not on what was published about Singapore but on the denial of the Singapore government's right to reply. Whatever the formal legal position, the government maintains that basic fairness, let alone courtesy, required the respecting of that right; and, indeed, even in law, the Fairness Doctrine in the United States specifies that broadcasters have an obligation "to afford reasonable opportunity for the discussion of conflicting views on issues of public importance." In practice, it is asked, would the American press ever deny an American president or member of the cabinet a right of reply? Why, then, treat the prime minister of Singapore and his colleagues differently?

"A Kind of Arrogance"

Even allowing for the touchiness and aggressiveness of the Singaporeans in responding to criticism, the editorial judgments of the publications involved do seem to have been poor. The correspondence between the Singapore government and the journals, which has been published by the former,[2] reveals an unattractive combination of arrogance, evasiveness, disingenuousness and irresponsibility on the part of the latter. After printing an article that, to the layman at least, seems clearly to defame the Singapore government, the *Asian Wall Street Journal* gave as a reason for not printing a reply the fact that it defamed the author. The AWSJ claimed to have the information to support one serious allegation but, despite repeated requests, refused to provide it. In several cases, articles that were clearly opinionated—if only in their very unbalanced and uncritical use of sources—were defended as examples of straight reporting. *Asiaweek* printed a letter under the name of the press secretary of the minister for home affairs which had not only been cut but had he several hundred words added to it, without consulting or informing the author.

The editors in question were, presumably, on sound grounds legally. But the would have done well to remember Edmund Burke's admonition to the British government in its dealings with the American colonies: "It is not what a lawyer tells me I may do; but what humanity, reason and justice tell me should do. Is a political act the worse for being a generous one?" And in standing on their legal rights, the editors would have done well also to remember that in this instance the) were dealing with a sovereign government other than their own, one which had legal means of retaliating.

As it was, the use by the Singapore government of a passage written by Vermont Royster, an editor emeritus of the *Wall Street Journal*, seemed entirely appropriate:

> Our craft is quick to correct the misspelling of a name or the wrong cutline under a picture. Most papers have a box nearly every day for such corrections. Let the complaint be, however, that a story was unfair to someone, that it contained unwarranted invasion of a person's privacy, that it was mistaken in some of its main facts-in those cases a wall of silence is likely to descend on the editorial sanctum. That kind of error is rarely apologized for, or even acknowledged. All too often the attitude is 'We stand by the story' no matter what. And that certainly is a kind of arrogance.

Singapore's case does not rest there. The government—and Lee Kuan Yew in particular—also responds at another level, one that invokes Singapore's circumstances rather than American standards of fair play. In fact it specifically rejects the notion that the U.S. model provides either a universal standard or one appropriate to Singapore. In a speech given to the American Society of Newspaper Editors in April, Lee observed that the media play different roles in different countries, reflecting different historical experiences, political systems and national temperaments. He referred to the BBC World Service, "which reports events impartially, but provides an interpretation from a definite perspective" as being more appropriate to Singapore than the American model. He also referred approvingly to the Japanese model, "which stays out of active politics, but goes beyond plain reporting to shape public opinion to help build up a national consensus on important issues."

According to Lee, the American ideal of an unrestricted contest in the marketplace of ideas is unsuited to newly independent nations. Where it has been tried the results have not been happy. In Sri Lanka and India it produced "confusion and dissension, rather than enlightenment and consensus." In the Philippines before the period of martial law, it resulted in "a wildly partisan press [which] helped Filipino politicians to flood the marketplace of ideas with junk, and confused and befuddled the people." In Singapore itself, with its volatile racial and religious mix, when the concept had been tried it had "time and again led to riots and bloodshed." Along with the "marketplace of ideas," Lee rejects the idea of the press as the fourth estate. The British never allowed it that status in the colony, and there are good reasons for not allowing it now. If the press were permitted to assume "the role of invigilator, adversary and inquisitor of the Administration," it would radically change the nature of Singapore society, said Lee, and "I doubt if our social glue is strong enough to withstand such treatment."

According to this view, no foreign publication has a right to circulate in Singapore; circulation is a privilege granted by Singapore on its own terms. It is denied to some. *Izvestia*, for example, is not allowed to circulate, and as Lee pointed out in his speech, in the interest of lessening intercommunal conflicts, Singapore and Malaysia have banned each other's newspapers for about twenty years. The essential condition is that there be no involvement in Singapore's domestic politics, and Singapore itself must be the sole judge of whether that condition is being met.

Circumstances and Statesmanship

For many Americans brought up on the First Amendment and accustomed, particularly in recent years, to regard freedom of the press as an absolute right, such a defense by Singapore of its actions will be unacceptable, perhaps even shocking. Others—those who believe that the application of principles should take account of circumstances and likely consequences—may react differently. For Singapore's circumstances are exceptional.

When the country became an independent state in the early 1960s, many good judges gave it virtually no hope of surviving, let alone prospering. It was tiny—one-fifth the size of Rhode Island. Its population, no larger than that of the Bronx, was composed of Chinese (themselves divided into several different dialect groups), Malays, Indonesians, Indians, Pakistanis, and Eurasians. These had never formed one community, and under the British they had occupied separate, officially demarcated segments of the island. There was no common language. The island had virtually no material resources whatsoever, apart from its people. Even its drinking water had to be piped over from the Malaysian mainland, as it still is today. Living standards were low.

This city-state came into existence in what was at the time the most turbulent, volatile and violent part of the world. Coups, insurrections, subversion, ineffectual central governments, and regional revolts were commonplace. To the north, a serious communist insurrection, supported by China, had just been quelled by the British with great difficulty. To the south, Sukarno was on the rampage and the largest communist party outside the Communist bloc was preparing to attempt a coup. To the northeast were the Vietnamese, and Singaporeans did not need much sense of history to remember the speed with which the Japanese had swept down from Vietnam two decades before to take the supposedly impregnable British fortress.

Given this set of conditions the subsequent history of Singapore—the sustained 7 percent growth rate; the creation of an educated middle class society with a per capita income higher than that of Italy; the provision of the best housing of any Third World country; the improved life expectancy and infant mortality rates that now almost equal America's; and, not least, the maintenance of internal order combined with a substantial level of personal freedom-is nothing short of miraculous. The people responsible for the miracle were Lee Kuan Yew and his colleagues. One could, indeed, mount a strong case that, pound for pound and measured in terms of the improvements they have wrought in the lives of ordinary people, Singapore has had the best government in the world over the last twenty years. Yet this is the government that is now being trashed by the American press.

Many of those who do the trashing concede the brilliant record of Lee's government—indeed, how could they not?—but use it against him in the current controversy. It is precisely because the Singaporeans have achieved so much and because so much is expected of them that their recent behavior warrants sharp criticism, it is argued. For they deserve to be judged by higher standards than most Third World countries, and recent behavior represents a backsliding or self-betrayal on the part of what is (with the possible exception of Japan) the most "modern" state in Asia. It is not a convincing argument.

First, given their outstanding record, the presumption must be that Lee and his colleagues are better judges than American editors of what is right for Singapore at this stage of its development. Second, far from backsliding, the Singapore government has been utterly consistent throughout concerning what internal security measures are necessary to ensure the country's progress. Over twenty years ago the then deputy prime minister of Singapore, Dr. Goh Keng Swee, spelled it out:

> The first and most important of the prerequisites to success is, I regret to say, an efficient secret police, or 'Special Branch' to use the delicate British colonial term for it ... It is however of the utmost importance that the highest standards of conduct on the part of the secret police are maintained ... checks should be real and not perfunctory measures. The secret police would, he said, arrest and detain those suspected of subversive activities and regrettably the due process of law could not be applied on these occasions for three reasons: legal procedures would blow the cover of the police operations; some forms of conspiratorial activities were not illegal; and the government could not afford to hold its hand until such times as crimes were actually committed.[3]

Lee's government has lived by these tenets consistently for the last quarter century. Repeatedly it has detained individuals believed to be agents of the

Communist Party of Malaya (CPM), sometimes seizing quantities of arms and ammunition in the process. Repeatedly it has exposed and shut down newspapers it considered subversive. These tenets have been part of an ethos stressing discipline, vigilance, control and restraint as essential ingredients of success for a society in Singapore's circumstances. Those who now accuse the Singapore government of betraying its own heritage and promise are either disingenuous or uninformed.

Third, and most compelling, it is not true that Singapore has now reached a position where it is free of danger and can afford to dispense with the procedures that have served it well in the past. The country still consists of a cluster of communities imperfectly joined. The CPM has not closed shop. The attraction of Islamic fundamentalism for Malaysia and the uncertain future of Indonesia after Suharto pose potentially serious threats to Singapore's internal stability. The current examples of the Philippines and Sri Lanka serve as reminders of the dangers posed by communist subversion and communal strife respectively. Vietnam, with the world's fourth-largest army, continues to menace its neighbors. To dismiss all this as "a deep Conradian fear of being swallowed up by the jungle" is not merely irresponsible but fatuous. Lee Kuan Yew has more to fear than the jungle.

His fears may yet turn out to have been exaggerated. The problem is that neither he nor anyone else can be certain, and he is in no position to take risks. Adam Smith once responded to a lament that Britain was ruined by observing calmly, "There is a lot of ruin in a nation." As far as large, powerful, cohesive nation states are concerned he was right. But small, internally divided states existing in insecure surroundings are a different matter. They work on very slim margins of safety, in an environment where conditions can deteriorate rapidly and a single serious error of judgment may have catastrophic consequences. This is true of Israel, and it is true of Singapore. For many Americans, living in a huge and powerful country well insulated by oceans, it is a truth that is difficult to appreciate. But what they readily dismiss as "paranoia," or "panic," or a determination to cling to power at all costs is sometimes the consequence of that "imagination of disaster" which is an indispensable prerequisite for statesmanship in managing the affairs of small and vulnerable countries.

Lee Kuan Yew has other qualities of statesmanship. In the current controversy, he has been the only one who has demonstrated any interest in keeping the issue in proportion and relating it to wider questions. While holding firm to the Singaporean position on the three issues in dispute, Lee has stated the U.S. position fairly and drawn a distinction between the reaction of the younger, second-generation Singaporean leaders (who include his son) and that of himself and his older colleagues. While he understood his younger colleagues' outrage at the intervention of the United States, he and the other elders were concerned to "register our protest in a way that does not damage the fundamentals of our relationship with the U.S. The U.S. role in the Western Pacific is vital to the security and stability of non-communist Asia, and therefore it is very much in Singapore's national interest." In his speech to Parliament, he quoted from a note he had written to all cabinet ministers:

> Of course, we must attack the Americans when they do us in, as they did over the GSP and Copyright. But we must use language which does not convey to our people that they have become our strategic enemies .... They are our friends and we are angry because they were behaving badly, or mistreating us, as friends."

He expressed concern at the xenophobia that is deeply embedded in much of Asian culture and the deliberate efforts both by communists and some non-communists to stir up anti-Americanism in Southeast Asia.

Anyone who has followed Lee Kuan Yew's career knows that these were not views fashioned for an occasion. They are consistent with the opinions he has expressed over the years, not only in Singapore itself but in international forums ranging from the Commonwealth to the Non-Aligned Movement, where expressing them has often carried a political cost. Because of his intellectual force, and because Singapore—which receives no aid from the U.S. and which has never hesitated to disagree with Washington on particular issues—cannot convincingly he depicted as an American lackey, he has probably been the most effective defender of the U.S. position in Third World debates.

Common decency requires that such a man receive more thoughtful and sympathetic treatment from America than he has recently been getting. But more than decency towards Lee Kuan Yew is involved here: small as Singapore is, the issue bears on a central theme of United States foreign policy. Americans of all political persuasions believe profoundly that it is their right and duty—indeed their destiny—to promote freedom and democracy in the world. It is a noble and powerful impulse, one not casually to be ridiculed or dismissed. But acting on it—if one is concerned to be effective and not merely to feel virtuous—is a complicated and delicate business, and the dangers are many. Success requires that this impulse be balanced against, and where necessary circumscribed by, other interests that the United States must necessarily pursue, more mundane ones like security, order and prosperity. For these represent not merely legitimate competing claims but the preconditions for a lasting extension of democracy.

Success requires, too, an awareness of the intractability of a world that does not exist merely in order to satisfy American expectations—a world that, for the most part, cannot satisfy those expectations in the foreseeable future. While determination and purposefulness are important ingredients in any effective policy, the attempt to force history in the direction of democracy by an exercise of will is likely to produce more unintended than intended consequences. The successful promotion of democracy calls for restraint and patience, a sense of limits and an appreciation of the wisdom of indirection, a profound understanding of the particularity of circumstances—all of which have been conspicuous by their absence in recent dealings with Singapore. As Carlyle once put it, "I don't pretend to understand the Universe—it's a great deal bigger than I am ... People ought to be modester." Indeed.

Notes

1. "Battle Against Leftism," *Asiaweek*, September 13, 1987.
2. *Singapore and the Foreign Press*, Ministry of Communications and Information, Singapore, March 1988.
3. Goh Keng Swee's speech, which was delivered in Canberra, Australia in 1967, is still a key document. It was quoted by Lee Kuan Yew in a major speech to the Singapore Parliament earlier this year and reproduced in full by the *Straits Times* in June.

22

The Idea of Human Rights

*Roger Pilon**

More than any administration in decades, perhaps in our history, the administration of Ronald Reagan has been characterized by its ideological orthodoxy. Not that its practice has always conformed to its principles—that is more than we should expect. But from the inception of the "Reagan Revolution" in the election-eve speech of the Goldwater campaign, Ronald Reagan has set forth a clear conception of the American order as envisioned by the Founding Fathers: limited but effective government, both at home and abroad. Speaking on Human Rights Day in the first year of his administration, he stated the matter plainly:

> Mankind's best defense against tyranny and want is limited governments government which empowers its people, not itself, and which respects the wit and bravery, the initiative, and the generosity of the people. For, above all, human rights are rights of individuals: rights of conscience, rights of choice, rights of association, rights of emigration, rights of self-directed action, and the right to own property. The concept of a nation of free men and women linked together voluntarily is the genius of the system our Founding Fathers established.

By contrast, Jimmy Carter promised us "government as good as its people." Whatever touchstone there may have been in that wonderful formulation, any similarity between it and the ideas of the Founders is doubtless coincidental. Nonetheless, this was the theoretical springboard of the Carter presidency—what one observer has called a campaign that never became an administra-

---

*Roger Pilon is the vice president for legal affairs and the director of the Center for Constitutional Studies at the Cato Institute. He served in the Reagan Administration as director of policy in the Bureau of Human Rights and Humanitarian Affairs of the Department of State.

This essay first appeared in *The National Interest*, no. 5 (Fall 1986).

tion—all of which helps to explain the election of 1980, and all of which is to say that in the end ideas matter, good and not-so-good ideas alike.

It is a central thesis of Joshua Muravchik's splendid study of Jimmy Carter's human rights policy (*The Uncertain Crusade: Jimmy Carter and the Dilemmas of Human Rights Policy*) that "a crucial determinant of the state of human rights in the world is the state of the *idea* of human rights." Although Carter is widely credited with placing that idea on the world agenda—especially as against the realpolitik of the Nixon-Kissinger era—it is well to remember the efforts of the Jackson Democrats of the early 1970s in the matter of Soviet and East European emigration, the UN addresses of Ambassador Daniel Patrick Moynihan in the mid-1970s, and various of the speeches of candidate Ronald Reagan leading up to the bitterly contested Republican primary of 1976, all of which raised the banner of human rights, albeit not from the pulpit of the American presidency. It fell to Jimmy Carter to do this. But so inartful was his administration's execution, because so confused its understanding of the idea, that Muravchik is driven to conclude that in this age, when

> the enemies of human rights all proclaim themselves to be its most ardent champions, . . . there is much less danger that the phrase, "human rights," will be forgotten or rejected than that its meaning will be lost. It follows that the highest task in the struggle to strengthen the idea of human rights is to defend it against impostors and to keep its meaning clear. At this task the Carter administration failed; indeed it may justly be accused of having added to the muddle.

This is a conclusion as provocative as it is trenchant, not least because it challenges the conventional wisdom, which would have us believe that whatever the failures of Carter's foreign policy generally, his human rights policy was not among them—indeed, that only lately has Ronald Reagan discovered the wisdom and use of a concern for human rights. Never mind that the human rights theme has been at the core of the Reagan administration's statements and has guided its practices from the outset. These "new revisionists," as Jeane Kirkpatrick has recently remarked, would attribute Reagan's successes in foreign policy to his having at last adopted the Carter human rights policy. Yet how could this be if Muravchik is correct—and he is—that Carter's human rights policy only added to the international muddle on the subject? From muddle one hardly expects to derive successes.

The answer is close at hand. It is that the human rights policy that Reagan has pursued is hardly the same policy that Jimmy Carter pursued, notwithstanding its invocation of the same label. Far from incorporating and continuing the muddle that was the Carter idea of human rights, the Reagan administration has returned to the wellsprings of the American order and formulated a policy consistent with that order.

The Reagan themes—limited government, the rights of individuals—are not to be found in the anthology of the Carter administration—not, at least, in so unambiguous and confident a fashion. No, these would never sell in the Third World, Carter's people believed, much less in the Soviet empire. This is not the stuff of accommodation and respect abroad, they thought. It is rather the stuff of the classical American ideology.

As these remarks suggest, Muravchik has set out to tell more than the Carter human rights odyssey alone. His aim, more deeply, "is to identify the critical dilemmas of our human rights policy as they were revealed by the experience of the Carter administration," the fundamental dilemmas that "will have to be confronted by any U.S. human rights policy." Toward that end, he takes up (1) questions about the relationship of human rights to political systems—and in particular the question whether our policy should endeavor "to transcend the ideological conflict between the democratic and the Communist worlds"; (2) questions about the definition of "human rights," whether we should promote those that are found in the American tradition or those that are embodied in international law and documents," in particular whether we should recognize so-called "economic and social rights"; (3) questions about consistency in the execution of our policy over myriad historical and factual circumstances; and (4) questions about the use of punitive measures in the administration of economic aid, security assistance, credits and financing, trade, or other forms of resource transfers.

Other reviewers will undoubtedly focus upon the third and fourth of these dilemmas since it is here that questions of policy are presented in their most concrete form. On the matter of policy generally, Muravchik is clear: "The principal medium of human rights policy must be words." Critical of a "heavy reliance on punitive measures," he observes that:

> In most of the unfree world today, the idea of human rights holds insufficient force over the minds of elites and of the masses, and its requirements are insufficiently understood. The goal of human rights policy is to change this.

In service of that goal, he concludes that four human rights policy should be aimed less at governments than at people." Taking Muravchik's prescriptions at face value, it is imperative that we be clear about the ideas that are the base of our hortatory efforts. Accordingly, the focus of this review will be upon the first and second of the dilemmas Muravchik has delineated, upon the philosophical foundations of our human rights policy.

Beginning with a brief discussion of the origins and operations of the Carter policy—how it was thrust upon the Carter campaign by the 1976 Democratic platform as "a rare point of unity in a bitterly divided party," how the program was staffed, after the election, not by the Jackson wing that had pushed so hard for its inclusion in the platform but by the human rights "movement" representing the party's McGovern wing, how the policy was launched and institutionalized, Muravchik turns next to the dilemma that is his central concern, whether the promotion of human rights can or should transcend the ideologies of political systems. Driven by a "deep yearning for reconciliation, even friendship, with the traditional antagonists of the United States, a yearning given voice in the President's declaration that we had as a people overcome our 'inordinate fear of communism,' " the new administration, Muravehik argues, sought at first to have it both ways, to speak out on behalf of Soviet dissidents, to respond to Andrei Sakharov's letter to President Carter, to entertain the recently released Vladimir Bukovsky, while at the same time pursuing "the overriding priority of its foreign policy," a new SALT agreement. "The key point," Muravchik notes,

> was that the administration rejected what had come to be called "linkage." It would protest Soviet misbehavior, such as violations of the Helsinki Accords, but it would not make any other aspect of U.S.-Soviet relations conditional on improvements in Soviet behavior.

In short order, history indicates, the Soviets put the new administration on notice: while the U.S. may not insist upon linkage, the Soviets were prepared to press for a linkage of their own, making U.S.-Soviet relations conditional on our not complaining about their misbehavior. Because the Soviets were thus prepared, the first mission to Moscow of Secretary Vance in late March of 1977 ended in "acrimony and complete failure," Muravchik contends. "From that moment, the administration was much more cautious in the application of its human rights policy to the Soviet Union." Not only did it move toward a "quiet diplomacy" reminiscent of the Kissinger era; more generally, it "took special pains to emphasize that its human rights policy was not an anti-Soviet policy"—indeed, that its concern to promote human rights transcended ideology. How better to profess perfect disinterestedness, to dissociate human rights concerns from our global interests? Thus the new assistant secretary for human rights, Patricia Derian, testified that "human rights violations do not really have much to do with the form of government or the political ideology or philosophy." In the same vein, UN Ambassador Andrew Young said that he sought to "break the sterile impasse between 'capitalism' and 'Socialism' that has for several generations served as an anesthetic to imagination as we are all caught up in one rigidity or another." And the president himself, upon his arrival in Poland in December 1977, remarked that "old ideological labels have lost their meaning," an assertion that First Secretary Gierek seemed to go out of his way to refute on the following day.

It is here that Muravchik launches into his sharpest attack on the Carter approach: "What Carter and his colleagues seemed to miss, indeed to deny," Muravchik claims, "is that the distinction between democracy and dictatorship is the 'great divide' when it comes to human rights." Whereas democracy is premised on the idea of human rights, "at least on that most basic right, the right of self-government," dictatorship is premised on the belief that some have authority over others: "the system itself is an inherent denial of human rights." In its attempt to "transcend" ideology, however, the Carter policy only obscured this distinction:

> It focused insistently on individual abuses rather than systemic deformities. It spoke always of "violations" of human rights, rather than of their "denial." What does it mean to say, for example, that the Soviet government "violates" the right of free speech? The Soviet government simply does not recognize that right. It denies it both in theory and in practice, and has done so for the better part of a century.

What can we say here? Muravchik's charge that the Soviet system is evil *by design* is absolutely correct. It is a system that from the very outset subordinates the individual to the group; the system begins not with the individual and his rights but with the group and its "rights. " As the Soviet Constitution makes plain, speech, association, artistic freedom are all "guaranteed'"—provided these "rights" are exercised "in accordance with the interests of the people and in order to strengthen and develop the socialist system." Speech in defense of the system, yes; in opposition, no. That is the very inversion—the very perversion—of what we mean by "a right." Indeed, coupled with other provisions of Soviet law, the idea of "a right" is made to stand on its head: a *right* becomes a *duty*, to support the system.

Yet the Carter administration was all but oblivious to this reality. In its attempt to achieve a pristine neutrality, in its attempt to rise above ideology, it failed to see that

> the struggle for human rights, far from being . . .indifferent to political systems, is fundamentally a struggle about political systems. It cannot sensibly be merely an endless chase after an infinite number of individual "violations." It must aim instead to erect political systems which have the idea of human rights, and the means for their protection, built in.

Clearly, Muravehik has reached a profoundly important conclusion here, hardly original, but one that bears repeated restatement all the same, for the "pragmatists" among us are perennially unable to give ideology its due in its bearing on human events. Whether and to what extent the Soviet rulers are any longer driven by Marxist-Leninist ideology is an open question, of course. That they are driven by the institutional constraints of their system, however, is not open to question; and those constraints are themselves the product of ideology. If we are to understand the struggle for human rights that is taking place in the world today, therefore, we have to address not simply the behavior of individual rulers but the systems that drive that behavior. In the case of the Soviet system, violations of rights are not aberrations; they are systemic imperatives.

Yet it was not the pragmatists who were principally responsible for the Carter muddle, Muravchik suggests, but the "movement" ideologues, especially those who pressed for recognition of "economic and social rights"—the "right" to a job, food, shelter, medical care, education, even "period holidays with pay," as called for in Article 24 of the UN Universal Declaration of Human Rights. We move then to the second of the dilemmas that concern Muravchik, how to define "human rights," which is intimately connected, of course, with the question of political systems. In fact, it is here—on this connection between the two issues—that Muravchik's thesis is at its most uncertain, wavering between rights theory, on one hand, and democratic theory on the other. They are not the same, of course, notwithstanding that the political philosophy that finds its roots in Benthamite utilitarianism and its flourishing in Progressive Era democratic theory has tended to conflate the two.

As Muravchik makes clear, these "economic and social rights" are not in the Anglo-American tradition. In the end, however, arguments from tradition will get us no further than the Carter administration's prudential argument, that by recognizing and promoting these rights we would better position ourselves to curry favor with the Third World, where such "rights" often seem to be the central concern. Indeed, in what must be dubbed a quintessential bootstrapping operation, the Carter State Department went so far as to assert: "First popularized by socialist thinkers, the [economic and social rights] eventually won universal approval."

Recognizing the limits of these "arguments," Muravchik lays out his own doubts. In the first place, governments often use the pursuit of such "rights" as an excuse to deny citizens their civil and political rights. Taken to its theoretical foundations—a sketch of which will be drawn shortly—this is a trenchant criticism; but Muravchik never takes his argument there. Instead, he simply denies that poverty necessitates the denial of freedom and political participation. He then goes on to note that "of all the desirable things in the world, there are only a few that we call 'rights.'" Moreover, "economic and social rights" depend on available resources; and they are enforced by different means than those used to enforce civil and political rights. Again, calling more and more things "rights" tends to cheapen the very idea, undermining respect for civil and political rights in the process. Yet again, recognizing that these rights entail "a government that is activist, intervening, and committed to economic-social planning," Muravchik notes that many economists believe "there are limits to the welfare state." Finally, a "more profound problem" arises when we realize that citizens, exercising their political and civil rights, may refuse to enact the legislation necessary to secure these "rights"; but if we insulate these "economic and social rights" from majority will, much as we insulate such "basic" rights as free speech, "then democracy will have been significantly truncated."

Muravchik is on to something very important with this final point, but unfortunately he has taken it in the wrong direction. He has drawn out a potential conflict between the democratic right of self-rule and these "economic and social rights," but he has simply assumed that the former is more "basic." Why is this? Why are these "economic and social rights" not on a par with the free-speech right—both insulated from majoritarian will? Alternatively, why is the free-speech right not itself subject to majority will? Indeed, if our right of self-government is our "most basic right," as Muravchik argued in his discussion of political systems, why is the free-speech right *not* subject to majority rule?

Answers to these questions would take Muravchik more deeply than he has gone in this essay. Yet answers are necessary if we are to get clear about some of the important and fundamental issues he has raised. In particular he has pointed, by implication, to the inherent tension between rights theory and democratic theory, which he has resolved without argument in favor of the latter. This resolution is all the more surprising because at several points he traces his views to the Declaration of Independence, where the issue is resolved, at least implicitly, in the other direction. As a corollary, and again by implication, by no means is it clear whether Muravchik thinks himself a legal positivist, in the democratic tradition, or a natural rights theorist, in the tradition of the Declaration. If the former is the case, as his emphasis on democracy suggests, then appeal to the natural rights tradition is misplaced—unless that tradition is so misconceived as to hold that our one natural right is the right to self-government, understood as majoritarian rule.

Let us begin, in the American tradition, with the Declaration, where it is clear that rights come first, democracy second. Indeed, not for several lines in that seminal writing do we get to any political or democratic considerations. The first considerations are of rights—more precisely, of the epistemological underpinnings of our rights, in the theory of reason, as self-evident truths, derived from a theory of moral equality and, implicitly, a principle of universalization. It is not from governments, the Declaration says, that we get our rights—no legal positivism here; rather, we have them prior to the existence of any government. Indeed, and now we come to the political derivations, it is in exercise of our rights that we *create* governments in the first place: the powers of the association we call "government" are "just" only if derived "from the consent of the governed." But there precisely, of course, is the rub; for majority will, even when achieved (and decision theorists have shown how rare this is *in principle),* will no more serve to bind the nonconsenting minority than the will of any other fraction of the whole—not, that is, if we take consent seriously. Nor will arguments from the fiction of prior unanimous consent to the process or the reality of "tacit consent" carry the day, this last because the argument comes down, in the end, to putting the individual to a choice between two of his entitlements—his right not to be subject to the will of the majority and his right to stay where he is.

What this all amounts to, then, is an insight the Founders seem keenly to have appreciated when they established *limited* government, but which modem democratic thinkers, including Muravchik, seem to have lost sight of—namely, that government, no matter how "democratic," is by definition a forced associations "necessary evil," in classical parlance—with an air of illegitimacy that surrounds everything it does—at least with respect to those who do not consent to its doing the particular thing it is doing, either to or on behalf of them. Democratic theory, in short, gives us a decision process- admittedly, one that recognizes to a greater extent than all other forms of political association our right to self-government; it does not give us a legitimating process-not, at least, when the governmental act that ensues from the process involves those who would wish to be left in peace.

With this brief sketch of the connection between rights theory and democratic theory, we can return to the dilemma we left above. Clearly, if the democratic right of self-government, understood as majoritarian rule, is basic, then there is no reason in *principle* for treating the free-speech right any differently than any other "right." Indeed, every other "right" becomes a function of the democratic right—which is to say no rights are safe save this one right to vote. That, surely, cannot be what Muravchik or any other advocate of human rights would want. Yet it is the ineluctable implication of those theories that put democracy first, individual rights second. This is hardly an original point, of course—its origins, by implication, are in Plato and Aristotle, its modern formulations in Montesquieu and Tocqueville; but it is easily forgotten. Nor is this to argue that democracy necessarily entails majorities running expansively over the rights of minorities. But the potential is always there; and in principle—save for the rare case of unanimity—the problem is always with us.

If rights come first, however, that leaves us still with the question *which* rights. The simple answer is those rights that alone can be justified as held "by nature," consistent with everyone else's enjoying the same rights. Take it on faith (this is not the forum for the full answer), those rights turn out to be just the ones held to be legitimate by the theorists of classical liberalism: the rights to life, liberty, and property. By contrast-and here we come to the point that Muravchik was almost upon—the so-called "economic and social rights" entail, for their realization, both the expansive, redistributive, welfare state, with all its inherent illegitimacy, and the further violations that are entailed by the need to *use* people, against their will, for the benefit of others, which is precisely the point that democratic theory obscures. In other words, it is not simply that other rights are "cheapened" by expanding the list of "rights," or that these "economic and social rights" are dependent upon the available resources to redistribute (as if those "resources," including labor, were all collectively held), or any of the other reasons that led Muravchik to his skeptical doubts. More fundamentally, any attempt to secure these *"rights" violates* rights—not the right of self- government, as Muravchik supposed, but the right to be left alone. If individuals count for something, and have a right to pursue their own peaceful ends, then we cannot use them for our own or even "society's" ends—not if we take seriously their right to independent lives. If it would not be right for an individual to so use another, why would it be right for a majority to do so?

So far-reaching are these conclusions that they would require Muravchik to recast his "great divide" between democracy and dictatorship. As a practical matter, this divide, for the most part, will do; for when we look at the world about us we usually see the more extensive violations of rights on one side, the less extensive on the other. As a theoretical matter, however, this divide is confused; for it subordinates the substantive rights of individual freedom to the process rights of democratic decisionmaking. This confusion becomes all the more striking when we realize that process rights are never ends in themselves: they are merely instruments, invoked to secure our substantive rights to life, liberty, and property. When these process rights are used by some as instruments to destroy the substantive rights of others, as can easily happen, then the rational order has been turned on its head.

A better divide, then, would be between limited government and totalitarian government. Not only would this help us to focus directly on substance rather than process—which after all is what rights in the end are all about—but it would help too to clarify the muddle that is created by the terms "right" and "left," especially when used to connote "authoritarian" and "totalitarian" regimes, respectively. These regimes are not "opposites." One is simply a more extensive—often much more extensive version of the other, usually because "justified" by an overarching ideology that extinguishes the place of the individual. On a continuum running from limited government to totalitarianism, then, authoritarian regimes, depending on the scope or extent of their authority, rest somewhere between the two. As such, they are "better" than totalitarian regimes. But in either case, improvement in the enjoyment of rights will take place only if the regime limits its control over the individual, only if it moves toward becoming a more limited government.

As noted earlier, this is a small but fundamental correction of Muravchik's thesis, aimed at getting the presumptions right—on rights rather than on democracy—not at calling into account the entire edifice. Moreover, since modern democracies tend also to be limited governments, the practical effect of this correction will not often be great. Nevertheless, it is important to see clearly the foundations of our undertakings, especially if the idea of human rights, on the international scene, is a muddle, as Muravchik has charged. In the case at hand, it is important to see that all the democratic theory in the world will not make a socialist regime any less authoritarian. That some of the people in such a regime exercise their political power over the property and economic affairs of others may not seem as disturbing as their exercising political power over the persons of others, but it is no less real a violation of rights.

These points in mind, Muravchik has given us a study that will go far toward clarifying the international muddle on the idea of "human rights." This is a perceptive and thorough account not only of the Carter human rights policy but of the dilemmas any such policy must address. Muravchik has helped us to see the place of that policy in our recent history. More, fundamentally, he has urged us to a keener appreciation of the place and importance of ideas-and of the idea of human rights in particular—in our practical affairs. By tracing the idea of human rights to its roots in classical liberalism, he has encouraged us to grasp its real meaning-as against the socialist aberration—and its real import in the world. This inheritance from the age of reason, and from our Founding Fathers in particular, is too important to be left unattended.

23

"Human Rights": The Hidden Agenda

*Irving Kristol**

To the best of my knowledge, the issue of "human rights" became a focus for a major foreign policy debate in a Western democracy occurred a little more than a century ago in Britain, when Gladstone divided the country because of the massacre of some 12,000 Bulgarians by their Turkish rulers. Gladstone was a believing Christian, with an intensity of religious commitment that, in the United States today, would surely be regarded as a disqualification for high office. He was appalled that the British government, under Disraeli, seemed unmoved by the massacre of Bulgarian Christians by Turkish Muslims.

And Disraeli was indeed unmoved. Though nominally a Christian, he could hardly be called a believer, much less a true believer. What he did care very much about was preventing Russia, the self-appointed Slavic "protector" of Bulgarians and other Balkan peoples under Turkish rule, from liquidating the Turkish empire and acquiring Constantinople and the Dardanelles in the process. He saw this as a serious threat to the new British empire he was in the process of creating—an empire that would include India and Cyprus, with the area in between (Afghanistan, Egypt, etc.) a British sphere of influence. For Disraeli, Russia's imperial ambitions were the main enemy, and it was to frustrate these ambitions that he tried to preserve the integrity of the Turkish empire—even if it meant a war with Russia, which he was prepared to contemplate. In the end, the Turkish Empire was beyond salvaging, but at the Congress of Berlin Disraeli was still able to come away with "peace with honor"—i.e., with Cyprus in hand and the Dardanelles out of Russian reach. As a concession to the Czar, the Bulgarians did get some dilution of Turkish sovereignty, but for Disraeli this was distinctly a minor matter.

---

*Irving Kristol was the publisher of *The National Interest* from 1985 to 2001.

This essay first appeared in *The National Interest*, no. 6 (Winter 1986/87)

In the brief period that intervened between the original Bulgarian massacre and the Congress of Berlin, Gladstone did more than denounce Disraeli for lack of Christian compassion. He elaborated an alternative view of Britain's role in the world and of an appropriate British foreign policy. It was, quite simply, an anti-imperialist view, a candidly "little England" view. He thought it ridiculous for Queen Victoria to become Empress of India, saw no point in having Cyprus as a colony or in establishing military outposts in Afghanistan. He believed in self-determination for the Christian peoples of the Balkans and did not give a damn for the Turkish empire, which he regarded as a barbaric relic—but he was not about to do anything to "liberate" those Christian peoples. And while he did not like the idea of Russia acquiring the Dardanelles, he did not think it was worth a war to prevent it. This was not just a point of view, it was a program.

When Gladstone returned to office in 1880, however, the "facts" that Disraeli had created, the public opinion that had been solidified behind them, as well as the coercive necessities of international power politics, prevented Gladstone from carrying out his program. He never left any doubt as to what he would have preferred to do, had he been free to do it. But he was not free, and the issue of "human rights" slid once again to the distant margins of British foreign policy.

When one looks back at this episode, one is struck by what one can only call the "innocence" with which the issue was raised and debated. Ever since the end of World War II, in contrast, when "human rights" again became of international concern, the entire discussion has been tainted with disingenuousness. For the past four decades, a concern for "human rights" has not simply and mainly been opposed to a hardheaded and hardhearted realpolitik. On the contrary, despite the sea of sentimentality on which the issue of "human rights" has floated, that issue has, as often as not, been an accessory to a certain kind of ideological politics.

Today, most discussions of "human rights" are misleading because beneath the surface there is almost always a hidden agenda. An issue of "human rights" today is all too likely to be an issue exploited in bad faith. Am I questioning the sincerity of the thousands of "human rights" activists in the United States and elsewhere? Well, sincerity in politics is a tricky affair. It is more common in politics than cynics think, but even political activists can have difficulty knowing what it is they are being sincere about. It is not always easy to distinguish between sincerity and a passionate self-righteousness that cares only for the purity of conscience that inhabits a posturing self. Many of the most ardent Northern abolitionists, prior to the Civil War, were so offended by slavery that they urged that the South be encouraged to secede. Were they being sincere about slavery, or about their own moral fastidiousness? God only knows.

There is no doubt that most Americans who exhibit a passionate interest in "human rights" are moved primarily by humanitarian motives—usually by an understandable, even commendable, outrage at one particular abuse directed against a particular person or group of persons. It is then very easy for them to slide into a feverish humanitarianism which disorients their senses when they confront issues of foreign policy. In such a condition, they are easily manipulable by those who have a professional, as distinct from a simple, humanitarian interest in "human rights."

Yes, one must certainly respect the courage of those human rights activists who live and operate in countries and under circumstances where self-sacrifice is a possible consequence of their commitment. Yet it also has to be said that even some of those who make this exemplary commitment do not necessarily care about "human rights" in any general sense. Thus, I do not share the widespread admiration for Archbishop Tutu of South Africa, because I am reasonably certain that if and when the African National Congress comes to power, he will be a vocal apologist for its tyranny and brutality. My certainty on this score derives from his placid acquiescence in the brutality and tyranny of existing black African regimes.

On the whole, then, I think the question of "sincerity" is best left aside when discussing "human rights" agitation. Much human rights agitation today appears to exemplify what Hegel called "negative activity"—a fanaticism of the abstract that assaults the actual without having in mind any practical plans for improving the actual. In politics such "negative activity," whatever its motivation, always ends up serving a positive political purpose. It seems to me that the key question today is whether such linked to a "hidden agenda." Much of the time, I would argue, this is the case. Moreover, it is this linkage that explains why the issue of "human rights" has achieved such extraordinary prominence in our time.

The era of bad faith in "human rights" began soon after the conclusion of World War II, with the United Nations' *Universal Declaration of Human Rights* in 1948. This document has been widely criticized for the bland way it equates "social and economic rights" (the right to a job, the right to medical care, vacations with pay) with the kinds of traditional political rights (government by consent of the governed, due process of law, etc.) that have prevailed in the liberal democracies. But there was more than intellectual error or enthusiastic idealism at work here. The document was an important first step in establishing something like a moral equivalence between liberal capitalist democracies and communist or self-styled socialist regimes. This was the hidden agenda that gave birth to this text.

It is probable that most of those in the West who endorsed the Declaration did not realize what was happening. They shortsightedly perceived only immediate advantages to their own political agendas. The trade unions were delighted to see their long-standing demands elevated to the level of "human rights." Liberals eager to construct a welfare state were pleased to think that they were now enlarging the sphere of "human rights." So, naturally, were social democrats, for whom the welfare state is a necessary transitional regime toward some kind of socialist society. To the degree that these groups shared a common ideological purpose it was the denigration of "old fashioned" property rights in order to create a more egalitarian society—and to this same degree, they were complicitous with the "hidden agenda," even if they didn't fully realize its implications. On the other hand, some of those involved in the composition and promulgation of this text knew exactly what they were doing, and were fully aware of its implications.

Those implications, spelled out over the succeeding decades, have been momentous. To begin with, the Declaration legitimized the notion that totalitarian or authoritarian societies that emphasize "social and economic rights" as part of an official egalitarian ideology have their own distinctive virtues as well as their obvious vices, to be balanced against the virtues and vices of liberal-capitalist societies. While this did not usually result in a literal "moral equivalence," it did frustrate any effort at a strong comparative moral judgment. It is not too much to say that what was involved was nothing less than a firm step toward the moral disarmament of the West.

Perhaps an even more important intellectual consequence of this new conception of "human rights" was the near-magical transvaluation of a venerable political idea: the idea of tyranny. Clearly, any authoritarian or totalitarian regime officially dedicated to an egalitarian ideology and officially committed to the entire spectrum of "social and economic rights" could not simply be described as a tyranny, even though the kinds of political rights distinctive of liberal societies were nonexistent. This helps to explain what to many thoughtful people is otherwise a mystery, or a sheer perversity: why the majority of liberals in the West extend such an extraordinary tolerance toward "left-wing" tyrants.

Traditional liberalism spoke not of "human rights" but of individual rights, these being almost exclusively rights vis-à-vis government. It explicitly recognized only one "social or economic right": the right to property, including the "property" of one's labor power. This right was thought to be the cornerstone of all those political rights that collectively defined a liberal order. In and of itself, of course, it was not a sufficient basis for those rights—but it was deemed a necessary basis for those rights. Nothing in the experience of the past three centuries has invalidated this thesis.

Political liberties exist only in societies that respect individual rights, including property rights. True, the degree of respect (or non-respect) will vary from country to country, and from time to time. Moreover, in all liberal societies today, property rights have been limited by various entitlements that some would call "social and economic rights," although they are never constitutionally defined as such. But wherever these entitlements are given a massive priority as part of an egalitarian ethos, a liberal society either will not exist or will not endure for long.

To put it bluntly: the effect of the "hidden agenda" was to help delegitimate the market economy ("capitalism") that is an indispensable precondition of a traditional liberal ("bourgeois") society. It had the further implication of casting into doubt the moral status of American foreign policy, which has never thought it appropriate to concern itself with "social and economic rights" in other countries. The importance of this latter implication has been gradually revealed over the course of the past two decades. It is today the primary "hidden agenda" of most activist organizations concerned with "human rights."

I have to emphasize (lest I seem paranoid) that many of the people involved in these organizations are naive innocents. But among the organizers and leaders there are always some full-time professionals who are sophisticated enough to know exactly what they are doing. "Human rights" indeed is only one aspect of their endeavors. It has been documented—though little notice has been taken of this—that many of the same people who are among the leaders of "human rights" agitation are also active in anti-nuclear agitation, arms control agitation, extremist environmentalist agitation, unilateral disarmament agitation, anti-aid-to-the-contras agitation, radical feminist agitation, as well as all sorts of organizations that sponsor "friendship" programs with left-wing regimes. Since these are not only energetic people but very intelligent as well, they have been very successful in giving the issue of "human rights" a special "spin" in a certain direction.

Take, for instance, the question of "torture" which has become so prominent in "human rights" agitation. Note that I put the word in quotation marks, because one of the successes of the "human rights" movement has been to broaden the definition of "torture" to include what would otherwise be classified as "police brutality." Americans would be disapproving of but not outraged at police brutality or the use of third-degree methods against prisoners in distant lands; we are, after all, familiar enough with this phenomenon at home, and would not be surprised to learn that it is far more common in "less civilized" (i.e., most other) countries. But torture, real torture, is an abomination to the bourgeois-liberal sensibility, a violation of that sense of human dignity which is at the very root of our liberal individualism. So a focus on torture is a brilliant bit of public relations.

The question that should be asked, but isn't, is: Why is torture such an issue now, when in years past it never even entered any discussion of international relations? Is torture more common today than it was, say, thirty years ago? There is no reason to think so. In a country like Turkey there has always been a thin line between sheer brutality and outright torture in its prisons. But Turkey, a member of NATO, is an important military ally of the United States. Are we really willing to help destabilize its government in the interest of prison reform? And are those who are so willing really more interested in prison reform than in such destabilization?

In fact, torture (and police brutality, too) may well be less common in the world today because of the power of the media to expose such abuses. In general, actual torture is used today mainly in countries where it has been a traditional practice for centuries. It is also likely to be used in circumstances of a guerrilla insurrection (urban or rural) where the police and military—themselves targets (and often victims) of assassination—are determined to acquire information that might help them suppress the rebellion. That there is provocation to torture is not, of course, a justification, since civilized opinion properly decided long ago that there is no justification, whatever the circumstances. But by focusing on instances of torture (or of police brutality now counted as torture) the "human rights" activists score an important point: They help legitimate the insurrection that today generally comes from the left, while doing their bit to discredit those governments that are trying to suppress the insurrection.

Critics of the "human rights" organizations assert that these organizations operate on a double standard—they seek out authoritarian governments that are on good terms with the United States and emphasize the violations (real or supposed) of "human rights" that occur there, but tend to be relatively unexcited, or at least much less excited, about violations of "human rights" by authoritarian or totalitarian anti-American governments. Indeed, the government that gains this privileged status need not even be left-wing, so long as it is clearly anti-American. Note the disproportionate lack of interest in the state of "human rights" in Syria or Iran, as contrasted with the intense interest in Israel.

To this the "human rights" activists reply, with plausibility, that it makes sense for them to direct their energies to situations where it is reasonable to assume that the United States government is capable of exercising some benign influence—and where, therefore, it bears a degree of moral responsibility for failing to exercise this influence. To which the critics retort that the "human rights" activists are themselves guilty of moral turpitude because of their failure to distinguish between what Joshua Muravchik calls "individual abuses" and "systemic deformities," the latter characterizing totalitarian communist regimes as distinct from merely authoritarian regimes. To which the "human rights" spokesmen then reply that this distinction between "totalitarian" and "authoritarian" regimes is a species of "cold war" sophistry, since the suffering of the victim of torture or police brutality under either regime is unvarnished, indistinguishable suffering.

I must confess that, though my sympathies are all with the critics of the "human rights" movement, I find this debate to be essentially sterile. To begin with, the perspective of the victim—whether in war or peace—is the stuff of which poetry (or perhaps theology) is made, not politics, and certainly not foreign policy. To invert Tolstoy's aphorism, all victims are alike in their suffering and humiliation. But not all political regimes in which suffering and humiliation exist are alike. The difference between totalitarian societies and authoritarian governments is obvious enough—though one of the purposes of focusing on the individual indignities suffered under both regimes is precisely to blur this obvious distinction. True, not all totalitarian societies are identical—there are important national differences that create shades and hues of totalitarianism—nor are they immune to change. But though there may arise an occasional instance where the distinction between an authoritarian and totalitarian policy is less easy to make, the distinction is of crucial significance for an understanding of twentieth-century history and politics.

Authoritarian governments have existed throughout history and may fairly be regarded as pre-liberal realities. Whether they are "destined" to become liberal or totalitarian societies, or to evolve into some social form still unimaginable, is an interesting question of political philosophy. But no one can seriously claim that the numerous authoritarian regimes now scattered all over the world constitute any kind of threat to liberal America or the liberal West. Totalitarian societies, on the other hand, are post-liberal realities—they emerge out of an explicit rejection of the Western liberal tradition, are the declared enemies of this tradition, and aim to supersede it. It is impossible to write a history of international relations in the twentieth century without making the rise of post-liberal totalitarianism (whether of the right or left) the central event of the era, or without making the "cold war" between the liberal democracies and the new states the central focus around which everything else revolves. It is, in contrast, perfectly possible to write a history of international relations in the twentieth century without ever bothering to mention something called "authoritarianism." In fact, the histories that have been written all do exemplify both this impossibility and this possibility.

It is not an accident that most "human rights" activists, and all "human rights" publicists or theorists, insist on denying either the existence or the importance of the totalitarian-authoritarian distinction. In the abstract, there would seem to be no need for them to do so. There are actually some "human rights" activists who do ignore this whole issue—like the clergy of yesteryear, they are impelled by the simple desire to alleviate human suffering, without paying attention to politics. But these are a minority, even among the clergy of today. The "human rights" movement is decidedly political. Its need to obfuscate the totalitarian-authoritarian distinction flows from its political intentions, its desire to deny that the "cold war" is anything but a paranoid fantasy of a bourgeois-capitalist establishment, to minimize the totalitarian threat to liberal-democratic nations, to unnerve American foreign policy by constantly exposing the "immorality" of its relations with authoritarian allies, etc. In short, to repeat—its purpose—the hidden agenda of its "negative activity"—is the moral disarmament of the bourgeois-capitalist West.

It is interesting, by the way, to note that the "human rights" movement is far less influential in Western Europe, and is taken far less seriously by governments there, than is the case in the United States. No European foreign office has to engage in the idiotic political arithmetic which Congress has imposed on our State Department, whereby every year it solemnly tots up the "human rights" situation in dozens of countries. It is an inherently absurd enterprise. If women in Switzerland don't have the vote, while they do in Rumania, does that make Rumania in any way more respectful of "human rights" than Switzerland? And how does one even apply the concept of "human rights" to Saudi Arabia—a medieval nation rather than a modern state? Why are we so silly as to get involved in this sort of thing, while European governments do not? Are the peoples across the Atlantic less concerned with human rights than we are?

I don't think so. I believe, rather, that the difference is that Western Europe has real, live, important socialist parties, while the United States does not. The result is that those Americans who, in Europe, would belong to socialist or social-democratic parties are forced to channel their political energies into "causes" which, in sum, approximate as closely as possible to those parties' programs. The upshot is that the European left is far more candid than its American counterpart, and has less need for any hidden agendas. When one reads books by European socialists on foreign affairs—the recent writings of Regis Debray can serve as an example—"human rights" is, at most, a very subordinate theme and the theme is sometimes not struck at all. These writings suffer from all kinds of illusions, but they are illusions that flow from avowed ideological convictions. In the United States, where it is imprudent to avow a socialist ideology, those convictions go underground and then emerge in "causes" such as "human rights" or "arms control" or "unilateral nuclear disarmament," which present themselves as apolitical or transpolitical.

Precisely because they seem so nonpolitical or transpolitical, they can actually be more radical in substance. No European country has an Arms Control and Disarmament Agency, whose function is presumably to thwart the militarist proclivities of our Defense Department. Similarly, no European country has an

Assistant Secretary of State for Human Rights, whose function is presumably to thwart the immoral proclivities of our State Department. True, the notion of negotiating an "arms control" agreement with the Soviet Union is at least as popular in Western Europe as in the United States. But in Western Europe this notion is often based on a real (or not-unrealistic) anxiety, that a conflict between the two superpowers could easily and quickly result in Western Europe becoming a devastated nuclear battlefield, even if the source of this conflict lies outside Western Europe itself or is marginal to Western European interests. It is this fear that motivates many of the more serious "anti-nuclear" activists over there. In the United States, however, "anti-nuclear" and "arms control" publicists are more akin to the anti-American, pro-Soviet left in Europe. They are persuaded that it is a "cold war" American foreign policy which threatens the world with nuclear devastation, and that a more "conciliatory" (i.e., appeasing) posture toward the Soviet Union and its allies will avert such a catastrophe. They display little fear of Soviet intentions, much fearful anxiety about our own White House, Pentagon, and State Department. It is this distrust of the United States and of its status as a world power—what in Europe would be called "anti-Americanism"—that motivates our more passionate "anti-nuclear" advocates and impels them to support any formula acceptable to the Soviets, and to adopt an appeasing mode in foreign policy. Such appeasement is their hidden—not deeply hidden, it must be said—agenda.

There is no other explanation, so far as I can see, for the pertinacity of various leading "arms control" advocates, when by now one would have expected them to be thoroughly disillusioned with the whole affair. This includes many who were involved in the negotiation of the SALT I agreement, an agreement that never would have been signed, never could have been signed, if it had been understood beforehand that the Soviets would promptly install over 500 intermediate range warheads aimed at Western Europe—something that, it turned out, was permitted (though certainly never envisaged) under the SALT I agreement. The lack of subsequent disillusionment among such knowledgeable people, the fact that their passion for the "arms control process" remains undiminished, is something that requires interpretation.

What makes American foreign policy so vulnerable to "human rights" agitation? The explanation is not far to seek: This foreign policy has—must have—an ineradicable moral-ideological component. We are indeed engaged in a profound ideological conflict with the Soviet Union, a conflict that dominates world politics. But it is both a simplification and a distortion to describe it as a conflict about "human rights." It is, rather, a conflict over the very definition of "human rights," and the point of this conflict is to determine who will have the power to define "human rights" for future generations. In that sense, the United States cannot evade the urgencies and the ambiguities of "power politics." The relation of such "power politics" to the American "public philosophy" makes for tension and complications in our foreign policy. Realpolitik a la Disraeli is unthinkable in America, since it runs against the very grain of our political ethos. Ours is a nation based on a universal creed, and there is an unquenchable missionary element in our foreign policy. We do aim to "make the world safe for democracy"—eventually, and in those places and at those times where conditions permit democracy to flourish. Every American administration in our history has felt compelled—though some have been more enthusiastic than others—to use our influence, wherever possible, to see that other governments respect our conception of individual rights as the foundation of a just regime and a good society.

On the other hand, only two presidents in our history have tried to emulate Gladstone in making the missionary element the very centerpiece of American foreign policy. The first was Woodrow Wilson, who believed that his enterprise would achieve its success by creating a world organization that in turn would form a "community of nations" pledged to respect the principles we hold dear—with disrespect being curbed by a broadened (Wilson would have said "heightened") definition of international law, to be enforced by this new "world community." It was a utopian vision, to which many eminent Americans still pay lip service, but which no serious person can any longer take at face value. Today, all that is left of the Wilsonian dream is a host of international organizations that are at best debating societies, at worst sinks of corruption. There is also an array of treaty obligations that the United States thoughtlessly entered into and from which we are now gingerly trying to free ourselves.

The second president, of course, was Jimmy Carter, who fully accepted the expanded version of "human rights" (including social and economic rights) and who then tried to give the American missionary impulse a unilateralist thrust. But he soon was forced to recognize that the world is a complex and recalcitrant place, full of other peoples with other ideas, and that while proclaiming high-minded principles was one thing, unilateral American efforts to reshape world realities according to our national vision were an enterprise necessarily limited in scope—often very limited. The rights of individuals in other lands are a matter of concern for Americans. One may even say it is an integral part of our national interest. But it is usually a concern that claims no centrality in our foreign policy, since it has to be weighed against all those other interests which make up our national interest. Secretary of State Cyrus Vance, one of the original "human rights" enthusiasts, was not in office more than a month before he felt constrained to issue the following statement:

> We will speak frankly about injustice both at home and abroad. We do not intend, however, to be strident or polemical, but we do believe that an abiding respect for human rights is a human value of fundamental importance and that it must be nourished. We will not comment on each and every issue, but we will from time to time comment when we see a threat to human rights, when we believe it constructive to do so.

Well—yes. If one is willing to stipulate that by "human rights" one means pretty much what used to be called "individual rights," then any American president could have endorsed that statement. Ronald Reagan, I am certain, would be happy to endorse it. The United States (in this respect like the Soviet Union) does stand for something in the world and its foreign policy must, to the degree that the world permits, respect the principles of its establishment. But it is the nature of foreign policy to operate, most of the time, in the realm of necessity rather than the realm of freedom. So while it is fair to assert that the ideological basis of American foreign policy gives it a permanent moral dimension which itself delimits the scope of any purely "realistic" policy, these limits have to be broad enough to permit foreign policy to be effective. Just how broad or narrow these limits are will depend on circumstances. Probably the "purest," most moral, least self-interested foreign policy action ever taken on behalf of "human rights" was the British navy's suppression of the slave trade in the nineteenth century. This action was made possible by many factors: Britain's massive superiority in sea power, the unimportance of the "Third World" countries involved, the non-existence (as compared with today) of a complex structure of international law and international organizations. So while Britain's action was wholly admirable, one also has to point out that it was costless, or as close to costless as makes no matter.

It is conceivable that the United States might, one of these days, find itself in a more or less comparable situation, and it is certainly to be hoped that it would then take a comparable action. But such situations are likely to be rare. Like all great nations, the United States does conceive itself as having some kind of "civilizing mission." But, lacking an "imperialist" impulse, we are not usually inclined to accomplish this mission through forceful intervention. Presumably if a Pol Pot regime came to power in Central America and began a genocidal campaign against its own people, we might very well intervene. On the other hand, we did not intervene in Cambodia, nor have we even dreamed of intervening in Africa, where tribal genocide is not uncommon. Unilateral military intervention by the United States on behalf of "human rights" would have to overcome resistance from both our enemies and our allies. And steps short of military intervention will almost always be more symbolic than real. True, symbolic action may sometimes be better than no action at all. But over time the impact, both at home and abroad, of a series of mainly symbolic actions will be negligible. Worse, they will be interpreted as a sign of weakness, not strength, of moralistic impotence rather than moral energy.

If this is our situation today—and the experience of the Carter Administration has confirmed that it is—why has the message failed to get through to the "human rights" constituency? The reason, I suggest, is that this constituency has its own agenda, and that "human rights" is a useful rhetoric in which to promote it.

A final point: There are some conservative (or non-left) "human rights" activists who feel that this theme can be exploited for purposes of anti-communist and anti-totalitarian propaganda. It is impossible not to admire the diligence with which they expose the sufferings of people under communism, and this kind of candid ideological warfare does serve to remind us of the nature of the enemy—a reminder that is always timely. But there is reason to wonder whether this strategy, on its own, can be effective over the longer term. There cannot be many people who do not already know about conditions in the Soviet Union. The question is: Why don't they care? Why are most of the major Christian churches in the United States so utterly indifferent to the persecution of Christianity in the Soviet Union and in Soviet-occupied Eastern Europe? If this be ignorance, it is a special kind of willful ignorance.

Such willful ignorance, I would suggest, has two sources. First, since the Soviet Union has its own (Marxist) conception of "human rights," about which it is brutally assertive and in no way apologetic, it does seem quixotically futile to criticize it for not sharing our traditional-liberal political philosophy. Second, and more important, there are many who believe the Soviet model is flawed but who nevertheless regard it as a respectable alternative to our own, which they perceive as at least equally flawed, or even flawed to a greater degree. The sad and simple truth is that, once one has lost faith in the traditional liberal model, one feels deprived of the moral authority to challenge the Soviet model and one then loses all interest in doing so. It is this loss of faith that feeds the organized "human rights" movement, and gives it an "anti-American" bias. To this loss of faith, mere anti-communism is no answer.

There is also a significant cost involved in such an anti-communist "human rights" campaign. To avoid accusations of unprincipled conservative bias, it is inevitably pushed toward making "human rights" a central issue in determining American policy toward South Korea, Chile, Indonesia, the Philippines, etc.—which is, after all, exactly what our anti-American "human rights" activists wish. In effect, the conservative campaign has the unintended consequence of legitimating the "human rights" efforts of the left. The so-called "human rights" activists inside the Soviet Union—or at least the more sophisticated among them—understand this problem well enough. They certainly do appreciate efforts in the West to alleviate the suffering of those who oppose particular policies of the Soviet system. This is justification enough for such efforts, whatever their limited success. But those activists inside the Soviet Union also have a hidden agenda, one of which I thoroughly approve. To the extent that the "human rights" issue offers them some protection as well as some leverage, they are morally entitled to use it. It is also politically prudent for them to emphasize it. Unfortunately, such hidden agendas are easily read by the Soviet authorities, who have had so much experience in writing them.